I0891110

Building the High-Performance Finance Function

André de Waal
Finance Function Research and Development Center BV, The Netherlands & HPO Center BV, The Netherlands

Eelco Bilstra
Finance Function Research and Development Center BV, The Netherlands

Jacques Bootsman
Finance Function Research and Development Center BV, The Netherlands

IGI Global
PUBLISHER of TIMELY KNOWLEDGE

A volume in the Advances in Finance, Accounting, and Economics (AFAE) Book Series

Published in the United States of America by
IGI Global
Business Science Reference (an imprint of IGI Global)
701 E. Chocolate Avenue
Hershey PA, USA 17033
Tel: 717-533-8845
Fax: 717-533-8661
E-mail: cust@igi-global.com
Web site: http://www.igi-global.com

Library of Congress Cataloging-in-Publication Data

Names: Waal, André de, 1960- author. | Bilstra, Eelco, 1969- author. | Bootsman, Jacques, 1967- author.
Title: Building the high performance finance function / by André de Waal, Eelco Bilstra, Jacques Bootsman.
Description: Hershey, PA : Business Science Reference, [2022] | Includes bibliographical references and index. | Summary: "In this book, the authors present their integrated view and knowledge on what they have learned so far on developing a high-performing finance function, to assist high-performance organizations develop strategic initiatives aimed at improving the finance function within an organization"-- Provided by publisher.
Identifiers: LCCN 2021029904 (print) | LCCN 2021029905 (ebook) | ISBN 9781799869290 (hardcover) | ISBN 9781799869306 (paperback) | ISBN 9781799869313 (ebook)
Subjects: LCSH: Business enterprises--Finance. | Corporations--Finance.
Classification: LCC HG4026 .W33 2022 (print) | LCC HG4026 (ebook) | DDC 658.15--dc23
LC record available at https://lccn.loc.gov/2021029904
LC ebook record available at https://lccn.loc.gov/2021029905

This book is published in the IGI Global book series Advances in Finance, Accounting, and Economics (AFAE) (ISSN: 2327-5677; eISSN: 2327-5685)

British Cataloguing in Publication Data
A Cataloguing in Publication record for this book is available from the British Library.

For electronic access to this publication, please contact: eresources@igi-global.com.

Advances in Finance, Accounting, and Economics (AFAE) Book Series

Ahmed Driouchi
Al Akhawayn University, Morocco

ISSN:2327-5677
EISSN:2327-5685

Mission

In our changing economic and business environment, it is important to consider the financial changes occurring internationally as well as within individual organizations and business environments. Understanding these changes as well as the factors that influence them is crucial in preparing for our financial future and ensuring economic sustainability and growth.

The **Advances in Finance, Accounting, and Economics (AFAE)** book series aims to publish comprehensive and informative titles in all areas of economics and economic theory, finance, and accounting to assist in advancing the available knowledge and providing for further research development in these dynamic fields.

Coverage

- E-Accounting
- Applied Finance
- Corporate Finance
- Ethics in Accounting and Finance
- Finance and Accounting in SMEs
- Development Economics
- Accounting Standards
- Economics of Natural and Environmental Resources
- Investments and Derivatives
- Finance

IGI Global is currently accepting manuscripts for publication within this series. To submit a proposal for a volume in this series, please contact our Acquisition Editors at acquisitions@igi-global.com or visit: https://www.igi-global.com/publish/.

The Advances in Finance, Accounting, and Economics (AFAE) Book Series (ISSN 2327-5677) is published by IGI Global, 701 E. Chocolate Avenue, Hershey, PA 17033-1240, USA, www.igi-global.com. This series is composed of titles available for purchase individually; each title is edited to be contextually exclusive from any other title within the series. For pricing and ordering information please visit https://www.igi-global.com/book-series/advances-finance-accounting-economics/73685. Postmaster: Send all address changes to above address.

Titles in this Series

For a list of additional titles in this series, please visit: www.igi-global.com/book-series

Stabilizing Currency and Preserving Economic Sovereignty Using the Grondona System
Patrick Collins (Independent Researcher, apan)
Business Science Reference • © 2022 • 244pp • H/C (ISBN: 9781799883029) • US $215.00

Transitioning From Globalized to Localized and Self-Reliant Economies
Ruchika Gupta (Amity University, India) Priyank Srivastava (Amity University, India) Shiv Ranjan (Amity University, India) and M. Affan Badar (Indiana State University USA)
Business Science Reference • © 2022 • 256pp • H/C (ISBN: 9781799887058) • US $195.00

COVID-19 Pandemic Impact on New Economy Development and Societal Change
Cristina Raluca Gh. Popescu (University of Bucharest, Romania & The Bucharest University of Economic Studies, Romania & The National Institute for Research and Development in Environmental Protection (INCDPM), Romania & National Research and Development Institute for Gas Turbines (COMOTI), Romania)
Business Science Reference • © 2022 • 425pp • H/C (ISBN: 9781668433744) • US $195.00

Microfinance and Sustainable Development in Africa
Yahaya Alhassan (University of Sunderland in London, UK) and Uzoechi Nwagbara (University of the West of Scotland, UK & Cardiff Metropolitan University, UK)
Business Science Reference • © 2022 • 368pp • H/C (ISBN: 9781799874997) • US $195.00

Redefining Global Economic Thinking for the Welfare of Society
Md Mashiur Rahman (Bank Asia Ltd., Bangladesh) Richa Goel (Amity University, Noida, India) Anthony P. Gomes (TeamPeople, USA) and Md Almas Uzzaman (Independent Researcher, Australia)
Business Science Reference • © 2022 • 268pp • H/C (ISBN: 9781799882589) • US $225.00

FinTech Development for Financial Inclusiveness
Muhammad Anshari (Universiti Brunei Darussalam, Brunei) Mohamad Nabil Almunawar (Universiti Brunei Darussalam, Brunei) and Masairol Masri (Universiti Brunei Darussalam, Brunei)
Business Science Reference • © 2022 • 269pp • H/C (ISBN: 9781799884477) • US $225.00

Evaluating Trade and Economic Relations Between India and Southeast Asia
Anita Medhekar (Central Queensland University, Australia) and Harpreet Kaur (Central Queensland University, Australia)
Business Science Reference • © 2022 • 347pp • H/C (ISBN: 9781799857747) • US $195.00

IGI Global
PUBLISHER of TIMELY KNOWLEDGE

701 East Chocolate Avenue, Hershey, PA 17033, USA
Tel: 717-533-8845 x100 • Fax: 717-533-8661
E-Mail: cust@igi-global.com • www.igi-global.com

Table of Contents

Foreword: Continuously Working on Future-Ready Finance Functions vii

Preface xi

Chapter 1
Introduction 1

Chapter 2
The Basis: The High Performance Organization Framework 16

Chapter 3
Current Situation of the Finance Function 28

Chapter 4
Ideas for Improving the Finance Function 43

Chapter 5
Design of the High-Performance Finance Function Framework 56

Chapter 6
Set-Up of the HPFF: Environments, Roles, and Profiles 93

Chapter 7
The HPFF Diagnosis 145

Chapter 8
Current HPFF State of Finance Functions 160

Chapter 9
Transformation Into the High-Performance Finance Function 179

Chapter 10
Best Ideas 206

Chapter 11
Future-Proofing the Finance Function 266

Appendix A: Benefits of the High Performance Finance Function 284

Appendix B: Overview Ideas for Creating the High-Performance Finance Function 286

Appendix C: Scientifically Developing the HPFF Framework 288

Appendix D: Overview of Roles in the HPFF Environments 293

About the Authors 294

Index 296

Foreword: Continuously Working on Future-Ready Finance Functions

THE FUTURE FOR THE FINANCE FUNCTION: THE NEED FOR A FINANCE TRANSFORMATION

High performance is the achievement of results that surpass expectations: a high-performance organization (HPO) performs exceedingly better than its competitors over the long term. But what does high performance mean for the finance function? Moving toward a high-performance finance function (HPFF) is generally referred to as finance transformation: overall, this involves the development of strategic initiatives aimed at improving the finance function within an organization. The transformation of the finance function may consist of restructuring the finance operating model, improving accounting methods, processes and systems, or re-platforming the finance and accounting systems. More specific examples include shortening a budget cycle, implementing new accounting software, adopting activity-based costing (ABC), reducing overhead costs, shifting to predictive accounting including driver-based budgeting and rolling financial forecasts. The goal of any financial transformation is the same: to align Finance and Accounting with the overall company strategy, to become more efficient as a function, and to provide better service and information to internal customers so they can develop clearer insights in the status and development of their organization and make better decisions.

Transforming the finance function has to be achieved in an integrated fashion, given that it entails a mixture of processes, systems, and professionals; this makes a financial transformation quite complex. Changing the finance function, or better yet, developing the finance function to achieve the next phase of quality and maturity is not blueprint change management, initiated by consultants or top-down management: it involves developing, learning, prioritizing, and focusing—in a step-by-step sequence—by the finance function leaders and financial professionals. Developing the finance function is a continuing journey with intermediate travel destinations. Once a destination is reached, the finance team formulates the destination for the next 'season' while learning from the previous stretch.

The future for finance functions is challenging. Information technology (IT) has turned out to be a game changer in improving processes. Developments in IT (such as digitalization, robotic process automation, predictive analysis, process mining, artificial intelligence, or blockchain) provide opportunities to improve reporting, planning, performance management, and workflow management as well as silo busting and resolving process inefficiencies. Although IT has enabled financial processes to become more efficient and effective, these processes still have to be executed by people. The notion that with the time regained from efficiencies the finance function can focus more on analysis and value-added activities should not be considered a given: this saved time could and should (also) be used for making the transformation a success. This is done by prioritizing the transformation, having a clear and inspirational view of the future finance function, having the courage to take the next steps (or leaps) forward, creating a superior finance team, being adaptable and flexible to new challenges and uncertainties, and constantly learning. In organizational changes, the people involved, i.e., the finance leaders and the finance professionals, play a pivotal role; therefore, sufficient time should be dedicated for them to develop.

CHANGING TO A HIGH-PERFORMANCE FINANCE FUNCTION

High performance and transformation are key words for the authors of this book. While the term "high performance" focuses on the end in mind, finance function transformation suggests a roadmap to a goal. However, once the transformation is achieved, this, of course, is not the end of the project; rather, it is a step to the next phase. Almost every organization that wants to transform its finance function has some form of a roadmap; high-quality organizations, in particular, typically view transformation as an ongoing and evolving process rather than as a defined project with a beginning, middle, and end.

"What would high performance mean for the finance function?": this is a question the authors have asked themselves over and over again in their professional lives. André de Waal first investigated, over many years, the ingredients that make organizations high-performing, i.e., so-called HPOs. Subsequently, the three authors—André, Eelco, and Jacques—together began to examine the finance function, starting with the following questions: What factors dictate the priorities for finance leaders to act upon? What is the correlation with HPO? What are the obstacles encountered by the finance function? What is the case for change? What are the expectations of internal customers? What are the megatrends and disruptors that have impact on the finance function? These are just a few areas they have researched in the context of the finance function; furthermore, it is not only research that the authors have undertaken—they have also developed instruments with the vision to put their insights into practice. As a result, this book is divided into two parts: the first, a synthesis of what a high-performance finance function should look like (the *what*); and second, cases and ideas from finance experts and professionals to inspire finance leaders and professionals in supporting the finance function's next steps into the future (the *how*).

In this book, the authors present their integrated view and knowledge on what they have learned so far on developing a high-performing finance function. They have translated their thoughts into insights, ideas, and a framework. They have published their insights in academic papers that are all aligned with the theory of HPOs. Their mission is to help finance functions improve and serve the community of finance professionals. They have built a robust piece of thinking, with concepts that have been academically reviewed and that provide novel insights representing the best ideas to put into practice. The concept of "best ideas" in itself is noteworthy: the authors define a "best idea" as the alternative between best practice and best guess. A best idea is a working idea in practice in a certain context, and may be of value when experimented with in the relevant context. The important lessons are not to simply copy best practices but to show boldness and initiative, constantly experiment, act while also learning, and evaluate the results along the way, in your own context.

WHY SHOULD YOU READ THIS BOOK?

This book is aimed at financial professionals with ambition: if you aim to initiate your journey and bring your finance function a step further than where it is today, the framework presented here (the *what*) is extremely useful for realizing an integral vision and serving as a reference point for the steps to be taken; and the transformation approach with its cases and best ideas (the *how*) will provide inspiration for your journey in the context of your own finance function. The book is full of examples and insights for you to take the next step in the journey to your own high-performance finance function and, at the same time, elevating your organization as a whole to the next quality level.

From my own career experience—40 years of experience in the finance function (initially as a financial controller and then with Deloitte, KPMG, EDS, and SAS) and as a thought leader and author on corporate and enterprise performance management (CPM/EPM) methods—I fully endorse the principle that change will only result when people feel compelled to change or when they are intrinsically motivated to change. To create change and overcome human behavior's natural resistance to change, it is necessary to create the need for change. One method to accomplish this is to leverage the existing high levels of dissatisfaction and discomfort of your colleagues and the executive team: this is your best lever for getting their buy-in for new ideas and innovation regarding the finance function. Ask your colleagues these questions: "How do we know what initiatives we should initiate first to grow as a finance function as a whole, to take a leap into the future, to fulfil the needs of our internal customers, to contribute to becoming an HPO? How much time should we spend to reach this point? How much effort should we put into the new direction?" In many cases, your colleagues will not have good answers. Then ask them: "Is that a good thing? How long do we want to perpetuate making decisions without knowing these answers?" If you ask these thought-provoking and deliberately disturbing questions in the right way, you will not need to spend much time on promoting the necessary changes.

A second method is having a vision of what "better" looks like. When people see a different view of their circumstances that can lead to an improved condition, they will consider changing. Do not spend too much time overpromoting this vision: this is because if people perceive the vision as being overly theoretical, complicated, costly, or impractical, this would discourage them from pursuing changes to realize that vision. Then, make the vision attainable. Take the first practical steps. Examples are pilots, proof-of-concept workshops, rapid prototyping with iterative remodeling, small process-improvement steps, learning-by-doing on the job, and experiments to demonstrate value and prove concepts. These activities accelerate learning and lead to more buy-in.

TAKE THE NEXT STEP

For finance leaders and professionals: this book incites, urges, encourages, and enables you to take the necessary next step. Finance leaders should start communicating the need for change; act as a change champion, including enrolling employees in idea generation, and ensure that finance teams have the right mix of digital, technical, business, and people skills to deliver insight, influence, and impact. Leading organizations take the initiative early; they are preparing their employees for new, yet undefined, future roles. Financial professionals will take the next step when recognizing that the skills developed through their professional training are no longer an automatic passport to a sustainable career: although these skills represent a foundation to build upon, the commitment to lifelong learning and embracing change remains the personal responsibility of every financial.

Learn from this book. I wish you success with your journey to the high-performance finance function.

Gary Cokins
Analytics-Based Performance Management LLC, Cary, USA
www.garycokins.com

Preface

Did you know that:

- the finance function is generally seen as one of the most if not *the* most important supporting function in an organization: it is regarded as the spider in the organizational web because it has relationships with every part of the organization and is also represented on the executive board;
- it therefore is for many organizations of the utmost importance that the finance function takes the lead on the journey toward high-performance, by transforming itself into a high-performance finance function (HPFF) and thus serving as a role model for other functions in the organization;
- however, in practice only a handful of finance functions have successfully mastered the mix of culture, talent, governance model, technology, and ability to improve necessary to become an HPFF;
- this is because finance functions experienced these past two decades many setbacks in their development efforts (accounting scandals, subsequent introduction of much new regulations, the dot.com bubble bust, several recessions, COVID-19 pandemic) causing them to reprioritize toward making primary financial processes more reliable and introducing new techniques such as risk management;
- as a result, many finance functions still spend too much time on routine activities and do not play an active role in strategic decision-making processes in the organization while the growth of financial professionals to business partners is also stalling;
- only 49% of finance leaders have started the transformation of their finance function to a higher quality level, while among these 80% indicate that they have not (yet) achieved noticeable results from the transformation;
- only one-third of organizations see their expectations regarding the results of a transformation met, while two-thirds state that their expectations are only partly or not at all satisfied;
- which results in less than 10% of organizations being satisfied with the effectiveness of their finance functions, and fewer than two out of 10 managers indicating that the finance function adds value to their organization;
- and a majority of finance functions are now struggling to keep up with digital developments and have great difficulty in attracting and keeping qualified finance professionals.

It clearly is a difficult time for the finance function. At the same time, many finance professionals are highly ambitious to make a difference in their organization. This book is aimed at those ambitious finance professionals. It addresses the above-mentioned issues in depth and shows how to deal with these in such a way that creating and sustaining an HPFF becomes a reality. In the book a framework is developed to help the finance function transform into an HPFF in a way that enables it to explicitly contribute to the organization in its endeavors to become a high-performance organization (HPO). In this way the added value of the finance function will increase even more and it will be regarded as being indispensable for the success of the organization. The book provides many examples and tools, techniques and tips & tricks, both from empirical research and case studies, with which finance professionals can take advantage for their own development and that of their finance function.

You can expect to find the following in the book. In Chapter 1 the need and the reasons for an HPO and an HPFF are discussed. The finance function is defined, its most important tasks, processes, and activities described, and its challenges in modern-day organizations reviewed. The current situation of most finance functions – which can be described as a "blood, sweat, and tears" environment which can just satisfy basic requirements of internal clients and external stakeholders – is compared to the desired HPFF state. A schematic reading guide is given and the justification for the book – the reason why it is important and how it came into being – starts the reader on the exciting journey toward high performance.

In Chapter 2, the high-performance organization framework (hereafter referred to as the HPO framework), a scientifically validated framework that enables and supports organizations in transforming themselves into a sustainable high-performing enterprise, is introduced. The HPO framework forms the basis for the HPFF. It consists of five factors, with 35 underlying characteristics, which are described. The HPO diagnosis, with which an organization can evaluate how far it is on the way to high performance, is discussed. This Chapter concludes with a listing of the benefits of using the HPO framework in practice.

Chapter 3 deals with the current situation of the finance function, which is explained from a historical perspective by first looking back several decades and then working toward the present time. Subsequently, the research into the trends in the finance function over that same period is reviewed. This research shows that there are specific "evergreens," i.e., activities that have taken up a significant proportion of the time of the finance function over the past decades, and in fact still do. These evergreens are described, and in addition the latest developments – identified from the professional literature – on activities that might become or possibly already are important to the finance function are discussed. This Chapter concludes with the core aim of the HPFF framework which is to support the finance function in dealing with current and future developments to meet and exceed its targets.

There is no shortage of ideas, especially in the professional literature, for elevating the quality of the finance function. However, it turns out that much of that literature focuses only on improving financial processes or on the question of how to develop financial professionals from scorekeepers into business controllers. There is limited literature that provides a glimpse of what a high-performance finance function looks like and what its place and role are within an organization. In Chapter 4 interesting studies from the literature from the past decade are discussed to develop an overall picture of the finance function of the future. First a look is taken at the benefits of an excellent finance function and then the most interesting ideas in the literature for creating such a function are discussed.

In Chapter 5 the movements are discussed that are currently shaping or that are expected to transform in the near future the finance function into a higher-quality finance function. Subsequently, these movements are converted in to a framework that can be used to create the HPFF. The HPFF framework is then extensively described, and its relationship with the HPO framework and its influence on the performance of the finance function are explained. Also the difference between the WHAT and the HOW of the framework is discussed, as are the obstacles that finance functions can encounter in practice during their transformation in to an HPFF. Courses of action to surmount these obstacles are also given.

Just as there is no "one financial" there is also no "one finance function." In fact, the finance function consists of several environments, each concerned with a different area of financial activities, in which financial professionals work in multiple roles. When setting up an HPFF, these different environments and roles have to be carefully taken into account. In Chapter 6, the environments of and the roles in the finance function are described, and their relationships with the HPFF framework are explained. In addition, the roles financials can have in the HPFF are given, the profile of the high-performance financial is described, and the implications for human resourcing are discussed. The Chapter also includes an overview of the digital transformation of the finance function: why it is important, what the status is, what skills are needed in the digital finance function, which obstacles are encountered during the transformation, and courses of actions that can be used to surmount these obstacles to achieve a successful digital transformation.

The initial step in the transformation to an HPFF involves performing an HPFF diagnosis. The diagnosis is the starting point for initiating change, prioritizing topics, and taking steps for improvement. For a process in which improvements take root, after a diagnosis and discussion of the outcomes, a follow-up is needed to continue the movement that has been initiated. This translates into concrete actions and projects. The focus must be on small improvement steps, so that employees save time for further improvement steps. In Chapter 7, what the HPFF diagnosis looks like is discussed. In addition, the experience of a finance function that conducted the HPFF diagnosis is related.

Since the development of the HPFF framework, extensive data collection by means of the HPFF diagnosis has taken place. This makes it possible to discuss how far in general finance functions are on the road to high performance. In Chapter 8 the average HPFF scores of finance functions worldwide are given and the reasons for these scores are discussed. Potential courses of action for improving and strengthening finance functions are described. This Chapter concludes with a discussion of a specific improvement opportunity: measuring and increasing internal customer satisfaction with the finance function.

In the literature to date, a generally accepted approach for the transformation of an finance function into an HPFF cannot be found. Therefore the approach for the transformation into an HPO was taken and adapted to an HPFF transformation. This approach, which encompasses a series of key steps and the use of so-called HPFF Coaches, is described in Chapter 9. In almost every organization, resources are scarce, which forces the finance function to compete for financial budget and people's time against the business (a battle often lost). Therefore the issue of how to secure a sufficient proportion of an organization's resources for the HPFF transformation is tackled. In addition, ideas from experienced financials how to realize the HPFF have been collected and are given in this Chapter.

During the research into the HPFF many fine ideas that finance functions have implemented, to strengthen themselves in order to become high performing, were collected. These ideas, that all can be tied to the HPFF factors and are thus useful to know about when undertaking an HPFF transformation, were gathered during interviews with financial professionals and many case studies conducted at finance functions. In Chapter 10, 50 of those best ideas are discuss. They are categorized according to the HPFF factor they most support and strengthen (some of the ideas can target multiple factors), and serve as inspiration for further strengthening finance functions.

The last task remaining for finance functions is to make themselves 'future-ready' so that they can deal with all kinds of changes in the environment. Such changes consist of threats caused by (worldwide) disruptors and megatrends, or opportunities provided by (mainly) megatrends. Unfortunately, there is limited literature on making the finance function future-ready, which limits the ability of the finance function to prepare itself for the future. This is illustrated by the COVID pandemic of 2020, which has shown that many organizations, and their finance functions, were not ready for the havoc it caused, resulting in considerable negative consequences. In this final Chapter 11, the fourteen most important megatrends and disruptors are described and courses of actions finance functions should apply, in order to adapt to these megatrends and disruptors in such a way that they can remain high-performing, are discussed.

Chapter 1
Introduction

ABSTRACT

In this Chapter the need and the reasons for a high performance organization (HPO) and a high performance finance function (HPFF) are discussed. The finance function is defined, its most important tasks processes, activities described, and its challenges in modern-day organizations reviewed. The current situation of most finance functions – which can be described as a "blood, sweat, and tears" environment which can just satisfy basic requirements of internal clients and external stakeholders – is compared to the desired HPFF state. A schematic reading guide is given and the justification for the book – the reason why it is important and how it came into being – starts the reader on the exciting journey toward high performance.

"The constant need to fail fast and relearn in a complex world, and the frequent upgrade of our skills, plays to the strength of the lifelong learning philosophy of the finance professional. It highlights the ever-growing importance of education on the quest to finding out what we don't know" (McCaffry, 2020).

1.1 THE NEED FOR A HIGH-PERFORMANCE FINANCE FUNCTION

As the world is starting to emerge from the deepest recession since the 1930s (at the time of writing this book, Spring–Summer 2021)—after years of financial scandals, economic shrinkages, cost reductions, and a global pandemic—it is time to look ahead by focusing with renewed energy on growth and adding value. Organizations—profit, non-profit, governmental—are again focusing on the future and their drive to build is returning. One manifestation of this focus is increased attention to the concept of the high-performance organization (HPO). The HPO is defined as "an organization that achieves financial and non-financial results that are exceedingly better than those of its peer group over a period of five years or more, by focusing in a disciplined way on that what really matters to the organization" (De Waal, 2012, p. 5). Core to the HPO idea is to create a strong internal organization that can easily and flexibly deal with both the threats posed and—in particular—the opportunities presented by the outside world. This can only be effectively achieved when all parts of the organization contribute to creating and sustaining

DOI: 10.4018/978-1-7998-6929-0.ch001

the HPO (He et al., 2018). This means that all departments, functions, business units, and divisions must transform themselves into high-performance entities (Mowbray et al., 2018).

Among the most important support functions of every organization is the finance function (Burgess & Bryant, 2001; CFO Innovation Asia, 2018; Dunk, 1999; Graham et al., 2012; Wolf et al., 2015; Zoni and Merchant, 2007). The finance function can be regarded as the spider in the organizational web, because it has relationships with every part of the organization and is also represented on the executive board. Therefore, it is of utmost importance that this function takes the lead by transforming itself into a high-performance finance function (HPFF) with urgency, serving as a role model for other functions in the organization. In practice, there appears to be only a handful of top-performing finance functions that have successfully mastered the mix of culture, talent, governance model, technology, and ability to improve necessary to become an HPFF (Roos et al., 2020). Most finance functions still spend too much time on routine activities and therefore cannot play an active and important role in strategic decision-making processes in the organization. In addition, many finance functions have more or less become stagnant in terms of their development because circumstances in recent years (see frame below) have forced them to concentrate mainly on getting their basic processes and reliability of their data and reports in order to allow them to meet the increasing compliance requirements. This has put a lot of pressure on the financial professionals who, thanks to their "blood, sweat, and tears", have often succeeded in only achieving the required basic performance: delivering reports, budgets, forecasts, and annual accounts in time and getting these approved by the external accountant. These pressures have prevented finance functions from investing sufficiently in the development of their financial professionals (McCaffry, 2020). In addition, operational managers and management teams increasingly require better service and support from the finance function to help them deal with organizational challenges (Lawson and Hatch, 2020). On top of this, many finance functions suffer from quality problems that have arisen because, since the financial and economic crises at the beginning of this century, often only basic investments have been made—often at the expense of the development of the financial professionals (Farrar, 2018)—while, at the same time, costs have been reduced by an average of 29% (Agrawal et al., 2020). The COVID pandemic and its economic consequences are expected to perpetuate such problems because organizations, and therefore also their finance functions, are anticipated to have to make (further) cutbacks (Lawson, 2020).

> "Many finance functions seem to be stuck in a rut. The symptoms are often easy to see. Teams manually produce the same reports, year after year—long after they have stopped being useful to management. Experts spend too much time making sure their numbers are right and not enough time figuring out what the numbers mean or what to do about them. And CFOs are often too caught up in their function's highly specific challenges to understand what best-in-class performance looks like and how to achieve it" (Roos et al., 2020).

However, working in such a way and in such a challenging environment cannot be sustained in the long term. Because of the great pressure, errors will inevitably creep into the work and people will become overtired and possibly leave the organization. This provides the first reason for finance functions to want to become HPFFs: financial professionals no longer have to work under immense strain in a fire-fighting mode; instead, they operate in a well-running finance function where it is enjoyable to work. The second reason to become an HPFF is the ambition of the finance function and its professionals to excel in their professional field, in order to make a significant contribution to the further development of both the finance function and the entire organization (see Figure 1).

Figure 1. The reasons for becoming a high-performance finance function

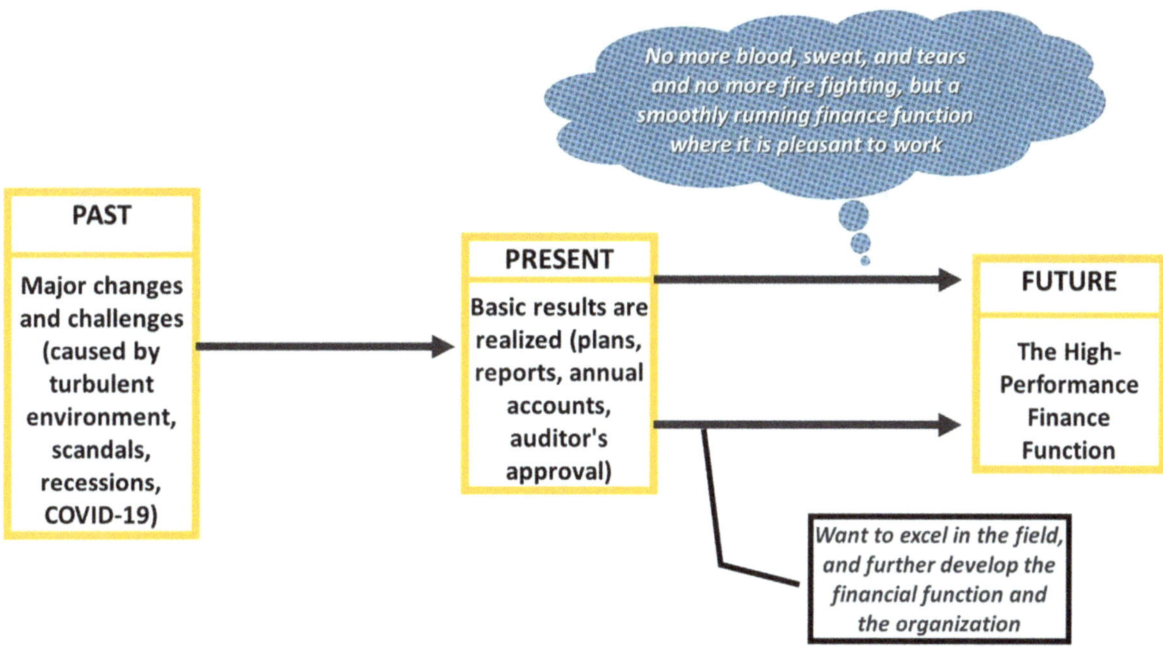

There is a third reason: it is very rewarding for finance functions to become HPFFs, given that HPFFs have lower operating costs; make fewer mistakes; have internal customers who are more satisfied; have more influence within the organization, especially during strategic decision-making; and spend more time in the business partnering role than average-performing finance functions (Accenture, 2014; O'Connor et al., 2014; PWC, 2014; Foged et al., 2018).

But what is a HPFF, and what does it look like? Daily life in the finance function is hectic: in addition to routine activities being carried out to an appropriate standard and on time, the finance function is also expected to respond quickly to ad hoc inquiries from the organization. In addition, the finance function must improve in order to become (even) more effective and deliver more added value to the organization. The finance function must achieve all this while 'normal work' (monthly, quarterly, and annual closings; internal and external reporting; administration) continues. It is therefore no wonder that many finance functions are structurally short of time and lack capacity to be able to continuously improve. This might also explain why, in a recent study (Rosvold, 2021), only 49% of the finance leaders surveyed had just started the transformation of their finance function. Among them, 80% indicated that they had not (yet) achieved noticeable results from this transformation!

As a result, the ability of the finance function to transform into an HPFF and support the organization in its transformation into an HPO is limited (see Figure 2). The available capacity can admittedly be increased by temporarily scaling up, but there is a "maximum to manage" that cannot be exceeded because people then risk becoming overloaded.

The challenges facing the finance function (Essaides et al., 2019)

- The finance function must make a greater contribution to the further development of financial employees to positions within and outside the organization, so that they gain broader knowledge and experience. Facilitating an active personnel policy is necessary because jobs for life no longer exist.
- The finance function has the ambition to offer the internal customer (generally the Board of Directors, the management team, and the line managers) more than mere satisfaction with the finance function, in providing greater involvement and self-steering by these internal customers in financial matters.
- The finance function wants to be able to cope with rapidly changing technologies, automation, and digitization because these provide many opportunities for further optimization.
- The finance function must deal with changing ways of working (such as more self-management/steering and, for example, "agile" working).
- Because of the constantly tightening legislation (also in an international context), the finance function requires increasing knowledge and flexibility in order to quickly adjust procedures and reports.
- The finance function wants to position itself differently in the organization (as a change agent) in order to be able to take a pioneering role in the transformation of the organization into an HPO, and with its current products, advice, knowledge, and prestige it has only been moderately successful in achieving this.
- The finance function has to take a leading role in looking ahead (forecasting) and scenario planning because these are increasingly important activities for the organization to survive and thrive.

Figure 2. Current situation of many finance functions

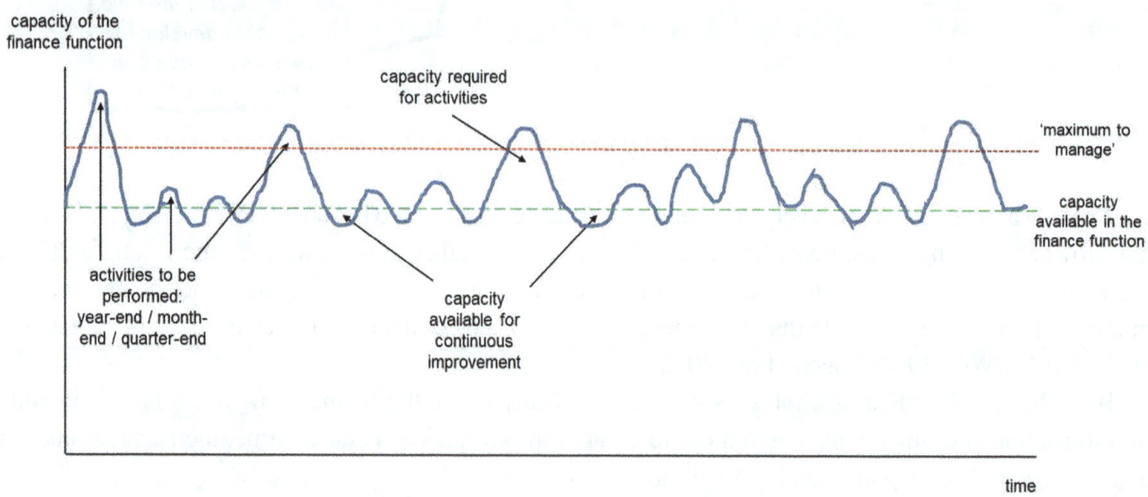

It is therefore necessary for the finance function to organize routine activities as efficiently as possible and to reduce the number of "peaks" in its activities. This means that the finance function must transform itself into a department that operates more efficiently and, above all, more effectively. In order to achieve this, many activities will have to be automated and non-routine activities will have to be designed and carried out in a different, smarter manner in order to create sufficient time and capacity for continuous improvement (see Figure 3).

The key question to address is how an HPFF can be created. In the literature, especially in practitioner contributions, a plethora of relevant publications can be found. However, most examine the finance function in isolation, focusing on its transformation to "world-class finance" or "best-in-class finance" with little regard to the function's role in the greater scheme of organizational workings and transformations (O'Connor et al., 2014; Wunsche, 2007). In this book, a framework is developed to help the finance function transform into an HPFF in a way that enables it to explicitly contribute to the organization in its endeavors to become an HPFF. As the foundation for this endeavor, this book takes the HPO framework (De Waal, 2012)—which is a scientifically developed and validated framework for transforming organizations into HPOs (Do and Mai, 2020)—and explicitly shows how the finance function can reshape itself in a manner that supports all factors of the HPO framework. In turn, the HPFF framework was developed on a scientific basis and tested in practice (De Waal et al., 2019). As such, this HPFF framework is the first practical and scientifically validated improvement framework for finance functions to build a solid foundation, thus finally giving practitioners a robust basis for improving their finance functions.

Figure 3. Desired situation of the finance function: HPFF

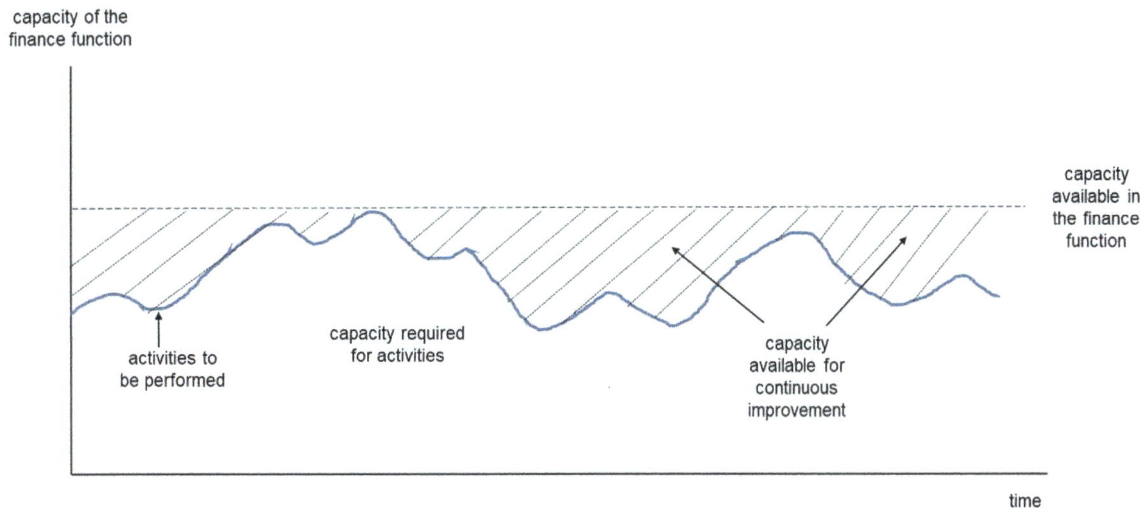

This book is intended for financial professionals who are willing to look beyond their own position, believe that the finance function has an important exemplary role within the organization, and seek to work in a highly professional environment. With the information in this book, these financial professionals can tackle the transformation of their finance functions by first getting colleagues enthusiastic about this and then working together on creating the HPFF and subsequently supporting the organization in its efforts to become an HPO.

> "Finance transformation doesn't just mean adopting or implementing a new technology. It also involves transforming systems, processes, the organization structure and the culture of the finance function itself. A successful finance transformation also involves foundational changes such as validating (and in some cases, defining) the strategic mission of the finance function within the organization, redefining the finance function's organization structure, roles and responsibilities, as well as reviewing and re-engineering processes. Altogether, these changes can lead to the redefinition of the finance function and its people" (Ferrin & and Wong, 2021).

1.2 WHAT DO WE MEAN BY 'THE FINANCE FUNCTION'?

Before we continue, it is useful to first discuss what exactly we mean by "the finance function." This term is used in this book for the entirety of financial processes that are performed in an organization, as well as for the group of people responsible for, and specializing in, the execution of these processes. The professionals responsible for the financial processes generally work in the finance function, but can also work outside of it. People within the finance function are often under the direction of the Chief Financial Officer (CFO) or the Director of Finance. In addition, there are people who work on financial processes but do not fall within the finance function, such as those in shared service centers that do not fall under the hierarchical line of the CFO. In various organizations, the business controller reports to the line manager and not to the CFO.

Every organization has financial processes and someone who is responsible for them; in other words, every organization has a finance function. The micro enterprise usually employs a part-time administrator, and the entrepreneur is often the one who keeps the finances in order. Small businesses have financial persons who mainly work in the financial operation, with a Financial Director as the person ultimately responsible. The finance function is compact and the finance function is close to the business. In a medium-sized organization more coordination, direction, and guidance is needed, because the logical cohesion of processes too often seems to be missing: thus, a Control department is created. For large companies, the question arises how the chain from transaction processing, via information delivery and sense-making, to providing advice can be shaped as effectively and efficiently as possible. In this book, we discuss the finance function as it exists in its fullest form. In practice, this concerns the finance function in most medium-sized and all large organizations. Depending on the size and specific situation of an organization, certain tasks will coincide between one or a few people, and certain ideas contained in this book may or may not be relevant. In the description of the finance function that we use, not all tasks of the CFO are part of that finance function because the CFO often has a seat on the Board of Directors. The CFO is then an executive with dual responsibility. We do not consider the CFO's management task to be part of the finance function, although the management tasks of the finance function are.

Which activities do we now include in the finance function? To arrive at a good overview, we consulted a Dutch and an Anglo-Saxon classification scheme that were both constructed after their authors consulted a large number of studies in the finance field. The Dutch professional organization of Accountants and the Association of Registered Controllers NBA/VRC mentions in its "Model of the finance professional" four core areas in which the financial professional works: Strategic Management; Performance Management; Finance Operations and Reporting; and Governance, Risk and Compliance (see Table 1). Finance Operations and Reporting and Governance, Risk and Compliance represent the "primary financial basis" for the finance function: providing reliable and relevant information to the organization. The financial administrative processes must be in order, and the internal control and risk management systems must work properly. Monitoring the continuity and controlling the organization is the main objective here. Strategic Management and Performance Management underline the increasing importance of decision support by the finance function. The roles of these areas are to facilitate insight and give advice to management, with the aim of making it possible for them to take the right decisions for the organization at both strategic and tactical levels.

The Institute of Chartered Accountants in England and Wales (ICAEW, 2011) distinguishes six groups of activities of the finance function in its framework: 1. Accounting (transaction processing activities, administration and reporting, financial control), 2. Compliance (regulations and tax), 3. Management

Table 1. The most important tasks and activities of the financial (NBA-VRC, 2014)

Role	Strategic Management	Performance Management	Finance Operations and Reporting	Governance, Risk and Compliance
Advisory / decision support	Strategic level: • Portfolio, acquisition and divestment decisions • Price, market, and customer strategy	Tactical level: • Capital investments • Working capital management • Increase effectiveness and efficiency of the organization	• Necessary (non) financial information for management	• Governance • Risk management and regulations
Primary financial	• Financing and tax strategies • Analysis and scenarios	• Effective management control systems, such as budgets and forecasts • Finance and treasury activities • Analysis and scenarios	• Taking care of internal and external reports ▪ Effectiveness and efficiency of administrative processes ▪ Analysis and scenarios	• Effective internal control framework • Implementation and application of the appropriate accounting and tax regulations

and Control (processes, applications, internal auditing, management accounting), 4. Strategy and Risk (strategy, risk management, M&A), and 5. Funding (investor relations and financing). As the sixth group of activities, organizational activities such as leadership and management and resourcing activities necessary for the finance function to function properly are included. The ICAEW mentions the following examples of this type of activity: the development, implementation, and management of financial systems; developing the financial professional; and outsourcing and shared services. The ICAEW framework emphasizes relationships between groups of activities that are highly interdependent: sometimes one activity informs another subsequent activity, sometimes it is more directive.

The organizational context (which is dictated by factors such as the size, history, and maturity of an organization) and the industry in which an organization operates result in differences in structure between finance functions of organizations. However, groups of processes can be distinguished, whereby one group of processes might be more represented in a certain type of organization than another group. The finance function in any organization generally includes the following transaction-processing financial processes (Perik, 2006): administration for the purpose of procurement (purchase administration, accounts payable administration); production (production administration, project administration, fixed assets administration, stock administration); sales (accounts receivable administration, invoicing, sales administration, quotation calculation); and internal control (administrative organization, cash management, general ledger administration, payroll). These administrative processes not only include transaction-processing activities but also activities that guide and facilitate, aimed at aligning the processes with the financial professionals who have to carry them out. For example, the Head of Accounting must have an overview of financial processes and systems, be accountable for the financial processing of the transactions, set out policies regarding the maintenance of financial records, and collaborate with other internal departments.

Treasury activities (managing the flows of cash in the organization) are sometimes treated separately in the Anglo-Saxon literature, with a distinction made between the controller and the treasurer: the treasurer is more externally oriented, while the controller is internally oriented (Gitman, 2011). Corporate finance, financing strategies, cash management, interest and currency management, and working capital management and insurance belong to the portfolio of the treasury function. The treasurer is responsible for the process of maximizing the profitability of the company and ensuring the strongest possible financial structure to safeguard continuity; this is also called financial management.

In addition to the transaction processing processes, an organization has planning and control processes such as budgeting, forecasting, cost price calculation, and internal and external management reporting. These processes are generally of a routine nature. Management reports are usually monthly and/or quarterly, and budgeting takes place annually in most organizations. The rhythm of forecasting often coincides with the rhythm of management reporting processes. External reports and internal reports clearly have a different dynamic, with external reports aimed at fulfilling accountability to external stakeholders while internal reports support internal decision-making. Group Reporting, i.e., the process from bookkeeping to annual accounts, is part of the external reporting process. In addition to the planning and control processes, with their recurring rhythm, the finance function carries out processes that do not have a fixed rhythm, such as cost modeling, key performance indicator (KPI) analysis, and planning. These processes are carried out to generate predictive data ("forecasting and predictive analysis") and provide new and better insights to management, and are therefore mainly aimed at supporting the tactical and strategic choices that management has to make. Special investigations are classified under "special processes"; these include investigations prior to acquisitions, mergers with other organizations, an IPO (initial public offering), a separation of organizational units, benchmarking studies, and the calculation of investment business cases. The planning and control and analysis processes are expected to enable management to make sound decisions. These processes mainly concern information that makes it possible to control decisions already taken (planning and control) and analyses that should lead to better or new insights. Both processes are assigned to the controller task part within the finance function.

Treasury and group reporting processes have a strong financial professional nature, in which knowledge of (working) capital flows, legislation and regulations, and International Financial Reporting Standards (IFRS) is very important. These processes are generally executed at the headquarters of an organization. Other specialisms with interfaces with the finance function may be situated at headquarters, such as:

- Tax planning and tax compliance: The process for complying with tax laws and regulations. This specialism performs, on behalf of the Board of Directors, the collection and processing of tax information, the elaboration of position papers during the processing of taxes, correspondence with tax authorities, and supervision and completion of national and international tax returns.
- Risk management: This process systematically and structurally identifies business risks that can threaten or cause damage to the organization (including operational and financial risks, and damage to its image). The risk management specialism supports the Board of Directors in identifying business risks, assessing their consequences, and assessing and monitoring (through the use of control measures and mechanisms) business risks. Policy-making to mitigate and insure against risks is also part of this specialism.
- Corporate governance: The process of proper management of the organization. This specialism provides the organization with the appropriate management policies and subsequent accountability toward stakeholders, including the owners (shareholders), employees, customers, and society as a whole. Stakeholders' expectations in regard to corporate governance are often set out in codes of conduct.
- Compliance: The process of complying with all laws and regulations set by society, the industry, and the professional field, as well as working in accordance with the standards and rules established by both the organization itself and those derived from legislation and regulations. This specialism supports the Board of Directors in ensuring that the organization operates in accordance with applicable laws and regulations, such as financial supervision acts and environmental legislations.

- Internal audit: The process by which the proper and reliable functioning of the internal organization is assessed in a systematic and disciplined manner, and which is carried out by auditors employed by the organization. This specialism assesses the design and operation of internal risk management and control systems on behalf of the Board of Directors. The purpose of the internal auditor is to provide additional certainty ("assurance") about the quality of the control measures (checks and balances) employed in various areas of business operations. Audits are performed on, for example, internal and external financial reporting (financial audit), business processes (operational audit), IT processes (IT or EDP audit), and safety, health, and environment (SHE) audit.
- Investor relations: The process that maintains relationships with potential and current investors of a company. This specialism is mainly responsible for communication with investors on behalf of the Board of Directors.

Laws and regulations, a stock exchange listing, the size of the organization, and societal developments determine whether or not these disciplines and specialisms are present in the organization and to what extent. Their positioning under the CFO depends not only on management decisions about the organizational structure, but also on the required independence of the finance discipline. For example, an Internal Audit department must operate independently and be independently positioned under the CEO or another member of the Board of Directors. In practice, the CFO and the Head of Internal Audit have many overlaps and interactions. The Head of Internal Audit reports formally to the CEO and to the Audit Committee of the Supervisory Board; in practice, the Head of Internal Audit also discusses the approach and results of audits with the CFO and often joins the management team of the finance function. Compliance is commonly also positioned outside the finance function. Table 2 provides a summary of the processes that we distinguish in the finance function.

Table 2. Processes in the finance function

Process	Explanation of type of process
Administration and book-keeping	Processes aimed at processing (the financial part of) transactions
Procurement (from purchasing to paying)	
Sales (from customer order to payment receipt)	
Internal control (ledger, administrative organization, invoicing, salary)	
Treasury	Processes aimed at corporate steering and management of the finances and risks of the organization
Group reporting (external reports)	
Other specialisms (Governance, Risk and Compliance, Tax planning and compliance, Internal audit, Investor Relations)	
Planning and budgeting	Processes aimed at planning and control of the agreed upon organizational goals
Forecasting	
Cost price calculation	
Management reporting (internal reports)	
Modeling costs	Processes aimed at analysis that should lead to new or better insights for decision-making
Scenario planning	
KPI analyses	
Special investigations	

In addition to organizing the processes as given in Table 2, the management of the finance function has other tasks, such as helping to develop the strategy of the organization; communicating with and being accountable to stakeholders such as the Supervisory Board, shareholders, regulators, and tax authorities; developing the employees of the finance function; propagating the vision of the organization and direction of the finance function, thus enhancing prioritization and focus; and improving financial processes, financial systems, data to be recorded, and projects to be executed. These tasks can be characterized as managerial in nature, in that their responsibility lies with a CFO or manager in the finance function. Therefore we have categorized them separately under the heading "managerial duties of the finance function." Information technology (IT) is indispensable in the provision of financial services. Reporting on existing data, as well as the generation of insights by combining internal and external data, is not possible without the application of IT. The finance function comes into contact with all aspects of IT applications, for example, in safeguarding data quality, data security, selecting (financial) software, architecture of financial data flows, and functional management of financial applications and reporting systems (if cloud solutions are not used). Collaboration with the IT department is therefore increasingly important. We categorize this under the heading "deployment of information technology." The groups of processes just discussed, together with those mentioned in Table 2, can be visually represented as a house: the so-called "House of Finance" (Figure 4).

Figure 4. The "House of Finance"

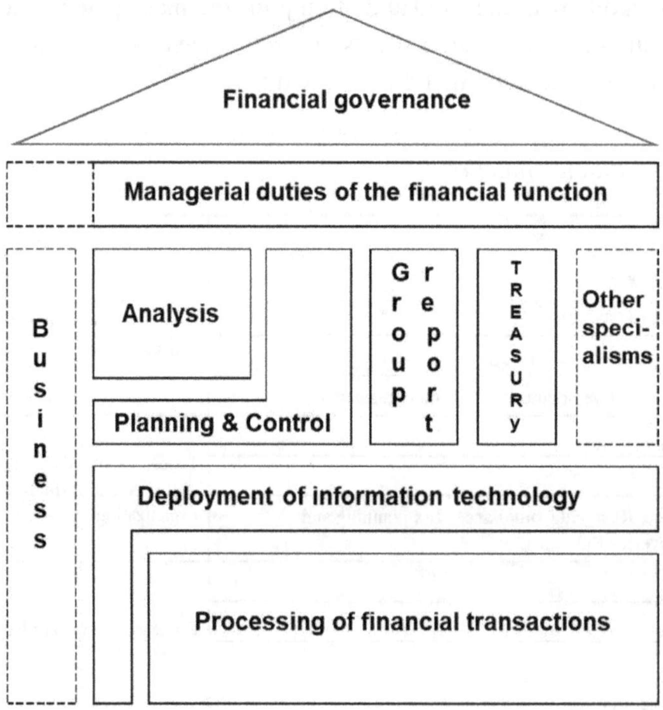

The foundation of the "House of Finance" is the processing of the financial transactions in the organization—both its own and the management of those by other departments (shown in orange in Figure 4). Two important financial processes of the finance function are Group Reporting and Treasury. These two processes have been established as separate processes because they are crucial for successful financial management. In addition to these typically specialist financial processes, other specialisms may fall under the CFO. Organizing sound financial governance is the process associated with managing the finance function. This not only concerns sound financial management but also the managerial tasks aimed at setting up and developing the finance function in regard to financial professionals, systems, data, and projects. These managerial tasks support and facilitate successful financial management of the entire organization. The planning and control and analysis processes can be combined under the term "controlling" or "management control." These are processes aimed at controlling processes and decisions made, and generating new and better insights. The finance function plays a major role in supporting the "business" or "operation" (the internal customers of the finance function) and coordinating organizational governance. The use of IT is part of this group of processes. IT is not only used to support its own management control processes, but also other processes in the organization. The use of IT plays such an important role within processes that we have also placed it under management control.

Naturally, the House of Finance is not a template that is applicable to every finance function or robust to all developments. For example, some organizations use an administration office situated outside the business units, such as a shared service center. In that case, the financial processes fall outside the finance function. In the banking sector, the risk function falls partly under the remit of the CFO and can even be divided into risk sub-processes such as market risk or credit risk. Some terms that are common in the finance function are not (yet) reflected in Table 2 or Figure 4. For example, the term "business partnering" does not appear in both because this term is used in different ways and requires more clarification, and because in this chapter we limit ourselves only to *processes* and do not yet focus on specific *roles* of financial professionals within the finance function. The same applies to the terms "business control" and "financial control."

1.3 READING GUIDE AND JUSTIFICATION

The remainder of this book is structured into two sections, each consisting of several chapters: "Designing the High-Performance Finance Function" (Section 1) and "The High-Performance Finance Function in Practice" (Section 2). Figure 5 schematically depicts the layout of the book.

As mentioned earlier, an important development is the transformation from an average organization to an HPO, which requires contribution from every function and department within the organization. In Chapter 2, we describe the HPO Framework that we used to create the HPFF, and we review the financial and non-financial benefits of being an HPO. In Chapter 3.1, we look at the current situation of the finance function, firstly from a historical perspective. We go approximately 30 years back in time to how the finance function stood at that moment, and work forward to the present day. The impact of various changes—mainly due to financial scandals, the pandemic, and various economic crises—on the finance function and the current state of the finance function are discussed. This current state is influenced to a great extent by the most important activities that the function has performed over the past decades and is expected to perform in the next decade(s). These "evergreens of the finance function" are dealt with in Chapter 3.2 and are the initial input for the design of the HPFF.

Figure 5. Schematic reading guide

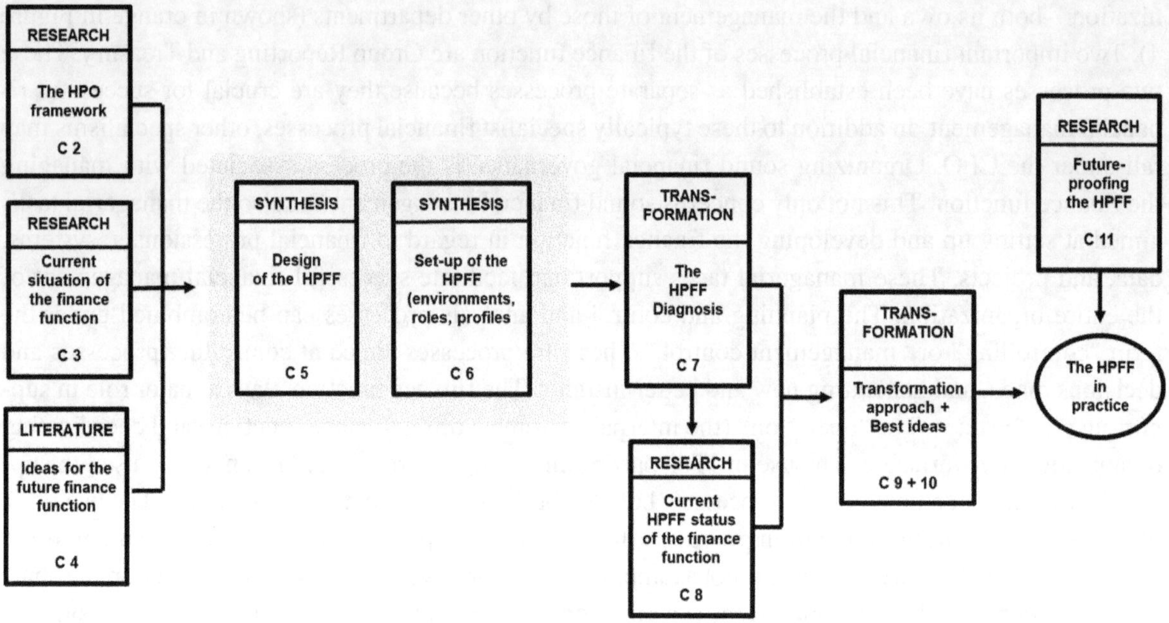

From Chapter 4 onward, we focus on the future finance function: we discuss the main ideas in recent literature for its development, and list these ideas as a second input for the design of the high-performance finance function. Chapters 5 and 6 are the synthesis of the previous chapters. The connection between the HPO Framework (C2), the current situation of the finance function (C3), and the ideas for the future finance function (C4) is made in such a way as to create a design for the HPFF. In addition, the environments that exist in an HPFF and the roles and profiles that financial professionals of an HPFF have are determined (C6). Subsequently, in Chapters 7, 8, 9, and 10, we focus on how to make this design reality and thus establish the HPFF in practice. We do this by presenting the HPFF Diagnosis, with which a finance function can evaluate how far along it is toward becoming an HPFF and what is needed to fully realize that status; describing the current HPFF situation of many finance functions and discussing the most common improvements needed; describing a transformation approach to the HPFF; and giving 50 "best ideas" of finance functions that have already transformed (parts of their function) into an HPFF. Finally, in Chapter 11, we discuss the future of the HPFF: in particular, what the influences of megatrends and disruptors in the environment (such as the COVID-19 pandemic) on the operations of the finance function are and how the finance function should deal with them. Regardless of what the future brings, it is indisputable that the performance level of the finance function is expected to be much higher than it currently is, and that the tools and ideas we provide in this book will be very useful to achieve the desired quality level.

Justification

This book is the amalgamation of two books we wrote in the Dutch language on the topic of the HPFF: *Hoe bouw je een high performance financiële functie?* [How to build a high-performance finance function?] (de Waal and Bilstra, Vakmedianet, 2016) and *De high performance financiële functie in de praktijk* [The high-performance finance function in practice] (de Waal, Bilstra, de Roeck, Vakmedianet, 2019). During and after writing these books, we documented the scientific foundation of the HPFF in several academic articles ("Identifying the characteristics of a high-performance finance function" in the *Journal of Advances in Management Research,* 2019*;* "Removing the barriers on the way to European high-performance finance functions" in *Problems and Perspectives in Management*, 2019). We also conducted several in-depth studies into the following topics surrounding the HPFF: how to measure internal client satisfaction with the finance function; how to obtain approval for the transformation to an HPFF; and what the influence of megatrends and disruptors is on the finance function. Armed with a new literature study, new cases and novel best ideas, we thought the time was ripe to write this book—not only to make our thinking and our experiences available in the English language but to also ensure that the HPFF becomes available to a wider audience. We hope you enjoy reading the book and that its content entices you to embark on the exciting journey toward high performance—both within your finance function and your organization!

REFERENCES

Accenture. (2014). *The CFO as architect of business value, delivering growth and managing complexity*. Accenture 2014 High Performance Finance Study, Accenture LLC.

Agrawal, A., Eklund, S., Waite, J., & Woodcock, E. (2020). *Finance 2030: four imperatives for the next decade*. McKinsey and Company.

Burgess, C., & Bryant, K. (2001). Revenue management – the contribution of the finance function to profitability. *International Journal of Contemporary Hospitality Management*, *13*(3), 144–150. doi:10.1108/09596110110388936

CFO Innovation Asia. (2018). *The changing role and mandate of finance: creating a vision for the future*. White paper, Chartered Global Management Accountant.

de Waal, A., Bilstra, E., & de Roeck, P. (2019). *De high performance financiële functie in de praktijk* [The high performance finance function in practice]. Vakmedianet.

de Waal, A. A. (2012). *What Makes a High Performance Organization, Five Validated Factors of Competitive Performance that Apply Worldwide*. Global Professional Publishing.

Do, T., & Mai, N. (2020). High-performance organization: A literature review. *Journal of Strategy and Management*, *13*(2), 297–309. doi:10.1108/JSMA-11-2019-0198

Dunk, A. (1999). The managerial roles of accounting: A value-adding perspective for the new millennium. *Pacific Accounting Review*, *11*(1/2), 77–88. doi:10.1108/eb037929

Essaides, N., Willman, T., & Dorr, E. (2019). *World-class finance: redefining performance in a digital era*. The Hackett Group.

Farrar, M. (2018). *Changing competencies and mindsets, creating a vision for the future research emerging themes*. Association of International Certified Professional Accountants.

Ferrin, M., & Wong, W. (2021). *Winning finance, Transformation harnessing the full value of the finance function*. Renoir Consulting.

ICAEW Finance and Management Faculty. (2011). *The finance function: A framework for analysis*. Accountancymagazine.com

Foged, B., Liu-Lindberg, A., Fynsk, H., & Codd, A. (2018). *Create value as a finance business partner: transforming the finance function into a profit centre*. Kindle Edition.

Gitman, L. J. (2011). *Principles of managerial finance* (13th ed.). Prentice Hall.

Graham, A., Davey-Evans, S., & Toon, I. (2012). The developing role of the financial controller: Evidence from the UK. *Journal of Applied Accounting Research*, *13*(1), 71–88. doi:10.1108/09675421211231934

He, C., Gu, J., & Liu, H. (2018). How do department high-performance work systems affect creative performance? A cross-level approach. *Asia Pacific Journal of Human Resources*, *56*(3), 402–426. doi:10.1111/1744-7941.12156

Lawson, R. (2020). The impact of COVID-19 on the finance function: The pandemic has changed how businesses around the world operate, and those within the finance function face cutbacks, lost compensation, and changing business needs. *Strategic Finance*, (November), 46–52.

Lawson, R., & Hatch, T. (2020). *Preparing the finance function for technological change: With the plethora of new technologies available to businesses and finance teams, determining where and how to begin a digital transformation can be a challenge*. Strategic Finance.

McCaffry, R. (2020). *Finance transformation: The human perspective*. Association of International Certified Professional Accountants.

Mowbray, P., Wilkinson, A. J., & Tse, H. (2018). High performance strategy: influence on HR department and line managers' design of employee voice. *Academy of Management Annual Meeting Proceedings*, *2018*(1), 11-34. 10.5465/AMBPP.2018.11034abstract

NBA-VRC. (2014). *Visiedocument over het beroep van de financieel professional* [Vision document on the profession of the Financial Professional]. Nederlandse Beroepsorganisatie van Accountants (ledengroep Accountants in Business NBA) and de Vereniging van Registercontrollers.

O'Connor, J., Schneider, L., & Willman, T. (2014). *The world-class performance advantage: how leading finance organizations outperform their peers*. Finance Executive Insight, The Hackett Group.

Perik, K. (2006). *Haal het beste uit je financieel manager* [Get the best out of your finance manager]. Pearson Education.

PWC. (2014). *Marktstudie financiële functie, goed voorbereid op de toekomst* [Market study of finance function, well prepared for the future]. PricewaterhouseCoopers Advisory N.V.

Roos, A., Tucker, J., Rodt, M., Stange, S., Ego, P., Boudadi, A., & Sheth, H. (2020). *Lessons from best-in-class CFOs*. Boston Consulting Group.

Rosvold, S. (2021). *The state of finance transformation*. CFO University. https://cfo.university/library/article/the-state-of-finance-transformation-march-2021-rosvold

Wolf, S., Weißenberger, B. E., Wehner, M. C., & Kabst, E. (2015). Controllers as business partners in managerial decision-making: Attitude, subjective norm, and internal improvements. *Journal of Accounting & Organizational Change*, *11*(1), 24–46. doi:10.1108/JAOC-10-2012-0100

Wunsche, A. (2007). The CFO as strategist and catalyst in building a high-performance culture. *Ivey Business Journal*, *71*(8), 1–10.

Zoni, L., & Merchant, K. A. (2007). Controller involvement in management: An empirical study in large Italian corporations. *Journal of Accounting & Organizational Change*, *3*(1), 29–43. doi:10.1108/18325910710732849

Chapter 2
The Basis:
The High Performance Organization Framework

ABSTRACT

In this chapter, the high-performance organization framework (hereafter referred to as the HPO framework), a scientifically validated framework that enables and supports organizations in transforming themselves into a sustainable high-performing enterprise, is introduced. The HPO framework forms the basis for the HPFF. It consists of five factors, with 35 underlying characteristics, which are described. The HPO diagnosis, with which an organization can evaluate how far it is on the way to high performance, is discussed. This chapter concludes with a listing of the benefits of using the HPO framework in practice.

2.1 HIGH PERFORMANCE: FIVE FACTORS AND 35 CHARACTERISTICS[1]

The HPO Framework, which was initially developed during a five-year academic study using data collected worldwide and then validated over another five years[2], consists of five factors and 35 accompanying characteristics and is depicted as a flywheel (see Figure 1). The HPO research shows that there is a direct and positive relationship between the five HPO factors and competitive performance: the higher the scores on the HPO factors (HPO scores), the better the results of the organization, and the lower the HPO scores, the lower its competitive performance. In fact, if an organization starts to work on (i.e., strengthen) one of the HPO factors, this will also have a positive impact on other HPO factors, which will, in turn, have a positive impact on all the HPO factors. Thus, this process is represented as a flywheel: as it starts to turn, it will go faster and faster: in a similar manner, as an organization strengthens its HPO factors, it will become better and better! The research also shows that the organization must have equal scores for all HPO factors in order to sustain high performance. For instance, if the organization scores an eight (out of ten) on four HPO factors and a five on another HPO factor, the organization will not be able to function as an HPO because it is out of balance. An easy way to visualize this is to imagine a pinwheel on a child's toy (see Figure 1). When exposed to the wind, it spins around at a constant speed.

DOI: 10.4018/978-1-7998-6929-0.ch002

However, if one of the blades breaks, the pinwheel will no longer turn around smoothly and will eventually stop. Like the wind on the pinwheel, an organization's attention should be distributed evenly across the five HPO factors to make sure none of them "break" and hold back the organization. Working on just one HPO factor or only a few characteristics without paying attention to the other HPO factors or characteristics in due course will not help the organization in the long run.

Figure 1. The HPO Framework

What vs. How
The HPO Framework is not a set of instructions or a recipe to be blindly followed: rather, it is a framework that has to be translated and applied by managers to the specific situation in their organization in order to design a specific version of the framework that is appropriate to their organization's context. Thus, after the *what* provided by the HPO Framework (as in, "we now know what has to be improved"), the tailoring of the organization, i.e., the *how* (as in, "how we should improve depends on the organization"), is done by the organization itself. Hence, the HPO Framework is not a silver bullet and does not provide a blueprint or recipe for high performance; it indicates the areas in the organization that are important for achieving excellent performance. It is then your task and that of your colleagues to undertake improvement actions that strengthen these areas and to maintain them when strengthened. Thus, the HPO Framework provides focus on the areas in your organization that really matter (the *what*). For the *how*, we have collected from practitioners various best ideas that could be of value when you realize your own *hows*.

Management Quality

HPO managers maintain trust with their employees by showing appreciation for their loyalty, treating them with attention and respect, and developing and sustaining good relationships with them. They encourage employees to have faith and trust in themselves and others, and they treat them in a fair and honest manner. They have integrity and act as role models for employees as well as their fellow managers through their honesty, sincerity, dedication, enthusiasm, respectful attitudes, strong ethical values, credibility, and consistent behavior. They are not afraid to show their weaknesses and they are neither complacent nor arrogant. They are also decisive: they avoid "paralysis by analysis" and propose quick and effective actions while stimulating others to also take action. HPO managers coach and facilitate employees in such a way as to enable them to also achieve better performance. They offer support and assistance and protect their employees from negative external influences (such as undue pressure from higher management echelons), when and where necessary. They are always approachable, but at the same time they hold their employees responsible for their results and take corrective action when they underperform. They put their focus on achieving results, emphasize to employees that they are responsible for their own performance, and are not afraid to make difficult decisions (such as firing an employee). They have an effective, self-assured, and strong management style that has been developed through continuous communication and enforcement of the values of the organization. They make sure that all their employees understand and support the organizational strategy. Where necessary, HPO managers coach their employees to enable their own activities to contribute to the achievement of the organizational strategy. HPO manager competencies are listed and described in Table 1.

Table 1. HPO characteristics belonging to the HPO factor 'Management Quality'

HPO characteristic	Description
The manager is trusted by employees	*Trust*: strong faith in the reliability, sincerity, and strength of a person
The manager has integrity	*Integrity*: moral sincerity
The manager is a role model for employees	*Role model*: a person whom other people look up to as an example in a particular role
The manager makes decisions quickly	*Decision-making*: the process of making decisions, whereby a conclusion is drawn or a solution is proposed
The manager takes action quickly	*Action-taking*: the process of doing things
The manager coaches employees to achieve better results	*Coaching*: training and supporting of employees
The manager focuses on achieving results	*Achieving results*: the attitude of wanting to achieve results (result oriented)
The manager is very effective	*Effective*: the ability to actually achieve desired results
The manager applies strong leadership	*Leadership*: the ability to lead a group of people or an organization - where that ability cannot easily be damaged or overthrown - and to resist external pressure, and to exude determination
The manager is confident	*Confidence*: a state in which one has (a strong) confidence in one's own ability
The manager is decisive with regard to non-performing employees	*Decisiveness*: The ability to make quick and effective decisions about employees who do not perform well
The manager always holds employees responsible for their results	*Holding responsible*: to be held accountable for one's own actions and the results achieved

Openness and Action Orientation

An HPO has an open culture, which means that extensive dialogue takes place between both managers and employees and among the employees themselves in exchanging knowledge and experiences, increasing commitment to the organization, and creating clarity on all organizational levels about what is important for the organization and what it wants to achieve. Managers explicitly ask for the opinions and ideas of their employees and act on that information. There is a large degree of mutual respect, and everyone is asked to get involved in the important affairs of the organization. There is room for experimentation and failure in the organization, and there is no fear of taking (calculated) risks and making mistakes (as long as they are not repeated): these are seen as opportunities for learning. People give each other honest and sincere feedback with the goal of making things better, and this feedback is interpreted and received as such. Knowledge in itself is not power in an HPO, but knowledge that is shared within the organization is, as then a '1 + 1 = 3' situation is achieved. The HPO culture is action-driven. Although there is plenty of deep thinking about issues, HPOs do not suffer from paralysis by analysis. They do not overanalyze, but balance thought with action. Thus, they allow enough time for adequate decision-making and then quickly turn their decisions into actions to solve problems. As a consequence, decisions can be made that are not optimal, and people understand that they may have to adjust a chosen course of action based on new information that becomes available. The relevant HPO manager characteristics are listed and described in Table 2.

Table 2. HPO characteristics belonging to the HPO factor 'Openness and Action-Orientation'

HPO characteristic	Description
The manager frequently engages in a dialogue with employees	*Dialoguing*: the activity through which the concept of a subject is exchanged with other people
Employees spend much time on dialogue, knowledge exchange, and learning from each other	*Knowledge exchange*: the activity through which the concept, knowledge and experience of a subject is exchanged with other people
Employees are always involved in important processes	*Involvement*: the act of participating and sharing of an experience by employees
The manager allows employees to make mistakes	*Allowing mistakes*: to allow an individual to do things incorrectly or to make errors of judgment without any consequences
The manager welcomes change.	*Welcoming change*: to allow employees the opportunity to do things differently
The organization is performance-driven	*Performance driveness*: to have a strong focus on doing things right and a need to achieve results

Long-Term Orientation

In the context of an HPO, long-term survival and benefits are far more important to stakeholders than short-term successes. The organization and its people are extremely client-oriented: they listen carefully to what clients want and need, they understand the values and interests of clients, they build excellent long-term relationships with them, and they have regular direct contact with them. HPOs directly involve clients in the organization's affairs (such as the development of new products and services or the best way to perform new tasks). They are open to their reactions and aim to increase value for clients. Their aim is that every party that comes into contact with the organization should have a good feeling about the interaction because the organization has added value and made things better for them: when this is the case, it is only natural for the organization to try to stay in existence as long as possible to make as many parties happy for as long as possible. The organization trains and grooms its people in such a way that new management can be promoted from within. Most managers have worked for a long time in the organization, albeit in different positions and possibly different locations, and thus know the organization, its stakeholders, its products and services, its employees, and its industry very well. Furthermore, because they are HPO managers, they can use this knowledge to good effect. HPOs are a secure workplace, both physically and psychologically. In regard to the latter, HPOs offer employees the confidence to make mistakes without having to be afraid of being fired. In fact, laying off people is the last resort for an HPO. These HPO characteristics are listed and described in Table 3.

Table 3. HPO characteristics belonging to the HPO factor 'Long-Term Orientation'

HPO characteristic	Description
The organization maintains good, long-term relationships with all stakeholders	*Relationships*: the aim to do good for all parties that are influenced by the success or failure of the organization
The organization is aimed at servicing customers as best as possible	*Servicing*: the attitude of an organization toward the individuals or groups that buy or purchase its goods and services
The manager has been with the company for a long time	*Long-time*: managers have a long career with the organization
New management is promoted from within the organization	*Promotion*: the career growth of a person who already works within the organization to a higher position
The organization is a secure workplace for employees	*Secure*: a stable workplace without risks or fears

Continuous Improvement and Renewal

HPOs have a strategy that is unique either in content (what the organization wants to achieve) or in execution (how the organization does things) or (ideally) in both. This means that it is very clear to potential clients why they should choose this organization over comparable organizations in the sector. An HPO also engages in the continuous development of new strategies to replace strategies that are no longer unique or no longer working. The organization then does its utmost to put these unique strategies into practice. It improves, simplifies, and aligns its processes to allow it to act quickly and effectively under changing circumstances. Unnecessary procedures and tasks are removed, and information overload is mitigated. The organization tracks the information that really matters by using critical success factors (CSFs) and key performance indicators (KPIs). It also precisely tracks whether objectives still contribute to the organization's strategy and goals and whether they are fulfilled. Difficult issues are immediately reported to both managers and employees so they can deal with them quickly and improve the way the organization works. An HPO perceives a moral obligation to continuously strive for the best results for its clients and its stakeholders. To this end, its products, processes, and services are continuously improved and renewed. This is supported by a commitment to continuously strengthen the core competencies of the organization and its people. The relevant HPO characteristics are listed and described in Table 4.

Table 4. HPO characteristics belonging to the HPO factor 'Continuous Improvement and Renewal'

HPO characteristic	Description
The organization has adopted a strategy that sets it clearly apart from other organizations	*Uniqueness*: a plan, with the intended course and objectives of an organization, of which only one exists
In the organization, processes are continuously improved	*Improvement*: the attitude and way in which internal business processes are always made better
In the organization, processes are continuously simplified	*Simplification*: the attitude and way in which internal business processes are always made simpler
In the organization, processes are continuously aligned	*Alignment*: the attitude and way in which internal business processes are always attuned to each other
In the organization, everything that influences the organization's performance is explicitly reported	*Reporting*: management of the organization through the systematic definition of mission, strategy and objectives of the organization, and by making these measurable with critical success factors and key performance indicators, so that remedial actions can be taken to keep the organization on the right path
In the organization, both financial and non-financial information is reported to employees	*Information*: providing everyone within the organization with both the financial and the non-financial information needed to achieve good results
The organization continuously innovates its core competencies	*Innovation of core competencies*: implementing new methods for and ideas about the competencies that the organization is best known for
The organization continuously innovates its products, processes and services	*Innovation of products/processes/services:* implementing new methods for and ideas about the products, services and processes of the organization

Employee Quality

An HPO has a diverse workforce in which employees' strengths complement each other. New people are hired who already have HPO traits, such as a high degree of flexibility and the resilience needed to recognize and address organizational problems in a creative way. Furthermore, these new hires will have different skills from the current workforce so that new competencies are continuously added to the organization's skill base. People are constantly developed through formal and informal training, on-the-job training, coaching, and through working with other organizations. In regard to the latter, the HPO has explicit goals to create high-performance partnerships (HPPs). In such an environment, employees, with the support of their managers, seek to achieve extraordinary results for which they expect to be held accountable and receive feedback. Their competencies are listed and described in Table 5.

Table 5. HPO characteristics belonging to the HPO factor 'Employee Quality'

HPO characteristic	Description
The manager inspires organizational members to accomplish extraordinary results	*Inspiration*: to make someone enthusiastic and inspired to achieve better and better results
Employees are trained to be resilient and flexible	*Resilience and flexibility*: the ability to easily and quickly recover from setbacks, and then tackle things in a different way
The organization has a diverse workforce with complementary strengths	*Diversity and complementarity*: employees of the organization differ from each other in many ways, providing the collective workforce with all the strengths the organization needs
The organization grows through partnerships with suppliers and/or customers	*Partnerships*: relationships in which employees from different organizations work together as partners to realize common goals

2.2 THE HPO DIAGNOSIS

Your organization can evaluate its high performance level and identify challenges and possible improvements by conducting an HPO Diagnosis. The HPO Diagnosis process starts with an HPO awareness workshop for management and other interested parties. During this workshop, the organization gets acquainted with the HPO Framework, the HPO Diagnosis, and the possible HPO transformation process. During the actual HPO Diagnosis, management and employees complete the HPO Questionnaire, which consists of statements based on the 35 HPO characteristics. The questionnaire has been validated and the statistics performed on data collected worldwide. Therefore, it is important to mention that the main principles of the HPO Framework remain unchanged, regardless of the type of company or industry being diagnosed. Respondents rate their organization on a scale of one ("we do not meet this characteristic at all") to ten ("we fully comply with this characteristic") on these statements. The individual scores are averaged to provide scores on the HPO factors for the complete organization. These average scores indicate which HPO factors and characteristics the company needs to improve in order to become an HPO. For these factors and characteristics, the organization drafts improvement actions that are incorporated into an HPO transformation plan. This plan is then executed during the year and updated when actions have been successfully wrapped up. The organization often installs an HPO Champion and HPO Coaches to guide this process. In principle, the HPO Diagnosis is repeated every one-and-a-half to two years to evaluate improvements in both the HPO score and the organization's performance and to identify new improvement areas.

2.3 ADDED VALUE OF THE HPO FRAMEWORK HPO-DIAGNOSE

Since the initial launch of the HPO Framework in 2007, many organizations have embarked on an HPO transformation, often using the HPO Diagnosis as the starting point of their journey to high performance. This yields the opportunity to perform an in-depth study of the application and performance effects of the HPO Framework at multiple organizations worldwide. We have shared many of our findings in a multitude of academic and managerial articles. Because we collected data from all HPO Diagnoses in our HPO database (which currently contains data from more than 60,000 respondents), we were able to confirm that the HPO Framework is generally valid for many countries and sectors. We attribute this universal applicability of the Framework to the HPO characteristics being what we call "evergreens of management": they are always important for creating and maintaining an excellent organization, regardless of the culture (country, industry, family/non-family) the organization operates in, and to which managers have to pay attention when devising the actions to undertake in order to lead their organizations to excellence and superior results (de Waal, 2013). We were also able to identify—using data from the past 20 years—the following benefits that organizations experienced as a result of transforming into an HPO (de Waal, 2020; de Waal and Goedegebuure, 2017):

Improved Attitude of Employees

Employees develop a stronger focus on improvement. They perceive and accept more responsibility for improving the products, services, and processes of the organization. They also take more initiative in these areas, which leads to a continuously improving organization. In addition, the degree of innovation increases because employees dare to experiment more. As a result, more new products and services can be brought to market in a shorter time span and with more success. There is also a more positive mentality and greater involvement and commitment. Employees become more solution-oriented: they think less in terms of problems and more in terms of solutions. They are proud of their organization and enjoy working there. They feel that the organization is doing a good job, which creates new energy in the organization. Employees feel that they are pursuing a common goal: to become and remain an HPO.

Improved Internal and External Collaboration

In an HPO, employees work better together, both internally with colleagues from other departments and externally with suppliers and customers. They are much more open to suggestions from others and no longer work on islands (or 'silos'), because they see themselves as part of the value chain of the organization that must function effectively in all areas. There is more trust, mutually between employees and between employees and managers, making it easier for them to build relationships and work together. Employees show more interest in each other, and managers are more sympathetic to employees: they do everything they can to bring out the best in them. In addition, there is more openness within the organization, and more often a good dialogue between managers and employees and also between the various business units.

Stronger Organization

The organization has a unique strategy compared with other organizations in the sector. This strategy can be unique in content and/or in execution. This clearly distinguishes the organization from the competition or its peer group (consisting of comparable organizations), making it more attractive to new customers and potential employees. The organization acts in a much more focused manner and has more discipline. Fewer projects and initiatives are developed; and if they are, these will be completed on time, within the set budget, and with the desired results. Employees also feel a stronger need to be socially responsible. When the organization shows commitment to all stakeholders, society benefits from the corporate social responsibility (CSR) activities undertaken by the employees of the organization. In addition, the organization has built a reputation for delivering high quality. This is a result of better service, fewer problems with quality, fewer errors, realizing organizational goals more often, and fulfilling the promises made to the customer to a greater extent. This not only gives the organization a better reputation in the sector, but in society as a whole.

Improved Financial Results

The non-financial benefits mentioned above translate into financial benefits. Productivity increases because the same number of employees do more and with more success. Profitability also increases because costs are lower and sales turnover higher. As a result, the organization climbs to the top of the industry as its market share continues to increase. Non-profit and government organizations do more, with higher quality, within the same budget. Finally, the financial situation of the organization not only improves but also stabilizes, because costs and budgets are better controlled.

Greater Competitive Advantage

Achieving higher HPO scores means better financial results, and when the organization achieves the highest average HPO score in the industry, it will also have the best financial results relative to the competition/peer group. The same is true for business units when compared inside an organization: those with the highest average HPO scores also exhibit the best financial performance of all units.

CASE: Successful Transformation - Pay Attention to the Undercurrent and the Upstream

A government organization was faced with a major challenge when a significant budget reduction of 35% was recently imposed by the Ministry. "Despite the fact that we are an IT-intensive company, personnel costs are still our largest cost item. With an imposed reduction of such a magnitude, you cannot avoid working more efficiently with fewer people," says the Director of Finance and Control. "Customer focus and efficient execution are and will remain key words in our service provision. We strive for an excellent service to more than 5 million customers. That is also, strange as it may sound, important to our costs. All benefit payments to the customers must of course be paid on time; if we pay an hour late, the call center will be overloaded with complaining people and that costs money. Another example is the number of questions from customers. If every customer calls us once a year, we can never handle it properly without incurring enormous extra costs. Our front is very customer-oriented, while we automate the back-office as much as possible. Moreover, we are very critical of anything that does not really contribute to our services."

The Director of Finance and Control, just like his fellow management team members, therefore faced a major challenge: total operating costs had to be reduced considerably because there was a significant savings target, while at the same time a high customer satisfaction score had to be maintained. To deal with this challenge, a major change had to be initiated. However, three years ago, when the Director of Finance and Control joined the organization, she found an organization that was tired of the many reorganizations and changes in management, with a culture that was insufficiently performance-oriented: "The morale and confidence among the employees was low and before me there had been several management changes in a short time." In this context, cost reduction had to be achieved and the number of people at the organization reduced from 3,000 to 2,400, with the finance department going down from 130 to 70 employees. "Finance and Control had and still has a dual role in this. First, the finance function itself had to contribute to the task. We did this by centralizing part of the financial administration and part of control. In addition, Finance and Control had to be at the forefront of the change, in order to create space to support the change process within the overall organization."

Undercurrent and Upstream

The bar was set high: the finance function wanted to become "best-in-class" to be able to deal with the changes and be the vanguard in that change. To achieve this, a multi-year change program "Finance of the Future" was started. At the start of this program, the aim was to increase efficiency as well as improve the quality of the function's services: "We wanted the finance function to professionalize, so that

Finance and Control would become a real partner with added value to the business and at the same time execute the transaction-oriented processes at a lower cost. For example, concrete goals were formulated for the integration of the information systems, for shortening the lead times in the planning and control cycle, for reducing the costs of the finance function, and for improving the control framework. In the first steps of the change process in the organization, we introduced the change from a blueprint approach. That gave us the framework for the needed change. With a small team, we shaped the changes of reduced head count and a change in structure."

The transition was performed top-down, which quickly turned out to be not so effective. The motivation and willingness among financial professionals to actually implement the changes was low. The Director of Finance and Control reflects on the start of the change: "The absenteeism rate was 12 percent and communication was difficult. There was also an insufficient feedback culture, which I believe is necessary for good collaboration and continuous improvement. We realized that our ambition could not be fulfilled without explicitly involving our financial professionals. That is why a distinction was made fairly quickly in the change program between the so-called "upstream" and "undercurrent" (see Figure 2).

Figure 2. Upstream and undercurrent in the transition at the governmental finance function

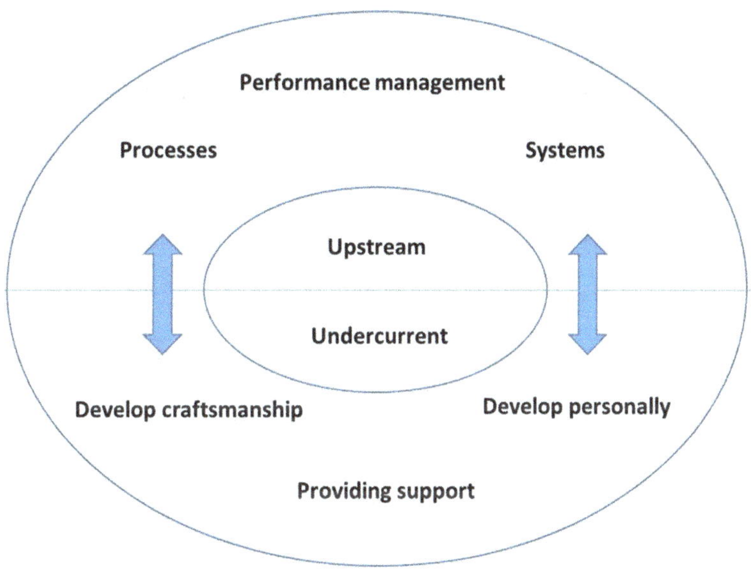

The upstream is about processes and systems, and about how the work can be done as optimally as possible. The undercurrent concerns the people who provide the services of the finance function. Craftsmanship development and personal development (and providing support to financial professionals through leadership) is the motor of concrete improvement themes in the upstream. The Director of Finance and Control puts it as follows: "As a management team, we initiated the change from two tracks. Both from the work that has to be done (the upstream) and from the way we do that work (the undercurrent). What we realized was that the change program would be a multi-year trajectory. We needed help in the beginning to initiate the undercurrent with the knowledge of the upstream. Knowing what is expected of you, for example process improvements, system implementations, and performance management, is necessary as a framework to focus on how you want to do this. We wanted to know how our financial professionals acted in their work, and whether that matched with our impression of this. In addition, we wanted to experience together where and how we could best work together. Increasing the learning capacity of the financial professionals is the most important flywheel for change. In this way we try to connect the upstream and downstream."

Now that the undercurrent has become stronger, the financial professionals are showing promising development, craftsmanship is increasingly shared with each other, and work attitude has improved — the improvements in the upstream are also coming more quickly. "Using an external benchmark, an upstream instrument, we now compare the performance of Finance and Control with a peer group of Finance departments of comparable government organizations. Also the results of the annual employee satisfaction survey within Finance and Control have considerably increased. And the customer satisfaction survey shows that the internal customer notices that the finance function increasingly delivers high-quality services in an efficient manner."

HPO as Starting Point

The people-oriented approach to the transition was prompted by the results of an HPO diagnosis carried out at the government organization just before the change process started. In this diagnosis, Finance and Control scored higher than the average for the organization; however, the results also yielded food for thought because low scores were achieved on 'continuously improving, simplifying and aligning processes,' 'employees are always involved in important organizational processes,' 'employees spend a lot of time dialoguing and exchanging knowledge,' and 'the leadership consists of strong leaders.' The Director of Finance and Control explains: "The results of the HPO diagnosis actually predicted how our organization would develop when we would start working on the areas for improvement. The diagnosis showed that we would lose employees mentally during the change if we did nothing. How do you ensure that these people get moving and learn to deal with changes?" Therefore, the finance function placed emphasis mainly on its financial professionals during the transition: not on using a "blueprint" as a starting point, but "action learning" by the financial professionals themselves. By combining professional knowledge with practical examples, and discussing together and learning from these examples, financial professionals started to better understand the change. As a logical consequence, the financial professionals showed increased willingness to change during the process. The Director of Finance and Control states: "I was told by my financial professionals that they were specialists; as professionals, I had to give them the confidence that they could make the change. Then they would get energy, they would also start the improvement dialogue with each other, and they would cooperate much more with the other departments."

The second HPFF diagnosis a year later showed that while the scores of the finance function had increased, to take a real step forward it was necessary to shift the focus of the change. "We concluded that financial professionals were still not involved enough in the decision making process," says the Director of Finance and Control. According to her, different approach was necessary, with the finance function now focusing on four areas:

1. The first focus area was entering into a continuous dialogue: "By conducting interviews, financial professionals can show that they stand for their promises and can find a good balance between the

interests of internal customers and their own financial expertise. More than before, the focus must be on the dialogue with the business."

2. The second focus area was the movement from contemplation to steering: "The finance function should not stand on the sidelines and assess what is not going well, but rather steer the business together with internal customers by oozing an attitude of 'we know and understand your business.' Investing in the expertise of the financial professional is not enough; the focus of training and professional development must be aimed at improving advisory skills."
3. The third focus area was working on continuous improvement within the finance function: "You improve by working together and coming up with solutions together. 'We invest in cooperation' is therefore an important starting point for us all."
4. The fourth and final focus area was achieving operational excellence in information provision: "We shouldn't spend too much time on creating reports and information, it should be organized as efficiently as possible by installing, for instance, an automated information supply."

REFERENCES

de Waal, A. A. (2013). Evergreens of excellence. *Journal of Management History*, *19*(2), 241–278. doi:10.1108/17511341311307408

de Waal, A. A. (2020). *High Performance Managerial Leadership*. Praeger.

de Waal, A. A., & Goedegebuure, R. (2017). Investigating the causal link between a management improvement technique and organizational performance: The case of the HPO framework. *Management Research Review*, *40*(4), 429–450. doi:10.1108/MRR-03-2016-0058

Do, T., & Mai, N. (2020). High-performance organization: A literature review. *Journal of Strategy and Management*, *13*(2), 297–309. doi:10.1108/JSMA-11-2019-0198

ENDNOTES

1. The text in this Chapter is based on Chapter 2 of the book *High Performance Managerial Leadership* (de Waal, 2020).
2. According to Do and Mai (2020, p. 305), "across the HPO literature, we found only the HPO framework developed by de Waal (2012) as an example of a scientifically validated conceptualization of high performance organizations."

Chapter 3
Current Situation of the Finance Function

ABSTRACT

This chapter deals with the current situation of the finance function, which is explained from a historical perspective by first looking back several decades and then working toward the present time. Subsequently, the research into the trends in the finance function over that same period is reviewed. This research shows that there are specific "evergreens," that is, activities that have taken up a significant proportion of the time of the finance function over the past decades, and in fact still do. These evergreens are described, and in addition, the latest developments—identified from the professional literature—on activities that might become or possibly already are important to the finance function are discussed. This chapter concludes with the core aim of the HPFF framework which is to support the finance function in dealing with current and future developments to meet and exceed its targets.

3.1 STATUS OF THE FINANCE FUNCTION

Sixteen years ago we published in the Netherlands the book *De Financiële Manager van de 21ste Eeuw* [The Financial Manager of the 21st Century] (de Waal, 2006). The Introduction in that book read as follows: "The finance function is one of the most important functions within an organization. It is estimated that companies in the world's five largest economies spend more than $200 billion per year on executing financial processes. Nevertheless, there is great dissatisfaction with the added value of the finance function and many organizations have worked in recent years to improve both the efficiency and the effectiveness of financial processes. It can now be said that transformation of the finance function is no longer an option but a necessity. The role of financial managers has been changing as a result of all this. Whereas in the past they were mainly expected to efficiently execute the financial administration, now financial managers have to focus primarily on the effectiveness of the finance function. This effectiveness is all about supporting the growth and prosperity of the organization. Costs, and especially cost reductions, are still an important means, but increasing sales and delivering added value have become the primary goal.

DOI: 10.4018/978-1-7998-6929-0.ch003

Financial managers are required to simultaneously perform a number of sometimes contradictory tasks: restore society's trust in the integrity of the organization, safeguard the profitability of the organization, enable further growth and shareholder value creation, and do more with less. They are no longer only responsible for the quality of the data and reported results, but now also for the realization of these results. In response to this development, financial managers have become professionalized at a rapid pace. In recent years they have grown from "the economic conscience of the organization" to individuals who are concerned not only with the traditional recording of historical data, but also with the business evaluation of current and future business activities. Financial managers are moving from "scorekeepers" to "business partners." This development has continued to date and will probably continue for some time to come." The book also included a schematic future vision of the costs of the finance function according to the type of activity (Figure 1).

Figure 1. Cost development of the finance function, as predicted in 2006 (de Waal, 2006)

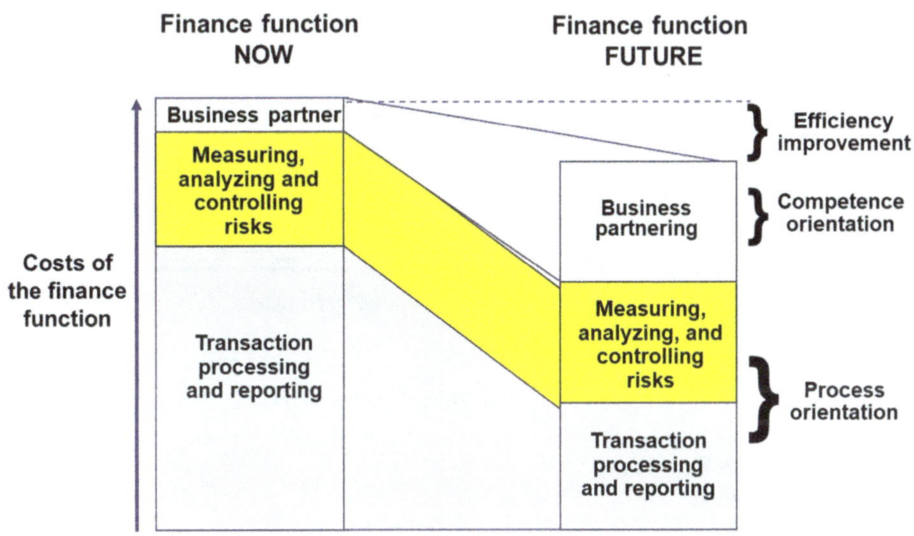

From Bean Counter to Bean Grower
The finance function is in general by nature conservative, detail-oriented, rule-oriented, and structured. To make the transition to a more forward-looking finance function requires a lot of innovative thinking and a structure to put this thinking into practice. Thus, over the next decade, finance functions will have to disrupt themselves to meet the demands of their customers who increasingly expect the function to serve as a true business partner, not a back-office department focused on transactional processing and historical reporting. It's a move from bean counter to bean grower (KPMG, 2019).

The clear prediction was that the emphasis in the time use (and thus the costs) for the finance function was shifting from transaction processing to business partnering, and that this would be done at a lower cost. As Figure 1 shows, the time that financial professionals spend on traditional activities would decrease because of increasing automation; they would instead spend more time analyzing data and sparring and consulting with line managers in the organization. This would result from a long-term development within the finance function, in which the focus shifts from purely financial administration to financial control and then business control. The reduction in transaction processing would be achieved through far-reaching information technology implementation and organizational changes such as setting up shared service centers. Figures 2 and 3, derived from more recent studies, show the situation a decade after the publication of Figure 1.

Figure 2. Shifts in the costs of the finance function (de Waal & Bilstra, 2016)

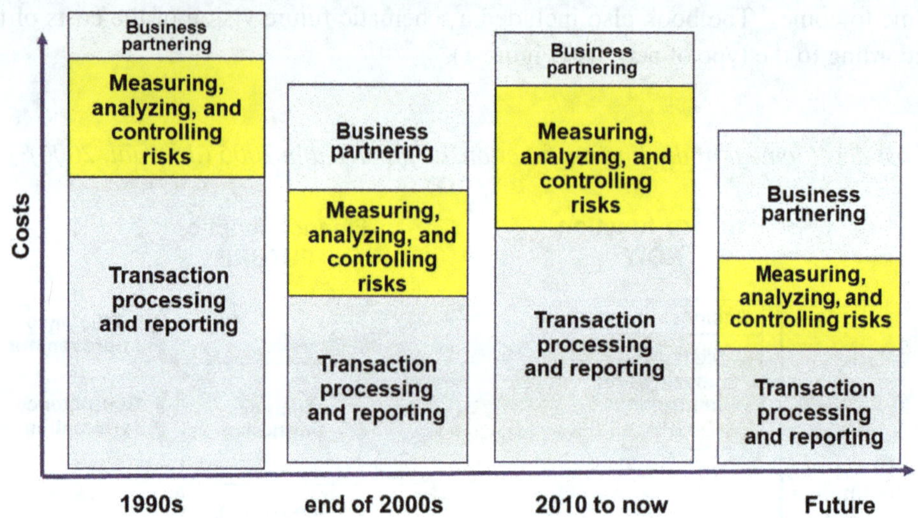

Figure 3. Impact of robotics on the finance function (KPMG, 2014)

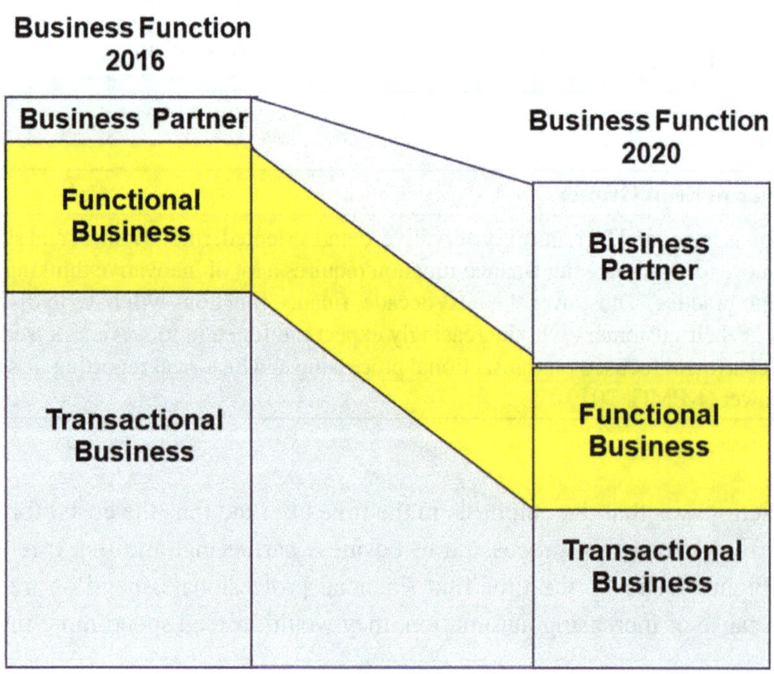

It is striking how much Figures 2 and 3 resemble Figure 1, with the main characteristic being that it looks as if the finance function in 2020 is more or less at the same point as it was fifteen years ago. How come? Indeed, since the 1990s, we saw that the emphasis in the work of the finance function was shifting from transaction processing to business partnering, and that this was happening at increasingly lower costs. The time that financial professionals spent on traditional activities decreased with increasing automation, and, instead, they spent more time analyzing data and becoming business partners of line managers in the organization. However, the accounting scandals, the subsequent introduction of new regulations (such as SOX, Basel III, IFRS), the dot.com bubble bust, and the severe economic recession at the beginning of the 21st century meant that the finance function had to reprioritize making primary financial processes more reliable and introducing fairly new techniques such as risk management (Davis & McLaughlin, 2009). On top of this, the COVID-19 pandemic and the economic measures that had to be taken, placed such a heavy time demand on the finance function that the growth from financial professionals to business partners stalled, mainly at the tactical level of measuring, analyzing, and controlling risk. This explains why so many articles in the financial professional literature are *still*—after all these years—about the need for more added value to be delivered by the finance function and for more business controllers (Accenture, 2014; CFO Research, 2013; Verbeeten & Heinen, 2019).

So little seems to have changed for the finance function in recent years. Is this a problem? It is, because the rest of the world continues to evolve. If we look at developments that are currently underway (Linthorst & de Waal, 2020)—continuous low growth in Europe, increasing globalization (despite COVID-19) and competition worldwide, pressure on profits, lots of money available but only limited opportunities for investment, more demanding and proactive customers, crumbling reputations and brand names, skills mismatch, changing demographics—it quickly becomes clear that the business environment is not getting any easier to succeed in. Thus, there is a strong need within organizations for a change from the transaction and report-oriented financial to the interaction-oriented financial professional, with the competencies of scenario-thinking, advising, analyzing, and anticipating organizational behaviors and changes. The role of controller has to transform from referee to playmaker at the strategic level, whereby they learn to master a new language: that of daring to challenge decision-makers in the organization when changes in strategy are needed. The next chapter provides a literature review of ideas for the development of the finance function to make the aforementioned possible. But first, in this chapter, a discussion of the "evergreens" of the finance function follows: the most important activities of the finance function over the past 20 years.

> The vast majority of organizations (89%) around the globe are finding that attracting and retaining appropriate talent is a challenge in today's finance function, which is grappling with evolving talent needs and shortages of the right skills (EY, 2019).

3.2 "EVERGREENS" OF THE FINANCE FUNCTION

Since 2002, we have regularly surveyed the trends in the finance function. The purpose of these studies is to identify which activities are performed by the finance function and seen as most important by financial professionals, how effectively these activities are performed, and which new activities are expected to play a role in the future finance function. The design of the studies has always been the same in order to enable comparison between the study results. As a first step, an inventory is made of the activities in the finance function that are written about in the financial literature. The idea is that these activities are likely or certain to become important activities on which the finance function will spend a considerable amount of time, given that they are considered worth writing about in the professional journals. A first conclusion that comes from this literature review is that the finance function—at least according to the professional literature—is getting busier. Fifteen trends were identified in the professional literature at the time of the first trend survey in 2002, and this number has since risen steadily to 50 in 2013 and 67 (!) in 2021.

In the second step, the trends are included in a survey in which the respondents are asked two questions: (1) indicate for each trend to what extent the respondent considers it important, on a scale from 0 (not important) to 3 (very important); and (2) indicate for each trend to what extent this trend is dealt with effectively within the respondent's own finance function, again on a scale from 0 (not effective at all) to 3 (very effective). Subsequently, the relative importance and performance effectiveness of each trend are calculated by adding the points awarded for each trend and dividing the sum by the maximum number of points to be obtained (= number of completed questionnaires times three points), and multiplying the result by 100%. For example, if a certain trend is indicated as very important by all respondents, this trend receives a 100% score for importance. Our analysis which now follows is based on the results of the last trend survey in 2013. We were planning to conduct the survey for the sixth time in 2021 but this was not possible because of the COVID-19 pandemic. However, given that the finance function has been especially busy with survival in the past two years, we expect that the current situation will not deviate too much from 2013. Furthermore, we used the 2013 trend results to develop the high-performance finance function framework, which we will discuss in Chapter 5.

Analysis of the Trend Survey Results

What can we conclude based on the results for the trends? The finance function has indeed become increasingly busy over the past two decades and is currently expected to deal with many activities at the same time. A number of "evergreens" can be distinguished: activities that have been important throughout the past two decades and which, therefore, in all probability, will continue to demand the attention of financial professionals in the foreseeable future. These main activities will remain part of the finance function in one way or another, which is why we refer to them as "evergreens."

It is striking that activities that have become less important do not really disappear from the finance function. We find that trends that score less than 50% are not that important for the finance function (anymore). However, only eight of the 50 trends score lower than 50%, which means that the financial professionals highlighted 42 trends important enough to (have to) spend time on them. Another striking conclusion is that the finance function has not become that much more effective over the past years, for example, scores of higher than 60% on performance effectiveness have hardly been observed. Although approximately half of the activities are handled more effectively, only six activities score higher than 60%. In other words, the result is essentially a meager pass for the finance function. Moreover, there are activities that have been performed less effectively over the years. This somewhat disappointing observation is undoubtedly related to the increased workload: by having to divide the same time over more activities, the time spent per activity decreases, leading to—as a logical consequence—decreasing performance effectiveness. In addition, society and the business world have become more complex and quality requirements have increased, which also requires more time to address, with a likely dampening effect on performance effectiveness. There are a number of specific activities that stand out, which we will now discuss.

Forecasting

Forecasting remains a difficult task. Although financial professionals find this the most important activity of the finance function, they remain less than fully satisfied with their ability to perform this activity. Forecasting was already high on the agenda in the 2002 survey, but in practice it appears to be one of the most elusive processes to implement. Granted, looking ahead in a turbulent environment is difficult: many employees are involved in a rolling forecast, and the interpretation of forecasting results requires a flexible way of thinking, recording, and reporting. However, the finance function has had plenty of time over the years to become better at it. A possible explanation for the difficulty the finance function faces in forecasting effectively is that it has a fixed rhythm of monthly, quarterly, and annual closing of figures, which leaves little room for the process of looking ahead. In addition, the large amount of structured information about the past (budget and actuals) fuels the tendency to record and report in detail. However, little is known about the future, which, in many cases, causes financial professionals to feel uncomfortable with the (excessively) high-level analyses involved. The forecasting process also needs space to discuss deviations and interpretations of the results. Finally, the pitfall of linearly extending the past to the future has to be avoided by thinking in long-term scenarios (after all: "past results are no guarantee of future results"), which requires a flexible way of thinking and reporting.

A North American consumer-goods company is using a forecasting tool that gathers and analyzes all types of data, including on variables such as macroeconomic conditions, geographic factors, and demographics. Armed with this information, the organization is able to alter pricing decisions in real time and as needed (Agrawal et al., 2020).

Budgeting

The respondents indicate that finance functions need to make the budgeting process more efficient, but that they are insufficiently successful in this. As a result, the budgeting process is increasingly seen as a bottleneck. Alternatives such as beyond budgeting, zero-based budgeting, or activity-based budgeting have, for various reasons, not seen widespread break-throughs in practice (Réka et al., 2014; Tugbay, 2020), and researchers and professionals are still looking for new, more acceptable alternatives.

Making Information Reliable

It is alarming that one of the basic roles of the finance function, namely that of making data reliable, is—despite the financial scandals at the beginning of this century and the subsequent great attention to this topic—still seen as very important to achieve, while the score for the corresponding performance effectiveness is not yet over 70%. Although it is true that this activity is the most effectively performed of all activities in the finance function, the general expectation of management was that data reliability would, by now, be close to 90 or even 100% because of the extensive attention paid to it. The lagging effectiveness may be caused by the fact that the amount of data has increased manifold in the past decades, the storage capacity to record data has increased enormously, and the number of IT systems in use within organizations has multiplied. Further developments in information and communication technology (ICT) (such as business intelligence and Big Data) has led to the generation of even more and new types of data. Outsourcing activities to shared service centers, with the associated data flows, also entail new data integrity issues.

The amount of data in the world is anticipated to reach 175 zettabytes (175 billion terabytes) by 2025, which is an annual growth rate of 66% over 2018 levels (Agrawal et al., 2020).

Improving Implementation Capability

The biggest gap between importance and performance effectiveness is found for the trend "improving implementations." The classic challenge for any organization is closing the gap between strategy (planning) and execution (implementation). The left half of the Plan-Do-Check-Act (PDCA) cycle—the Plan and Do phases—is often well taken care of within organizations: there is no lack of plans and their implementation is often started with great energy (Paraschivescu, 2018). However, the right half of the cycle—the Check and Act phases—generally receives too little attention, as a result of which necessary adjustments are not made or are made too late, and the desired results are not sufficiently achieved. The crux is that most organizations make too many plans, for which additional activities often have to be undertaken "on top of" the organization's regular activities; as a result, there is simply too little time for the implementation of those plans. In addition, these plans often lack ownership of the implementation process; as a result, no one is responsible for monitoring the progress of their implementation. Because the finance function, from its position as the "spider in the organizational web," is involved in many projects, it suffers excessively from these problems. It will therefore have to devote more time and attention to "improving the process of process improvement" (de Waal, 2020).

Ability to Bring About Change

The ability of an organization to bring about change is crucial, certainly when it comes to dealing effectively with the many trends in the finance function. This ability depends strongly on how the finance function deals with the behavioral aspects of change. Our trend research shows that although the finance function has long recognized the importance of this skill, it does not think very highly of its own ability to deal effectively with the related behavioral aspects. This may explain why, as discussed earlier, implementations are so slow and ineffective. This needs to be remedied quickly as organizations increasingly strive to become HPOs, as mentioned in Chapter 1.

Summary of the Most Important Activities

We now list and briefly describe the 21 most important activities (those with more than 70% importance in our last trend survey) as performed by the finance function, in order of importance, as the first input for the design of the HPFF.

- *Promoting forecasting* - The finance function promotes an organization-wide focus on the longer term by introducing rolling forecasts.
- *Making information more reliable* - The finance function works on creating reliable internal and external information flows within the organization.
- *Optimizing business processes* - The finance function focuses on profound simplification and optimization of business processes and business systems in order to achieve cost benefits.
- *Improving ICT usage* - The finance function ensures a greater role for information and communication technology, both within the function itself and throughout the entire organization.
- *Improving implementation capabilities* - The finance function focuses less on making plans and more on implementing and realizing those plans to the highest possible standard.
- *Including non-financial information* - The finance function focuses on reporting and controlling non-financial indicators, for example by introducing a balanced scorecard.
- *Making budgeting more efficient* - The finance function strives to optimize the budgeting process by adjusting this process or eliminating it entirely (beyond budgeting).
- *Implementing standardization* - The finance function focuses on far-reaching standardization of business processes and information, with the aim of improving quality and speeding up processes.
- *Reducing costs* - The finance function works emphatically on cost reduction, both in the organization and within the finance function itself.
- *Increasing innovation* - The finance function pays specific attention to the implementation of innovative solutions, in the form of the application of new tools or innovative execution of processes.
- *Developing talent* - The finance function focuses on the (further) development of the talents of financial professionals to enable them to produce higher-quality work and promote their retention the organization.
- *Improving behavioral aspects* - The finance function focuses specific attention on the role of the behavior of financial professionals in business operations and improvement initiatives. An example of this is increasing interest among financial professionals in developing change management capabilities.
- *Attracting and hiring good people* - The finance function makes every effort to attract talented people, thereby winning the "war for talent."
- *Strengthening risk management* - The finance function explicitly maps out the risks that the organization faces or may face.
- *Reporting from standard applications* - The finance function develops an integrated vision of the systems and processes used for reporting throughout the organization, and then further reduces reporting from spreadsheets and increases reporting from standard applications.
- *Paying more attention to program and project management (project control)* - The finance function coordinates projects and programs in a professional way to stimulate high performance within the organization.

- *Increasing attention to cost management* - The finance function increases transparency and insight into costs for the purpose of correct cost determination and transfer pricing.
- *Strengthening ethics* - The finance function pays specific attention to integrity issues and works on improving ethics within the organization.
- *Strengthening knowledge management* - The finance function records financial knowledge in systems in order to share this knowledge more efficiently throughout the organization.
- *Applying best practices* - The finance function focuses on identifying best practices in well-performing organizations within and outside the organization's own sector/industry, and then implements these in the organization.
- *Increasing trust* - The finance function helps to increase trust in the organization by providing reliable information and monitoring the quality and integrity of processes.

3.3 FUTURE DEVELOPMENTS

As mentioned before, we were planning to conduct another survey in 2020 but could not do so because of the COVID-19 pandemic. However, we did identify from the professional literature the latest developments on activities that might become—or possibly already are—important to the finance function. To make the list of activities in the previous section complete and up-to-date, we briefly describe the additional 16 activities here. The activities have been alphabetically ordered because they have not been validated in terms of their importance to financial professionals yet.

- *Applying agile working* - Agile working is about bringing people, processes, connectivity and technology, time, and place together to find the most appropriate and effective way of working to carry out a particular task. It is working within guidelines (of the task) but without boundaries (of how one achieves that task). Agile working in Finance aims to improve the operation and its process.
- *Applying dynamic reporting* - Dynamic (or real-time) reporting offers 24/7 access to the most up-to-date information. Furthermore, it enables users to interact with data through interactive functionalities in order to conduct basic and advanced analysis of data. Dynamic reporting, powered by machine-learning capabilities, aims to be insightful, intuitive, and enables the user to use data as a past, predictive, and live decision-making resource. Examples in finance function are a financial KPI dashboard, or a sales and order dashboard.
- *Applying e-invoicing* - Electronic invoicing is the digitization of the entire process of incoming and outgoing invoices. E-invoicing digitizes parts or even the entire Purchase-to-Pay process which covers activities of requesting (requisitioning), purchasing, receiving, paying for, and accounting of goods and services.
- *Applying robotic process automation (RPA or robots)* - Robot Process Automation is software that allows organizations to perform certain tasks through the use of virtual robots. Virtual robots consist of software that log in and automatically follow all kinds of routine processes, without human intervention. In repetitive rule-based environments, these virtual assistants can perform administrative processes, finance and IT support, and back-office activities.

Robotization—also known as robotic process automation (RPA) or robotics in short—enables organizations to transfer repetitive and labor-intensive administrative work to smart software, increasing productivity and quality of work and thereby reducing the need for rework including error recovery. Some examples of applications of robotics in the finance function are automatic invoicing, automatic checks based on data analysis, automatic reports, automatic links between various transactions, updating customer profiles, and credit card checks. Organizations that apply robotics have lower costs. For example, an organization with robotics can go from 5,000 to 500,000 invoices per FTE (Kieft, 2020).

- *Defining the roles within the finance function better* - Role clarity provides employees with a clear understanding of their tasks and responsibilities as well as the processes they need to perform. This clarity is not limited to their own role; it also includes their colleagues' roles. Clarity is an essential precursor of productivity, and a lack thereof can cause stress and confusion in people. Role clarity creates more motivated employees, more efficient cooperation between the different groups in the finance function, and a better understanding of the external stakeholders of who does what in the finance function.
- *Experimenting with blockchain technology* - The concept of smart contracts and consensus protocols in blockchain technology creates immutable data and a transparent process for all parties in a process chain. This increases trust between parties and additionally creates an efficient process. Example of an application in Finance is creating consensus during inter-company deliveries when the organizational units use different financial ledgers.

A blockchain is a distributed database that maintains a steadily growing list of data items resistant to manipulation and forgery. The database is essentially a ledger with transaction data. This digital transaction data is stored in a distributed manner. This means that there is no central point where this is checked. The lack of a controlling central party appears to be a risk, but it is actually a safety mechanism. The control is in the ledger itself. The information in the ledger is encrypted, and with many blockchain applications a part of the ledger is even available to end users. A complete version of the general ledger ("Full Nodes") is available in many places. This means that if someone tries to falsify a transaction, many ledgers are checked for accuracy (Kieft, 2020).

- *Implementing workflow automation (incl. process mining)* - Process Mining is a technique to map and analyze the course of business processes with the help of a program developed for this purpose, so that the disruptions in the process can be remedied and a "happy workflow" (i.e., a process without disruptions) is created.
- *Introducing artificial intelligence* - Artificial Intelligence (or as it is better known by its abbreviation, AI) refers to the simulation of human intelligence in machines that are programmed to think like humans and mimic their actions. Areas where AI can support the finance function are, for example, risk management, fraud prevention, and credit decisions.
- *Making more use of advanced data analytics* - This is the autonomous or semi-autonomous examination of data or content using sophisticated techniques and tools, typically beyond those of traditional business intelligence (BI), to discover deeper insights, make predictions, or generate recommendations. Advanced analytic techniques include data/text mining, machine learning, pattern matching, forecasting, visualization, semantic analysis, sentiment analysis, network and

cluster analysis, multivariate statistics, graph analysis, simulation, complex event processing, and neural networks.

> A services company uses algorithmically derived forecasts to enable forward-looking financial steering. The company has developed a calculation engine that applies machine learning to generate a fully data-driven, unbiased forecast faster and with less effort than that required for forecasts developed by experts. Instead of analyzing deviations between targets and actual performance, the company compares past forecasts with actual forecasts. Armed with these rapidly produced forecasts of how conditions will change, the company can take action to preempt unfavorable outcomes and promote competitive advantage (Roos et al., 2020).

- *Making more use of SaaS (software as a service)* - SaaS, also known as software-on-demand or web-based software, is a software licensing and delivery model in which software is licensed on a subscription basis from a vendor and is centrally hosted by that vendor. Organizations choose SaaS because it offers them a lower or a more stable cost level, and software applications in use are always maintained and kept up-to-date.
- *Moving to cloud computing* - Many organizations are transferring their core IT capabilities from on-premise to the cloud. This choice is often made from a cost perspective (costs better under control) and a maintenance perspective (continuous monitoring and updating of software by hosting providers).
- *Optimizing business intelligence* - Analytics and business intelligence (ABI) is an umbrella term that encompasses the applications, infrastructure and tools, and best practices that enable access to and analysis of information in order to improve and optimize decisions and performance. Solutions include corporate performance management and analytics, data warehouse/data infrastructure, and data quality areas. ABI is the foundation by which the finance function generates the insights that help management steer the organization.
- *Paying more attention to (the consequences of) pandemics* - Pandemics (such as COVID-19) greatly disrupt organizational processes: they not only force changes to the working environment (working from home) but also affect the way of working together in Finance teams and with clients; even service delivery to (and revenue from) clients can seriously be harmed. To deal effectively with a pandemic, robust IT facilities, flexible processes, and adaptable professionals are required.
- *Paying more attention to sustainability* - Sustainability refers to meeting current energy and health needs without compromising the ability of future generations to meet their needs. Sustainability has three pillars: environmental (balance in ecological systems), social (universal human rights and basic necessities attainable by all people), and economic sustainability (long-term economic growth without negatively impacting social, environmental, and cultural aspects of the community). Organizations are part of society and should contribute to those pillars, which is what the public increasingly expects them to do.
- *Placing more emphasis on stakeholder management* - Stakeholder management is the process of maintaining good relationships with the people who have most impact on the work of the finance function or are most affected by that work. Knowing what the internal stakeholder expects from the finance function means maintaining regular contact with the internal customer to discuss their

experiences, needs, and wishes as well as what the finance function can offer and the direction of development of the finance function.

Careful What You Wish For (Or Rather: Predict!)

Validation of trends is always a good idea, as recent research shows (Essaides et al., 2020). In 2018 Deloitte made predictions about the finance function which were checked three years later. Even in this short time span several predictions turned out to be inaccurate in the sense that they did not (yet) became true or were surpassed by further or other developments. This makes one humble and careful about making predictions. At the same time, the research of Deloitte does show that the finance function is in constant flux and development, and thus finance leaders should always continue "sticking out their feelers."

Table 1.

Aspect	2018 prediction	2021 status	New prediction
The finance factory	Transactions would become touchless because of innovation in automation and blockchain's deployment. Finance would focus on designing and maintaining systems that automate business practices and governance models.	What's changed: A slower-than-expected rate of investment in data architecture, combined with absence of standardized processes, causes finance to only now shift from automating activities to focusing on more complex processes. And without proven use cases, blockchain's momentum has stalled.	Few finance functions will likely have a truly touchless back office by 2025, but ERP systems and other tools can enable CFOs to apply automation to high-value activities, such as planning and forecasting.
The role of finance	The way we foresaw it, Finance would focus more on service, analytics, and business insights, developing new capabilities that would enable the function to supply management with an integrated view of business performance for "just-in-time" decision-making.	Faced with the pandemic finance has mainly focused on strengthening its agility and adaptability.	As real-time information becomes reality and business analysis becomes automated, finance will bolster its efficiency by offloading some responsibilities to centers of excellence and outsourcing vendors. Lower costs enables finance to invest in work that is building organizational value.
Financial cycles	Finance goes real-time, producing actuals and forecasts on-demand, thereby making traditional finance cycles less relevant. There is no close, and forecasting happens in real time.	The close has not disappeared. Organizations have tried to speed it up, but key information is still often only available on a monthly basis.	The demand for off-cycle reporting will accelerate while new business models are created and the post-pandemic economy takes shape.
Operating models	Robots and algorithms will join an expanded finance workforce that already includes gig workers, freelancers, and others; new service delivery models will emerge. Such models will be driven by the need to expand the function's core capabilities.	What's changed: The pandemic underscored the benefits of being able to support remote workers by proving effective collaboration tools and clearly defined work responsibilities. Challenges also emerged, such as the criticality of keeping data secure in an environment where the workforce is distributed.	With many organizations having difficulty hiring employees via traditional channels, finance will use technology to access global talent pools and specialized resources.

continues on following page

Table 1. Continued

Aspect	2018 prediction	2021 status	New prediction
Enterprise resource planning	New ERP vendors would enter the market by offering specialized applications and microservices that sit atop—and integrate with—platforms.	Current ERP providers have added new features, including cognitive functionality, and/or bought competitors to incorporate their technology.	Big vendors will continue embedding more advanced capabilities, bringing more data into ERPs, while dispatching any threats to their business model. Cloud-based financial ERPs may migrate from back-office cost centers to drivers of finance automation and digital transformation.
Data	Many finance functions would still be struggling with questions of data integrity and completeness. Automation and cognitive tools would help, but a not enough.	Not much.	To realize its digital transformation goals, finance needs an organizational data strategy with a strong leader. Without the appropriate skills, workaround solutions will only grow that much more complex.
Workforce and workplace	Finance talent models will put a premium on data scientists, business analysts, and storytellers, who, combined with tools such as predictive modeling, will enrich the function's ability to provide strategic advice.	With new business and revenue models emerging and the pace of change accelerating, the war for talent has intensified. Organizations are hiring more data scientists, but not necessarily in finance.	Finance needs to sharpen its value proposition and expand its sources of talent to draw the people it needs most: with business acumen, a service mindset, digitally savvy, and possessing knowledge drawn from operations, engineering, and other functional areas.

The COVID-19 pandemic is shaping finance priorities for the coming years. For instance, before the crisis, 4% of financial professionals worked primarily from home and 13% had hybrid arrangements working between their homes and the office. Post-crisis, these percentages are expected to rise to 25% and 33% respectively, which will have many consequences for office space; thus, work-from-home facilities and appropriate arrangements and leadership styles are necessary (Gartner, 2021). When asked how CFOs see the new post-pandemic normal the majority stated that to be an opportunity redesign the business (Deloitte, 2021). As part of this redesign they especially want to focus on increasing the quality of forecasting processes so the organization will be better prepared on future disruptors and not be overwhelmed by over- or under-demand; adjust M&A processes to the new environment; remove growth anchors and preserve growth ladders by specifically focusing on transformational innovation and reintroducing capital expenditures faster after a recession than their peers; and focus on building scale, not scope, in the cost structure by reducing the complexity that inflates cost structures and weakens competitive positions and concentrating spending in scale-building investments. In addition, they want to tackle the inefficiencies in analyzing huge volumes of data so they get more time to perform in-depth analyses, increase data accuracy and the use of visualization, improve cross-functional collaboration and cooperation across organizational boundaries, remove outdated or siloed technological solutions, clarify lines of accountability in the organization, simplify processes in general, and introduce a constantly evolving strategy (Financial Director & Workday, 2021).

3.4 DEALING WITH THE ACTIVITIES AND DEVELOPMENTS

How should the finance function undertake its (main) activities and deal with current and future developments to meet and exceed agreed-upon quality and productivity targets so that (internal and external) customers are satisfied and the people working in the finance function experience great fulfilment at work? In the next chapter, we identify from the literature and discuss many ideas to achieve this state; this discussion eventually leads to the development of the high-performance finance function (HPFF) framework. It is important to realize that the HPFF framework is not a structure nor a set of procedures:

rather, it is a framework that helps financial professionals develop a way of thinking and then a way of working that becomes ingrained in their attitudes and behaviors, leading them to focus on achieving the best results that they possibly can for their customers. Many, if not most, finance functions will already have projects underway to improve themselves and help them achieve a higher quality of work. However, all of these projects, although worthwhile in themselves, run a high risk of coming to nothing if the mindset needed to execute them successfully is largely missing. It is this very mindset that the HPFF framework aims to develop in financial professionals to foster in them the attitude and inclination needed to approach these projects with high quality and success being foremost in their minds, followed by developing the skills they need to infuse high quality into their way of working (see Figure 4).

Figure 4. Depicting the core aim of the HPFF framework

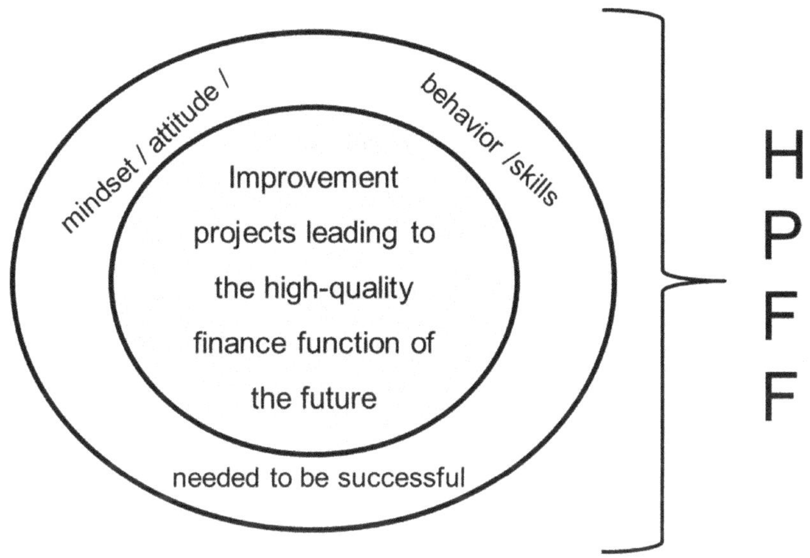

Goal vs. Means
Becoming an HPFF is not a goal in itself. It is a means for achieving the ultimate goal: becoming a finance function that can be of the utmost value to its internal and external customers. The HPFF Framework helps you to develop a mindset and way of thinking that enables you to achieve high performance in everything you do. This makes it possible to serve your customers as best as you can, and, in the process, enable the finance function to become highly attractive to its employees and achieve exceptional results.

REFERENCES

Accenture. (2014), *The CFO as architect of business value, delivering growth and managing complexity*. Accenture 2014 High Performance Finance Study, Accenture LLC.

Agrawal, A., Eklund, S., Waite, J., & Woodcock, E. (2020). *Finance 2030: four imperatives for the next decade*. McKinsey and Company.

Davis, T. R. V., & McLaughlin, L. P. (2009). Is finance a business partner yet? *Strategic Finance*, (March), 35–40.

de Waal, A. (2006). *De financiële manager van de 21e eeuw* [The financial manager of the 21st century]. Controlling en Auditing in de Praktijk no. 74. Kluwer.

de Waal, A., & Bilstra, E. (2016). *Hoe bouw je een high performance financiële functie?* [How to build a high performance finance function?]. Vakmedianet.

Deloitte. (2021). *Finance 2025: Looking ahead with the benefit of hindsight*. CFO Insights, Deloitte Development LLC.

Essaides, N., Willman, T., & O'Connor, J. (2020). *2021 key issues*. The CFO Agenda, The Hackett Group.

EY. (2019). *Reimagining the tax and finance function, find your path forward*. Ernst & Young LLP.

Financial Director & Workday. (2021). *The future of finance 2021 and beyond*. Financial Director and Workday.

Gartner. (2021). *2021 Gartner CEO Survey: The CFO Perspective*. Gartner Inc.

Kieft, R. (2020, Nov.). Disruptie van de financiële functie: stimulans voor het leven lang leren [Disruption of the finance function: incentive for lifelong learning]. *CM*, November.

KPMG. (2014). *The view from the top. CEOs see a powerful future for the CFO, are CFOs ready for the challenge? An Asia Pacific survey*. KPMG International Cooperative.

KPMG. (2019). Finance disrupted, how should the CFO respond to a business environment in turmoil? *Future of Finance*. KPMG LLC.

Paraschivescu, A. O. (2018). Hoshin Kanri and Total Quality Management. *Economy Transdisciplinarity Cognition*, *21*(1), 91–98.

Réka, C., Ildikó, Ş., Pete, D., & Cardoş, V. (2014). Traditional budgeting versus beyond budgeting: A literature review. *Annals of the University of Oradea, Economic Science Series*, *23*(1), 573–58.

Research, C. F. O. (2013). *Shaping the finance function of tomorrow: finance's strategic mandate - and the innovations that will help them meet it*. CFO Publishing LLC.

Roos, A., Tucker, J., Rodt, M., Stange, S., Ego, P., Boudadi, A., & Sheth, H. (2020). *Lessons from best-in-class CFOs*. Boston Consulting Group.

Tugbay, E. C. (2020). Better budgeting or beyond budgeting? An analysis of Turkey's top 500 industrial companies. *FP&A Trends*. https://fpa-trends.com/article/better-budgeting-or-beyond-budgeting-analysis-turkeys-top-500-industrial-companies

Verbeeten, F., & Heinen, J. (2019). *Finance transformation in the digital era, acquiring new skills to drive the digital transformation*. Finance on a Mission (University of Amsterdam/Workday/PLUC!/Finance Transformation Forum).

Chapter 4
Ideas for Improving the Finance Function

ABSTRACT

There is no shortage of ideas, especially in the professional literature, for elevating the quality of the finance function. However, it turns out that much of that literature focuses only on improving financial processes or on the question of how to develop financial professionals from scorekeepers into business controllers. There is limited literature that provides a glimpse of what a high-performance finance function looks like and what its place and role are within an organization. In this chapter, interesting studies from the literature from the past decade are discussed to develop an overall picture of the finance function of the future. First a look is taken at the benefits of an excellent finance function and then the most interesting ideas in the literature for creating such a function are discussed.

It has become clear from the previous chapter that the finance function has not entered calmer waters in recent years; quite to the contrary, the requirements that both the internal organization and external stakeholders place on the finance function have tightened and increased. In the meanwhile, the finance function has developed the lofty ambition to become a valued partner to the business. Unfortunately, it appears, in practice, that these two developments have not been reconciled by many finance functions. For example, in a study that was first conducted in 2003 and repeated in 2010, IBM noticed limited growth in the time spent by the finance function on value-added activities. Only one-third of CFOs who participated in Ernst & Young (2010) and Oracle and Accenture (2013) surveys said their finance function played an important role in the development of organizational strategy. In addition, the majority of respondents in a survey by Accenture (2011) were disappointed to find that the organization does not even use the "products" of their finance function, such as better data, reporting, and analytics; nor is the finance function automatically asked to participate in strategy development or decision-making processes. Studies of a later date (Agrawal et al., 2020; Caswell-LaPierre et al., 2020; Essaides et al., 2020; KPMG, 2019) reflect the same sentiments and indicate that not only does something fundamental has to change within the finance function but also that something must be done about the position and image of the finance function within the organization. To our knowledge, there is no academic research

DOI: 10.4018/978-1-7998-6929-0.ch004

into the benefits of creating a high-performance finance function. To obtain information about these potential benefits we turned to studies performed by consultancy firms and benchmark organizations.[1]

4.1 BENEFITS OF AN EXCELLENT FINANCE FUNCTION

We collected and summarized the benefits as mentioned in the professional studies in Table 1 (the details can be found in Appendix A).

Table 1. Benefits of being a high-performance finance function vs. being an average-performing finance function

Criteria	Benefit
For the finance function itself	
Internal client satisfaction	65% more likely to meet stakeholder expectations
Time spent	Up to 50% more on activities that add value
Business partnering	Up to 41% more likely to be seen as valued business partner by the operation
Cost level	Up to 60% lower
Productivity improvement	Up to 34% higher, mainly due to a higher level of automation
Capabilities	Financials seen as more innovative, knowledgeable in terms of operations, agile, proactive and commercial-minded
Talent development	Up to 24% more training hours; 60% more retention of financials
Self-service for managers	Up to 50% higher availability
Projects	Up to 50% more successful, with a higher ROI
For the organization with a high-performance finance function	
Financial	Higher revenue and market share (up to 20% higher), margin (6.7% higher), earnings before interest tax depreciation amortization (EBITDA, 4.0% higher), return on equity (ROE, 5.9% higher), and total shareholder return (TSR, 10.7% higher)

A clear conclusion can be drawn from Table 1: creating a high-performance finance function offers many benefits to the finance function itself as well as to the wider organization. The big question now is: how can such a finance function be created?

4.2 IDEAS FOR THE HIGH-PERFORMANCE FINANCE FUNCTION

In this section, we discuss the most interesting ideas—identified in the literature from the past decade (2010–2021)—that could serve as ingredients for creating the high-performance finance function. We included only literature sources that were based on actual research in the finance community, either using a survey, interviews with financial professionals, or roundtable sessions. In this way, we could be certain that these ideas originated from practice, i.e., from financial professionals who deal day-to-day with activities in the finance function and who have a view on the developments that are needed and desired in their finance function. In total, we identified 34 studies on the (ingredients of a) high-performance finance function. All ideas were collected and tabulated in Table 2, which can be found at the end of this chapter. We first discuss the most interesting studies in more detail, because these might have some out-of-the-box creativity in them; and all of them would make the reader think.

Based on a global survey of senior finance executives from 440 organizations on "the intelligent finance function"—defined as a finance function that is "best-in-class" in terms of operational efficiency, effectiveness in supporting the business, and capability to deliver added value to stakeholders—KPMG (2013) proposed a 'vision picture,' which can be seen in Figure 1.

Figure 1. Building blocks of the intelligent finance function

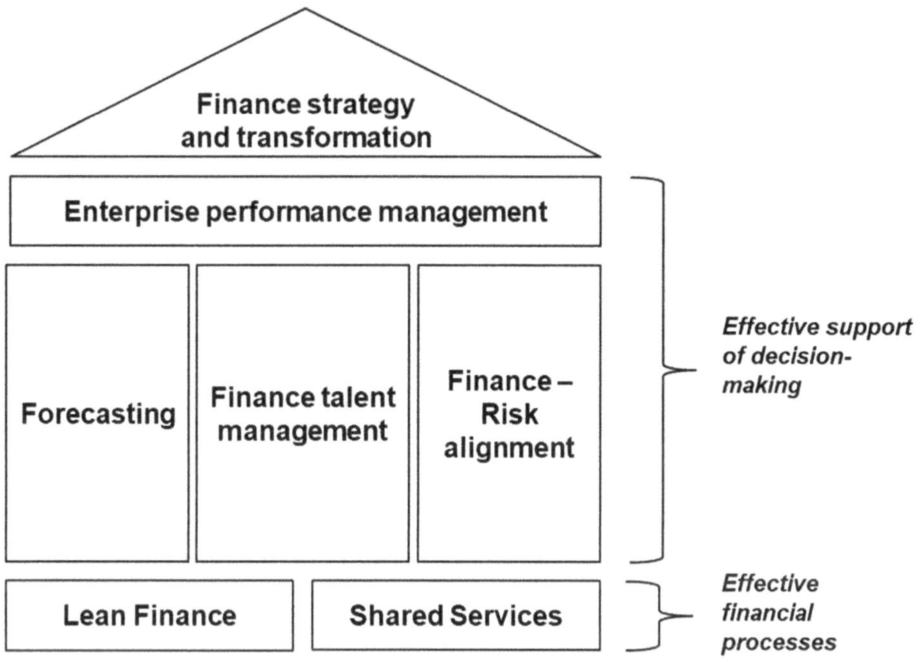

The building blocks of the intelligent finance function are as follows:

- Lean Finance: Tools and techniques that optimize operations in the finance function and ensure that there are only a few inefficiencies left in the basic financial processes;
- Shared Services: The basic financial processes are carried out at a location where this can be done most cost-efficiently, so that the finance function is free to spend time on value-adding activities;
- Forecasting: New business intelligence systems and analytics make it possible to integrate planning and control and make reliable predictions;
- Talent Management: An organization-wide HR framework is created with which the best financial talents can be attracted, motivated, and retained for a long period of time;

- Alignment of Finance with Risk Management: Risks and opportunities are balanced in such a way, for both the short and the long term, that strategic and tactical decision-making is significantly improved.

The Hackett Group (O'Conner et al., 2014) identified three areas in which the finance function can and must immediately recalibrate in order to transform itself into a "best-performing finance function": (1) talent management; the finance function must rapidly hire and train people with analytical and business partnering skills, in consultation with the human resource department; (2) service delivery; through the increased use of shared services, cost savings can be achieved which can then be used for undertaking higher added-value activities; and (3) financial processes; through the use of technology, even more routine transactions can be eliminated while the other activities can be carried out at any physical location by means of standardized workflows (see Figure 2).

Figure 2. Schematic overview of the redesign of the finance function

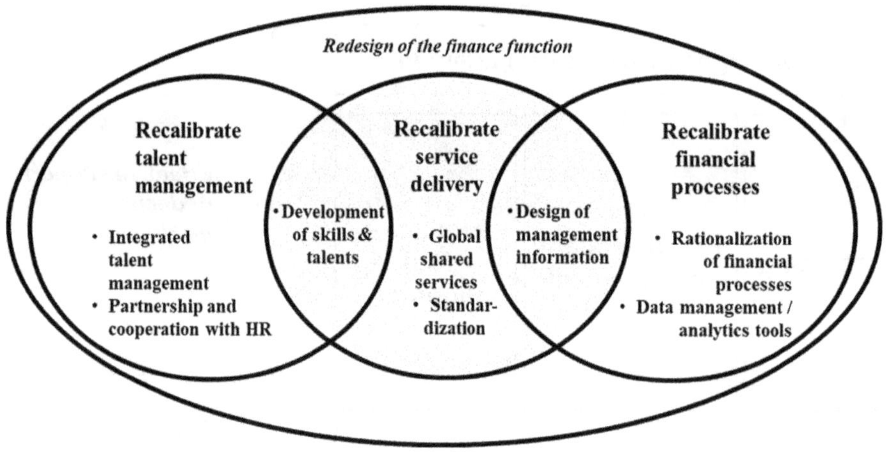

PWC (2014a) made a number of predictions of what the finance function could look like in 2030. The CFO will become the CPO (chief performance officer); the finance function will be in charge of the organization's sustainability agenda; and it will not focus anymore on managing risks but rather on coping well with uncertainty while strengthening the resilience of the organization. Robots will scan reports for fraud, inaccuracies, and lies; technology will become even more important (with technologies such as 100% cloud-based ERP systems and a seamless harmony between man and machine), with big data being routinely used to identify opportunities for performance improvements. Financial skills will be mainly found in the operation and are therefore no longer the domain of the finance function; and stakeholders will receive real-time financial, economic, social, and tax performance information about the organization. In order to make this happen, the finance function has to focus on four main tasks: (1) enable good navigation by providing real-time reporting, rapid (predictive) analyses based on big data, as well as dynamic and integrated forecasting—all aligned with the growth strategies of the organization; (2) mediate between the organization on the one hand and interested parties on the other, by providing information to a wide range of stakeholders and entering into dialogue with them; (3) increase resilience, by planning for contingencies, using predictive analytics, and developing plans for mitigation; and (4) strengthen connectivity, by designing systems and processes that promote collaboration between operational departments and between the organization and its suppliers and customers.

PWC (2014b) stated that the answers organizations provide to the question "How can the finance function add more value?" are hopelessly outdated: organizations tend to respond that this can be achieved by reducing costs and providing the business with more financial insight. However, the correct response, according to PWC, should be a counter-question: "Do we really need a finance function?" After all, the operational managers are increasingly responsible for budgeting, performance measurement and reporting, and strategic decision-making, and are now beginning to acquire the skills previously reserved for financial professionals (through "self-service" regarding financial services). This means that, in time, a separate finance function will not be needed anymore. The only way to survive for the finance function is to play a more dynamic and facilitating role, evolving away from static and rigid processes and controls to more adaptive, agile, and resilient financial processes for which the finance function will be the "conductor" on behalf of the business.

According to Eklund et al. (2018) financial professionals have to make two core shifts if they want to keep pace with changing expectations and opportunities in a digital world:

- *Shift 1: Adopt an agile operating model.* This new operating model is intensely focused on stakeholders, which would allow the finance function to sense and quickly respond to changes in the financial environment; it would comprise a flat network of teams rather than a traditional hierarchy; have clear division in transactional tasks—handled by a small cadre of individuals using standard, streamlined, repeatable processes—and higher-level strategic tasks, managed by staffers drawn from one or more "communities of interest" (which are the home base for financial professionals rotating in and out of small teams that are tasked to high-priority finance projects); it is made up of small, focused project teams staffed by financial professionals with cross-functional skills who are dedicated to a single project at a time, with full accountability for a clearly defined scope; and fosters an entrepreneurial mindset in financial professionals while requiring finance leaders to act as coaches who empower employees to stretch their skills and serve as proactive advisors to the business units.
- *Shift 2: Build finance capabilities for the digital age.* The finance function's role no longer entails simply reporting facts with accompanying recommendations; its new role is to interpret and present data accurately and persuasively, and then coach people, both inside and outside the finance function, on using digital tools and data effectively. This requires financial professionals to have a deep understanding of strategic principles and how the organization creates returns for shareholders; and an ability to lead "the case for change" and, for this, gain the trust required to influence their peers in making difficult decisions to help improve financial performance.

Verbeeten & Heinen (2019) gathered input from over 75 CFOs and finance executives during various roundtables and interviews, in which they identified key issues about the finance function in the digital era. Subsequently, they sent out a questionnaire to more than 100 finance professionals. They then developed the following conclusions and recommendations for the finance function:

- *Drive digital strategy initiatives.* The finance function must actively engage in digital strategy initiatives because these are likely to influence the long-term viability of the organization. It must challenge the business to invest sufficiently in digital innovation. This requires the finance function to understand the market well, to think creatively, and to persuade people in multi-functional teams.

- *Focus on value-adding technologies*. Organizations should set clear goals for technological solutions, balance their investments in legacy systems and new technologies, and select technology projects that bring the most value. The finance function should develop clear decision criteria on how to successfully select and adopt or stop and discard technologies.
- *Accelerate the closure of the skills gap*. The finance function should adopt a team-based approach, thus making sure that the team as a whole—rather than each individual—is future-proof; this requires developing a structural training program for financial professionals as well as succession planning for specific functions in the finance function. This approach requires all financial professionals to have a basic skill set in several areas (e.g., data management, agile/lean/scrum, data science, core accounting skills) so that they will be comfortable speaking the languages of data, business, and finance and accounting. It also means that it will be necessary to establish new roles and responsibilities in the finance function, with possibly changed job descriptions.
- *Develop a data-driven decision culture*. In a data-driven culture, the key question in solving a problem is "what do we know?" not "what do we think?" To be able to establish this culture, the finance function has to solve several practical and operational problems (such as capturing reliable data and hiring/retaining finance professionals with the right skill set); and start challenging the business on the basis of data and insights rather than opinions.

Based on trend-watching research, Gartner (2021) identified 10 trends to watch:

1. *A skills disconnect created by digitalization.* Talent-management strategies have to evolve to meet emerging competency requirements of digital transformation. Revised competency models and associated behaviors will lead to the hiring and development of employees in such a way that enables the finance function to make better business decisions.
2. *High demand for decision-ready data.* As organizations grow increasingly global and the speed of business increases, data are sourced and captured in a distributed fashion. This requires abandoning the notion of the "one-size-fits-all centralized data governance model" and instead distributing governance to data owners, where appropriate, in order to capture "sufficient versions of the truth" that will improve the quality of decision making.
3. *(Re)centralization of finance analytics.* As the finance function seeks to reduce costs while improving analytical insight, many organizations are relocating finance analytics in scalable, centralized models. This entails shifting the front-office paradigm toward shared delivery models, for instance by setting up a hub-and-spoke model, with strategic data analytics located in the center of excellence (COE) hub and "business interpreters" from the finance function collocated in the business and the COE.
4. *Reporting goes on-demand.* Internal clients are gaining real-time access to self-service data, complemented by advanced analytics.
5. *An emerging fourth era for ERP.* Enterprise resource-planning (ERP) vendors are offering core finance applications in the cloud, where intelligence systems like automation and artificial intelligence (AI) are embedded in the ERP.

6. *The AI revolution has begun.* In the coming decade, AI will optimize or transform nearly every activity in finance. This requires the finance function to educate itself on how the function will change, develop new skill sets, make more investments to deploy AI, and reconstitute the data infrastructure to support AI.
7. *Internal controls at risk because of RPA.* As robotic process automation (RPA) and other digital technologies become commonplace, the appropriate internal controls must be established to assure against financial reporting risk with minimal reduction of implementation speed.
8. *Growth through supplier collaboration.* Organizations are increasingly reliant on suppliers for providing key capabilities and support; as a result, the finance function must support the establishment of new supplier relationships and contribute to strengthening existing ones. Better supplier collaboration will help the organization gain a competitive advantage and uncover additional growth opportunities.
9. *Growing use of shared services.* Shared services have moved beyond regular finance transaction processing to include value-added services in finance and beyond. This supports the focus shift from cost reduction to value delivery. Process experts become digital experts, who not only understand process strategy and problems and current solution options but are also expert in "digital sensing."
10. *Cost scope harms efficient growth.* Build scale, not scope, into cost structures to achieve long-term revenue growth, long-term cost reduction, and short-term simultaneous growth and margin expansion.

> In one company, instead of relying on manual analysis of spreadsheets, the finance function used artificial intelligence (AI) in its quarterly forecasting activities. This development was driven by the exponential growth in the volume of data available and the ability AI offered to use a variety of modeling approaches, including time series and regression analysis, to visualize the data and provide richer analyses. The approach was also automated through machine learning. Using AI enabled the production of forecasts with an average accuracy of 98–99%. Interestingly, the purpose of using AI was not to replace human judgment but to supplement the finance team's perspective and support higher-quality discussions when discussing forecasts with other business functions (ICAEW/ISCA, 2019).

Roos et al. (2020) distilled three key success factors from their research on best-in-class CFOs:

1. *Break the compromise between efficiency and effectiveness.* Top performers do not see achieving both efficiency and effectiveness as a zero-sum game. They achieve efficiency by eliminating or automating nonvalue-adding activities, while simultaneously achieving effectiveness by ensuring that the finance function focuses on activities such as forecasting and analytics that help the business identify and pursue opportunities to create value.
2. *Aim higher for efficiency.* Top performers see many more opportunities for achieving best-in-class efficiency than just the traditional savings levers and questioning whether existing legacy systems are still fit for purpose. They apply nonstructural improvement levers, such as service level optimization, process simplification, and next-generation digitization. They also revisit the overall operating model and shared-services setup of their finance function.

3. *Focus on business impact, not finance expertise.* Top performers emphasize business-oriented performance management activities, such as forecasting, ad hoc analysis, and business intelligence, rather than the classic areas of finance expertise such as treasury, investor relations, or M&A.

The finance function of a global health care company increased efficiency and effectiveness by employing agile organization principles. The function divided itself into two units: one focused on end-to-end finance transactions and the other on business partnering. In the business-partnering unit, the finance function greatly expanded value-adding activities, such as analytics and scenario modeling, and focused on developing new skills. To free up resources for these activities, the finance leadership team carefully scrutinized each of more than 50 existing finance tasks. The assessment uncovered the opportunity to improve efficiency by 30% by eliminating duplicative work and introducing automation and robotic process automation (Roos et al., 2020).

McCaffry (2020) researched the development of the finance function structure, which initially followed a "hierarchical triangle" model with a broad base and just a few roles at senior levels. Then, the shape evolved into a segregated triangle; because of advances in information and communications technologies, routine transactional processes were migrated to shared service centers placed in the bottom part of the segregated triangle, while value-adding activities were performed in the upper part of the segregated triangle. In the current digital age, the growth of automation and artificial intelligence (AI) is eroding this traditional triangular base to form a pentagonal shape, as can be seen in Figure 3. At the lower levels, this change has implications for succession planning as the basic finance activities that are being increasingly automated have historically provided training ground for new finance professionals.

Figure 3. The shape of the finance function in the digital world

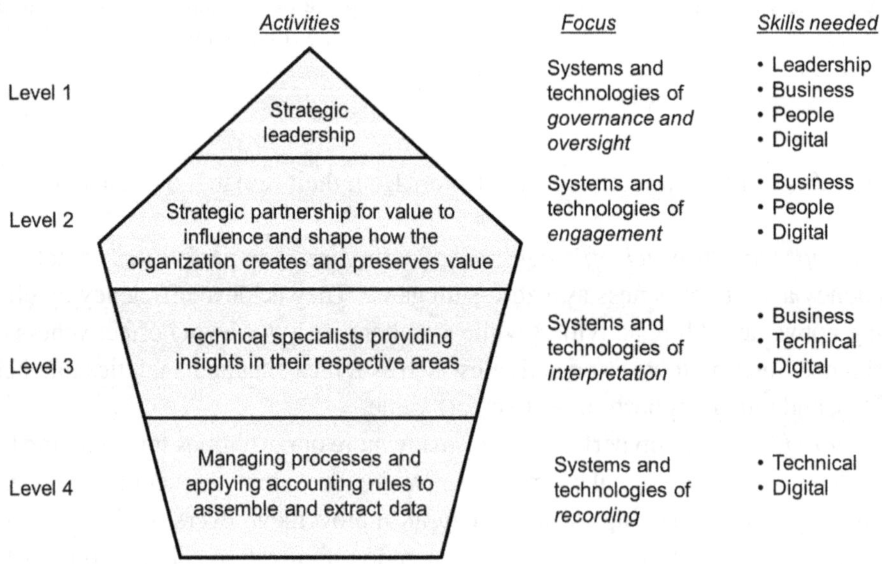

Tjandra et al. (2021), in their research of the nature of the CFO and finance function of the future, put the development of the finance function in a historical perspective and then produced a slight variation on Figure 3, as Figure 4 depicts:

Figure 4. Evolution of the shape of the finance function

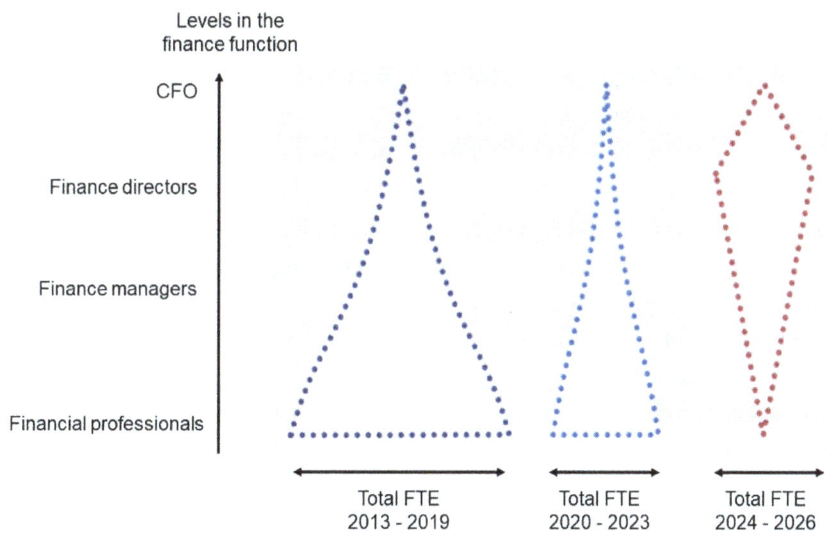

According to Tjandra et al. (2021), in the last decade the shape of the finance function evolved towards a "tear drop" shape with a bottom-heavy end consisting of financial professionals. This shift is caused by the increased adoption of centralized and functional organizational structures and shared service centers. In this decade this shape will again shift but now towards a "kite" shape because of tighter spans of control, centralized processes, and connected enterprise in which front, middle and back offices will be increasingly merged.

Attention for the environmental, social and governance (ESG) performance of organizations has risen sharply this decade and, based on the results of Grant Thornton's 2021 CFO Survey (2021), many organizations are now looking beyond compliance and are seeking to differentiate themselves as ESG leaders. An increasing number of CFOs now see ESG as a fundamental driver of financial success while the majority of CFOs state that ESG is either a top consideration or equally as important as financial success. Many CFOs cite ESG compliance, reporting and disclosures as a growing concern. At the same time they are more and more integrating ESG expectations into both performance evaluations and compensation. The biggest driver of the increased focus on ESG comes from inside the organization: the main stakeholders that are pushing their organization to enhance the maturity of their ESG programs are employees. These want to work for organizations that share and take meaningful actions that support employees' values, embrace diversity and demonstrate real care for their well-being and advancement. Therefore, finance functions are increasingly reporting on ESG issues such as employee retention and development; diversity, equity and inclusion;, and employee health and safety.

Based on exchanges with leading CFOs, Hippe et al. (2021) developed a near-term vision for the future finance function, which will make it possible for the function to become the "custodian of organizational performance" that steers performance holistically and objectively in the best interest of the entire organization. The vision rests on four pillars:

- *Becoming a hybrid finance function.* After standardizing, optimizing, and almost fully automating the main finance processes from end to end, finance functions move toward "hybrid finance" which entails a symbiosis of finance specialists and the digital ecosystem (that includes artificial intelligence, machine learning, and advanced analytics). "Hybrid finance" creates new roles in the finance function, as finance employees need to administer the digital ecosystem and perform "sanity checks" to ensure the quality of for example forecasts and simulations. Examples of how "hybrid finance" delivers value include: providing initial hypotheses on appropriate actions to take based on data-driven insights, performing independent tasks that do not entail repetitive work or clear rules, and conducting complex simulations relating to, for example, the interrelationships among cash, taxes, and the balance sheet.
- *Seeing the organization as a living system.* The end-to-end optimization and digitization of processes give rise to a networked organization that forms a living system. Remaining manual tasks are fully transferred to global business services as well as to shared resources, such as automation experts, project managers, or business process owners. The boundaries between functions and business units further diminish. In this organization, the finance function consists of bundles of cross-functional support that pool data, tools, and systems to fully own end-to-end processes and their outcomes; expert functions (such as tax, treasury, and HR) that support the cross-functional bundles; and business partners that support business leaders by not only providing appropriate answers but also asking the right questions.
- *Accepting responsibilities beyond core topics.* The networked organization makes it possible for the finance function to extend its responsibilities into adjacent topics previously managed by other support functions. This enhances the finance function's ability to steer performance holistically and promote optimal outcomes.
- *Acquiring advanced capabilities.* Every financial professional will need a differentiating expertise. They will increasingly serve as the connection between technical analysis developers and results-oriented business people, facilitating their interactions and translating their terminology. As a result, finance know-how will remain essential, and the ability to continuously improve technical and digital skills will gain importance, even as transactional tasks diminish or become automated. Analytics, mathematics, and technical skills will become commonplace, so that finance specialists can also serve as data scientists or developers of the digital ecosystem.

> Rather than lowering personnel costs by moving operations to low-wage countries, automation is now increasingly the main source of cost savings. Decisions about staff deployment will therefore be less about location and more about access to talent. In contrast to the current model of large transactional centers in low-cost locations, offshore centers will, in the future, be smaller, more specialized, and more automated for high-added-value services (KPMG, 2019).

Results of the Literature Review

We have listed, counted, and bundled the developments as the second input for the design of the high-performance finance function and presented the results in Table 2; in Appendix B, the detailed results of the literature review can be found.[2] Ideas that appeared five times or fewer were not included because these ideas are not widely supported in the literature. The ideas are listed in the order of the number of times mentioned in the literature, with idea 1 being suggested the most.

Table 2. Ideas for an excellent finance function derived from the literature

Ideas for an excellent finance function
1. Increase the efficiency and effectiveness of the finance function.
2. Apply even more IT to automate processes.
3. Create closer cooperation with the business by being a business partner.
4. Place greater focus on the execution of value-adding activities.
5. Develop a specific behavioral profile for each financial role.
6. Pay more attention to the personal development of financial professionals.
7. Place greater focus on looking ahead and forecasting.
8. Achieve greater involvement in the strategy and decision-making processes.
9. Apply more outsourcing and shared services.
10. Create financial self-reliance in the line.
11. Gain deeper knowledge of IT.

REFERENCES

Accenture. (2011). *Delivering value in a complex world: the next battleground for the finance organization*. Accenture LLC.

Accenture. (2014), *The CFO as architect of business value, delivering growth and managing complexity*. Accenture 2014 High Performance Finance Study, Accenture LLC.

Accenture. (2018). *From bottom line to front line*. CFO Reimagined. www.accenture.com

Agrawal, A., Eklund, S., Waite, J., & Woodcock, E. (2020). *Finance 2030: Four imperatives for the next decade*. McKinsey and Company.

Caswell-LaPierre, A., Kracklauer, S., Essaides, N., Dorr, E., Hall, B., & Willman, T. (2020). *Transforming finance to prevail in the next normal*. The Hackett Group.

Economics, O. (2018). *How finance leadership pays off, six ways CFOs stay ahead of the pack*. www.oxfordeconomics.com

Eklund, S., Tam, M., & Woodcock, E. (2018). *New technology, new rules: Reimagining the modern finance workforce*. McKinsey and Company.

Ernst & Young. (2010). *The DNA of a CFO: a study of what makes a Chief Financial Officer*. Ernst & Young.

Essaides, N., Willman, T., & Dorr, E. (2019). *World-class finance: redefining performance in a digital era*. The Hackett Group.

Essaides, N., Willman, T., & O'Connor, J. (2020). *2021 key issues*. The CFO Agenda, The Hackett Group.

Gartner. (2021). *The digital future of finance, 10 CFO opportunities to accelerate digital transformation*. Gartner for Finance, Gartner Inc.

Hippe, A., Roos, A., & Oberauer, A. (2021). *The Future of the Finance Function*. Boston Consulting Group.

IBM. (2003). *CFO survey: current state and future direction*. IBM Global Services.

IBM. (2010). *The new value integrator: insights from the Global Chief Financial Officer study*. IBM Global Business Services.

ICAEW/ISCA. (2019). *Digital transformation in finance functions: ASEAN and UK perspectives*. ICAEW thought leadership in partnership with The Institute of Singapore Chartered Accountants. ISCA.

KPMG. (2013). *Being the best: inside the intelligent finance function*. KPMG International Cooperative.

KPMG. (2019a). *Future ready finance survey 2019*. KPMG International Cooperative.

KPMG. (2019b). *De toekomst van Finance: transformative van de finance functie, bouwen aan het dienstverleningsmodel van de toekomst* [The future of Finance: transforming the finance function, building the service delivery model of the future]. KPMG Advisory N.V.

McCaffry, R. (2020). *Finance transformation: the human perspective*. Association of International Certified Professional Accountants.

Mirvis, P. H., Albers Mohrman, S., & Worley, C. G. (2021). *How to do Relevant Research, From the Ivory Tower to the Real World*. Edward Elgar Publishing Limited. doi:10.4337/9781788119405

O'Connor, J., Schneider, L., & Willman, T. (2014). *The world-class performance advantage: how leading finance organizations outperform their peers*. Finance Executive Insight, The Hackett Group.

Oracle & Accenture. (2013). *The CFO as catalyst for change*. Oracle and Accenture.

PWC. (2014a). *Marktstudie financiële functie, goed voorbereid op de toekomst* [Market study of finance function, well prepared for the future]. PricewaterhouseCoopers Advisory N.V.

PWC. (2014b). *Finance matters, finance function of the future*. PricewaterhouseCoopers LLP. www.pwc.co.us/finance

Roos, A., Tucker, J., Rodt, M., Stange, S., Ego, P., Boudadi, A., & Sheth, H. (2020). *Lessons from best-in-class CFOs*. Boston Consulting Group.

Thornton, G. (2021). *Values driving value, CFOs looking to lead on ESG*. Grant Thornton LLP.

Tjandra, J., Swaminthan, A., & Jing Yi, P. (2021). *Finance of the Future: Being a resilient CFO*. KPMG Services Pte Ltd.

Verbeeten, F., & Heinen, J. (2019). *Finance transformation in the digital era, acquiring new skills to drive the digital transformation*. Finance on a Mission (University of Amsterdam/Workday/PLUC!/ Finance Transformation Forum).

ENDNOTES

1 According to Mirvis et al. (2021) practice-driven management research in general identifies real-life phenomena much quicker than theory-driven management research which is generated in "university-time." Thus, practice-driven management research is mainly aimed at generating timely knowledge for practitioners, as opposed to timeless knowledge sought by organizational scholars.

2 The bundling took place for the ideas we found in the literature up to 2015, as in that year we initially developed the HPFF Framework. For the purpose of this book we updated the sections in this chapter with ideas with literature over the period 2016 – 2021. We also checked whether these ideas from recent literature are aligned with the ideas initially identified.

Chapter 5
Design of the High-Performance Finance Function Framework

ABSTRACT

In this chapter, the movements are discussed that are currently shaping or that are expected to transform in the near future the finance function into a higher-quality finance function. Subsequently, these movements are converted into a framework that can be used to create the HPFF. The HPFF framework is then extensively described, and its relation with the HPO framework and its influence on the performance of the finance functions are explained. Also, the difference between the what and the how of the framework is discussed, as are the obstacles that finance function can encounter in practice during their transformation in to an HPFF. Courses of action to surmount these obstacles are also given.

From the studies discussed in Chapters 3 and 4, we can observe the following:

- The most important activities of the finance function are still the provision of reports and associated analyses, and the provision of support to the business with financial issues. The use of ICT, especially in the form of cloud computing and big data, is receiving increased attention.
- The finance function is still struggling to find the right balance between the roles of scorekeeper and business controller. Risk management is an increasingly important task for the business, which, at the same time, requires more and more strategic and tactical support.
- The finance function sees its future in providing more value-adding services to the business, although the function is currently still largely engaged in transactional activities of relatively low added value.
- There is a (slow) shift from financial activities that were previously the exclusive domain of the finance function to the operational level where line managers gain more financial control and where the finance function provides support to them.

DOI: 10.4018/978-1-7998-6929-0.ch005

- The finance function will become more involved in the external world, with both the internal and external stakeholders of the organization.
- The finance function will have to deliver more output with a higher quality and decreased budgets.

We can now start shaping the HPFF based on this sketch of the situation.

A German industrial conglomerate employed an innovative approach: a zero-based organizational redesign of its finance function. It categorized the activities of the finance function as governance, service, or advice, and applied a zero-based mindset to determine which ones were truly required. For governance, it considered what type of minimum governance and control was really needed. For service activities, it asked the business units to define the type and level of support services they required. For advice activities, it considered what central entrepreneurial guidance and recommendations were needed from a business perspective and what would be the most effective way for the finance function to provide that support. This approach helped the organization analyze the value of finance activities and align those activities with business needs and Board priorities (Roos et al., 2020).

5.1 IDENTIFYING THE MOVEMENTS TO THE FUTURE FINANCE FUNCTION

When we combine the ideas for a best-performing finance function (Chapter 4, Table 2) with the main activities of the finance function (Chapter 3, section "Summary of the most important activities"), it turns out that all 'evergreens' are covered by the suggested ideas (see Table 1). This allows us to conclude that the future finance function will probably broadly perform the same activities as in past decades, but that there are enough ideas to execute these activities in different, better ways that will lead to a higher quality level of the finance function.

Table 1. Activities of and associated ideas for the future finance function

Ideas	Evergreens
1. Increase the efficiency and effectiveness of the finance function	▪ Make information more reliable ▪ Optimize processes ▪ Add more non-financial information ▪ Make budgeting more efficient ▪ Implement standardization ▪ Reduce costs
2. Place greater focus on the execution of added value activities	
3. Apply even more IT to automate processes	▪ Improve ICT systems and architecture
4. Creating closer cooperation with the business by being a business partner	▪ Improve implementation capabilities
5. Place greater focus on looking ahead and forecasting	▪ Strengthen looking ahead
6. Apply more outsourcing and shared services	
7. Create financial self-reliance in the line	
8. Pay more attention to the personal development of financial professionals	▪ Develop talent ▪ Hire good people
9. Gain greater involvement in the strategy and decision-making processes	
10. Develop a specific behavioral profile for each financial role	▪ Strengthen innovation capabilities ▪ Improve behavioral aspects
11. Gain deeper knowledge of IT	

With the activities and ideas from Table 1, we can now identify the movements that will transform the current finance function into the future finance function, and thus the HPFF. During several roundtable meetings with finance professionals, these were categorized into three groups of interrelated movements: enhanced **IT** (ideas 3, 7, and 11 from Table 1) linked to changing **behavior** (ideas 4, 8, 9, and 10) leads to more effective **processes** (ideas 1, 2, 5, and 6).

Effective Processes

- *Movement 1: Shifting focus from going-concern to continuous improvement of the finance function.* The core of the future finance function is formed by this movement. The finance function still devotes much time to handling current processes within the organization, often performing extensive "firefighting" to put current processes in order in the current organizational situation. In the future, the finance function will be devoted to continuously improving its efficiency and effectivity. Organizations are constantly in flux, with "change" being the normal status that influences financial processes. The finance function will anticipate these changes and ensure that its processes and services are suitably prepared. It will, for instance, use a delegation of people from the business who, under the guidance of well-trained experts (for example, green belts), will help the finance function implement the correct adjustments (that is, desired by the users in the operation) in the financial processes.
- *Movement 2: Shifting the focus from executing routine transactions to executing value-adding activities.* This move makes it possible to free up financial professionals from their current routine work to become real business partners of operational managers.
- *Movement 5: From looking at what happened in the past, rooted in the nature of the financial profession, to looking to the future with more proactivity and forecasting.* The organization will, therefore, be quicker to identify risks and dangers requiring it to act, as well as opportunities of which it can take advantage as a first-mover/frontrunner. When discussing the past with line management, the information is too often outdated, while the business itself already has more recent information. Therefore, looking at the past should be limited to the level where future projections can be updated and improved. Through working with models and scenarios aligned with the strategy developed by business units, the need for financial interventions can be detected earlier.
- *Movement 6: From doing everything in-house to shared services and outsourcing.* This move has been ongoing for quite some time now, but will accelerate as increasingly more activities qualify for delivery through shared services or outsourcing, thus freeing up further time for the finance function to execute value-adding activities.

> At one company, a "One Standard" initiative was initiated to create standard tools, data, and even meeting formats for the finance function. This approach trickled down into all finance processes, including the standardized measures for performance reporting. Likewise, another company standardized end-to-end finance processes for high-volume activities such as procure-to-pay, order-to-cash, and record-to-report. The centralization of transaction processing has streamlined work and ensured adherence to standard operating procedures. Its standardized software further simplifies these efforts. At yet another company, the "Core Finance" initiative brought uniformity to finance through standardized reporting systems and consistent taxonomies across the organization. Bringing uniformity to the company's financial data enabled other functions to more easily access and interpret data, which freed up finance professionals to focus on more value-adding activities (APQC, 2018).

Enhanced IT

- *Movement 3: From manual operations to full automation.* Although the finance function has been greatly automated in recent years, many organizations still suffer from legacy systems. These will be replaced by integrated IT systems, thus seamlessly integrating financial processes across units and functions.
- *Movement 7: From financial knowledge and expertise being concentrated in the finance function, on which the business is entirely dependent regarding financial matters, to shifting (routine) financial processes to operations and more financial self-reliance in the business.* This move creates increased financial self-sustainability in the operation, which is supported by experts from the finance function and by elaborate but user-friendly IT architecture.
- *Movement 11: From IT laymen to IT application experts.* Increased automation and more complex questions from the business require specialist knowledge in the finance function on the availability and functionality of IT applications. The IT department will handle the installation of hardware and software, but the finance function must know in detail what this new software can do, so as to optimally support the business.

> "Surprisingly, top performers are not distinguished by their finance IT systems. Our research shows that IT systems and architecture need improvement at most companies. The key to success is having a clear IT target picture and a roadmap that is focused on creating incremental business impact over time" (Roos et al., 2020).

Changing Behavior

- *Movement 4: From being internally focused, mainly involved in maintaining order in financial processes, to more cooperation with and, thus, more support of the business.* For this purpose, support tools (e.g., business intelligence tools, smart reporting) must be introduced and improved, and the number of fixed reports must be decreased in volume and number, to allow both the business function and the finance function to have sufficient time to conduct meaningful dialogue. It will be assumed that line managers only need detailed information on matters that greatly influence their achieving specific objectives and targets. As management of the finance function, it is necessary to ensure that there is a correct match between the level of employees and the work they carry out. It is still too often the case that lower-educated employees spend too long analyzing complex matters while highly trained employees spend too much time making routine reports.
- *Movement 8: From professional and knowledge training, which financial professionals only receive as and when financial issues arise or when taking the next step in their financial career, to continuous personal development.* Because many routine tasks will be automated, only complex activities that require higher levels of expertise will remain. Furthermore, working more often and more closely with the business also requires different skills. These challenges can only be met when financial professionals continue to proactively develop themselves, rather than undertaking education only when circumstances dictate. The finance function will, in collaboration with the human resource department, have a talent development process to guarantee meeting future demands for financial experts (and in the process making sure that financial professionals stay motivated as they can develop themselves and more easily move around in the finance function).

- *Movement 9: From a mainly tactical role to a more strategic role in the organization.* The finance function will have a greater influence on strategic planning and decision-making processes to safeguard the financial component therein. Financial professionals can use their expertise to analyze in-depth the financial consequences of certain decisions and activities, and provide business managers with the right advice. Rather than offering mere reflections or remarks ("cost has risen, revenue has fallen"), this advice should pose inquisitive questions to initiate dialogue. By challenging the business to produce its own scenarios and solutions, the quality and effectivity of financial professionals' advice will increase. In particular, the finance function will lend support to the business in addressing complex and major problems, stepping back once these have been solved. Through this support and education process, the finance function advances the organization as a whole. Therefore, management of the finance function must pay attention to developing and strengthening the communication and dialogue skills of financial professionals.
- *Movement 10: From "one size fits all" development programs for financial professionals, which are often strongly technically oriented, to specific behavioral profiles for each role that a financial professional performs within the finance function during a specific time period.* In Chapter 6, we will discuss these behavioral profiles more in-depth.

In the service delivery model of the future, as part of a virtual Center Of Excellence, financial professionals will be able to use machine learning to analyze various data sources and thus produce faster and more accurate forecasts. The financial professionals will spend less time producing the forecast and have more time to help management analyze and interpret it (KPMG, 2019a).

Relationship Between the Movements and the HPO Framework

Table 2 matches the movements of the future finance function with the HPO factors to evaluate whether all of the latter are "covered" by the former. The relationship between them is examined from the perspective of the HPO factors, given that the finance function's role is to support these with its movements.

Table 2. The relationship between the HPO factors and the finance function movements

HPO factor	Movement
Management Quality Employee Quality	▪ From "one size fits all" development programs to a specific behavioral profile for each finance function role. ▪ From mainly knowledge training to continuous personal development. ▪ From IT layman to IT application expert.
Continuous Improvement & Renewal	▪ From a focus on going concern to continuous improvement of the finance function. ▪ From manual operation to full automation. ▪ From doing everything in-house to shared services and outsourcing.
Openness & Action Orientation	▪ From financial knowledge, traditionally concentrated in the finance function, to financial self-reliance by the business. ▪ From internally oriented to more cooperation and therefore more support of the business.
Long-term Orientation	▪ From a focus on performing routine transactions to a focus on performing value-adding activities. ▪ From a tactical role to a more strategic role. ▪ From looking at the past to a focus on proactivity and looking ahead.

- *Management quality* - Managers of HPOs are responsible for creating the preconditions for their employees to achieve extraordinary results. In a high-quality finance function, this can be achieved through continuous attention to developing financial professionals and managing talent, thus ensuring that the personnel have the requisite skills to create and maintain such a high-quality finance function. Managers should also ensure that there are different behavioral profiles for financial professionals, so that each can develop in the direction best suited to them.
- *Employee quality* - Employees of HPOs want to have responsibility, be held accountable for their results, and achieve extraordinary performance. For the finance function, it is important for employees to have these traits, so that financial activities are executed at the highest quality level. In addition to managers of the finance function seeking to ensure that finance professionals develop in the right direction, finance professionals themselves should take personal responsibility for their own development. This especially includes developing more sophisticated IT knowledge and skills.
- *Continuous improvement and renewal*: HPOs continuously improve and renew their processes, products, and services. Because this makes change the norm rather than the exception, the finance function must ensure that it can not only handle this change but also take the lead in the process of continuous improvement and renewal, both of the organization overall and of the function itself. Specifically, the function must explore the possibilities offered by IT, shared services, and outsourcing.
- *Openness and action orientation* - Because the finance function will be increasingly in contact with the business—regarding transactional financial or complex, high-impact activities—it should ensure that financial professionals have the right communication and dialogue skills to talk to the business and to help managers when and where needed.
- *Long-term orientation* - HPOs always prioritize long-term continuity and sustainability over short-term financial gain. The finance function exists to support the business in its survival and long-term growth; it does this by supporting management during strategic, planning, decision-making, and forecasting processes, providing the information needed to make decisions that promote the organization's long-term future.

The information in Table 2 gives the basis for defining the HPO: *the HPO supports the organization in becoming and remaining an HPO by ensuring that its people, processes, and systems are of the highest quality.* It also provides the starting ground for developing the HPO framework.

5.2 DESIGNING THE HIGH-PERFORMANCE FINANCE FUNCTION FRAMEWORK

To develop the HPFF framework, we sought to relate the 11 movements to the performance of the finance function and to the HPFF factors (de Waal et al. 2019).[1] Unfortunately, we were unable to identify a suitable questionnaire in the literature to allow this. Therefore, during several brainstorming sessions with finance professionals, we designed a questionnaire ourselves: we did this by converting the movements into HPFF statements with which respondents could assess their own finance function. Ultimately, the 11 movements were converted into 34 statements. In addition, we developed a number of statements that could be used to measure the performance of the finance function. The HPO, HPFF, and performance statements were included in a questionnaire that was sent out to our network of financial professionals.

These were mainly CFOs and managers in the finance function of profit and non-profit organizations. They were asked to distribute the questionnaire to as many professionals as possible working in the finance function of their organizations.

The HPFF Factors and Characteristics

Based on a factor analysis, five HPFF factors were identified from the collected questionnaire data: Finance function Improvement, IT Focus, Personal Development, Role Clarity, and Strategic Role. These five factors include a total of 28 characteristics.[2] In addition, a Finance Function Performance Factor was also identified that can be used to evaluate the performance of the function, using five characteristics. In Table 3, the HPFF factors and accompanying characteristics are listed; in addition, the movements to which the HPFF characteristics relate are given.

Table 3. The HPFF factors and accompanying characteristics and their originating movements

HPFF factors and characteristics	Movement
Factor 1. Finance Function Improvement	
1. In the finance function, improvement efforts are tracked and evaluated using performance indicators	1. Increase efficiency and effectiveness of the finance function
2. In the finance function, improvements are implemented in a structured way	1. Increase efficiency and effectiveness of the finance function
3. In the past year, financials have had enough time to make their work activities more efficient and effective	1. Increase efficiency and effectiveness of the finance function
4. In the finance function, implementing improvements is actively encouraged	1. Increase efficiency and effectiveness of the finance function
5. In the finance function, processes are executed as much as possible in a uniform way and in one place, so that expertise of these processes is bundled and centralized	6. More outsourcing and shared services
6. In the organization, managers engage in financial self-service	7. More financial self-reliance of operational managers
Factor 2. IT Focus	
7. The finance function is capable of implementing the latest IT software	11. More knowledge about information technology
8. In the finance function, all routine processes have been fully automated	3. More use of information technology to automate processes
9. The finance function has (a lot of) IT application knowledge	11. More knowledge about information technology
10. The finance function has sufficient budget at its disposal each year to accelerate automation and digitalization of the function	3. More use of information technology to automate processes
11. In the finance function, automation and digitalization have a high priority	3. More use of information technology to automate processes
12. The finance function is aware of the current and newest applications and possibilities afforded by IT software	11. More knowledge about information technology
13. The finance function spends less and less time on routine activities	2. More focus on performing value- adding activities and business partnering
Factor 3. Personal Development	
14. In the past year, financials have received sufficient technical training to be able to excel in their work activities	8. Continuous attention to the development of financial professionals and talent management

continues on following page

Table 3. Continued

HPFF factors and characteristics	Movement
15. In the past year, financials have undergone personal development training to be able to excel in their work activities	8. Continuous attention to the development of financial professionals and talent management
16. In the finance function, everyone has a personal development plan	8. Continuous attention to the development of financial professionals and talent management
Factor 4. Role Clarity	
17. In the finance function, there is a clear description of the behavioral requirements for each financial role	10. Different behavioral profiles for financial professionals
18. In the finance function, there is a clear description of the technical requirements for each financial role	10. Different behavioral profiles for financial professionals
19. In the finance function, there are specific development programs for each financial role	10. Different behavioral profiles for financial professionals
Factor 5. Strategic Role	
20. The finance function is seen as a serious partner during strategic discussions	9. More involvement in strategic and decision processes
21. The finance function has important input into each decision of strategic importance	9. More involvement in strategic and decision processes
22. Other departments regularly and spontaneously ask the finance function for advice when taking important decisions	9. More involvement in strategic and decision processes
23. The finance function is actively involved in all the important processes conducted in the organization	4. More cooperation with the business
24. The finance function actively searches for possibilities for cooperation and collaboration with the business	4. More cooperation with the business
25. The finance function performs more and more value-adding activities for the business	2. More focus on performing value- adding activities and business partnering
26. The finance function, together with the business, regularly examines possibilities of creating more value-adding activities for operations	2. More focus on performing value- adding activities and business partnering
27. The finance function proactively adapts prognoses on the basis of important developments	5. More focus on looking ahead
28. The latest prognoses, as developed by the finance function, are given priority during important decision-making by management	5. More focus on looking ahead

Finance Function Improvement

This factor revolves around the extent to which financial professionals have the ability and the skills to improve their function. The associated characteristics are: improvement measures in the finance function are monitored and evaluated using performance indicators; the implementation of improvements is tackled in a structured manner in the finance function; the financial professionals have been able to spend sufficient time in the past year on making their activities more effective and efficient; and the implementation of improvements in the finance function is actively encouraged. In addition, this factor contains a characteristic that is aimed at increasing the process knowledge in the finance function: in the finance function, processes are carried out as uniformly as possible and in one place, so that expertise about these processes is bundled. Finally, there is a characteristic that describes an activity that makes line managers less dependent on the finance function for assistance in finance-related matters while, at the same time, giving the finance function more time for more complex tasks; this is achieved through the use of financial self-service by managers in the organization. "Self-service" means that line managers can prepare their own reports without assistance from the finance function.

> At Microsoft, leaders from any department can directly access key financial information. Thanks to its standardized reporting system, the company has only the one source of data that the managers can access on their own. Instead of answering e-mail queries and performing low-level research tasks, financial professionals focus on providing analysis, offering suggestions, and engaging in work that adds value to the company (APQC, 2018).

IT Focus

The 'IT Focus' factor puts emphasis on the importance of automation for strengthening the finance function. The characteristics of the finance function required for this are as follows: sufficient annual budget to accelerate the automation and digitization of the finance function; and automation and digitization are given a high priority. Also important for this factor is the knowledge that financial professionals have of IT applications that could be implemented in the finance function and the organization as a whole: the finance function is aware of the latest applications and capabilities of IT programs; the finance function has extensive IT application knowledge; and the finance function is able to implement the most recent IT applications. "IT application knowledge" means knowledge of applications, i.e., how functionalities of the application can be effectively used for the improvement of work processes. Finally, this factor contains characteristics that reflect the results of the focus on IT: all routine financial processes are fully automated; and the finance function spends less and less time on routine activities.

> Research shows that a large number of financial professionals underestimate the impact of technology on their job. If they do not move quickly, disruption is just around the corner for them. Employees must have a number of competencies and character traits that give them the ability to be versatile. In this way, they contribute to the agility of the organization as a whole. This is called "employagility" (Kieft, 2020).

> "I strongly believe in the power of technology to automate, to achieve better data quality, reduce error margins, manage risks better and so on. However, I don't believe that people will become redundant. Rather than talking about artificial intelligence, I prefer to call it computer aided intelligence. People become smarter and more efficient thanks to the computer and will have to perform less routine work themselves. For us that means absolutely no threat, on the contrary. Technology ensures that we can handle the growth of the organization and are able to provide an answer to new needs" (Holvoet, 2021).

Personal Development

The focus here is on the development of financial professionals, as is apparent from the characteristics of this third HPFF factor: in the past year, financial professionals have followed sufficient technical training courses to be able to excel in their position; in the past year, financial professionals have had sufficient personal development training to be able to excel in their position; and financial professionals all have a personal development plan. "Plan" should not necessarily be taken literally here: the point is that the finance function spends time in a structured way on gaining insight into how the financial employee wants and should be developed, and then works on that development in a structured way. Whether this employee development is recorded in a "PDP" (personal development plan) or monitored in some other way is less relevant.

"Financial professionals would do well to ask themselves the following questions and take action accordingly: 1. Where is my added value?; 2. Which of the new developments will most influence my role in the future?; 3. What do I need to be able to keep up with these developments?" (Kieft, 2020).

"One stumbling block for C-suite leaders is the idea that investments in capability building must show immediate payoffs. In reality, most of the value accrues over time. Capability building never ends. So you have to look for markers along the way that make you feel comfortable you're moving in the right direction. Those markers of success might include an increase in the number and quality of customer engagements and higher employee satisfaction scores. The likelihood is that these markers will point to more tangible measures: sales, deposit growth, loan-balance growth" (Abdelal et al., 2021).

Role Clarity

The HPFF factor 'Role Clarity' clarifies the different roles that exist within the finance function. After all, "*the* financial" does not exist because there are different environments within the finance function in which financial professionals perform different roles. And these different roles come with different requirements. The associated characteristics are: in the finance function, there is a clear description of the technical requirements for each financial role; in the finance function, there is a clear description of the desired behavior per financial role; and, in the finance function, specific development programs have been established for each financial role.

A leading telecom player found that almost half of its financial professionals lacked the technical skills needed to execute future roles, and 42% were in roles that were unlikely to exist in a decade's time. Rather than eliminate staff, the company encouraged employees to assess their own capability gaps and learn new skills. In its first year, the program enabled the company to fill 40% of new job openings in the finance function with internal candidates (Agrawal et al., 2020).

"CFOs should walk the walk, completing capability programs themselves. Apart from role modeling the desired mindsets and behavior, they can also, better than most, help business-unit and fellow C-suite leaders think about strategic imperatives as a cohesive whole, the skills needed to execute the plans, and the impact of these activities on the financial health of the company" (Agrawal et al., 2020).

Strategic Role

The HPFF factor 'Strategic Role' relates to the way in which the organization, and especially the operation, views the finance function. The relevant characteristics are as follows: the finance function is a full-fledged discussion partner at the strategic level; the finance function has an important say in all decisions of strategic importance; the finance function is spontaneously asked for advice by other departments when making an important decision; the finance function is actively involved in all major projects and processes of the organization; and the finance function is increasingly adding value to the business. In the context of this factor, there is also a great deal of emphasis on the collaboration between the finance function and the business: the finance function actively seeks opportunities for collaboration with the business; and the finance function also regularly examines—together with the business—the possibilities of adding value to the business. Enabling foresight and forecasting is an important part of fulfilling the strategic role: the finance function adjusts the forecast proactively based on important events; in addition, the forecast most recently adjusted by the finance function always leads important management decisions.

> The role of finance executives has greatly evolved in the last 60 years. From the 1950s to the 1980s, CFOs were essentially accountants. Then, from the 1990s to the 2010s, they ascended to the level of business partners. From 2020, CFOs will increasingly be strategic enablers, going beyond a supportive role to a proactive one. In virtually every company we look at, the CFO is becoming the second most important C-suite executive, sitting at the right hand of the CEO and articulating a story about the financial results they expect to realize. An effective leadership team relies on the CEO and CFO being a great double act (Accenture, 2018).

Finance Function Performance

Our research also highlighted how the performance of the finance function can be measured and tracked. The 'Finance Function Performance' factor contains the following characteristics: the internal customer is very satisfied with the finance function; financial professionals themselves are very satisfied with the finance function; the finance function is very efficient; the finance function is highly effective; and the finance function always has an important say in the decision-making process that takes place in the organization.

5.3 RELATIONSHIPS BETWEEN THE HPO, HPFF, AND FINANCE FUNCTION PERFORMANCE FACTORS

After determining the HPFF and Finance Function Performance factors, we looked at how these factors are statistically related to each other and to the HPO factors. Figure 1 shows the results of this analysis.

Three of the HPO factors have a direct positive influence on the performance of the finance function: Continuous Improvement and Renewal, Long-Term Orientation, and Management Quality. This result means that the finance function will always benefit if the organization as a whole decides to transform into an HPO. This was to be expected from the HPO factor Continuous Improvement and Renewal:

Figure 1. Overview of the HPO and HPFF factors that positively influence the performance of the finance function

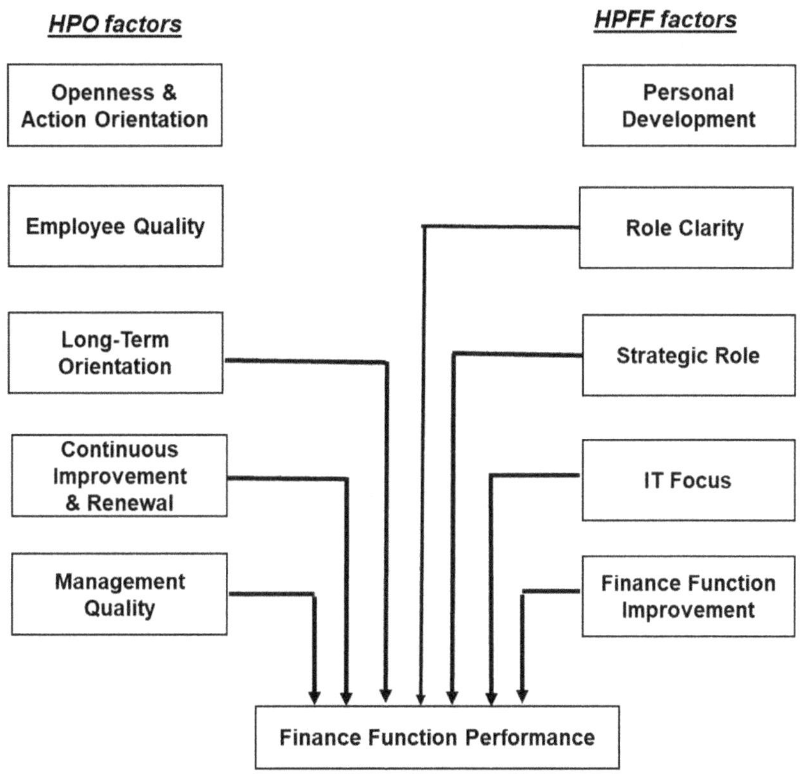

continuous improvement is an important activity for the finance function to be able to efficiently execute financial processes and generate reports, and to be able to become more effective because of continuous renewal. Long-Term Orientation is important for the finance function to safeguard the continuity of the organization and maintain stable relationships with both internal and external customers (after all, they are the stakeholders of the finance function). Finally, high-quality management is always necessary to create and maintain a smoothly running organization and thus also to ensure a smoothly running finance function. The HPO factor 'Openness and Action Orientation' mainly concerns the relationship between (individual) managers and employees and applies to all people in the organization, not just the finance function; thus, there is no direct specific effect on the finance function performance. Finally, HPO factor 'Employee Quality' also has no direct effect; this is because this factor affects the quality of financial employees through HPFF factors 'Personal Development' and 'Role Clarity' (of which the latter does have a direct influence on the performance of the finance function).

At most organizations, the finance function overemphasizes operational and cost-reduction-focused initiatives relative to the priorities of executive management; however, at high-performing organizations, the opposite is the case, with Finance placing a higher priority on planning and insight generation for executive management (KPMG, 2019b).

HPFF factor 'Strategic Role' has the strongest positive relationship with the performance of the finance function. Thus, performance in regard to one of the most important activities of a support function such as the finance function—namely, providing the best possible support to the business and its management—is *the* measure of a successful finance function. The strategic role of the finance function is mainly experienced by the internal customer in the organization, i.e., management. If management is satisfied, served well, and even involved in the further development of the finance function, then the strategic role of the finance function is properly fulfilled. In order to get a good idea of what this internal customer wants, a formal survey of internal customers must be held regularly (see also Chapter 8 on our survey of internal customer satisfaction with the finance function). In addition, there must also be a regular informal dialogue about the quality of services delivered by the finance function. The increasing role of information technology in the organization, and therefore in the finance function, is also apparent from our research. The HPFF factor 'IT' has a strong positive influence on the performance of the finance function: the better the IT architecture and the knowledge of financial professionals about IT, the better the performance of the finance function. This is important because a finance function that invests in applications with which data can be collected and processed efficiently and effectively, will have time for other more value-adding activities. HPFF factor 'Finance Function Improvement' logically has a positive effect on the performance of the finance function: an improvement of processes in the function always has a positive effect on daily practice and effectiveness of the activities executed by the function. HPFF factor 'Role Clarity' also has a direct impact, albeit weaker, on the performance of the finance function. This means that it is important for a well-functioning finance function to actually distinguish the different roles in the function and match these with specific financial professionals. This puts "the right person in the right place," in other words the best person is chosen for a specific role and thus is enabled to excel in the corresponding activities of that role. Finally, HPFF factor 'Personal Development' does contribute to the development of financial employees, but does not in itself improve finance function performance. This is because "the proof of the pudding is in the eating" applies: someone may have followed a good course or training, but if this person does not put what s/he has learned into practice (or cannot put it into practice due to organizational circumstances), then there will be no positive effect to be noticed on the performance of the finance function.

We then looked at the mutual relationships between the HPO and HPFF factors, to see which factors influence each other (see Figure 2).

As can be seen in Figure 2, there are strong mutual relationships to be found between almost all HPO and HPFF factors; this was as expected because we developed the HPFF factors in such a way that they would be related to high performance (see Table 2). We will now take a closer look at the relationships in Figure 2 from the perspective of the HPO factors:

- *Openness and Action Orientation.* Because financial professionals, owing to their strategic role, are increasingly coming into contact with (management of) operational departments, they must have good communication and dialogue skills. These skills that can already be "trained" within the finance function itself, between manager and employee and among employees themselves. In addition, financial professionals must ensure that they have so much business and IT knowledge that operational departments want them to be involved in important business processes. Subsequently, they can take that knowledge back to their own finance function to use it to improve the function itself.

Figure 2. The relationships between the HPO and HPFF factors

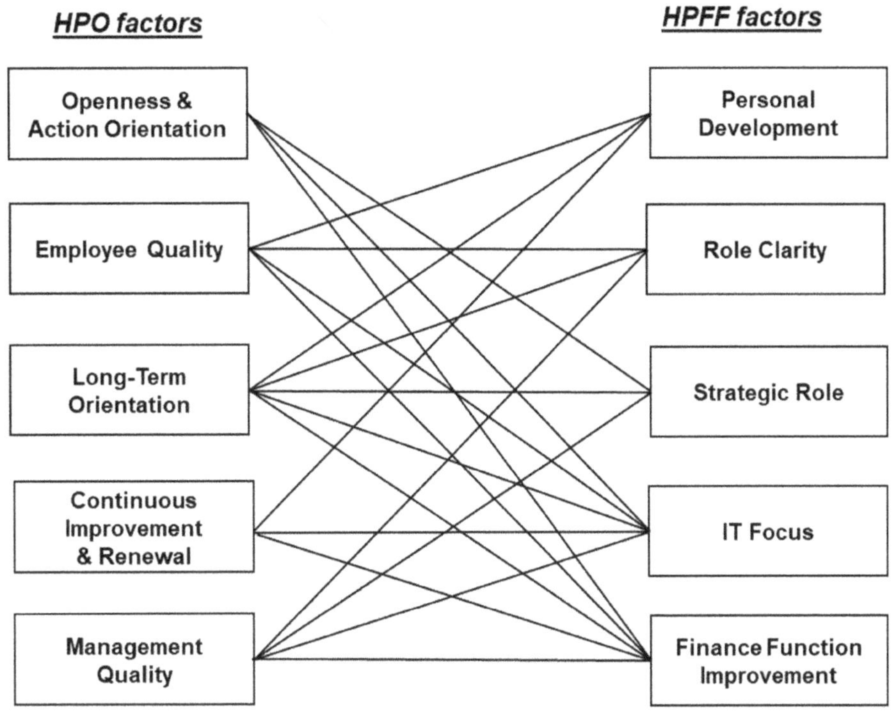

- *Employee quality.* Employees of an HPO want to have—and then be held accountable for—their results, and they want to excel. They therefore will play an important role in improving the finance function, both in carrying out improvement activities and in acquiring IT knowledge. In addition, they take responsibility for their own personal development and role clarity.
- *Long Term Orientation.* For the HPO, continuity and sustainability of the organization are very important, something that is reflected in its focus on the long term instead of on the short term—as is the case for many "ordinary" organizations—and in its attention for customers and stakeholders. It is therefore no wonder that this factor has a relationship with all HPFF factors because these factors are all in the service of both the continuity of the finance function (among other things by continuously improving it) and the internal (the business managers) and the external (the stakeholders) customers.
- *Continuous Improvement and Renewal.* HPOs are constantly improving and innovating their processes, products, and services. This "mindset" will help the finance function to continuously improve itself. IT plays a major role in improvement and renewal efforts, which means that a great deal of IT knowledge and focus will have to be present within the finance function. The mindset of continuous improvement will also help financial professionals to (continue to) develop themselves.
- *Management quality.* HPO managers are responsible for creating the conditions in which their employees can excel. In the case of the finance function, managers must ensure that finance professionals know what is expected of them in their role, and further encourage and coach them to gain IT knowledge and actively participate in improving the finance function. They themselves

will fulfill an important strategic role toward the business managers, often as part of or advisor to the management team.

Our statistical analyses also show that the HPFF factors positively influence each other. For example, HPFF factor 'Personal Development' has a strong relationship with HPFF factors 'Role Clarity', 'Finance function Improvement', and 'IT Focus'. This indicates that financial professionals must develop appropriately, in terms of both technical and behavioral skills, in order to perform their work successfully in the role they have. HPFF factor 'IT Focus' has a strong relationship with HPP factor 'Finance function Improvement' because IT plays a major role in many improvements undertaken in the finance function. HPFF factor 'Finance function Improvement' has a strong relationship with HPFF factor 'Strategic Role' because a finance function that is constantly improving can better fulfill its supporting role toward the Board of Directors and line management.

5.4 THE HPFF FRAMEWORK

In Figure 3, we have provided a simplified schematic overview of the most important relationships in the so-called HPFF framework. We also place the five HPFF factors into the three categories that we previously applied to identify the 11 movements (see Chapter 5.1).

Figure 3. The HPFF framework

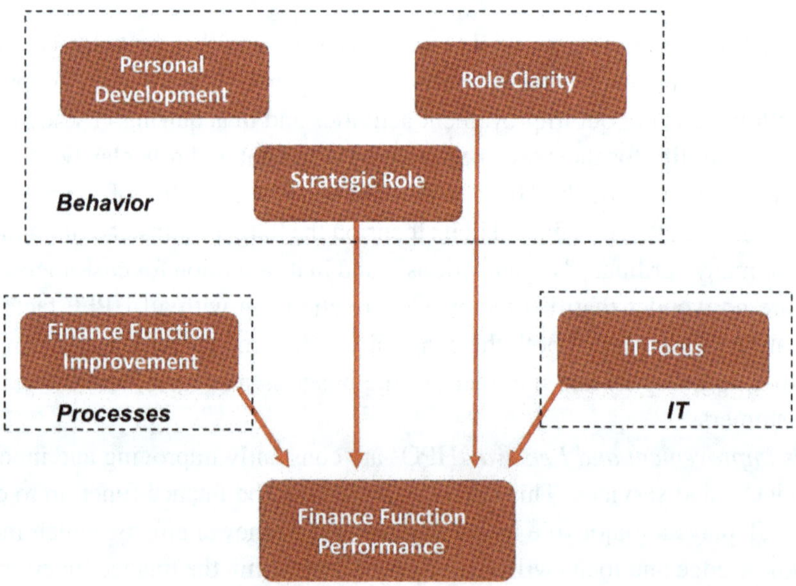

By applying the HPFF framework, finance functions can get started in their journey of transforming themselves into a high-performance finance function. A tool for this is performing the HPFF diagnosis on a regular basis, preferably every 1½ to two years. Here, we will briefly discuss the diagnosis so that it is clear to the reader what it entails when reading the case studies at the end of this chapter; Chapter

7 discusses the HPFF diagnosis in more detail. The purpose of the HPFF diagnosis is to evaluate how far a finance function is in its journey toward becoming an HPFF, i.e., the extent to which the function has already been set up and behaves like an HPFF. The diagnosis yields information that is then used to determine opportunities for making the finance function stronger to such an extent that it is (even) better able to support the operation and be a valued business partner of management. The HPFF diagnosis is therefore *not* an assessment of the current performance of the finance function, because it strictly looks at the progress made toward becoming an HPFF.

In the diagnosis, *all* people working in the finance function complete the HPFF questionnaire, which consists of the 28 HPFF characteristics, the five performance characteristics, and the 10 obstacles that most hinder the transformation of the finance function into an HPFF (see Chapter 5.6 for a detailed description of these obstacles). Based on the data collected with the HPFF questionnaire, average scores for the HPFF factors are calculated and displayed in a graph. This graph indicates how far along in becoming an HPFF the finance function currently is. The graph shows which factors need to be strengthened to improve the performance of the finance function. In a workshop, there is discussion about the diagnosis results: in particular, do the financial professionals recognize and acknowledge these results; what are the possible causes of the scores ("root cause analysis"); and—most importantly—what can be done to strengthen the factors. The outcome of the HPFF diagnosis is an HPFF action plan in which the improvement activities are listed, prioritized, and assigned to financial professionals, who then execute these to transform their finance function into an HPFF.

What vs. How
The HPFF Framework—just as the HPO Framework—is not a set of instructions or a recipe that can be blindly followed. Rather, it is a framework that must be translated by the financial professionals to the specific situation of the finance function. Thus, after the *what* provided by the HPFF Framework (as in, "we now know what has to be improved in our finance function"), the tailoring of the finance function, the how (as in, "*how* we should improve depends on the situation of our finance function"), is done by the financial professionals themselves. Hence, the HPFF Framework is not a silver bullet and does not provide a blueprint or recipe for high performance; rather, it indicates the areas in the finance function that are important for achieving excellent performance. It is then the task of the financial professionals working in that finance function to undertake improvement actions that strengthen these areas. Thus, the HPFF Framework provides focus on the areas in the finance function that really matter!

CASE: IT Pays to Become an HPFF at Legrand the Netherlands

Although there are many *internal* benefits to becoming an HPFF—such as lower operating costs, fewer errors, and more satisfied internal customers—there can also be *external* benefits. This could include a growing reputation among financial professionals working at other organizations, for example by winning prizes. An example of an external benefit is the case of the company Legrand the Netherlands, which has been engaged in an HPFF transformation for several years and—although not yet being a full HPFF—has already won the Best Finance Team of the Year Award in the Netherlands. According to the jury report, "Legrand the Netherlands was chosen by the jury as the winner in the middle/large organization category because they are very clearly a team that is working on improving the Finance function. The jury was impressed by how Legrand the Netherlands' finance function, with a relatively small team, has an enormous impact and very good collaboration with the business and functions as a true business partner. The Legrand data warehouse is a textbook example of a modern finance team. This team exudes enthusiasm for the work they do and that was very much appreciated by the jury." As the CFO explained during the award ceremony: "Our finance team has improved significantly over the past years in terms of IT, processes and behavior. As a result, we have actually transformed from traditional transaction processing, cost focusing and looking back, to more analysis, looking ahead, collaborating with other departments and greater involvement in strategic projects." In this case study, we will discuss how Legrand's finance function has managed to achieve the aforementioned.

Legrand the Netherlands and its Finance Function

Legrand the Netherlands is part of the worldwide operating French multinational Legrand Group, a specialist in electrical and digital infrastructure for buildings. Legrand focuses on residential and commercial construction, machine and panel construction, and industrial applications. The company supplies systems for energy distribution, communication networks, and building automation, wherein all systems are optimally aligned and can therefore be installed easily, safely, and quickly. The organization strives for a leading position as a total or one-stop-shop supplier within the electrical and digital market. The company has been operating since the 1950s and has grown steadily ever since, reaching global sales of 5.5 billion euros in 2017 with 37,000 employees. Legrand the Netherlands was founded in 1972 and now has 150 employees. The Dutch company focuses on increasing the ease of installation and use of its products for end users, installers, advisers and logistics partners with aligned systems and services that contribute to the improvement of energy consumption, communication, safety and design within buildings. To this end, Legrand has developed four core values: ethics, innovation, customer focus, and sustainability and environment.

Legrand's finance function is organized both centrally and locally. The head office in France has financial specialists in areas such as tax, treasury, and internal control. The operational side of the finance function is organized in the countries themselves. Legrand The Netherlands' finance function consists of eight people: a CFO, two business advisers, two administrators, an information architect, a legal counsel, and a financial specialist. The department has developed its own mission, which it propagates in all its communications: "An excellent Finance team (HPFF) that realizes reliable reporting and acts as a full-fledged business partner for other disciplines in order to create value for our organization." Legrand's four core values have been translated into specific values for the finance function: ethics means proactive cooperation and committed and reliable action; innovation is the pursuit of continuous improvement and renewal of processes and reports; customer focus is realized by providing reliable and timely management information and being a business partner for the business; and sustainability and environment means consciously dealing with materials, processes, and colleagues in an environment-conscious manner.

The Impetus for the HPFF Transformation

A few years ago, the CFO of Legrand the Netherlands decided that it was time to further develop the finance function. Although it was operating adequately, the function had to improve and strengthen itself if it was to be able to guarantee reliable reporting (internal and external) in the future and to actually act as a full-fledged business partner to the other disciplines. In addition, the finance function had to continue to meet the financial (reporting) requirements within an increasingly complex and competitive environment (due to competitors who operate increasingly cost-consciously). For these reasons, the finance function decided to embark on an HPFF transformation. The first step in the transformation was to organize a study day for the financial employees where they were introduced to the HPFF and HPFF frameworks. The workshop started with an explanation by the CFO of his vision on and the necessity of creating an HPFF. Subsequently, the design and structure of the HPFF framework was discussed. Then the financial professionals got to work addressing the following questions: How can the HPFF be defined at Legrand? How can the characteristics of the HPFF be fulfilled at Legrand? How can the HPFF be set up at Legrand? What needs to be done to implement the HPFF at Legrand and how can that be achieved?"

During the study day, the employees decided to first adjust the definition of the HPFF for their own finance function to: "The HPFF works proactively with the organization to become and remain an HPFF, by always having the right people, processes, and systems at a high quality level." The function then chose the following attention points as priority:

- *Focus more on carrying out activities that add value and do more business partnering.* The finance function wanted to position itself more emphatically as a partner of the business, by making it clearer what value the function could add to the business. The function aimed to create greater financial awareness among managers by making financial matters more understandable for them, proactively giving advice (and not after the fact), participating more in discussions taking place in the business so that the financial component is more explicitly present and taken into account during discussions and decision-making, giving and asking for more feedback, creating win-win situations, better conveying what the function is doing, and by finishing what it promised and started with (note: this attention point is related to the HPFF factor 'Strategic Role')
- *Strengthening the employee's behavioral profile.* The finance function wanted to strengthen its own communication skills. Employees had to learn to connect with other disciplines and to communicate more effectively, to let what was said/asked sink in first and then to come back to it later, not to be overwhelmed, to be more assertive, profile themselves more and show self-confidence, and give and ask for more feedback (note: this attention point is related to the HPFF factor 'Personal Development')
- *Increase the efficiency and effectiveness of the finance function and make more use of IT to automate processes.* Processes that should be addressed first were as follows: ensuring the continuity and backup of the financial processes (having financial professionals perform more different tasks so that they can act as backup for each other), more dynamic reporting, and even more standardized and automated processes (note: this attention point is related to the HPFF factors 'Finance function Improvement' and 'IT Focus')

The Transformation

Three years after the start of the transformation into a higher-quality finance function and after winning the Best Finance Team of the Year Award in the Netherlands, we spoke to the CFO about how Legrand Netherlands has approached the transformation. His story is below.

Starting and Approaching the Transformation

'The HPFF workshop made my employees feel enthusiastic about the HPFF framework. We concluded in the first finance monthly work meeting after the workshop that we, as a function, were going to use the framework to determine which areas to improve and develop further. We saw, and see, the HPFF framework as a structured way to ensure that we continue to improve in the three areas of IT, processes, and behavior. Because, to be honest, in itself, it was an eye-opener that you have to keep developing simultaneously in all areas to improve your overall performance. So it is not the case that you should only focus on IT or only on processes, it is about the cohesion between the three areas and you have to initiate improvement actions in each area. We already did a lot, but the HPFF framework made it possible to assess whether we have given all the essentials sufficient attention.

I asked my people to think about what we could do specifically and concretely. We then made a list of improvement actions for the three areas. All employees were involved in this and we always discuss status and progress with everyone during our monthly work meeting. The actions and associated goals have been included in the finance function's annual plan. Naturally, we also take the strategy of the entire company into account: we align with the most important strategic and commercial targets so that we, as finance function, are in step with the rest of the company. This also gives us the opportunity to inform employees about, and involve them in, new products and customers that are coming, the market that is becoming increasingly demanding and wants faster delivery times, the fact that there are more deviations and specials compared to the standard range of products we carried in the recent past, which will require more project-based work. It is important that the financial professionals know that these things are about to happen so that they can prepare.'

Behavior

'Behavior is becoming increasingly important when you look at the profile of the financial professionals and therefore also for our employees, which is why behavior has received more attention since the HPFF workshop. The role of the financial is changing: more demands are being made on communication skills and connecting with other disciplines. You are, as a financial professional, no longer in an ivory tower where you produce figures and reports and that is it. As a finance function department, we meet with Operations every two weeks to discuss the performance in the factory and the warehouse. We also have monthly meetings with Sales. In addition, the involvement of Finance is increasingly demanded, also from Legrand Group, in several topics, including non-financial topics such as CSR (Corporate Social Responsibility) and Health and Safety.

Various employees suggested that we, as a finance function, should profile ourselves more and increase our visibility in the company, so we are taking steps there. One step was to create the theme of "personal empowerment" and we looked for suitable training in the field of connecting and effective communication with people in which every financial, including myself, was going to participate. To increase our visibility, we made a very simple A3 sheet with our photos accompanied by a few sentences what we do. We hung that A3 sheet next to all coffee machines and also put it on the intranet. We received nice responses to that, especially along the lines of "Gosh, are you doing this also?" Another campaign was to visit people physically at their workplace more often instead of sending an email. If you walk around the company for half an hour, you will hear a lot and quickly know what is going on in the company.

We have different positions within finance: the subject specialist, the business advisor, the information broker—and these all require different training. For example, one of the administrators often goes to VAT training and both of them go to the National Administrators Day, the controllers recently went to an Excel dashboard course, and I myself always go to the National Controllers Day to get inspiration and follow developments that I can potentially include in our function plan. We look consciously at the profiles and decide which, especially professional, training courses are appropriate for them. We mainly try to match with the strengths of the individual; we believe that it is better to let people do what they are good at and what they enjoy than to focus too much on subjects in which they are less adept.'

Processes

'In regard to processes we started with a lean management course. The aim was to learn to structure and organize processes more easily and efficiently. For example, we tracked for six months on what activities we spent our time. It showed that the month-end closing process, which we thought was in good order because we usually reported to our French headquarters on working day 6 while we were given eight days to do so, took many more hours—hours spent on tasks that contributed little or nothing to the process. We then focused on improving this by, for example, standardizing more and further automating the process. In addition, we worked on having a backup for 80% of our basic processes. I wanted to create as many "duo's of financial professionals" as possible in these processes. This means that if someone drops out, another financial can take over the work so that everything can basically continue.

We are also increasingly moving toward self-service reporting for managers. For example, we have introduced dynamic reporting. Before, we had many static reports containing the usual actuals compared to budget and last year. Now, in Excel, we have built dynamic dashboards in which managers can select and filter data themselves. The interesting thing is that managers now come to us with questions that are of a higher difficulty level than before. You have to coach and support the managers in building self-reliance, though. You have to explain it well and the penny drops a bit faster with some people than with others—that differs from person to person.'

IT

'With regard to IT, we had already done quite a few things before the HPFF workshop. We had already set up a data warehouse and implemented an IT solution for the purchase-to-pay process, in which incoming invoice streams were fully automated and digitized. But here, too, we used the HPFF framework to see which IT buttons we had to press to improve further. With regard to increasing IT knowledge within the finance function, we realize that we did not need eight IT experts within the team, but that we needed only one or two persons who have an affinity with IT. We have identified these individuals and they now follow specific courses in this area. We still need to do more about that. For example, we let trade magazines circulate in the controller department and we subscribe to e-alerts about developments in the financial field. We could be more proactive in also bringing in specific IT knowledge, to allow us to follow developments in the IT market more actively.'

Experiences and Results So Far

'The decision to start the HPFF transformation three years ago now appears to have been a very timely one. The requirements that head office places on us in the field of reporting, internal control, compliance, forecasting, etc., have been considerably increased in recent years. Today, everything has to be faster and better to guarantee the desired quality level. We can say that if we had not started with HPFF at the time, we would have been in trouble now. Partly because we currently have things better organized in all three areas—IT, processes and behavior—we were able to make time to tackle these improvements properly, to standardize and automate more, to set up a good compliance program, and to contribute to other matters such as CSR. In fact, you can say that as a finance function you *have* to become an HPFF because otherwise you will not be able to meet the higher requirements placed on you, let alone fulfill a leading role within the organization.

Another advantage of the HPFF framework is that it gives financial professionals more structure and clarity, and that benefits them. For example, the HPFF action plan makes it possible to reflect, every quarter, on how we are doing and what is still needed. In fact, the HPFF framework has become in our function the internal communication vehicle. We did experience that one financial gets out of his or her comfort zone more easily than another. One of the financial professionals, for example, remained a bit more critical and wanted to return to his comfort zone sooner rather than later, while another liked to work on these kinds of improvement projects. I see it this way: you need attackers and defenders. The attackers like HPFF because it brings innovation, renewal, and improvement. The defenders feel more comfortable with the structure they already have and the things they do every day and in which they are often very good. The finance function needs both, with the defenders guarding the base. So it is not the case that all financial professionals put in the same amount of energy and proceed as fast as possible, but everyone went along with it, no one showed any resistance. Interestingly, the attackers are more likely to adopt new things, such as purchase-to-pay and dynamic dashboarding, than the defenders. The latter, in contrast, say: "It is great that those attackers improve things in my domain and in my processes, but I leave all those new things to those people for a while because they can do that much better." The defenders will eventually take up the new things if these have yielded good results, when they see the benefits for their own work. The consequence of this is that if you are going to embark on an HPFF transformation, you must emphasize that you do not assume that everyone in the finance function must now go and tackle everything. You distribute improvement activities based on the roles and personalities of the financial professionals. But you have to emphasize that everyone within the department has to act on the results of the improvements.

We've been at it for three years now and I think we're going at the right pace. The most important thing for me is that the function continues to develop. Yes, some improvements simply go faster than others. But I have noticed that you should not always go too fast, you should not want to completely turn the entire function upside down, because financial professionals in particular naturally like a certain degree of structure and security. The most important thing is that you keep developing, and that can be done step by step. It is better to do two to three projects a year well than many projects only half baked. Ultimately, it is important that you continuously improve. That improvement does not always have to be in the form of a big project, it can also be small things that you just almost casually start so that you can take another small step. So for me the pace in itself is not decisive, but it is that you keep developing.

If I look at the results we have achieved, it is in a nutshell: a stable, efficient, and proactive finance team; basic processes that are in order and, where possible, automated; a transformation from a more traditionally oriented to a more business-partner-oriented position; and a function that creates added value for the organization. To elaborate on the latter: we clearly work better together with the other disciplines. We also ask them more about what we can improve and how we can make their work easier, something they generally eagerly respond to with all kinds of suggestions to us. We are now also doing much more forecasting, an activity that is becoming increasingly important in the current era. We are not only making them more often for our own Dutch management but also for the head office in France, and we are making them more reliable and accurate. By the latter, I mean that the assumptions under the forecasts are increasingly substantiated on the basis of market and organizational knowledge and developments. What we now experience is that other disciplines are really happy with the finance function, in the sense that we provide them with a lot of correct management information. They now also regularly come to us with things to check or think along with certain issues; they trust us.'

Future Plans

As part of our case study, we asked Legrand to complete the HPFF diagnosis. The results are depicted in Figure 4.

Figure 4. HPFF scores for Legrand the Netherlands

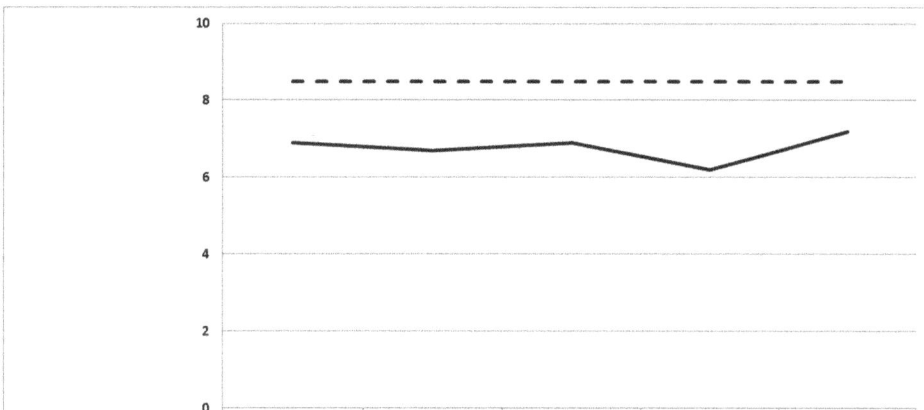

	Finance Function Improvement	IT Focus	Personal Development	Role Clarity	Strategic Role
HPFF (AVG>=8.5)	8,5	8,5	8,5	8,5	8,5
Legrand (n=6, AVG=6.8, PERF=7.3)	6,9	6,7	6,9	6,2	7,2

Figure 4 shows that although Legrand the Netherlands is not yet an HPFF, it is on its way to becoming one. Legrand's finance function scores on average (AVG in Figure 4) a 6.8 on the HPFF factors and a 7.3 on the Finance function Performance factor (PERF in Figure 4). It can be seen in Figure 4 that the focus on the development of financial professionals in particular is paying off in terms of Legrand's score on HPFF factor Personal Development. Undoubtedly, this attention resulted in the formation of the strong team that impressed the jury of the Best Finance Team of the Year Award Netherlands.

The CFO of Legrand responds to the results of the HPFF diagnosis as follows: 'Of course we are not there yet, in fact you never really are with a transition to HPFF. We still have a number of spearheads for the coming years. We have an issue in particular with the integration of the processes. Because we are part of a group consisting of many acquired companies, we do not have a uniform IT architecture and therefore no integrated processes. In the coming period, the focus within the group will be placed on achieving more integration. We want to achieve continuous improvement and renewal of processes and reports through further process optimization, further rollout of dynamic dashboards, and streamlining of information exchange and online collaboration within the organization. We want to communicate even better and further increase our visibility by, for example, developing our own corporate identity and regularly giving presentations to the other disciplines. We will continue to develop the role of business partner, especially in non-financial matters. The quality of financial professionals continues to receive attention through follow-up training in Collaboration and Effective Communication training sessions, and by having employees attend conferences, do company visits and follow additional training sessions. The further development of the forecasting process remains important and we will ensure that we are fully involved in the strategic orientation of the company. We were happy and proud to have won the Best Finance Team Award because it was a great recognition for the growing process we went through together. At the same time, it is an incentive to continue on the path toward HPFF. In addition, we will discuss the HPFF framework within the entire organization. Within Legrand we have a lot of freedom to take initiatives and we have made good use of it with HPFF, and now is the time to share our experiences with the rest of the Legrand group.'

5.5 WHAT'S NEW ABOUT THE HPFF

At first glance, one might think both the movements leading to the HPFF and the HPFF factors themselves are not necessarily new; in fact, many of them have been around for years. However, the difference our research makes is that, based on the information gathered and our extensive knowledge of HPOs, we have been able to design a structure for the future finance function that:

- has a solid academic foundation, both in its development and because of the peer-reviewed journals in which we published articles about the framework;
- is based on the evergreens, i.e., activities of the finance function that will always be important, which we have identified in longitudinal research over 15 years;
- encompasses current and future developments;
- has a direct link with the HPO factors and therefore explicitly supports the transformation into and continued existence as a high-performance organization;
- recognizes that there are different environments within the finance function (not a 'one size fits all') and has developed specific behavioral profiles for them (see Chapter 6);
- ensures that financial professionals need to develop not only professionally but also behaviorally;
- gives substance to the HPFF factors by describing "best ideas" for them which financial professionals can use to strengthen them (see Chapter 10);
- leads to doing more with higher quality at a lower cost.

CASE: Bringing Multiple Finance Functions Simultaneously to a Higher Quality Level at an Investment Company

Investment company ICo Ltd.[3] is specifically looking for participations in companies that not only have growth potential but also want to develop themselves sustainably with a focus on long-term value creation. To this end, ICo orchestrates the management of its participations to demonstrate entrepreneurship and to actively respond to social themes. This results, on the one hand, in an investment company that does not have a fixed period to make an exit (i.e., selling off the participation), and, on the other hand, in participations that all find innovation and sustainability to be of paramount importance. ICo is explicitly involved in the participations by supporting them in the area of management and with certain central services. The participations themselves remain responsible for their own performance at all times and in that respect operate completely independently of ICo; they make use of the support services when it suits them. One of these support services is in the financial field. ICo has its own finance function that provides consolidated reporting on all participations based on the information provided by these participations. In addition, ICo's finance function supports the finance functions of the participations in complex financial matters as well as with their quality development. With regard to the latter, ICo's CFO and controller organize a knowledge exchange meeting for the CFOs of the participations several times a year. During each meeting, a topic that is relevant to all participations is discussed.

An HPFF session was organized as part of these CFO meetings. The aim of this session was to introduce the CFOs of the participations to the HPO and HPFF frameworks, and make them enthusiastic about transforming their own finance function into an HPFF. The latter was important because if the finance functions of the participations succeeded in transforming into HPFFs, they could play a pioneering role within their organizations in the transformation of those organizations into HPOs. This would not only increase the value of the participations, but—more importantly—enable the participations to achieve their innovation and sustainability objectives.

In preparation for the CFO session, ICo's finance function first decided to organize an HPFF workshop itself in which the function could become better acquainted with the HPFF philosophy. The intention was for ICo's finance function to improve itself toward becoming an HPFF, thereby 'setting a good example' for the participations. In addition it would give ICo's controller the opportunity to acquire the HPFF knowledge needed for her to support the finance functions of the participations in their transformation into an HPFF. In preparation, employees of ICo's finance function completed the HPFF questionnaire. Their scores were then discussed during the HPFF workshop, possible improvements were identified, and priorities set.

The CFO meeting was held shortly afterwards. In preparation, all participating CFOs received a link to the internet-based HPFF questionnaire, along with a request to complete it for their own finance function. The questionnaire was anonymous; none of the respondents were asked to provide their names. The meeting consisted of the following parts:

- A lecture on the HPO and HPFF frameworks.
- Discussion of the HPFF results (these were averaged across all participating CFOs to form a virtual finance function that could serve as an example for all attendees).

- Interactive break-out in groups about the HPFF results: Is there recognition and acknowledgment of the results and what they mean for the finance functions of the participations? What improvements are needed? Are there good examples within the participations that can help in this respect?
- Presentations of the break-out groups to each other.
- Discussion about the possible roll-out of the HPFF framework within the participations, and the role that ICo's finance function could play in this.

The outcomes of the break-out session were discussed per HPFF factor, in which best ideas were also exchanged. A number of points that emerged from this are described below.

Finance Function Improvement

- The CFOs were satisfied with how they improve their processes, but felt that they still paid too little attention to the evaluation of these improvements (how it went, what was delivered, what was learned). They therefore wanted to make this evaluation a standard part of the implementation.
- The CFOs were of the opinion that adding milestones and key performance indicators (KPIs) to improvement processes could help them maintain more focus on and control of those improvement processes.
- The CFOs realized that it is important to structurally set aside time to work on improvements and not indulge passing whims.
- Involving long-term employees in improvement plans and change processes proved difficult for many CFOs. They therefore felt that it is the finance manager's responsibility to provide feedback and urgently encourage these employees to change. Finance functions who want to become HPFFs should not be afraid to say goodbye to people who do not want to change, because resistance to change can have a major positive impact on the function and the organization.

IT Focus

- Automating routine processes remained an important base for all CFOs. At the same time, it turned out to be difficult to write a financial business case for increased automation in the smaller organizations.
- The CFOs saw IT as a means to implement uniform and standardized processes. A good example of this is the implementation of an ERP package, in which the finance function and the organization do not take existing processes as starting point but instead regard the processes as "prescribed" by the ERP package (which, after all, contains the best practice processes of the sector). In this way, desired process changes within the organization can be "enforced."

Personal Development and Role Clarity

- The CFOs considered it important to continue to stimulate personal development in their financial professionals. They therefore felt that they should maintain dialogue with them and ensure open feedback in which the wishes of the financial professionals and requirements of the organization could be aligned.

- It is also important to (continue to) pay attention to one's own development as a CFO, for example by participating in network clubs, roundtables, professional training, and by receiving coaching.

Strategic Role

- The CFOs were satisfied with the role they play in supporting important decisions within their organization. They have found that it is essential to understand the business well in order to successfully fulfill that strategic role.
- In order to ensure the fulfillment of the strategic role at various organizational levels, it can help to have the controllers and financial professionals become a permanent part of a strategic project team.

Comments from ICO's CFO and Controller on the Usefulness and Necessity of the HPFF Diagnosis

"We conducted an HPFF workshop in the run-up to the CFO session. At first we had the feeling that ICo could already reasonably be considered to be an HPFF, but while we talked about the diagnosis results quite a few improvement opportunities came up, and there were some surprising ideas. The power of the HPFF diagnosis as we have experienced it lies mainly in the discussion within the team. By talking about the various factors in a structured manner, you uncover many things. Through the discussion we experienced a positive energy and a good commitment to actually become a full-fledged HPFF in the near future.

During the CFO session itself, we also had good discussions with each other on the basis of the HPFF factors. Here too we experienced the discussion as very positive. No standard solutions such as "implement an ERP package" emerged, but rather tips about what works and what does not work during an implementation. Or discussions about how to make development programs for every level of employee in the finance function. Good best ideas were shared through the open and honest discussion. The HPFF diagnosis may not be really innovative in this respect, because you can always have a good discussion. But what the diagnosis is strong in is: it helps you to look at your processes and the business from a distance and some detachment, focus on the what is really important, and then come up with good recommendations."

5.6 REMOVING THE OBSTACLES TO BECOMING AN HPFF

Before the finance function can transform into an HPFF, it is important to have a clear picture of the obstacles specific to this transformation process. Leading financial teams know how to proactively anticipate these obstacles in order to increase the chances of a successful transformation process. In practice, however, there is only a handful of high-performing finance functions that are successful in terms of the mix of culture, talent, management model, and technology necessary to become an HPFF (PWC, 2017; Zoni and Pippo, 2017; Essaides et al., 2020; Ferrin & Wong, 2021). This is perhaps because finance functions are still lacking awareness of the obstacles that may await them while improving, with the result that they are insufficiently prepared when these do occur. This might explain why a majority of CFOs complain that the transformation of their finance function goes too slowly or even fails.[4] Because of the slow pace of transformation, the finance function is not able to keep up with the many changes internal and external to the organization, and it thus misses chances to deliver more added value to the business. We conducted a study to gain more insight into these obstacles by attempting to answer the question: What are the main obstacles that need to be addressed so that the finance function can transform into an HPFF? In addition, we looked at how these obstacles could be removed so that the probability that a finance function successfully transforms increases significantly.

Most CFOs agree that legacy data, process, technology, and skills are key impediments to their ability to adopt new ways of working. This finding is revealing when learning how Fortune 2000 companies actually run (Reilly, 2018):

- "We track over 3.5 billion dollars of labor spend on spreadsheets."
- "We produce over 4,000 reports. We have no idea who uses them and if they are valuable."
- "Business performance discussions are often done in silos—we utilize less than 10% of the data we generate of which most is historical in nature."
- "We have over 27 Business Intelligence tools and don't have any executive-level dashboards."
- "We define advanced analytics as doing variance analysis faster."

The Obstacles Questionnaire

Our study began with a study of the academic literature on the obstacles that finance functions face on their way to achieving a higher quality level. However, we did not find any relevant articles, so we decided to consult the finance management literature. Because consultants and professional associations in general conduct a lot of research into the finance function, we identified a few obstacles reported in this stream of literature.[5] We did not stop there, however: we additionally decided to distribute a survey on obstacles among finance professionals. The reason for this was that in today's "VUCA" (Volatile, Uncertain, Complex, Ambiguous) world things are changing so much and so rapidly that not all obstacles that finance functions might encounter are already covered in the literature. Through our survey, we aimed to make the list of obstacles fully up to date. The survey consisted of just one question: What are the three main obstacles, that is, the three issues that you need to tackle and fix before you start your finance function on a journey to at a higher quality level?" The responses of the financial professionals were grouped according to similar obstacles. In total, the survey revealed 24 obstacles, including all 10

The Delphi Method

The Delphi method is particularly suitable as a research tool when there is insufficient knowledge about the problem being investigated. The method structures and facilitates group communication that focuses on one complex problem, whereby consensus of the group regarding a solution can be reached over a series of iterations of expert feedback. The Delphi method has five characteristics (Loo, 2002; Okoli and Pawlowski, 2004): (1) there is a panel of careful selected experts who have a broad spectrum of opinions on the research topics; (2) the panel experts generally remain anonymous, so they cannot influence each other; (3) the researchers create a series of structured questionnaires and feedback reports to which the experts respond; (4) the responses of the experts are collected in a number of iterations; and (5) the result is a report or article containing the results of the research.

obstacles we had identified from the professional literature. This list of obstacles formed the basis for the Delphi research—a research method that we explain in more detail in the frame.

The Delphi Rounds

We choose a group of 14 financial professionals from our networks who were operating at a high level in the finance function (average working period in finance was 28.3 years) and who had experience with improving their function. Figure 5 schematically shows our research approach, listing the number of Delphi rounds.

Figure 5. Schematic overview of the Delphi investigation process

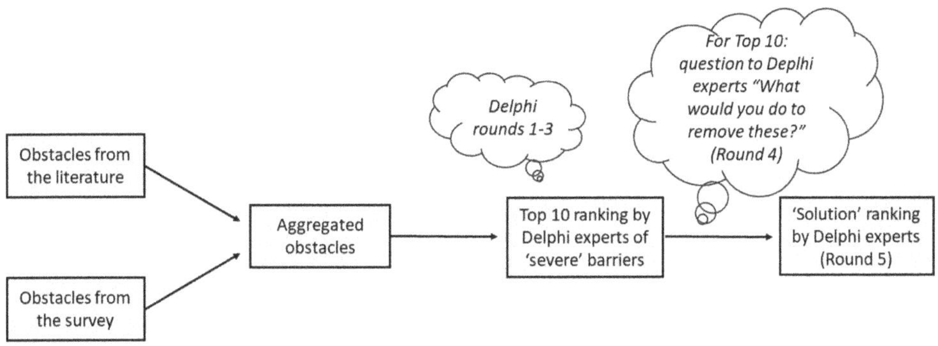

During Delphi round 1, the list of obstacles was sent to the expert panel, along with a question asking the panel to sort the obstacles according to "severity." A "severe obstacle" meant that it was an obstacle that absolutely had to be addressed for the finance function to be able to transform into an HPFF. The experts were also asked to add obstacles to the list that they had themselves experienced and that were not in the list. The feedback from the experts was merged and sorted in a first ranking of the obstacles according to their severity. There were several low-scoring obstacles which, in the experience of the experts, were apparently not that important; these were removed from the list. Additional obstacles, suggested by the experts themselves, were added to the shortened list, which subsequently was sent again to the Delphi experts for review. In Delphi round 2, although no consensus was yet reached by the experts, once again obstacles emerged that were considered to be less important; these too were removed. Finally, in Delphi round 3, consensus was reached by the Delphi experts on a clear list of top 10 most severe obstacles.

Top 10 Obstacles and Corrective Actions

Upon completion of Delphi round 3, the experts were asked in round 4 about how, in their experience, these obstacles could best be addressed and "removed," in such a manner that the obstacle would no longer hinder the transformation to HPFF. This resulted in a multiple of practical measures that the experts had taken. Similar corrective actions were merged and the resulting action list was sent to the experts in Delphi round 5, with the request to assess the proposed actions per obstacle according to effectiveness:

which corrective action was it that they expected, possibly on the basis of previous experience, to most effectively tackle the obstacle? This round immediately led to a consensus because it yielded a clear top three of the most effective corrective actions for every obstacle. These top three lists of measures thus form a good starting point for every finance function to tackle its own obstacles on the way to HPFF. Below, the top 10 obstacles are discussed in more detail and the corresponding top three corrective actions given.

Obstacle 1. Inefficient and Non-Integrated Processes in the Organization

Supporting the organization and the internal customers (Board of Directors and line management) with valuable insights requires both data and processes as well as supporting systems to be in order. After all, the finance function is highly dependent on reliable and aligned processes to yield the integrated data needed for management information to be put together. However, many organizations struggle with process management—in particular, mastering the processes in the organization to ensure that they are properly aligned and can be executed efficiently. Without good process management, it is difficult to extract reliable data quickly and efficiently from the processes in the organization. In addition, the financial processes also suffer from faltering input from operational processes: "garbage in, garbage out."

The Delphi experts consider the following actions most effective to address this obstacle:

1. Designate people as "owners" for the improvement of processes, applications, and data. When people become responsible for processes, the chance that these will be looked after and improved increases considerably as these process managers can be held accountable for their improvement results. Also, they usually have an allocated budget to enable them to improve the processes assigned to them, which increases the chance of successful improvement.
2. Assemble a multidisciplinary team to map the processes, data, and systems throughout the organization, identify bottlenecks, and build and implement solutions. The fact that people from different disciplines are involved in this multidisciplinary team processes will itself ensure better alignment of processes, data, and systems between and across disciplines. Improving those processes, data, and systems will also be more effective, because such a team takes the interests of all disciplines into account.
3. As a finance function, make an improvement plan together with the business and implement it step by step and consistently. Because the finance function is so dependent on the quality of the processes as they are carried out in and by the business, it is wise to work proactively with that business to determine how certain processes can jointly be improved.

> A global food provider transitioned its finance function to a consolidated corporate model, with the accounting and finance function centralized, to standardize processes and achieve top-quartile performance. Previously, the company's major divisions included a multitude of business units, each with a finance function. The shift to centralization enabled finance to move from a generalist model to a much more specialized approach using global process owners to ensure best-practice, standardized finance processes. The driving focus in restructuring finance into a process organization has been on building capabilities regarding people, processes, data, and technology. This has enabled the assignment of centralized process owners who could focus on continuously improving processes (APQC, 2018).

Obstacle 2. Data are not (yet) in Order in the Organization

Finance functions have traditionally focused on data management, i.e., ensuring the reliability, security, and privacy of the data as it is generated and collected in the organization. This is because the reliability and relevance of the reporting and management information provided by the finance function depends to a large extent on "good" data. In practice, however, it appears that many organizations have difficulty with "data governance": having and keeping clear who in the organization owns and is therefore responsible for what data (and its quality). There is often a lack of unambiguous data definitions that apply to the entire organization.

The Delphi experts consider the following actions most effective to address this obstacle:

1. As a finance function, define the data model, creating "one single version of the truth." This means: establishing data definitions, installing a master data management process, building a data warehouse, creating unique source files, and then constantly monitoring and regularly updating these.
2. Analyze the data and use kaizen solutions for improvement. To be able to fundamentally improve the data, the finance function will first have to map the available data, analyze them, and then thoroughly improve its quality using quality methods such as the kaizen method. Subsequently, these data will be included in the aforementioned data model and the data quality thereof will be monitored.
3. Establish a multidisciplinary team that maps out processes, data, and systems, identifies bottlenecks, and builds and implements solutions (see obstacle 1).

Obstacle 3. Insufficient Leadership and Desire to Change from CFO/Manager F&C

In general, the management of the finance function is under great pressure to comply in a timely manner with the legal reporting requirements and the requirements of the internal client, the Board of Directors, and the line management. On top of that, there is extensive fire-fighting because data are not being delivered correctly, IT systems are malfunctioning, and information has been lost between different processes. The result is that the finance function in general meets its requirements through "blood, sweat, and tears" every month, but that insufficient time is spent on implementing improvements that will increase the quality of the processes and the delivered products. To free up time for this, which generally requires the management of the finance function to say "no" to the internal client more often, takes courage and leadership and the absolute will to change and improve. In practice, this is often lacking in management[6], with, as a consequence, a finance function that keeps on "muddling through."

The Delphi experts consider the following actions most effective to address this obstacle:

1. Show the finance function's management how successful peers improve their finance function. After all, a good example is worth following. In addition, these peers also show that the path from a regular finance function to an HPFF is indeed possible: they can discuss with management and emphasize the importance of an HPFF transformation, and they can share tips to tackle and manage the transformation.
2. Make sure there is a financial with authority at the top of the organization, i.e., on the Board of Directors. This generally is someone with authority on the Board who is responsible for Finance,

and who is listened to by the finance function's management when he/she insists on improving the finance function and who, in addition, has the authority to initiate the transformation into an HPFF.

3. Create urgency for changes to the finance function with the CFO/Manager F&C. This can be done by showing, for example, how the circumstances of the organization and its environment are changing and how satisfaction among financial employees or internal customers is declining. In addition, potential cost savings that are currently not achieved must be identified and the quality problems in the finance function have to be measured in order to show the organization that the finance function is a professionally run department.

Obstacle 4. Insufficient Change and Improvement Culture within the Finance Function

Obstacle 4 is in line with obstacle 3, but now applies more or less to all employees of the finance function. The insufficient change and improvement culture is reinforced by the fact that financial professionals are generally not trained in change management skills because little attention is paid to this during their education and training programs. As a result, there is often a lack of change management skills within the finance function.

The Delphi experts consider the following actions most effective to address this obstacle:

1. CFO/Manager F&C leading by example with regard to change and improvement. This means that the management of the finance function must be visibly engaged in working on the transformation into an HPFF, thereby indicating as a role model how important the transformation is to management.
2. Management of the finance function making it clear that making mistakes and learning is crucial, but sitting still is not an option: This will allay financial professionals' fear of making mistakes, which inevitably accompany change and improvement. At the same time, management makes it known that it is expected from employees that they will get moving and start with that change and improvement, and that experimentation is an integral part of an HPFF.
3. Appointing change/improvement teams that include financial professionals who have the "improvement gene" and who therefore have no problem taking the lead in the transformation to HPFF; management of the finance function must give these teams sufficient space to actually and visibly realize changes and improvements.

Obstacle 5. Inadequate IT Systems in the Organization

This obstacle is caused by two situations. The first situation is where organizations struggle with "legacy systems," i.e., outdated IT systems that were implemented a long time ago and/or that came with acquisitions and mergers and that are no longer relevant to the current situation of the organization and no longer meet the current requirements of users. The second situation is often a result of the first situation. To remove the legacy systems, organizations are starting to implement new IT systems; however, unfortunately, these implementations regularly do not go well or even fail. As a result, the organization, and especially the finance function, is stuck with a half-baked system that requires extensive manual activities to make available relevant information of the appropriate quality.

The Delphi experts consider the following actions most effective to address this obstacle:

1. First, processes must be improved before acquiring a new ICT system. If the processes do not run smoothly or align well, they cannot be properly automated. Once again, the principle of "garbage in, garbage out" applies: the manual inefficient and ineffective way of working then becomes an automated inefficient and ineffective way of working. The finance function can, with its "helicopter view" of the organization, take the lead in improving processes.
2. Management of the finance function should ensure that ICT is placed higher on the strategic agenda of the organization. It should be ensured that colleague managers no longer see ICT as a cost but as a "business enabler," and are therefore prepared to invest more in the ICT architecture.
3. Analysis should be undertaken of whether the ICT problem lies with the ICT systems themselves or with its architecture and embedment within the organization. This makes it clear whether the problem lies in the first or second situation described above, which allows the finance function to provide the appropriate corrective action advice to the Board of Directors.

Using ICT in the Finance Function
A high-tech manufacturer is using machine-learning algorithms and analytics to monitor financial and business-continuity risks. This has reduced staff time needed to complete an audit while at the same time allowing the organization to better target units that pose the greatest risks. As a result, the manufacturer has reduced the total cost of internal audits by 15 to 20%. A global consumer-packaged-goods company uses natural-language generation to generate drafts of the management discussion and analysis for the monthly operational reviews. This technology converts structured data into meaningful financial prose that summarizes and synthesizes insights. Automating sections of the reports frees up considerable time of the financial professionals (Agrawal et al., 2020).

Obstacle 6. Lack of Buy-in from Line Management for the Development of Finance into an HPFF

As the finance function develops into an HPFF, it increasingly functions as a business partner of line management. This means that the finance function becomes more concerned with consulting on operational matters, in particular with the financial consequences of operational decisions. This is not always appreciated by line management because managers may perceive it as interference in their area. Furthermore, the finance function is also not always regarded as a sparring partner with sufficient understanding of operational and commercial matters. Yet another reason for this obstacle may be that line management is afraid of (too many) critical questions from the finance function and therefore prefers to keep the finance employees at an arm's length and in the dark.

The Delphi experts consider the following actions most effective to address this obstacle:

1. Management of the finance function must regularly explain to the business what the finance function is doing and how the business can benefit from a properly functioning finance function. This should be done in the form of a dialogue in which the business can immediately make its wishes known. In this dialogue, management should regularly check how satisfied the business is with the support it is receiving from the finance function.
2. The Board should testify openly that a strong finance function is important to the business. When the importance of the finance function for the proper functioning of the Board of Directors itself,

and thus also for the organization, becomes clearer to the business, it will be more willing to make use of the support from the finance function and to invest more in the "upgrading" of the finance function.
3. The business should be more involved in processes within the financial domain. After all, "unknown makes unloved." Therefore, management of the finance function should encourage line managers and operational employees to work together with financial employees during the implementation of financial processes and in the aforementioned multidisciplinary teams.

Obstacle 7. Insufficient View on or Understanding of the Business Among the Financial Professionals

Because of the constant pressure on the finance function, financial professionals generally do not have enough time to frequently or closely interact with and immerse themselves in the operation. In addition, many financial professionals have little operational experience, because on the one hand their training has paid little attention to this and on the other their career path has likely mainly taken place in the financial domain. This makes it difficult for them, for example, to convert financial data into business insights, which means that the possibility of becoming a real business partner in the HPFF is not that high.

The Delphi experts consider the following actions most effective to address this obstacle:

1. Having financial professionals pay regular working visits to the business; by talking to operational staff and line managers, financial professionals will gain on-site knowledge and understanding of operational processes and the decisions taken by the business.
2. Letting financial professionals participate in management teams and/or undertake an internship in the business.
3. Having CFOs talk more with the financial professionals about the business; because the CFO has a lot of contact with operational colleagues on the Board of Directors and generally also line managers, she/he will gain extensive knowledge of the operation which then must be shared with the employees in the finance function. This must be done regularly so that financial professionals are kept informed of the most recent developments in the business and can respond quickly or deal with them proactively.

In a large manufacturing multinational, the local finance functions in various regions are aligned through biannual "open line" discussions with the company's CFO. All finance functions join in on these calls to discuss priorities and strategic planning. Regional functions also have quarterly face-to-face meetings and monthly virtual meetings to discuss strategy, business performance, and the ongoing digital transformation. These efforts help the company's finance function to align its strategy with the business so that it can act as not only financial controller but also a business partner by providing integrated forecasts, analytics, sales, and operational planning, as well as inventory management and manufacturing resource planning (APQC, 2018).

Obstacle 8. Insufficient Financial Professionals with the Right Knowledge and Skills Available

Financial professionals require specific competencies in order to transform their function into an HPFF. In particular, more all-rounders with advisory skills, who can provide high-quality strategic and operational financial advice, are needed. After all, routine financial activities are all automated in the HPFF. Many financial professionals are not trained at all for this purpose (see also obstacle 7) and, moreover, because of the aforementioned "blood, sweat, and tears" approach, they do not have enough time to develop the desired profile. The shortage of financial professionals with such profiles severely hinders transformation into an HPFF.

The Delphi experts consider the following actions most effective to address this obstacle:

1. Mapping out the competencies necessary for being able to properly fulfill all roles in the HPFF, and selecting and recruiting new staff who have these competencies.
2. Management of the finance function should be open and transparent toward financial professionals about their lack of necessary knowledge and skills. Management should not ignore the fact that the finance function must spend more time and effort to develop financial professionals with the right profiles. Furthermore, it should also be made clear to the financial professionals themselves that they have an obligation to develop the competencies necessary to excel in their role.
3. Management should use HR instruments such as "the fleet review." In doing so, the quality of the financial professionals is structurally and regularly reviewed, and can be structurally addressed.

Obstacle 9. Insufficient/Unclear Business Objectives and Priorities within the Organization

The finance function exists to support the internal customer, for example, the Board of Directors and line management. Its task is to provide them with relevant management information. However, when business objectives and priorities are unclear or perhaps nonexistent, it becomes very difficult for the finance function to meet the current needs of the business (because these are not clear). Furthermore, it becomes virtually impossible to properly develop and structure the HPFF, in particular the HPFF factor 'Strategic Role,' because there are no benchmarks for this.

The Delphi experts consider the following actions most effective to address this obstacle:

1. The finance function should take the lead to develop the organizational mission/vision/strategy/objectives together with the business. In this context, the most important financial and non-financial key performance indicators must be derived in dialogue with the business, ensuring that there is consensus about them within the organization.
2. The finance function should, together with the business, determine what is really important for the organization and focus on this in the management reporting rather than striving for 100% completeness.
3. The finance function should ask the business to explain the purpose of doing certain things, and then determine if these things are worth tracking and reporting in management reports.

The finance function of a large manufacturer has a mix of efficiency and effectiveness metrics to track its global processes. The function sets targets annually and ultimately aims for 10% year-over-year improvements in efficiency and top-quartile performance in the costs ratio to total spend. The metrics feed several dashboards:

- Efficiency metrics feed a productivity dashboard. This dashboard tracks the value of improvement initiatives and technology implementations to evaluate how they deliver against preset targets.
- Operational metrics feed a dashboard focused on bottom-line savings. Metrics such as overdue results, average days outstanding, error rates, number of transactions processed, and excessive credit are filtered by the shared service center, by business, by region, and at the corporate level.
- A financial risk dashboard gauges macroeconomic drivers to track the overall health of the working capital. By tracking risk profiles such as debt reserves, the finance function can determine what factors or events affect risk outcomes and what the organization needs to mitigate (APQC, 2018).

Objective 10. The Board of Directors and Line Management do not Focus Sufficiently on Analyses and Insights Provided by the Finance Function

There may be several reasons for the Board of Directors and line management paying insufficient attention to the "products" delivered by the finance function. Some of these reasons will undoubtedly be related to the obstacles discussed earlier. Regardless of the reasons, the effect is that the finance function is not seen as a full (business) partner, certainly not at the strategic level. Therefore, support from top management for the finance function's transformation into the HPFF will be minimal.

The Delphi experts consider the following actions most effective to address this obstacle:

1. The CFO should lead by example by using the analyses provided by the finance function during management team meetings. Colleagues should be shown what these analyses can be used for, which strategic and operational decisions can be taken on their basis, and how the analyses can serve as "early-warning signals" to the business.
2. The finance function should start with small improvements in the business and "score" with small projects based on the analyses. In doing so, line managers should be shown what role the financial analyses played in those projects and be gradually familiarized with the use of these analyses for their own purposes.
3. Management of the finance function should emphasize the importance of exemplary behavior by the Board of Directors and the management team with regard to the use of the analyses and insights. When the top managers of the organization show that the analyses provided by the finance function are important to them in their steering of the organization, lower management levels will be more inclined to use these analyses as well. In addition, if the top levels use the financial analyses in dialogue with managers, the latter will have to delve into them (so that they will soon see the possibilities and added value of those analyses).

REFERENCES

Abdelal, R., Carmody, K., Hill, M., & Pearson, W. J. (2021). *The CFO's role in capability building*. McKinsey & Company.

Accenture. (2018). *From bottom line to front line*. CFO Reimagined. www.accenture.com

Agrawal, A., Eklund, S., Waite, J., & Woodcock, E. (2020). *Finance 2030: four imperatives for the next decade*. McKinsey and Company.

APQC. (2018). *Ten characteristics shared among best-in-class finance functions*. American Productivity and Quality Center.

de Waal, A., Bilstra, E., & De Roeck, P. (2019a). Identifying the characteristics of a high-performance finance function. *Journal of Advances in Management Research*, *16*(3), 352–377. doi:10.1108/JAMR-08-2018-0066

de Waal, A., Bilstra, E., & de Roeck, P. (2019b). *De high performance financiële functie in de praktijk* [The high performance finance function in practice]. Vakmedianet.

Essaides, N., Willman, T., & O'Connor, J. (2020). *2021 key issues*. The CFO Agenda, The Hackett Group.

Ferrin, M., & Wong, W. (2021). *Winning finance, Transformation harnessing the full value of the finance function*. Renoir Consulting.

Gartner. (2019). *Hallmarks of Winning Finance Transformations*. Gartner, Inc.

Holvoet, M. (2021). Manier waarop mensen samenwerken, bepaalt succes van finance [The way people work together determines the success of finance] [published with kind permission of Financial Media]. *CFO Magazine*, (235), 31–34.

Kieft, R. (2020, Nov.). Disruptie van de financiële functie: stimulans voor het leven lang leren [Disruption of the finance function: incentive for lifelong learning]. *CM*.

KPMG. (2019a). *De toekomst van Finance: transformative van de finance functie, bouwen aan het dienstverleningsmodel van de toekomst* [The future of Finance: transforming the finance function, building the service delivery model of the future]. KPMG Advisory N.V.

KPMG International. (2019d). *Future ready finance survey 2019*. KPMG International Cooperative.

Loo, R. (2002). The Delphi method: A powerful tool for strategic management. *Policing*, *25*(4), 762–769. doi:10.1108/13639510210450677

Okoli, C., & Pawlowski, S. D. (2004). The Delphi method as a research tool: An example, design considerations and applications. *Information & Management*, *42*(1), 15–29. doi:10.1016/j.im.2003.11.002

PWC. (2017). *Stepping up: how finance functions are transforming to drive business results*. Finance Effectiveness Benchmark Report 2017. PricewaterhouseCoopers.

Reilly, A. (2018). *Accelerating the digital agenda in finance: Part 1*. Accenture.

Roos, A., Tucker, J., Rodt, M., Stange, S., Ego, P., Boudadi, A., & Sheth, H. (2020). *Lessons from best-in-class CFOs*. Boston Consulting Group.

Yacht. (2016). *More finance or no more finance? Bepaal uw focus voor de toekomst*. Research report. Yacht.

Zoni, L., & Pippo, F. (2017). CFO and finance function: What matters in value creation. *Journal of Accounting & Organizational Change*, *13*(2), 216–238. doi:10.1108/JAOC-12-2014-0059

ENDNOTES

1. The scientific research approach used to develop the HPFF framework is described in Appendix C and in even more detail in de Waal et al. (2019a+b)
2. Six statements were rejected because they did not fit on any of the five identified HPFF factors.
3. This organization, just as almost all case companies, has been made anonymous upon request.
4. See Yacht, 2016; Gartner, 2019. Gartner reports, based on research, that seven out of 10 finance transformations fail.
5. We only studied literature not older than ten years, to be sure that the obstacles that were mentioned in that literature were still valid for contemporary finance functions.
6. In all fairness, the service attitude which characterizes most financial professional also gets in the way of saying no, which after all basically means not providing support in the case of the particular request.

Chapter 6
Set-Up of the HPFF:
Environments, Roles, and Profiles

ABSTRACT

Just as there is no "one financial," there is also no "one finance function." In fact, the finance function consists of several environments, each concerned with a different area of financial activities, in which financial professionals work in multiple roles. When setting up an HPFF, these different environments and roles have to be carefully taken into account. In this chapter, the environments of and the roles in the finance function are described, and their relationships with the HPFF framework are explained. In addition, the roles financials can have in the HPFF are given, the profile of the high-performance financial is described, and the implications for human resourcing are discussed.

6.1 ENVIRONMENTS IN THE HPFF

The field of activity of the finance function is situated between the CFO and the operation on the one side (*internal*) and customers, suppliers, and other stakeholders of the organization on the other side (*external*). The CFO manages and directs the finance function. The finance function is a staff function tasked with supporting the primary, operational processes. The operation organizes its processes to serve the (end) customers of the organization, and suppliers are part of these processes. In addition to customers and suppliers, the organization deals with parties to which it is accountable, such as shareholders, regulators, analysts, and the Supervisory Board. We also place the latter among the bodies to which accountability is required, although the Supervisory Board is formally positioned within the organization. As indicated in Chapter 1, we do not classify the CFO's management team tasks under the finance function, although the CFO's steering of the finance function is part of this function. The primary task of the finance function is to take responsibility for the financial administration, to provide financial reports to internal and external stakeholders, and to comply with financial laws and regulations. The responsibility for adequate control measures to minimize business risks, which can be characterized as Compliance, Risk Management and Accounting, also falls under the range of duties.

DOI: 10.4018/978-1-7998-6929-0.ch006

The above activities can be clustered into two work environments for the finance function: (A) an environment based on administration and processing of data, and (B) an environment based on judgment, compliance with laws and regulations, and the delivery of added value to the operation in financial terms (see Figure 1). The activities in these two environments form the core activities of the finance function. If these core activities are not performed adequately, the expertise and competency of the finance function comes under scrutiny; therefore, these activities must at least be in order and of a minimum quality.

Figure 1. The core activities of the finance function

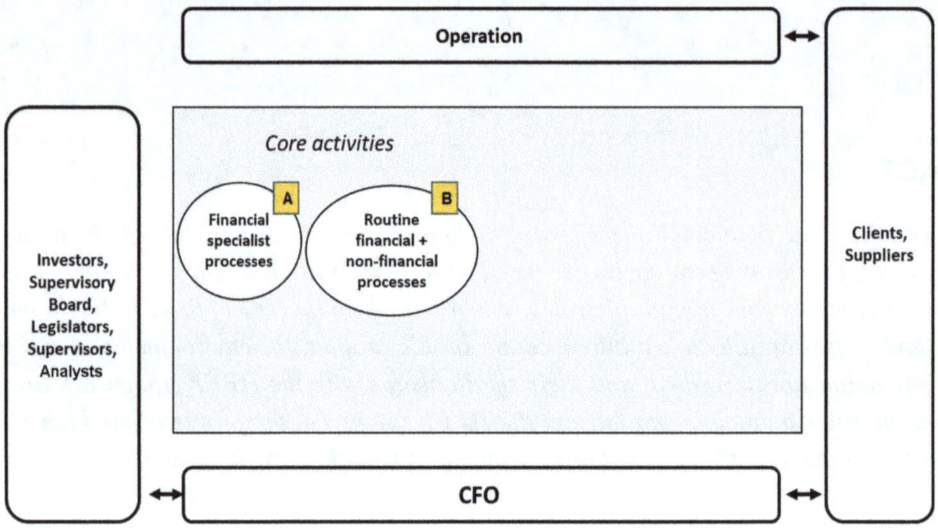

With the emergence of the field of Controlling in the 1980s, internal information provision and support for internal decision-making have become increasingly prominent in the duties of the finance function. The controlling activities generally fall within the finance function; sometimes a business controller is directly responsible to an operation manager. Over the past decades, the concept of "added value" has become increasingly important. This concept expresses the essence of producing, namely adding value to a good or service. What the added value really turns out to be, is determined by the recipient of the service or good provided: the difference between the market value and the production and the raw materials purchased for it. The added value of services is more difficult to determine because the production process is less visible. This is no different for the recipients of services from the finance function, the business, or internal customer. The added value of the finance function is therefore a somewhat abstract concept. We give that concept meaning by seeking the added value in the contribution of the finance function to achieving organizational goals, generating and interpreting information for the operation and line management, providing support and advising the operation during decision-making by supplying and monitoring of the financial components of doing business, and being a "reliable financial source of information" at all times for management and operations. The value-adding activities of the finance function can be classified under two additional environments: (C) an environment based on fixed methods and rules and the production of information; and (D) an environment based on judgment and working with information.

Because of developments in information technology, it is necessary for the finance function to build up expertise in structurally and efficiently establishing an information architecture that optimally supports decision-making in the organization. This can be placed within or outside the finance function. First, let us assume a separate environment C in the finance function, because this represents the intersection of financial and non-financial information in the organization. Many finance functions do not distinguish a separate environment C or are still in the early stages of setting up this environment. We zoom in a bit more on this "new environment" (Figure 2).

Figure 2. The environment in the finance function where self-service and data analytics come together

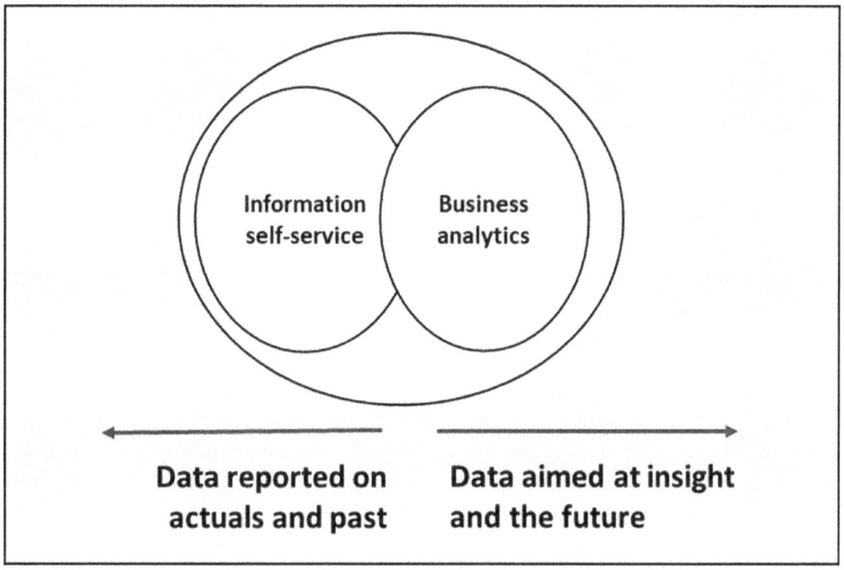

The combination of financial and non-financial data flows translates into an information architecture and data management environment that makes a structured and efficient link between the data from source systems and bundled information for all kinds of target audiences in the organization. An environment where (the reporting of) historical data comes together with (the generation of) predictive future-oriented data, all for the benefit of effective decision-making in the organization. Many developments in environment C have an IT-technical nature (terms that are common in this environment are information management, master data, data warehousing, data mining, data governance, Business Intelligence, Enterprise Performance Management) and are (usually) too far removed from the finance function's own expertise. However, two developments in environment C will have such an impact on the activities of the finance function that we are obliged to discuss them here.

The first development is the self-service concept: the IT tools are designed in such a way that line managers can be in the lead themselves with regard to using the financial services they need at the time they need it. They are increasingly able to themselves request reports, make data and reporting selections, "drill down" to answer their own information requests, in the form and at the time that they themselves want, instead of having to ask for these from the IT department or the finance function. To make this self-service possible, as many routine activities in the reporting process as possible have been automated. The finance function ensures that the data and information in those systems have a high degree of reliability. The advantage of the self-service concept is that line managers become more financially skilled and familiar with managing based on financial and non-financial figures. The financial professionals in environments C and D can then focus on more complex financial activities that have a high organizational impact.

The second development is "big data" or "business analytics." Increasing amounts of data, storage capacity, and computing power of software tools mean that more and more data can be combined. The main characteristics of big data are that it is only valuable for the business if it is available quickly, if it comes from multiple sources, and if it can be flexibly enriched with other (unstructured) data. These characteristics are summarized in three v-words: high-volume, high-velocity, and high-variety (Beyer, 2011). Two other v's are now regularly added: variability (changeability of data) and veracity (fidelity of data). Unfortunately, the definition of big data is not always clear and the term big data is often incorrectly used for all kinds of data collection. As far as we are concerned, the term "business analytics" is better suited and we will use this term in this book. The line manager is supported by the finance function with business analytics that combines data sources and generates new and in-depth business insights. These activities require specialist knowledge that line managers do not have; in addition, they need those services less frequently and more on an on-demand basis. The finance function can thus concentrate on the really difficult and thus more value-adding activity of business analytics and thereby develop into specialists in this field who are valued by the line managers.

One company organized a big-data competition to encourage its finance team to think about problem-solving using data. After initial training, financial professionals were given a data block to play with and the challenge to present new business insights drawn from the data. This competition proved so popular among the financial professionals that the company plans to repeat it frequently. Another company had developed a series of "belts" around skills in data—from red to black—to provide a structured approach to learning and ensure the right level of data analytics skills for different roles. For example, red represented the skills needed of a basic end-user of tools, such as the ability to access and analyze detailed breakdowns of data; a green belt meant that the person had the skills to build dashboards; and a black belt showed that "the wearer" is able to build data cubes (ICAEW/ISCA, 2019).

Self-service development forces the finance function to consider how it wants to support its internal customers during the provision of information: by offering ready-to-use reports or by offering high-quality datasets where the internal clients determine themselves what they need and want? The business analytics development ensures that experts from environment C, currently still mostly working in IT departments, will increasingly transfer to the finance function. This will have an impact on the (team) composition of financial professionals in this position, the recruitment and selection of this different type of financial professionals, and different routes of knowledge training and personal development. In Figure 3, we place the two environments C and D next to the two previously discussed environments.

The four environments together form the finance function. In large organizations, the day-to-day management of the four environments is often not united in one role. It seems obvious to manage the environments functionally: after all, the environments differ in the nature of their activities, each environment requires different skills, and each environment experiences different developments that influence its activities. Despite these differences, there are many dependencies, connections, and relationships between the environments. These dependencies argue for the so-called chain management of the processes (from data capture, via data processing, to reporting and analysis) running through the four environments. In Figure 4, we show these relationships.

Figure 3. Core and value-adding activities of the finance function.

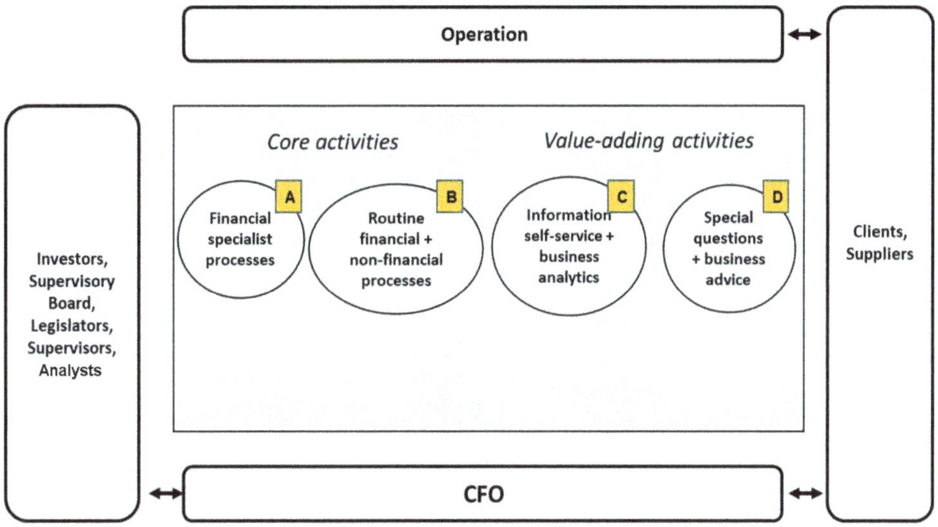

Figure 4. The set-up of the HPFF based on the four environments

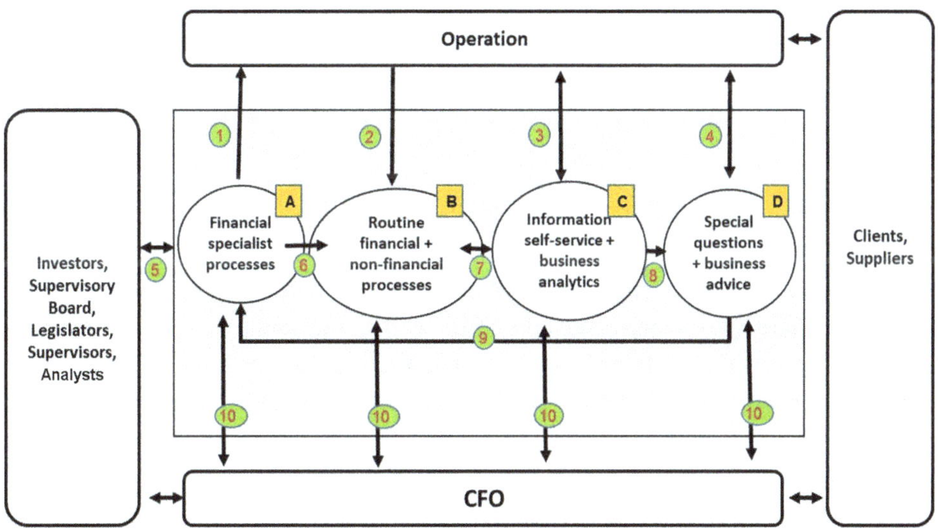

The relationships between the environments differs: sometimes generating insights involves one-way communication of guidelines, and at other times a two-way dialogue between two environments. Environments B, C, and D in any case form an information chain: from data capture in environment B via data processing and reporting in environment C, to interpreting and giving meaning in environment

D. Table 1 summarizes the most important relationships between the four environments with each other and with stakeholders. The relationship numbers in this figure can be traced back in Figure 4.

Table 1. Relationships between the four environments of the HPFF

Relationship number	Between ...	... And	Topic of the relationship
1	Environment A	Operation	Guidelines with regard to risk management and administration
2	Environment B	Operation	Invoices, invoice approval, commitments entered into, administrative questions
3	Environment C	Operation	Making standard reports available (whether via self-service or not) and making use of these reports
4	Environment D	Operation	Advice on management decisions, financial and non-financial information, (un)solicited advice, story behind the figures, business cases, (coherence of) management indicators in the business
5	Environment A	Stakeholders	Guidelines, legislation and regulations, developments in the professional field
6	Environment A	Environment B	Guidelines with regard to risk management and administration, and recorded data per discipline
7	Environment B	Environment C	Data processing, (standard) financial reporting, reporting non-financial information, data quality
8	Environment C	Environment D	Predictive analyses, analyses aimed at new insights, cost allocations, insights via business analytics, visualization of data, translating new information demands from the business into data management, data quality
9	Environment D	Environment A, B, C	Feedback on questions from the operation, control role of the provision of information to the business for reporting, budgeting, forecasting, and scenario planning
10	CFO	Environment A, B, C, D	Leading, inspiring and motivating, advising, giving direction, coaching, exemplary behavior

6.2 ROLES OF THE FINANCIAL PROFESSIONALS IN THE HPFF

The financial literature has, for decades, been full of articles about the desired characteristics of CFOs, controllers, and financial professionals, and it therefore seems unnecessary to pay attention to this subject in the present book. However, if anything has thus far become clear in this book, it is that the requirements of the finance function, and thus by definition also those of financial professionals, have changed and increased significantly in recent years. That is why it is still interesting to look whether these requirements have already been worked through in the recent literature on the desired skills and knowledge that is required of the modern financial. This is all the more necessary because the HPFF described in this book makes demands not only of the knowledge and skills, but also of the attitude and behavior of financial professionals. Recent research shows that finance functions that report to be substantially above average in effectiveness spend a lower percentage of their time on statutory and external financial reporting and a higher percentage on strategy development and improving finance operations. These last include the high-value activities for which employers pay a premium and require accounting and finance professionals to possess a skill set that is harder to automate (Lawson et al., 2019). The general expectation of finance functions is that recruiting and development strategies are going to change: 42% of respondents in a recent survey expect their finance function to transition their financial professionals into a broader business analytics role, and 39% expect to provide significantly more technology training for staff. Only 23% expect to hire more employees with additional technical skill sets, suggesting finance functions will go for a combination of upskilling of current staff and acquiring skills from the outside (Kaplan, 2021).

In this section, we list the job requirements for financial professionals as they can be found in the recent literature. In the subsequent sections, we discuss the profiles desired by the different environments of the HPFF, and what these profiles can mean for the human resources policy of the finance function. In the last section of this chapter, we deal with the question of whether financial professionals should not only show leadership in their own field of the finance function but also whether they can or even should be the initiator of HPO in the organization. A study of mainly the professional literature shows that there are different types of research that examine profiles of and in the finance function. We cluster these studies into research into a. roles in the finance function; b. roles of the CFO; and c. the skills and profiles of the financial. The studies are summarized underneath and summarized in Appendix D.

A. Studies on the Roles in the Finance Function

We start with an older literature source that is still relevant. Wunsche (2007) states that the finance function has four "faces," which means that the traditional financial accounting role can be linked to the new role of the finance function as a driver for a high-performance culture. Wunsche (2007) names these faces and describes them as follows, in the form of the two main challenges that each "face" must face (so to speak):

- *The steward.* This face encounters a challenge with regard to internal controls, risks, and liability, and will ask itself: "How can I reduce the risks and the burden of enforcing controls for the organization, without compromising integrity?" The second challenge has to do with the quality of the information: "How do I ensure that the data the organization relies on is accurate and provides the best and most insightful reporting and information?"
- *The operator.* This face has a challenging task when it comes to cost reduction: "How can I reduce costs while adding value at the same time?" The second challenge has to do with the business model: "How can I organize the finance function in such a way that it can optimally meet the needs of different stakeholders?"
- *The strategist.* Talent management is the challenge encountered by this face of the finance function. The central issue is: "Given the great diversity of roles in the finance function, how can I attract, develop, and retain the right talent?" The second challenge relates to linking business activities to shareholder value: "How can I develop a common language between management and investors so that they can communicate at the same level?"
- *The catalyst.* This face has an investment management challenge: "How can I ensure that our investments in innovation and growth deliver the greatest possible return?" Implementing the strategy is the second challenge: "How can I partner with senior managers to jointly promote strategy delivery throughout the organization?"

A well-known classification of the roles present in the finance function is that of Ernst & Young (2008): the "scorekeeper" with a focus on administration and accounting; the "commentator" with a focus on reporting and explaining the figures; the "business partner" with a focus on value creation; and the "custodian" with a focus on governance (Figure 5). The scorekeeper and custodian roles must be in order before the other two roles can be taken up: first, controls and compliance have to be in order before the finance function can work out how to add value to the business. The four roles are often linked to the changing role of the CFO. According to Ernst & Young (2008), there is movement from scorekeeper to business partner (from bottom left to top right in Figure 5); the development of the CFO thus symbolizes the development of the finance function.

Figure 5. The four roles of the finance function according to Ernst & Young

Business skills

Reactive | ***Proactive***

Commentator	**Business partner**
• Focuses on explaining the figures • Tells the business story with figure • Analyzes variances in the results • Makes management reports	• Focuses on value creation • Acts as advisor to and integrator of the business • Provides insight and challenges for better decision making
Scorekeeper	**Custodian**
• Focuses on administration • Processes transactions accurately • Matches financial data • Makes Profit & Loss statements and balance sheets	• Focuses on governance • Works with the business to safeguard compliance and effective controls • Acts as keeper of property and protector of financial value • Is the conscience of the organization

Accounting skills

Fourné et al. (2018) distinguish, based on their multiyear panel data analysis, three different roles that financial professionals can exercise:

- *The business partner.* The financial professional in this role is expected to enhance managerial decision-making. The business partner works on scenario analyses to support strategic planning purposes, discusses future business perspectives with management, conducts sensitivity analyses on key drivers of business performance, pro-actively explains to management how changes in non-financial performance measures affect profitability, discusses strategic issues with senior management, and joins steering committees to present the financial implications of strategic options.

- *The watchdog*, sometimes labeled the corporate policeman. The financial professional in this role is primarily responsible for monitoring managers and ensuring that they adhere to set performance standards and internal regulations. The watchdog identifies the organizational units in which performance targets were not achieved, analyzes variances between actual and planned performance of organizational units for control purposes, informs accountable managers and their superiors about variances from budgeted targets, highlights negative budget variances within official reports to ensure that higher-level managers notice them, and revises budget targets to ensure they serve as an up-to-date basis for control purposes.
- *The scorekeeper*. The financial professional in this role takes care of routine reporting duties and the administration of an organization's internal financial systems. The scorekeeper instructs others how to enter data correctly within the internal financial systems, checks whether interfaces between data systems work correctly, cooperates with colleagues from the financial accounting department to clarify data entry errors in financial systems, updates cost center plans within the financial systems of the organization, corrects data entry errors within the financial systems of the organization, and collects data on operational processes that will be included within periodic reports.

Fourné et al. (2018)'s comparison of roles over time suggests that these are only changing slowly, and that dramatic changes in the composition of the financial professionals' role sets are thus unlikely to be expected. Accordingly, they predict that the business partner role will most likely have its place in the future and that the watchdog role will also survive mainly because of regulatory requirements. However, the future for the scorekeeper is uncertain, mainly because of the digital revolution. Standardized reporting is already declining because managers increasingly rely on self-service tools that enable ad-hoc reporting and provide individualized options for managers to decide upon and access a desired level of detail and content. Scorekeepers can in this respect still be useful when they focus on making sure that accounting data are reliable and available across departments, which enables further streamlined decision-making processes.

Eklund et al. (2018) state that organizations increasingly develop into network-based organizations and that this requires finance functions to have four distinctive groups of financial professionals:

- *The core*. A small team of financial professionals that is responsible for most of the accounting and bookkeeping activities, and transactional processes such as invoice-to-pay and revenue management, that have not been (already) automated.
- *The problem-solvers*. A larger group comprised of financial professionals who can be assigned on short notice across the organization to projects addressing specific financial challenges. Moving in and out of project teams gives these financial professionals a broad appreciation of the business, with opportunities to develop a wide range of finance and business-advisory skills.
- *The specialists*. A group of financial professionals with deep technical and analytical skills, organized into centers of excellence (COEs). Each COE focuses on a particular aspect of financial performance (such as customer and revenue analytics, liquidity, tax planning, and working-capital management).
- *The value leaders*. A small group of financial professionals consisting of highly skilled finance value leaders, who have free range to tackle the most pressing business opportunities and challenges across the organization. These leaders have capabilities in problem solving, collaboration,

financial and business acumen, and technical and data analytics. They serve as integrators across the organization, collecting and analyzing insights from the core team, the problem-solvers, and the specialists, and then developing action plans for improving the organization's financial health.

Verbeeten & Heinen (2019) distinguish several future roles in the finance function:

- *Financial professionals as decision shapers.* To be able to facilitate the digital finance transformation, this type of financial needs to be able to translate the purpose, mission, and strategy of the organization into facts; strong storytelling skills to translate the purpose of the organization into performance measures and decision rules for measuring long-term success; and business acumen and HR skills to bring the vision forward and establish a data-driven decision culture.
- *Financial professionals as agile change enablers.* This type of financial supports the agile organization by finding ways to shorten planning cycles; constantly scanning the business environment; increasing execution speed by breaking through the traditional silos; using lean to increase the efficiency of processes; using technology such as process mining and RPA to optimize these processes even further; and using a cross-functional end-to-end approach to detect and tackle inefficiencies in the organization's core processes and to increase the overall execution speed of the organization.
- *Financial professionals as information architects.* This type of financial safeguards the quality of data in the organization by making sure that the information flows in the organization are under control; striving for clear data definitions and single versions of the truth, although the reality is that the data landscape is often scattered—especially outside the Finance domain; and, in general, improving data quality organization-wide in order to leverage data analytics opportunities.[1]

According to KPMG (2019) changing circumstances and priorities lead to changes in the roles in the finance function to ensure readiness to support necessary new capabilities and skill requirements:

- Financial data modelers/scientists will implement complex financial models and advise on the consequences of different scenarios for the organization's finances and business activities.
- Business solutions architects, with experience in managing a digital workforce and general knowledge of the systems landscape, will identify the required changes in the financial and administrative process and implement new and relevant technologies.
- Innovation and investment strategists will identify changes in customer and competitor behavior and its implications for the business through an outside-in approach that develops insights based on trend signals.
- Business planning analysts will guide interactions between different business groups and communicate information effectively. They are likely to have extensive business knowledge as well as in-depth finance and administrative processing knowledge.
- Business partners will use their understanding of external markets to investigate and leverage threats and opportunities for the purpose of supporting the strategic direction of the organization.

Tjandra et al. (2021), based on a survey into the maturity of the digital function in finance, listed five existing roles and five new roles in the finance function:

Existing roles

- Business planning analyst: interacts across business groups and communicates information effectively; has extensive business knowledge and deep technical financial expertise.
- Strategic business partner: has strong understanding of external markets, to provide strategic direction; is a co-pilot to the business and is able to navigate ambiguity and influence potential shifts in business models.
- Commercial finance: is the finance liaison for sales, marketing and commercial departments, utilizes internal and external expertise to drive business decisions through customer financial planning, scenario modelling, and customer and product profitability analytics.
- Financial & regulatory accountant: is focused on delivering core reporting and analytics to the business; has a deep finance and accounting background.
- Global process architect: defines the mission, strategy and vision of business processes across geographies, business units and functional areas; provides global oversight and is responsible for driving continuous improvement initiatives across the organization.

New roles

- Transformation architect: leads special projects driving change across the organization; architects project strategy and vision through execution, deployment and value realization; quantifies value drivers and articulations results to stakeholders.
- Innovation & investment strategist: takes an outside-in approach to develop insights from trend signals and identifies changes in customer and competitor behaviors and possible business implications.
- Business solutions architect: has experience with managing a digital workforce and knowledge of the systems landscape; is able to translate process changes and implement required solutions.
- Intelligent automater: is able to automate different finance processes and to leverage various levels of smart automation.
- Financial data modeler/architect: executes complex models and advises on financial and business impacts of different scenarios.

CFOs have an increasingly difficult task this decade: to accelerate growth and digital initiatives, preserve/restore the organization's financial health, and improve the effectiveness of the finance function. These priorities for CFOs are derived from the value proposition that the finance function in general offers the organization—bringing back the right costs to support growth—therefore, it must improve its structure, talent, and capabilities. What makes it all the more difficult for them is that the CFOs expect most digitalization efforts to take up more time than they have in the past, with it being increasing challenging to accomplish successful transformation results (Gartner, 2021a).

B. Studies on the Roles of the CFO

Hope (2006) distinguishes seven roles for the CFO: "freedom fighter," "analyst and adviser," "architect of adaptive management," "warrior against waste," "master of measurement," "regulator of risk," and "champion of change." As a freedom fighter, the CFO has to fight against details and complex systems that deprive the finance function of time for reflection and analysis. As an analyst and advisor, the CFO must do everything possible to retain the best professionals and put together the right team so that the finance function has such a high analytical level that it leads to ideas for improvement. As an architect of adaptive management, the main task is to return decision-making to line managers. As a fighter against waste, the CFO must primarily propagate the "lean philosophy": eliminate, as much as possible, activities that add little or no value. As the master of measurement, the CFO must provide a framework of coherent KPIs that contribute to the organizational goals. As a "risk adjuster," the CFO must ensure an effective framework of proper corporate governance and risk management. As "champion of change," the CFO is the person to transform the finance function, who starts with a vision and the goals set by the management team, who ensures buy-in of employees, and who, above all, implements changes pragmatically.

KPMG (2014) surveyed senior executives in Asia about their views on the CFO and the finance function in their organization and what they expect from both in the future. The sobering outcome was that 32% of those surveyed said their CFO did not understand them enough and thus did not provide adequate support in the challenges that these executives faced while managing the organization. Furthermore, 72% of those surveyed believed that the role of the CFO and the finance function would become much more important in the coming years—even more so than that of other staff departments. The areas in which the finance function could have the greatest added value were identified as performance and result growth (M&A, business partnering, strategy support), governance (regulations, Board requirements, risk management, compliance), efficiency/cost control (cost optimization, working capital, sourcing), control (IT, internal audit), and innovation (new products and services, new business models, new markets). The main attributes that the senior executives were looking for in their CFO was having a big-picture vision and ability to undertake strategic thinking, and the technological skills to deal with increasingly important technology and ICT. The executives urged their CFOs to become more involved in talent management to safeguard future talent for the finance function. Another important question was which shortcomings, according to the respondents, did CFOs have to overcome to be eligible for a CEO position; the responses were as follows: weak interpersonal skills (40%), weak leadership skills (35%), lack of commercial experience (32%), being too focused because of having a narrow view (30%), not having a big-picture vision (24%), or focusing too much on value and efficiency and not enough on growth (19%).

> Managing and measuring organizational performance and added value will be a top priority for the CFOs of the future. They will be expected to support their organization with one common goal: to understand inputs, perspectives, and challenges in order to make the right strategic decisions for both investment and growth. For this, CFOs will have to recognize and exploit their unique position within the organization. They are at the hub of organizational performance, connecting finance, operations, and strategy (KPMG, 2019).

According to Accenture (2014) the modern CFO wears three hats:

1. The accountant hat, with a main focus on the past: characteristics are accounts-centric, descriptive, backward-looking, with a focus on financial data, having mainly accounting skills, functionally siloed.

2. The business partner hat, with a main focus on the present: characteristics are business-centric, predictive, forward-looking, with a focus on financial and operational data, having mainly analytical skills, business aligned.
3. The strategic enabler hat, with a main focus on the future: characteristics are finance productivity-centric, retool and retain talent, focus on becoming a data-driven organization and applying digital technology, adopting an agile operating model.

Accenture (2014) also states that the CFO of today and of the high-performing digital business of the future should:

- focus on securing critical business outcomes and economics by enabling strategy
- partner with the CEO to deliver those outcomes
- embrace new technologies and evaluate enterprise-wide investment to support the velocity required for tomorrow's business
- own the data agenda and wield the power of data, for instance by controlling the one version of the truth
- build new talent with the agility, skills, and experience needed in the HPFF.

In an update of the aforementioned Accenture study, Campagne et al. (2021) defined CFOs as the "architects of business value" by putting focus on the following activities:

- Collaborating frequently with colleagues in the "C-suite", by putting in place management rhythms that create cross-functional dialogue on strategic priorities, investments, initiatives and decision-making.
- Being the "keeper of one truth" for the organization, by using cross-organizational insights to bridge gaps with senior stakeholders and inform strategic decision-making.
- Providing insightful and sophisticated perspectives and knowledge, by understanding the most critical issues for each senior business partner, tailoring insights in order to build relevance and influence decisions, and using AI and machine learning to unlock deeper insights.
- Taking ownership for harmonizing technology and data platforms, working closely with the CIO/CTO to improve end-to-end capabilities, drive cross-pollination of ideas and deliver outcomes for all stakeholders.
- Engaging in managing risk through data security to a meaningful degree.
- Bringing the full power of the finance capability to strategic initiatives inside the organization, by promoting finance as an end-to-end advisor on strategic and digital initiatives across the enterprise.
- Taking responsibility to create societal value through environmental, social and corporate governance (ESG) performance of the organization, by addressing pressing societal and environmental challenges and disclosing and optimizing stakeholder outcomes in these areas.

The Dutch Professional Profile Committee of the Association of Registered Controllers (2021) suggested a new profile, with accompanying skills, for CFOs as the finance function is changing in several ways that the CFO has to be able to deal with:

- providing increasingly frequent and close support to the other departments;
- supporting the organization in continually developing and adapting structure and business models;
- shifting from post-hoc accountability to prudent forecasting of financial and non-financial results
- helping the organization to respond more quickly to new developments by providing excellent data analysis;
- becoming more externally oriented and maintaining close ties with external stakeholders.

The Committee propose five roles for the CFO of the future:

- *Paragon of integrity*: The CFO is a role model of integrity and ensures that the design and operation of the organization promotes integrity. To this end, the CFO has the ability to work in accordance with rules, act ethically, deals well with tensions, and displays a healthy self-knowledge; and is good at acting with integrity and setting an example, cultivating trust in others, being transparent and aware of social issues, and reflect on own and others' behaviors.
- *Leader/connector*: The CFO provides leadership to the finance function, and also to the wider organization. To this end, the CFO has the ability to provide leadership, cooperate and consult well, establish contacts, maintain networks, negotiate, and present arguments; and is good at communicating, delegating, listening, guiding others, giving trust, storytelling, bringing people together, being diplomatic and giving presentations.
- *CEO's co-pilot*: The CFO is a co-pilot to the CEO and shares responsibility for defining and adapting the organization's strategy. To this end, the CFO has the ability to think ahead, discover and explore, renew, being entrepreneurial and being customer focused; and is good at translating abstract conceptual thinking into concrete solutions, offering ideas, daring to go against the crowd, expressing opinions, and exploiting business opportunities.
- *Change architect*: The CFO contributes to adapting the organization's structures, business models, processes, and projects to ensure that the organization functions efficiently and effectively. To this end, the CFO has the ability to plan and organize, convince and influence others, manage change, and think logically; and is good at structuring, being flexible and determined, resolving conflicts, motivating and supporting others, advising, and showing determination.
- *Enabler*: The CFO enables effective decision-making by highlighting issues, putting these on the agenda, and sharing responsibility for resolving them within the finance function and the organization as a whole. To this end, the CFO has the ability to analyze, take decisions, dealing with adversity, being result-focused and monitoring quality; and is good at getting results, setting priorities, assessing risks and opportunities, delivering results, solving problems, promoting quality thinking, and monitoring productivity.

Personal Effective CFOs
Gartner for Finance (2021) defines highly personal effective CFOs as CFOs that are able to simultaneously encourage organizational behaviors that sustain top- and bottom-line growth while outperforming expectations for short-term financial outcomes. A CFO can achieve this level of effectiveness by demonstrating the following controllable behaviors: • Closing the distance between CFOs and customers by spending more time with them and personally prioritizing pricing strategies and working capital. • Going beyond relationship-building to create constructive tension with the CEO and board, by challenging them on their assumptions about major decisions. • Plugging into the business performance by personally prioritizing business performance management and securing strong relationships with managers and their business units. • Allocating their personal time with the same rigor they ask their organization to allocate capital (i.e. explicitly announcing and discussing own personal focus areas, "zero-basing" their calendar to remove low-return uses of time, dedicating time for focused sprints to increase the speed of their own impact, and using post-audits to create a learning loop on their own time spend.

Webb and Lawson (2021) see six major shifts in the areas of attention for the CFO of the future:

1. Stakeholder focus: the CFO will change the current focus on safeguarding and reporting to focusing on stakeholder and investor management;
2. Strategy formulation: the CFO will have a leading responsibility for business strategy formulation, validation, execution and achievement;
3. Growth optimization: the CFO will change the current focus on cost control to growth and revenue optimization;
4. Wide view of performance: the CFO will focus on measuring all aspects of the strategic objectives of the organization;
5. Forward insights: the CFO will change the current focus on retrospective reporting to forward insight and becoming a chief performance officer;
6. Career progression: the CFO will increasingly have the CEO role as the next career progression.

These shifts have implications for the skills needed by the CFO of the future (Webb and Lawson, 2021):

- *Financial acumen (technical and ethical skills).* It is not so much the intention that the CFO does the 'number crunching' but s/he needs to have the expertise to understand the issues that lie behind the numbers and the disclosures. In addition, the CFO needs to have the ethical skills that ensure that "the one version of the truth" is conveyed to the organization's stakeholders and that the right context for the subsequent discussion about that information is provided.
- *Strategy acumen (business skills).* The CFO needs to have a strong ability in business strategy and knowledge and have a good practical understanding of the business. This makes it possible for the CFO to provide a check and balance to the CEO. A good and healthy relationship between the CFO and the CEO forms the key to the success of the organization.
- *Risk management and governance skills.* The risk management aspects of the CFO role will increase in importance as businesses seek to recover and achieve stability from the turbulent last few years. The CFO thus needs to be better and more rigorous in planning and risk assessments.

- *Data and technology skills.* The changes in data availability and technology have a strong influence on the finance function. The CFO therefore needs to have (or develop) a working knowledge of the technological possibilities for the finance function and the organization as a whole.
- *Leadership and communication skills.* The CFO has a leadership role not only in the finance function but also in the organization at large. To fulfill this role adequately the CFO needs to have the following leadership attributes: through coaching and mentoring provide effective leadership to the team; the ability to develop meaningful narratives and use these to lead to desired outcomes; challenging accepted views and developing alternative viable solutions to problems and issues; having a global view and being able to apply this view locally; being able to innovate and to think ahead in relation to viable opportunities; resilience in achieving tasks and driving to conclusions and results no matter the obstacles; recognizing a range of ideas from a variety of perspectives and encompassing these in the decision-making process; embracing the evolving nature of the workforce; embracing the evolving nature of the customer base and placing the (internal and external) customer at the center of attention.
- *Supply chain skills.* The CFO has to be able to align the supply chain to the organization's purpose and cost model, make it more resilience and making sure it satisfies ethical sourcing considerations.
- *Investor management skills.* Investor management and the broader stakeholder agenda are increasingly important aspects of the CFO's role. Thus the CFO needs to be able to tell the organization's story well and address sustainability concerns of people/planet/profit these external parties might have.
- *Consulting skills.* As the strategic advisory role is growing in importance, the CFO needs to be able to provide strategic advice to management, and act as a super-connector across the organization. And as the CFO becomes increasingly involved in the overall execution of the organization's strategy, s/he needs to be able to consult the business on organizational integration or divestment issues.

Tjandra et al. (2021) listed, based on a survey into the maturity of the digital aspects in finance, several main activities for the CFO in the digital finance function:

- being a co-pilot with the other management team members in leading the transformation of the organization's business model and cost structure
- being closely involved in the digital transformation of the organization, entailing amongst other replacing legacy systems and upskilling staff
- being a Chief Data Steward who develops strategic and commercial analyses based on rigorous data management, data governance and data insights.

> At a shipping company, finance leaders attend a business finance college that offers dedicated leader training such as cross-functional collaboration, problem-solving, leadership skills, and change management skills. The training culminates with team-building sessions and a real-world case to work through using a problem-solving framework. A manufacturer multinational provides its finance leaders with rotations throughout the company every three to five years to provide a better understanding of business needs (APQC, 2018).

C. Studies on the Skills and Profiles of Financial Professionals

Ten Rouwelaar (2018) conducted research into what is referred to in the literature as "Controller Involvement in Management" and, in particular, studied the degree of involvement of financial professionals in decision-making. Financial professionals have a dual role: on the one hand a "management service" role, also known as the business partner role or "business advocate"; and, on the other hand, an "oversight role," also known as the control role or "corporate policeman." The business partner role is aimed at helping managers with their decision-making and in performing their management functions. The control role means ensuring that the actions of all employees in the organization are legal, ethical, and in the best interests of the organization. The business partner role is becoming increasingly important in the development of the finance profession. As financial expert, the business controller should be able to make a critical contribution to operational decision-making. The degree of involvement in strategic decisions (strategy, investments, and marketing) seems less dependent on the manager of the business unit, but more on the personal characteristics of the business controller (high degree of extraversion, high emotional stability).

The Royal Dutch Association of Accountants (NBA, 2019) defined in their vision of the profession of the financial professional five main roles and accompanying competencies that the financial can have in the future finance function:

- *The navigator*. In the navigator role, the financial is the helmsman who directs the organization in the right direction. He/she does this based on broad knowledge of finance, control and scenarios, and is a driver in the field of ICT. Constant alignment of a long-term vision and short-term action is crucial in this role. The required competencies are initiative (identifying opportunities and acting on them); entrepreneurship (identifying and, business-wise, weighing up opportunities in the market both for existing and new products, taking risks in order to achieve a business advantage); and vision (distancing oneself from daily practice, concentrating on main points and long-term policy).
- *The sensor*. The sensor role involves picking up important signals within and outside the organization, on whose basis of which the organization may need to take action. This role is highly interactive. Required competencies are creativity (coming up with original solutions to problems, thinking up new methods to replace existing ones); awareness of the environment (being well informed about social, political, and economic developments and using this knowledge effectively for the organization); and networking (building relationships and networks that are useful in achieving goals, using informal networks effectively to get things done).
- *The coach*. In the role of coach, the financial makes sure that the finance function runs smoothly by creating the right conditions, motivations, and enthusiasm for others to do their jobs well and maintaining good relationships with other functions. Required competencies are: coaching (giving direction to employees in the context of their tasks and required performances; using a style adapted to particular employees and their situation so that they can develop optimally); group-oriented management (giving direction to a group of employees in the context of their group task performance; establishing and maintaining partnership in order to achieve the stated goals); and organizational sensitivity (recognizing the influence and consequences of one's own decisions or activities on others, recognizing the interests of other parts of the organization).

- *The analyst.* The analyst is mainly a researcher, clarifier, and reporter. This role includes performing data analysis of internal and external information to provide a clear picture of how the organization is doing in relation to the set goals. Required competencies are problem analysis (identifying problems, recognizing important information, making connections between data, detecting possible causes of problems, searching for relevant data); judging (drawing correct and realistic conclusions based on available information); customer focus (researching the wishes and needs of the customer and acting accordingly, anticipating needs of customers, giving high priority to service and customer satisfaction).
- *The gatekeeper.* The gatekeeper ensures that the organization has a sound foundation, monitors the control environment, and is an important part of the organization's moral compass. The gatekeeper develops an ethical standards framework and ensures that the outside world is not harmed by the activities of the organization. Required competencies are integrity management (maintaining generally accepted social and ethical standards); independence (taking actions that are based more on one's beliefs than on the desire to please others, setting one's own course); and tenacity (sticking to a particular action plan or view until the intended goal is achieved or cannot be reasonably reached).

Caswell-LaPierre et al. (2020) describe six capabilities a finance function needs to have to be able to successfully go through the digital transformation that essentially every finance function needs to go through now and in the coming years:

- Digital engagement - The ability to design and optimize stakeholder experiences through digitization and integration of interactions across channels and leveraging data.
- Digitally enable workforce and organization - Maximizing productivity, intellectual property creation, and value contribution of individual workers and the (virtual) teams they operate in through the use of digital tools and platforms.
- Digital service optimization - Maximizing efficiency and effectiveness of the delivery of business services and execution of underlying processes through the use of digital tools and platforms.
- Digital ecosystem - The ability to create value through interactions in a highly scalable, digitally interconnected network of businesses, customers, service providers, individuals, and devices.
- Analytics-driven business insight - The support of business decisions with advanced analytical capability based on real-time, high-quality data, which is managed throughout the life cycle as a strategic asset.
- Digital information technology capabilities - The digital architecture and capabilities of the internal information technology organization that are needed to support and sustain digital transformation of the organization, including cybersecurity management, agile service delivery, advanced data stewardship, and provision and technology innovation.

Successful organizations are those that have invested in the finance skills that support digital business models; yet only 10% of CFOs believe that their finance teams have the skills needed to support their organizations' digital ambitions (McCaffry, 2020).

The Association of International Certified Professional Accountants (2020) developed a competency framework to help management accountants and their employers understand the knowledge requirements and assess the skills needed for both current and desired roles of trusted finance and business strategist:

- Technical skills - responsibility for monitoring the implementation of strategy
- Business skills - understanding of the organization's environment, current strategic position and direction, with strong analytical skills and the ability to advise on strategic options for the business
- People skills - using proper influencing skills to obtain positive outcomes and make decisions that align with the organization's strategic direction
- Leadership skills - expert knowledge to develop strategic vision and provide unique insights to guide the overall direction and success of the organization
- Digital skills - formal responsibility for business areas, actions, and decisions with a high-level strategic impact.

Gartner (2021b) distinguishes five digital competencies that the finance function should have: technological literacy, digital translation, digital learning and development, digital bias management, and digital ambition. Finance leaders seeking to prepare finance talent for digital opportunities should therefore:

- overlay digital competencies onto the finance function's current competency model to identify shared objectives between existing and new digital competencies and roll out competency upgrades faster;
- set achievable digital competency goals by using employee feedback to check that the new digital competencies are achievable in the near future and relevant to the finance function's current needs;
- teach financial professionals the observable behaviors associated with digital competencies to help them understand the relevance of these competencies for both finance and business processes.

> In the digital age, technology is crucial to success and is often seen as a driver of change. While advances like artificial intelligence promise to change the way we work, it is easy to forget that new technologies are driven by human responses to a changing environment. New software solutions promise better data management, faster analysis, and real-time reporting. However, underinvestment in people and resources, lack of training, insufficient and inconsistent communications, no clear change management framework, and/or the absence of a talent pipeline can all spell disaster for an organization (McCaffry, 2020).

6.3 PROFILE OF THE HIGH-PERFORMANCE FINANCIAL

In this section, we outline the profile of a professional in the HPFF. In a curriculum vitae, the profile is a piece of text in which a professional makes the connection between his/her personal and training information and his/her work experience. Just like in a curriculum vitae, we will use the profile of the financial to make the connection between their knowledge and skills on the one hand and personal characteristics and motivations on the other.

> Surveyed potential future CFOs state that when they become CFOs they will spend most time on value creation across the wider business ecosystem (92%); will champion, together with the finance function, a new way of operating across the business (78%); furthermore, they believe the finance function should be proactive and connected in its operations alongside business partners across the wider business ecosystem (77%); and that the finance function should empower other functions to take on all finance activities (66%) (Accenture, 2018).

What is noticeable in the literature is that in profile sketches of the financial, the business partner (often equated with the business controller) is usually the center of attention. However, this does not do justice to professionals from the other finance function environments; moreover, we have already concluded that "the one financial" does not exist. After all, the HPFF consists of four environments, each with its own characteristic activities. In each of those environments, different themes and IT developments are topical:

- The environment based on administration and processing of data (transaction-based). In this environment, the theme of efficiency is central, in terms of achieving as many error-free actions as possible through first-time-right, smartly designed processes. Automation, robotization, and digitization are developments that play a role in this environment.
- The environment based on fixed methods and rules and the production of information (rule-based). Themes in this environment are smart deployment and functional use of IT tools, efficient data flows and architecture, and effective reporting processes aimed at generating (new) business insights. Big data, business analytics, self-service, and business intelligence are developments that play a role in this environment.
- The environment based on judgment and working with information (judgment-based). Themes in this environment are advisory skills, business insight, combining the roles of "corporate policeman" and "business advocate," and delivering added value. IT developments in this environment are limited. It does help if the professionals in this environment understand IT developments and the consequences thereof for the internal customer.
- The environment based on judgment and compliance with laws and regulations (a combination of rule and judgment-based). Themes in this environment focus on advisory skills, business insight, vocational expertise, and the delivery of added value. The IT developments in this environment are limited.

We now provide an outline of what can be expected of a financial professional in each environment in the finance function. Aside from an employment contract there is also a psychological contract, i.e., the unwritten expectations for mutual relationships that apply at all times between employees, managers, and colleagues. These expectations are an important determining factor for behavior in organizations. The organization expects, among other things, honest professionals who will first share their criticism with the organization (rather than going directly to the public), act in the interests of organizational goals, and are willing to work overtime if necessary. Employees, in turn, expect to have a good workplace and to be consulted in the event of organizational changes. Expectations of professionals are in regard to their personal characteristics, motivations, skills, and knowledge. Many (HR departments of) organizations work with competencies and a framework of competency profiles. Competency is the ability to perform effectively in a given situation. Competencies are generally made up of four types of building blocks: personal characteristics ("who am I"), motivation or drives ("what do I want"), skills ("what can I do"), and knowledge ("what do I know"). Competency management is often used as a foundation for a coherent design and application of HR instruments. A detailed elaboration of tasks, skills, and competencies in the finance function or the ability to develop competencies will differ by organization and finance function; we leave that to the HR experts—our aim is to use the profiles to provide an indication of the expectations of the financial in a specific HPFF environment.

General Personal Characteristics ("Who Am I") and Motivations ("What Do I want")

Although we distinguish four environments in the HPFF, which each environment having its own profile, there are personal characteristics and motivations that every professional in the finance function should possess:

- Integrity: have an ethical and positive critical attitude.[2] This means complying with the values and standards of the vocation and the codes of the organization, and acting accordingly. Organizational interests come first. Encouraging ethical behavior in the organization and helping colleagues deal with (financial) dilemmas is crucial.
- Having a feel for numbers and financial processes: being able to deal well and accurately with numbers and having basic knowledge of financial processes. Financial professionals must have a certain foundation when it comes to working with figures; therefore, at least a minimum of knowledge about finance and accounting processes is a prerequisite. Controllers who are relatively distant from operational financial processes are expected to know how an administration works, how entries are processed in the general ledger, and how reports are generated. A feel for numbers also means working to a certain degree of accuracy, because if numbers do not add up in a presentation, it will not benefit the credibility of the finance function.
- Clear communication: being proactive and transparent about one's own actions and being accessible when dealing with fellow professionals. Extensive collaboration takes place in every environment and between the environments; therefore, keeping each other informed proactively is important to maintain speed in processes and projects. Clear communication means accessible communication: giving information from the perspective of the environment where the other financial works, giving and receiving feedback, responding to the experience of others, using accessible language, and giving examples.
- Passion and drive: being driven, having a passion for the profession, and being curious about the possibilities for improvements in the financial field. This also includes seeking improvements together with fellow professionals and being open to carrying out the work as optimally as possible together with colleagues. Learning ability, self-reflection, drive to grow personally, social involvement, and willingness to share knowledge are qualities that every financial must possess.

Specific Skills ("What Can I Do") and Knowledge ("What Do I Know")

We can focus on the profiles of financial professionals in terms of the environments they work in when we take the previously mentioned themes and developments in those environments as a starting point. Each environment then has its own profile with its own areas of knowledge and skills. In this way, we arrive at four profiles in the HPFF (see Figure 6): the "corporate specialist," focused on judgment and compliance with legislation and regulations; the "finance service provider," aimed at processing operational transactions; the "information expert," aimed at developing fixed methods and rules and producing information; and the "trusted finance lead (or business partner)," focused on judgment and working with information.

Figure 6. The four profiles in the HPFF and accompanying required skills

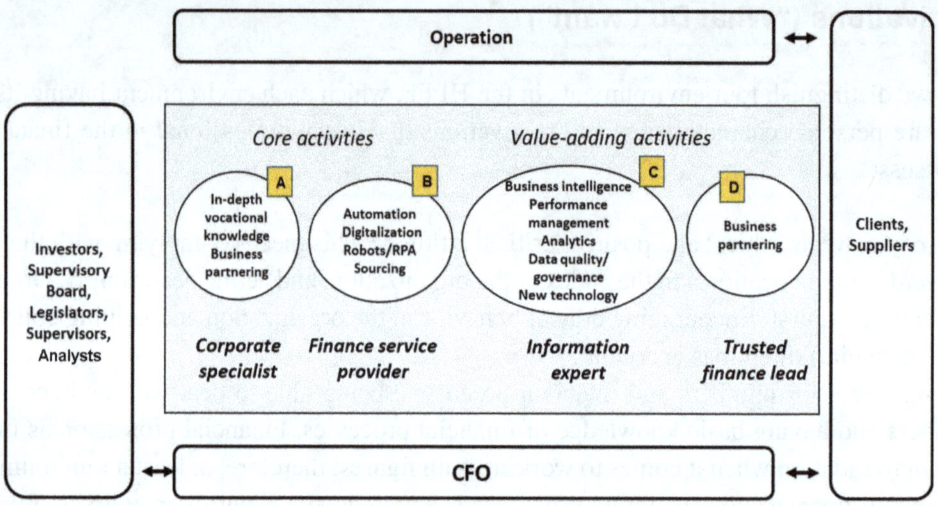

The Corporate Specialist

The corporate specialist possesses the following combination of knowledge and skills:

- Strategic insight: Thinking from an organizational perspective, understanding the business model and the strategy of the organization, being able to translate strategic organizational choices into organizational actions and consequences for one's own role and specialization.
- Thorough knowledge of the area of specialization: deep knowledge and understanding of the specialist subject, being able to communicate as an equal with external counterparts, being able to sketch future scenarios and formulate visions in the own area of specialization.
- Creativity: combining various options within the boundaries of legislation, regulations, and market situations; finding the best solution for the organization, while keeping in mind the interests of the organization and society.
- Influencing and convincing skills: persuasiveness in explaining proposed solutions to senior management.

The profile of the corporate specialist then looks like this: a professional who is a specialist in the chosen field, follows developments in this field closely, thinks in the interest of the organization, has strategic insight, advises on compliance with the law and regulations, can explain developments in the field, and is clear and convincing in presentations (Figure 7).

Figure 7. The profile of the corporate specialist

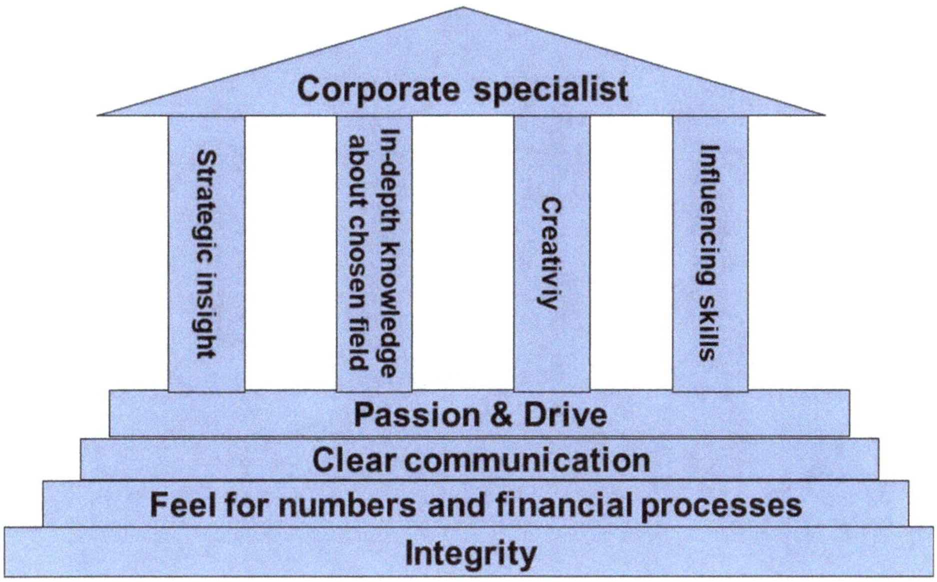

The Finance Service Provider

The finance service provider has the following combination of knowledge and skills:

- Administrative expertise: thorough knowledge of the operation of the administration, tax and ledger processes, focus on unambiguous recording of financial data.
- Operational insight: understanding of (exceptions in) accounting processes, able to address inconsistencies in order to improve controls, proficient in lean methods and continuous improvement.
- Accuracy: keen eye for detail, working accurately, skilled in dealing with systems, constantly looking for opportunities to achieve efficiency in processing, skilled in processing large quantities of transactions, "first-time-right" work attitude.
- Service orientation with a customer focus: service-oriented attitude toward both internal and external customers, sense of balance between "you ask, we do" and the importance of following own financial professionals processes and procedures, taking responsibility for properly answering questions from internal and external customers, aware of one's own contribution and role in the communication within the organization, identifying opportunities for improvement, active listening and conversation skills.

The profile of the finance service provider then looks like this: a professional with administrative knowledge, who is disciplined in processing data, works accurately, strives for 'first-time-right,' knows what recording is for and able to translate this into his or her own processes, proactively indicating opportunities for simplification and automation, a service-oriented and positive attitude, helps internal and external customers with their questions, and provides feedback (Figure 8).

Figure 8. The profile of the finance service provider

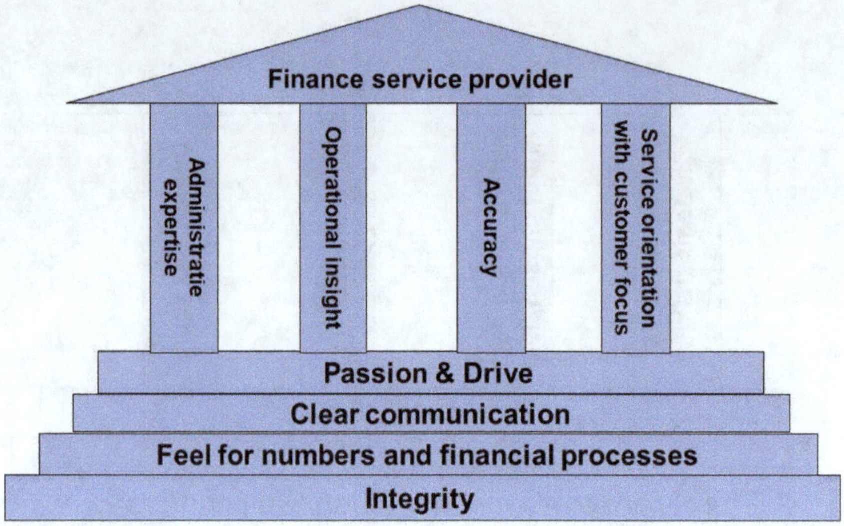

In paragraph 6.6 we discuss how digitization, digitalization and digital transformation affects Finance to a high degree. Processes of digitization (think of converting paper invoices into digital invoices) and digitalization (digital information used to simplify and make current ways of working more efficient) are often started in finance processes like accounting, accounts payable and accounts receivable. The finance service providers are therefore, generally speaking, the first in the finance function that are confronted with technology in their activities. Working with data, IT and systems is thus a crucial component in the skills of the service provider. Technological literacy and business knowledge help the finance service provider to perform the job well.

The Information Expert

The information expert has the following combination of knowledge and skills:

- Strategic insight: ability to think from an organizational perspective, demonstrate future-oriented thinking in relevant scenarios, show understanding of the business model and the strategy of the organization.
- Data analysis skills: expertise in data analysis, data structures, data quality, and data management; skill with (new) tools and business analytics; follower of technological developments in the field of business intelligence.
- Creativity: ability to tackle issues facing the organization and deal with these in a targeted manner; substantiate analyses with data from internal and external data sources; test insights from the analyses in the organization in order to adjust and refine the analyses if needed.
- Influencing skills: proficient in advising, anticipating different interests in the organization, demonstrating persuasive power in explaining the proposed solution to senior management.

The profile of the information expert then looks like this: a professional with creativity and analytical skills, who exhibits perseverance in discovering the "question behind the question," who can quickly convert the information needs of internal customers into useful insights, who works well with the IT department, seeks cooperation with the business partner and line management, can prioritize questions from operations according to importance and urgency, knows how the business works, has insight into the data architectures of the organization, knows the market for software applications in the field of performance management, is an expert in business intelligence and business analytics, knows what the ICT developments are, and can communicate well (Figure 9).

Figure 9. The profile of the information expert

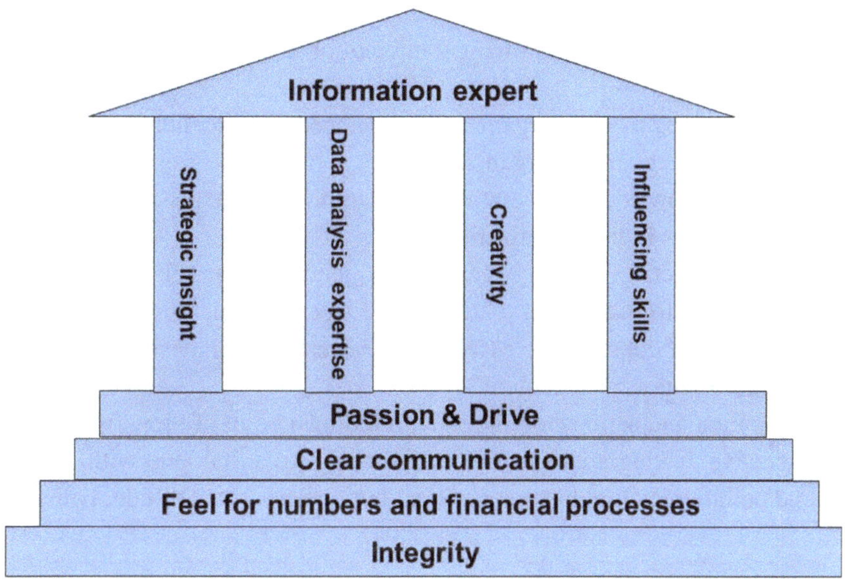

The development of digitization via digitalization to digital transformation has been going on for quite some time now and of course this transformation also effects the finance function. In publications about this transformation new proficiencies and knowledge areas are listed that are needed for finance professionals to cope with and be successful in a digital transformation of the finance function. Skills that are mentioned are:

- technological literacy: having insight and knowledge about IT-systems and applications, to be able to detect risks, identify benefits and implement IT solutions for the finance function
- data skills to collect and process data efficiently, to use data transformation and data mining tools, transform data into information, and link financial data analysis with business data
- technical skills, such as being able to do scenario planning, statistical analyses, predictive modelling, and program algorithms
- IT-systems skills, to understand and work with artificial intelligence, machine learning and programming languages (low-code/ no-code tools)

- business skills, to be able to communicate with senior management and also with operational-oriented colleagues, create a story out of data, analysis, work cross-functional, understand and contribute to strategic planning.

As a finance information expert one cannot have these skills without having knowledge of tools, the working of (finance) IT systems and applications, databases and cyber security (data controls, integrity controls, governance, risk management). Combining the aforementioned knowledge and skills with personal agility (adaptive, anticipatory, logical and critical thinking), yields the profile of a future-ready finance professional.

The Trusted Finance Lead

The trusted finance lead possesses the following combination of knowledge and skills:

- Strategic insight: thinking from an organizational perspective, excellent understanding of the business model and the strategy of the organization.
- Operational insight: knowledge of operational and administrative processes, skilled in embedding (improvement) measures in the organization.
- Influencing skills: proactively giving feedback, a good feel for relationships, skilled in advising and coaching, able to make interventions, able to communicate with operational and senior management, capable of constructive escalation if necessary, persuasive powers in explaining the proposed solution to senior management.
- Autonomous thinking and acting convincingly: building a point of view from both a financial and business perspective, having a clear opinion, entering into a dialogue with 'presence,' skilled in presenting and communicating, having a critical but constructive attitude, being right and getting it right.

The profile of the trusted finance lead then looks like this: a professional with boldness and courage, who knows what is going on in the organization, knows the background of the business and is intimately familiar with the business, has an opinion and makes it known to management, makes choices and completes projects satisfactorily, alternates a critically positive attitude (control role) with a helpful attitude (support role), and is very adept at dealing with changing circumstances and new techniques in the financial field. It is someone the business cannot and does not want to ignore, and who is therefore seen as an equal partner of management, and even as a "partner in change." After all, a good financial creates space in the agenda to work on improving the finance function and thus sets an example for the rest of the organization (Figure 10).

The trusted finance lead plays an important role in digital transformations. The trusted finance lead - also called the business partner of management - is synonym for the value-adding role that the finance function wants to fulfil in the organization. Business partnering is about servicing management and creating insights for them. Data and IT are a big part of that servicing. Not only the traditional processes as reporting, planning, budgeting, forecasting and cost accounting have a large IT component (business process automation implemented with enterprise management software); "new" processes such as predictive modeling, process mining and data analysis basically depend on the use of IT tools. Thus, the foundation of the work of a trusted finance lead can be found in data and IT.

Figure 10. The profile of the trusted finance lead

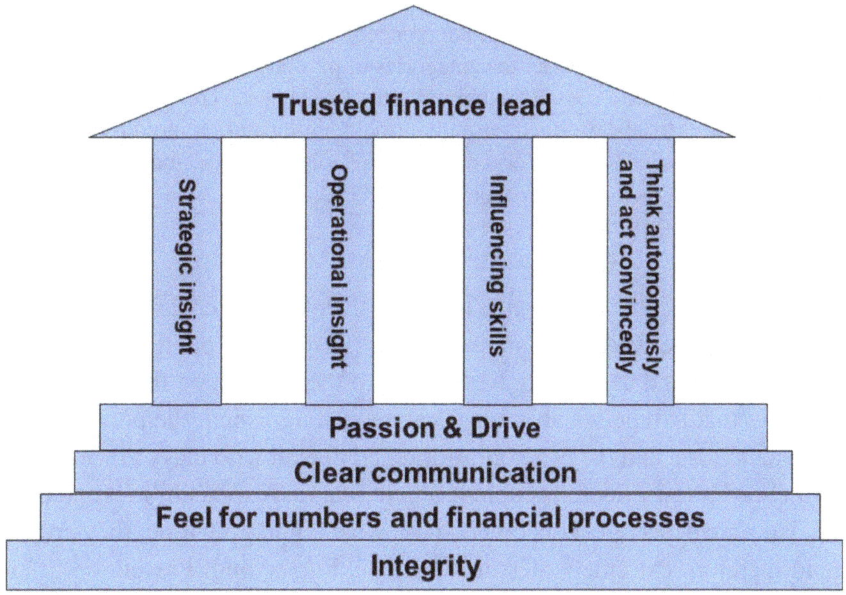

Business knowledge is the core skill of a trusted finance lead. Combined with technological literacy, data skills, IT systems skills and personal agility a trusted finance lead is of great value to an organization. A business partner needs to move away from the spreadsheet and instead needs to increasingly think in terms of data input, business rules and calculations and presentation layers. A business partner needs to strive for less manual work, and thus actively promote and help to automate manual process steps. Cooperating and knowledge sharing with the information expert is also crucial for fulfilling the business partner role successfully.

6.4 THE PROFILES AS THE BASIS FOR HUMAN RESOURCING

As the HPFF framework shows, the development of financial professionals is an important spearhead for every finance function, especially because the finance function increasingly wants to move toward the role of added-value supplier to the organization. The importance of the financial as a business partner for management is increased. As discussed earlier, ICT developments follow each other in rapid succession; these are developments that not only change the operational processes in the organization but also the administrative and reporting processes in the finance function. Specialization in the finance function will also increase. In short, the financial must prioritize and make choices that result in a finance function which, at all times, has the right people in the right functions so it can deal with all eventualities and quickly anticipate developments in the (near) future (see Chapter 11 for these developments).

Financial professionals at Maersk are encouraged to acquire operational skills for a better understanding of the business and its finance responsibilities. This is supported with a dedicated training program in which financial professionals gain a clear sense of specific stakeholders' needs and how to support the business. The program is based on a model of 12 competencies under the categories of partnering, analytical, leadership, and technical skills. All financial professionals are assessed on their maturity level in each competency, and Maersk focuses on two to three core competencies to be developed through formal training and six months of face-to-face coaching. Three days of formal training include a real-world case study to solve business and financial issues. Participants then write a paper reflecting on their learning experience (APQC, 2018).

It is necessary to appreciate that the finance function always experiences certain tensions: on the one hand, finances must be in order and laws and regulations must be complied with; on the other hand, the business must be supported and developed. Research into the motivation focus of employees and their personality type shows that two personality types can be distinguished: the prevention-oriented person who plays in order not to lose, and the promotion-oriented person who plays to win (Grant Halvorson & Higgins, 2013a+b). Prevention-oriented people see their goals as responsibilities and they aim to achieve them at all times. They are especially concerned about what could go wrong, they are accurate, careful, and deliberate and therefore extremely alert to what could go wrong. Prevention-oriented people are risk-averse—not too creative but very analytical. In fact, this is the profile of the traditional controller. Promotion-oriented people see their goals as a means to progress and they concentrate on the rewards that can be expected. They have little difficulty in taking risks, they think positively and are creative. They make more mistakes and often do not have a Plan B, but that is the price they are happy to pay for their progress. The researchers therefore recommend that managers would do well to adapt their managerial style to the type and focus of an employee. Promotion-minded employees thrive with "transformational" managers who value creative solutions, have a long-term vision, and like to shake things up. Prevention-minded people function best with "transactional" managers who emphasize rules and standards, protect the status quo, tend to micro-manage, avoid mistakes, and focus on more immediate goals.

Now that we know that the HPFF has four different profiles and that there are generally two types of personalities, management can focus on developing high-quality financial professionals. The profile for each financial environment can help with this, both in terms of the financial professionals anticipating and planning their own development, and for the finance function to set up HR instruments accordingly. The latter is a necessary precondition for developing financial professionals. Recruitment and selection, collaboration, training and development, and growth and succession are processes that the HPFF cannot pass on to the HR department; HPFF management must have an opinion on issues such as: How do we hire the right people?, How do we develop our people?, and How do they continue to grow? These are strategic HR questions; management must work closely with the HR department to find answers to these questions that permanently increase the quality and thus effectiveness of the financial professionals.

Recruitment and Selection

For the recruitment and selection of new candidates, the four profiles of the financial, as developed in the previous section, work well as a guideline when preparing recruitment advertisements and conducting interviews. The profiles also give direction to the financial professionals themselves: they make clear what is required in each environment in the finance function, what the relationships are with the other environments, and what developments are taking place in the environment a financial chooses to work in. Financial professionals can anticipate and successfully handle the challenges of working in a certain environment through targeted education, training, and gaining specific experiences. The different profiles also reinforce the call for different skills for each environment. Both the organization and the finance professionals themselves must take these profiles into account during the application procedure. However, although assessing potential new employees on the basis of the profiles does help in the selection process, it does not guarantee that the right people will be hired. A potential candidate must also have the 'DNA' that the finance function is looking for and the work attitude and ambition that the organization's finance function requires. It is therefore important to test not only for knowledge and skills but also for personal characteristics and motives.

Collaboration

The profile sketches make it possible to assess the composition of the teams in the finance function. The existing situation can be compared with the desired one, so better teams can be put together. In addition, the profiles give direction to expectations around collaborations between employees and teams in the finance function. Collaboration can improve significantly if organizations think in terms of roles instead of functions. In general, people increasingly fulfill multiple roles in organizations. In addition to their regular work activities, they often participate in improvement projects. In addition, more than before, they are invited to think about the organization's strategy and its operational translation. In short, employees have a portfolio of roles in an organization; this is also the case in the finance function. Combining roles, instead of executing one after the other, is called having a role portfolio. A financial is often working in multiple partnerships across the organization. This brings with it entering into dialogue with different people and discussing conflicting perspectives. This leads to personal growth and to being able to add value to those work partnerships. If the management of the finance function decides to work with a role portfolio, the aforementioned four profiles of financial professionals can serve to design and fill those roles and thus also to further develop the competencies of the financial professionals.

Training and Development

Financial professionals must be offered sufficient time and support for personal development. Financial professionals are often highly analytical and tend to learn through knowledge, and spend less time on developing skills and reflecting on their own attitude and behavior. As described earlier, in the HPFF, the distinctive capacity for financial professionals will mainly lie in the development of their attitude and behavior. However, formal vocational training (such as becoming a chartered accountant) does not always adequately address attitude and behavior, but rather focuses on developing knowledge and analytical skills. An education in general management or change management provides a broader perspective and teaches the financial to assess financial situations from different perspectives. A training where "action learning" and self-reflection are the starting point will help to develop the required interpersonal skills needed in the HPFF. The profiles can be used by management to see what the specific development points of a financial are, on the basis of the skills that are important for the specific environment in which this financial works. The profiles also provide managers with guidance in their work review and development discussions with employees and can be used by the finance function when starting a corporate university, i.e., an internal academy for the finance function.

> A manufacturing multinational expects its finance talent to progress through rotational assignments every three to five years. This includes exposures to various country-level finance functions and a mix of responsibilities in frontline, back-office, manufacturing, R&D, and operational business unit work. This helps to develop business acumen as well as soft skills such as communication and dialogue. As a result, financial professionals have a more comprehensive sense of the business when conducting higher-level work (APQC, 2018).

Development and Succession

It is of interest to investigate how financial professionals grow in a finance function set-up consisting of four environments and four profiles. In practice, few financial professionals make the switch from, for example, finance service provider to trusted finance lead or from corporate specialist to information expert. This is in itself not surprising because the profiles for these roles vary quite a bit, and a switch would therefore require a substantial investment in retraining of and adaptation by the financial making the switch. Nevertheless, a move from one environment to another can be useful for financial professionals from the point of view of learning the other perspectives of the financial professional field and thereby developing themselves. The progression from corporate specialist to business partner is more common. This is primarily a movement from a specialist to a more generalist role. A specialist starts in a specific activity of the finance function (for example treasury or corporate reporting), often at head office, develops specialist knowledge, becomes increasingly skilled in the chosen area, and grows in seniority. In the course of his/her career, a specialist will sometimes hit the ceiling, for example because broader, more comprehensive topics require knowledge of other disciplines or must be approached from different angles than the financial professional is used to or because younger colleagues now have to be managed and coached. In that case, additional training in the broadest sense is possible by following courses in business administration, human resource management, psychology, or by undertaking skills training in management, change management, or coaching. As a result, the specialist becomes more generalist and better at the role of business partner.

A generalist, on the other hand, starts relatively quickly in a broad position (such as that of business partner). In the course of her/his career, the generalist—who is good at making connections with other people, applying a helicopter view on different topics and specializations, and managing complex matters—can also hit a ceiling. One cause may be having to work with people who know more about certain topics, as a result of which the generalist is not taken seriously by their more knowledgeable colleagues or even subordinates. Then it may be time to choose a direction: specialization or expertise. Both specialists and generalists are equally valuable to organizations and the finance function. Every finance function should ask itself what type of specialists are needed in which environment, and what type of generalists are needed to bring and keep those specializations together.

If financial professionals continue to work in one environment for a longer period of time, they naturally become more and more of an expert and therefore a specialist. In many organizations, growth up the hierarchy consists of the movement from specialist to generalist. For the financial, seeking to grow to the top of the finance function, if that is the ambition, having experience in only one environment of the finance function is too limited a background. If the financial wants to become a CFO, it is necessary to have worked in several different environments of the finance function, and preferably also to have held a position outside the finance function, for example in operations, sales, or marketing. For the management of the finance function, it is necessary to actively think about the careers of the financial professionals, and to stimulate and coach these with career guidance. Appointments and successions from within then become a logical consequence of an active and targeted personnel policy within the HPFF.

Nearly two-thirds of CFOs are worried that talent shortages will impair their organization's ability to meet short-term strategies. However, contrary to the situation before the COVID-19 pandemic, they now face a different war for talent. In this 'new' war financial professionals are reluctant to surrender the flexibility they gained during the pandemic (for example, almost 49% of U.S. millennial and Gen Z workers would consider quitting their jobs if their employers were not flexible enough about remote work), and they have, because of the increasing talent scarcities, increased leverage as they consider their employment options. Thus, recruiting and retention becomes tougher for the finance function. In addition, cyber security concerns are increasing because of the increase in malware attacks, to which remote workers were particularly perceptible, during the pandemic. Therefore organizations, and their finance functions, have to plan for a long-term, secure hybrid workforce. For example by providing workers with company-owned laptops, moving workloads and applications to the cloud, developing new strategies to protect data and web applications, and educating workers in cyber security issues (Grant Thornton, 2021).

Summary

In Figure 11, we have summarized the four roles and associated behavioral skills.

Figure 11. Summary of the four profiles of financial professionals in the HPFF

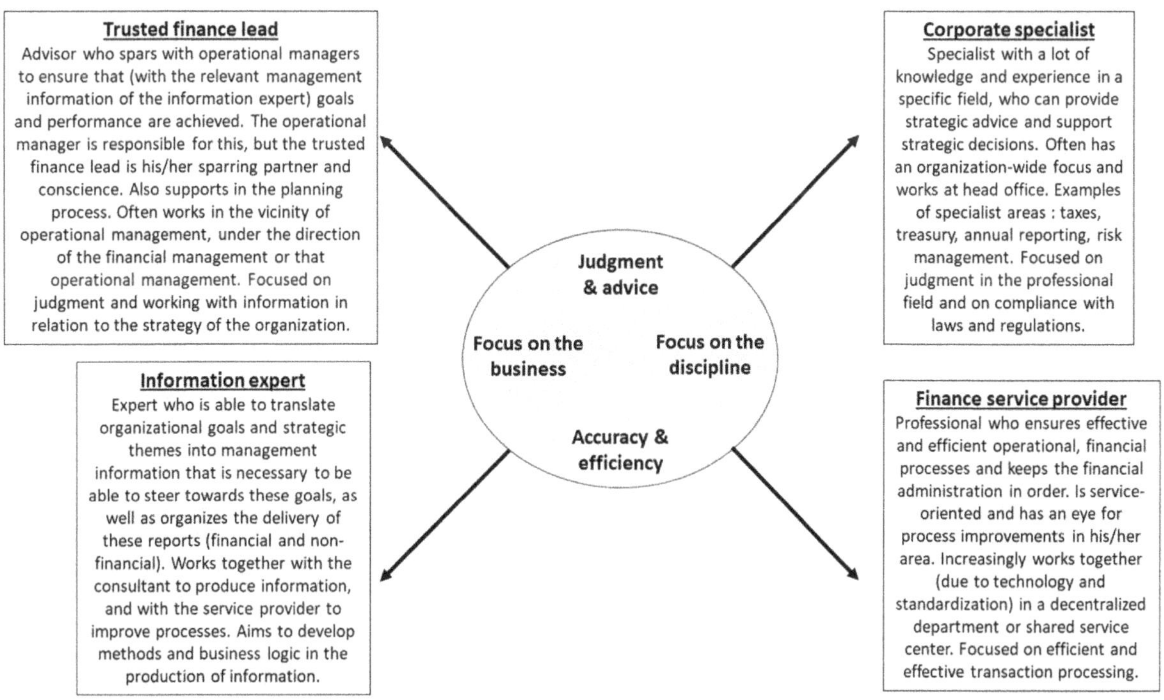

6.5 THE FINANCE FUNCTION AS PIONEER OF HPO

"At the frontiers of effectiveness, finance leaders deliver far more than core financial skills: their work guides the functioning of the entire organization" (Agrawal et al., 2020).

When studying organizations that have undertaken a successful transformation to HPO, it turns out that there is always at least one person who acted within the organization as the champion of the HPO philosophy. This person is the promoter and champion of HPO and ensures that colleagues become and remain enthusiastic about the prospect of becoming an HPO. This is a person who does not give up, who effortlessly overcomes obstacles, has perseverance, and finds great satisfaction in seeing the organization and its people grow. This person generally has such a high position in the organization that decisions can be enforced, resources and time can be freed up for the transformation to HPO, and people can be held accountable for keeping their promises regarding executing the transformation actions. The big question is of course: who should this spider in the HPO web be in your organization?

The logical answer is the chief executive officer (CEO); however, this person is mainly externally oriented as the representative of the organization to the outside world and has little time to get involved in internal affairs, let alone in such an important process as the HPO transformation. The next logical position that qualifies is the chief operations officer (COO) because she/he focuses on the operational affairs of the organization. However, not every organization (and certainly not the small and even mid-sized ones) have a COO position. In addition, operational matters can be so time-consuming that the COO also has too little room to get involved in more holistic matters such as HPO. That brings us to the next logical person: the CFO. When we look at the HPO factors (Chapter 1), we see a logical connection between the finance function and the HPO (Table 2).

Table 2. The connection between HPO and HPFF

HPO factor	Connection with the HPFF
Management Quality (characteristics include: integrity, fast decision-making and action-taking, result-oriented)	Integrity is paramount for the HPFF, both as a guardian and a promoter of that integrity within the organization. With regard to decision-making and action-taking, the HPFF is the primary provider of the information needed for these activities.
Openness and Action-Orientation (characteristics include: sharing knowledge and involving people in important business processes)	The HPFF has relationships with all organizational units and can therefore promote knowledge sharing between those units by acting as a facilitator and intermediary. In addition, the HPFF often coordinates organization-wide projects in which many people can be involved.
Long-Term Orientation (characteristics include: the conviction that the customer is always No. 1, maintaining excellent relationships with stakeholders)	The HPFF provides the information that management and the operation need to properly interact with the stakeholders of the organization.
Continuous Improvement and Renewal (characteristics include: having a unique strategy, continuous process improvement, process alignment)	The HPFF is involved in strategy setting, and process measurement and improvement, as information provider, information analyzer, and idea generator.
Employee Quality (characteristics include: having flexible and resilient people, good collaborators)	The HPFF financial keeps up to date with the professional literature and regularly ventures outside his/her own field, to learn new things (permanent education). The HPFF financial also collaborates extensively with the internal organizational units as well as with external customers and suppliers.

Table 2 shows that the finance function should be ideally suited to take the lead in the transformation of the organization into an HPO. The function can achieve this in collaboration with the HR department, given that three quarters of the HPO characteristics are related to behavior. However, in our financial trend survey (see Chapter 3), only 22% of financial professionals were of the opinion that the finance function should take the lead in the transformation into HPO. The first reason for this was that the finance function itself is not yet high performance (enough) and therefore does not feel inclined to take this pioneering role just yet. After all, the pioneering nature of the role undoubtedly means that the finance function will first be assessed by the other departments as to whether the function itself is a role model in the field of HPO. The finance function therefore has to first convert itself into an HPFF. The second reason is that the finance function must also have a natural position to be the pioneer. In an organization that focuses on technological innovation, for example, it might make more sense if the HPO idea originates from the R&D department. The third reason may be that in the finance function, no "natural leaders" have (yet) stood up to take on the pioneering role. The fourth reason is that the finance function is both a business challenger of and supplier who provides the resources and information to enable operational managers to undertake HPO transformations. This is a dual role that is potentially difficult to reconcile when being the HPO pioneer.

The question of whether a financial can be a pioneer of HPO is not only one of knowledge and skills, but also of personality traits. In order to become a high-performance financial, the financial professional will have to adopt less of a wait-and-see approach and focus more on developing the right motivation focus. Promotion-oriented people seem therefore ideally suited to be the pioneer in the transformation to the HPO. This means that the CFO does not necessarily have to be the pioneer; the pioneer could very well be a program manager or manager of Finance Transformation within the finance function.

However, in our opinion, the finance function, especially if it is (becoming) an HPFF, will have a head start to take on the pioneering role toward HPO. If the management of the finance function challenges, supports, and facilitates its employees, skillfully balancing between prevention-oriented and promotion-oriented management, then the finance function automatically becomes HPO's "frontrunner." This challenge, support, and facilitation is reinforced by being fully committed to the development of the financial professionals and by embracing the possibilities of IT. Effective and efficient processes are then a result of the chosen course of the CFO and the finance function: high-performing in terms of behavior, IT, and processes. This is the direction the finance function has to take, both for itself and for the benefit of the organization.

6.6 DIGITAL TRANSFORMATION AND THE FINANCE FUNCTION

The HPFF factors 'Finance Function Improvement' and 'IT Focus' emphasize the importance of automation for improving and strengthening the finance function. This fits well with the digital transformations many if not most organizations, and their finance functions, nowadays are undertaking. *Digital transformation* is a change in how the organization employs digital technologies to modify existing or create new business processes, new business models, culture, and customer experiences, with the purpose to meet changing internal business and external market and client requirements. Digital transformation changes the way operations gets done and, in some cases, creates entirely new classes of businesses. It fundamentally alters how the organization delivers value to customers, and it is a cultural change that requires the organization to continually challenge the status quo, experiment, and even be comfortable with failure. In general the transformation is made possible by many areas of new technology. *Finance digital transformation* is the implementation and use of digital technologies to specifically improve efficiency, efficacy, insight, agility and quality of finance processes and systems, in order to create time for the finance function to support the business with better information and insights (these definitions have been composed on the basis of the descriptions and definitions given in: CFO Community & Unit 4, 2020; Gartner, 2021c; Horváth & Partners, 2019; ICAEW & ISCA, 2019; Morgan, 2020; Pratt & Sparapani, 2021; Salesforce, 2018; The Enterprisers Project, 2021; Trianz, 2020; Verhoef et al., 2021; Workday, 2020; Yooz, 2019).

No modern-day organization can function without an effective IT architecture, thus there is a great need for successful digital transformations. Unfortunately, many of these digital transformations are not very successful or are very difficult. In fact, the professional literature reports that only one-third of organizations had their expectations regarding the results of the digital transformation met, while two-thirds state that their expectations were only partly or not at all satisfied (Blackline, 2020; Morgan, 2020; Trianz, 2020; Workday, 2020). In this section we look at the nature of a digital transformation, i.e. the difference between digitization/digitalization/transformation, the drivers for a digital transformation, what the benefits of a digital transformation are, what the status regarding digital transformations worldwide is, what skills in the finance function are needed to deal adequately with a digital transformation, and what bottlenecks finance functions can encounter while embarking on a digital transformation. Regarding the obstacles, we will report on the discussions we had with experienced finance professionals on their experiences and ideas how to deal adequately with these obstacles on the way to a successful digital transformation of the finance function.

Research Approach[3]
For our research we relied mostly on the managerial literature. The main reason is that developments in the IT field and with digital transformations are going so quickly[4] that academic literature cannot keep up. In addition, Verhoef et al. (2021) found that, despite the visible impact of digital transformation on organizations and their finance functions, the academic literature has paid surprisingly little attention to this development and has only recently started to address the topics of digitization, digitalization, and digital transformation. Therefore, we needed to turn to so-called practice-driven management research as, according to Mirvis et al. (2021), this type of research – which is generally reported in white papers and research reports by consultancy and professional associations – identifies real-life phenomena much quicker than theory-driven management research which is generated in "university-time" – and which is reported in academic journals. We selected mainly literature on digital transformations in the finance function; some sources were on digital organizational transformations (to obtain an all-encompassing overview of the obstacles). All sources reported on recent empirical research, not older than 5 years with the emphasis on the past two years. In total 82 sources were used. From these sources we collected information on the status and progress of digital transformations worldwide (with emphasis on the Americas, Europe and Asia).   For the discussions on the obstacles with experienced financial professionals we used three meetings. The first one was the Nationale Controllersdag 2021 [the Dutch National Controllers Day] where, during a breakout session, we had a discussion with 28 professionals about the obstacles. Subsequently we organized in Autumn 2021 three roundtable discussions with in total 34 professionals (CFO's, business controllers, managers Finance & Control). In these meetings we concentrated on the courses of action the professionals used during digital transformations they undertook with their finance functions. Each meeting built on the results of the previous meeting.

Difference Between Digitization, Digitalization, and Digital Transformation

Quite a few organizations confuse digital transformation with digitalization, in fact, many use these terms as synonyms. However, they in fact – together with digitization – indicate various stages of technology development of an organization (and its finance function) and can be described as follows (Salesforce, 2018; Verhoef et al., 2021):

Digitization

Digitization is the process of converting analog information into a digital format so that computers can store, process, and transmit such information. Organizations used to keep records on paper, handwritten in physical ledgers or typed into physical documents. When computers became mainstream organizations converted most or all of their ink-on-paper records to digital computer files. Digital data was exponentially more efficient for businesses than analog papers had been, but business systems and processes were still largely designed around analog-era ideas about how to find, share, and use information. Digitization is also refered to as a change of analog to digital tasks, or as the integration of IT with existing tasks. Digitization is mainly focused on achieving cost savings.

Digitalization

Digitalization is the process of using digitized information to make established ways of working simpler and more efficient. In this process IT serves as a key enabler to optimize existing business processes by allowing a more efficient coordination between processes and creating additional customer value through enhancing user experiences. IT is also used to seize new business possibilities by changing existing business processes. Digitalization is not only focused on cost savings but also includes process improvements that enhance customer value.

Digital Transformation

Digital transformation is the process of changing the way business gets done and, in some cases, creating entirely new classes of businesses using IT. It entails an organization-wide change that leads to the development of new business models, which may be new to the organization itself and even its industry. Digital transformation affects the whole organization and its ways of doing business. It rearranges the processes to change the business logic of a organization and its value creation process. Digital transformation is focused on operating in novel and innovative ways by answering the questions "What is our technology really capable of?" and "How can we adapt our business and processes to make the most of our technology investments?"

Drivers for Undertaking a Digital Transformation

Digital transformations have become increasingly important and urgent for organizations because of a variety of reasons (EY, 2021; EY Singapore & ACCA Singapore, 20121; ICAEW & ISCA, 2019; Lawson et al., 2019; Liu-Lindberg, 2021; Moll & Yigitbasioglu, 2019; Oesterreich et al., 2019; Pratt & Sparapani, 2021; The Enterprisers Project, 2021; Verhoef et al., 2021; Workday & Deloitte, 2021; Yooz, 2019):

- The transformation to Industry 4.0. This generated the introduction and subsequent rapid adoption of technology-based techniques such as e-commerce, digital marketing, and social media. The sheer number of new technologies and the huge amount of data nowadays available put big pressure on organizations to incorporate these in their operations. Industry 4.0 also originated integrated ecosystems, formed by the close collaboration of organizations in the same value chain. Organizations have to go along with other organizations that introduced these techniques and they also have to become part of these ecosystems, in order to survive and stay relevant. This has generated the idea of Finance 4.0 (Liu-Lindberg, 2021; Sablinskiene, 2021) which entails incorporate intelligent and innovative visualization technologies into the finance function. These technological solutions first "take-over" core financial activities – processing, recording, correcting and controlling – allowing finance departments to spend minimal time dealing with daily operations and more space for focusing on value enhancing activities and working as business partner to the business.
- Increasing competition through increased streamlined operational processes causing higher productivity levels. Competitors are increasingly using digital technologies and digital operating models to streamline their operation and become more efficient and effective, i.e. productive. In order to match these increased productivity levels organizations have to at least match these digitalization efforts.
- Increasing competition through the entrance of industry disruptors. An increasing number of industry disruptors enter the market; these start-ups and scale-ups are often solely based on technology platforms which makes them more agile and flexible in offering products and services with shorter lead-times than traditional companies (which thus have to digitalize their operations quickly).
- Increased demands and expectations of customers. The trend to 24/7 availability of products, services and access to organizations has created the expectation among customers that *every* organization can do the same and instantly satisfy their needs. This can only be achieved by digitalizing the organization's client-facing processes.
- Government schemes and support for digitalization. Increasingly governmental institutions are requiring that interactions between them and organizations proceed digitally. Examples are online filing of documents and digital tax returns. And in various countries governments offer subsidies and grants for digital transformation projects, with the aim to increase the level of digitalization (and thereby the productivity) of the country.

Description and Benefits of a Digital Finance Function

As could be expected with a relative new concept as the digital finance function, its shape and looks are not yet crystallized into a definitive form. Based on the professional literature (BearingPoint, 2020; Essaides et al., 2019; Farrar, 2019; Gartner, 2021d; Grund et al., 2020; Horváth & Partners, 2019; Liu-Lindberg, 2021; Ramakrishnan, 2021; Reilly, 2018), we have summarized its main features upon which the literature agrees, see Figure 12.

In the core the digital finance function has digitalized, automated the entire finance value chain – from order to cash, procurement to payment, employee on-boarding to separation, treasury, taxation, governance, internal controls and so on – and hosted it in the cloud while using shared and open platforms and ecosystems; all interactions across the value chain are covered, including customers, suppliers and partners, financial services entities and regulatory agencies; organizations with a digital finance function do not have pieces of the value chain that are manual and/or paper-based. It then keeps investing in state-of-the-art technology and digital applications, in developing the skills of its financial professionals, and in making sure digital strategies are aligned with organizational strategies. In the core the digital function also consists of people that use the digital capabilities and access to organization-wide data to, with a forward-looking and continuous improvement mindset, integrate and optimize processes across the organization, and to communicate results in a comprehensible manner to the business.

Figure 12. Depiction of the digital finance function

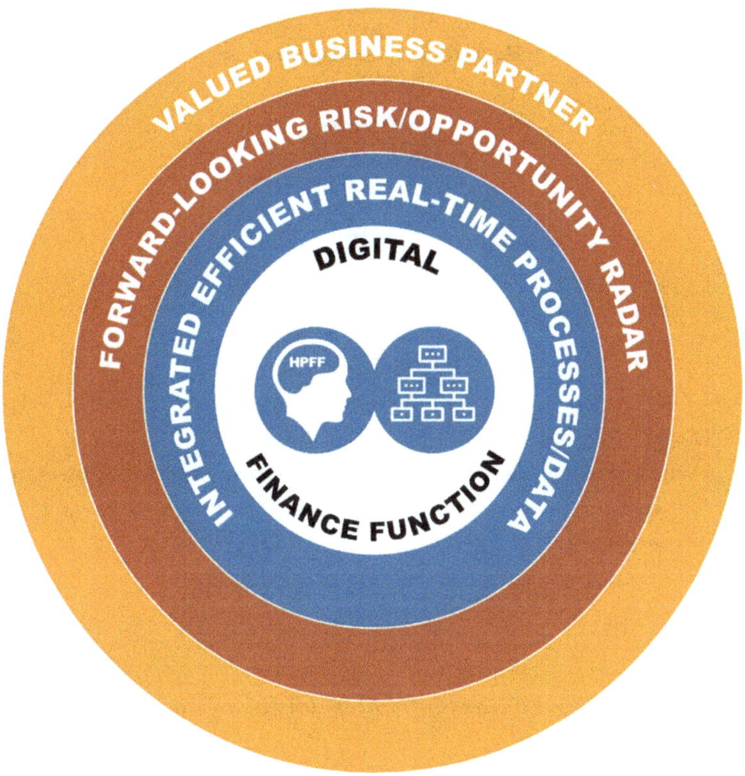

Based on this dual core of technical capabilities and digital high-performance mindset, the digital finance function ensures prompt availability of business performance data, establishing a (near) real-time, indisputable single version of the truth based on the highest data reliability; closes the books and reports financial results publicly on time and without manual effort, helping to reassure stakeholders that the organization is operating smoothly no matter the (external) circumstances; continuously identifies, tracks and acts upon non-financial performance indicators (such as customer demand, customer satisfaction and retention, project delivery, employee satisfaction and retention) that are leading indicators of future financial performance; easily identifies troublesome business areas, offers the business helpful ideas for addressing their challenges, acts quickly on critical issues, and takes proactive steps to mitigate risks; and makes it possible for the financial professionals to produce outcomes (such as financial statements) regardless of the physical place and time they are working.

The digital finance function embeds its financial professionals in business units as valuable business partners; this ensures that each business unit adheres to corporate governance and finance guidelines, robust cost and profitability management, and effective administration of internal controls; helps the business unit manage its business; increases understanding how to use financial data to target growth; and sustains profitability.

Undertaking a digital transformation has many benefits for organizations and their finance functions, as can be seen from Figure 13 and 14.[5]

Figure 13. The main benefits of digital transformations for organizations

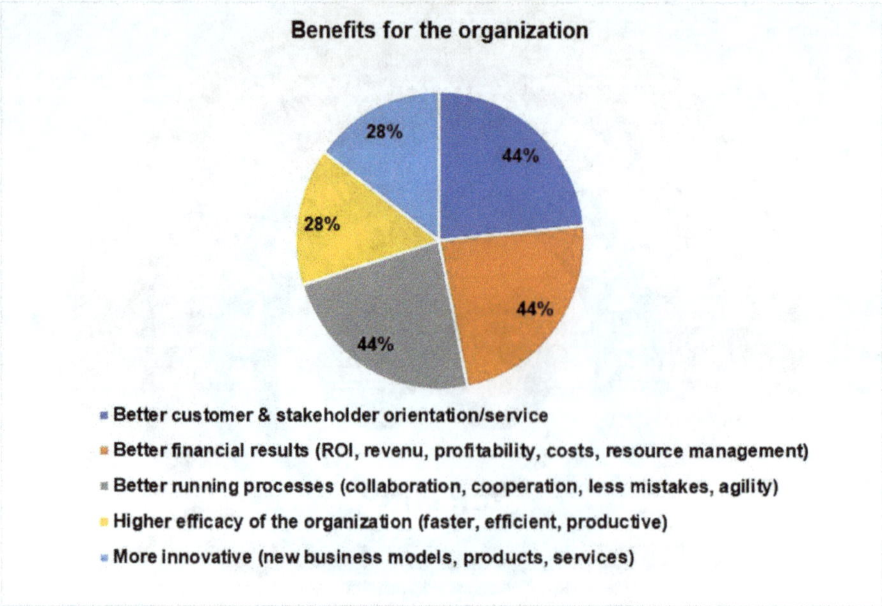

Figure 14. The main benefits of digital transformations for finance functions

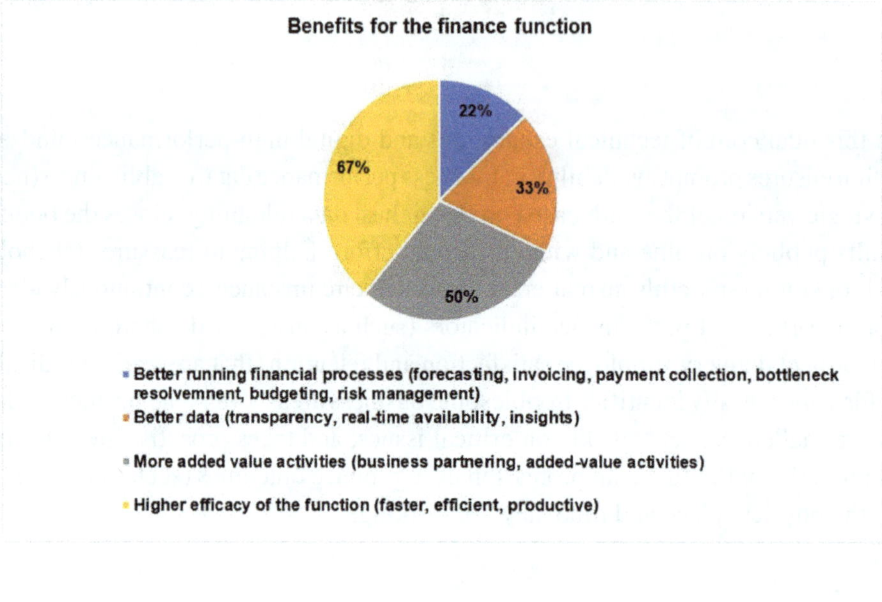

Main Skills Needed in a Digital Finance Function

"Formerly, it was the profession itself which determined what defines a qualified controller. With the introduction of information systems and later of ERP systems, this changed profoundly. Companies like SAP and Oracle became more prominent in defining and deciding what types of skills were needed in order to succeed as a business or financial controller in a large multinational company. We believe that digital transformation will further reinforce this trend" (Glader & Strömsten, 2020).

"The results from the literature analysis indicate that the financial of the future is expected to combine the functions of a strategic thinking business partner with selected functions of a data scientist" (Oesterreich et al., 2019).

Under pressure from the digital transformation the skills that finance functions need are changing. In Sections 6.2 and 6.3 we discussed the various roles and profiles financial professionals can have in the HPFF. In this section we add to this discussion by listing the skills finance functions, according to the professional literature, need in order to manage the digital finance function well (see Figure 15).[6]

Figure 15. Skills needed in the digital finance function

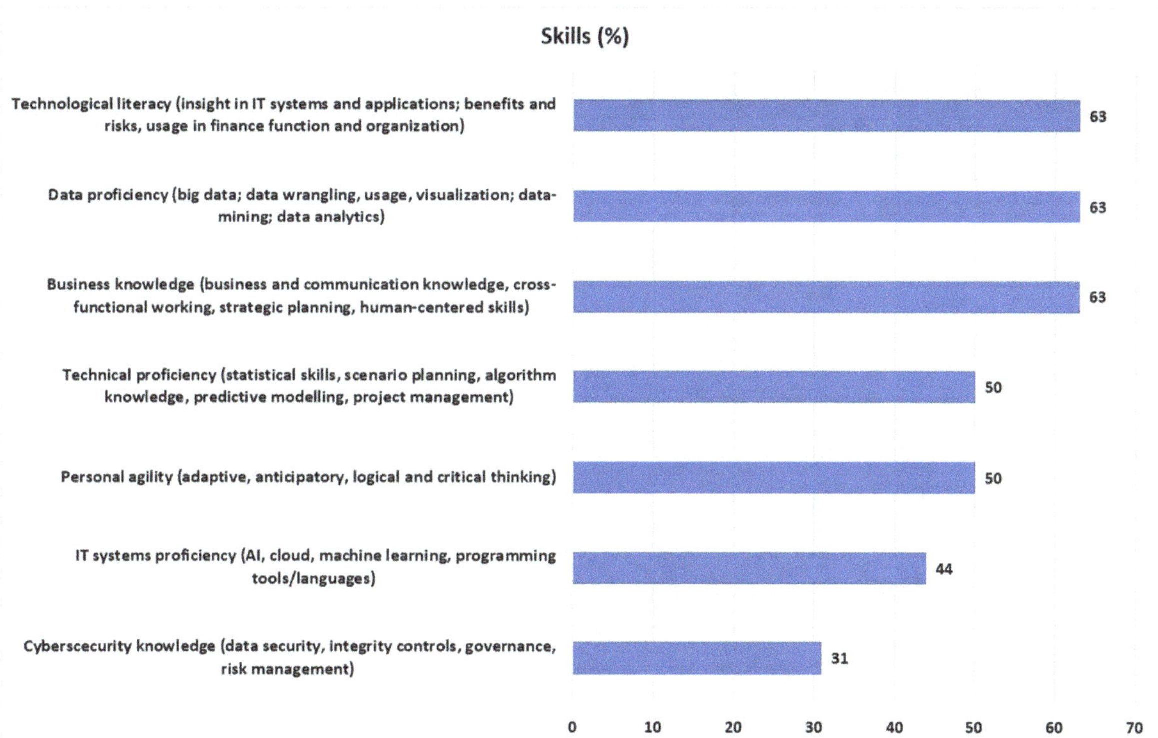

Planned and Actual Investments in Digital Transformations

The benefits of digital transformations are increasingly acknowledged by organizations. In fact, the literature review shows that worldwide 76% of the surveyed organizations are planning to invest more in digital transformations, while only 24% report to invest the same or less. It is interesting to see in which IT applications organizations and their finance functions are planning to invest, and what they have actually invested in in recent years (Figure 16).[7]

Figure 16. Planned and actual investments in IT in the past five years

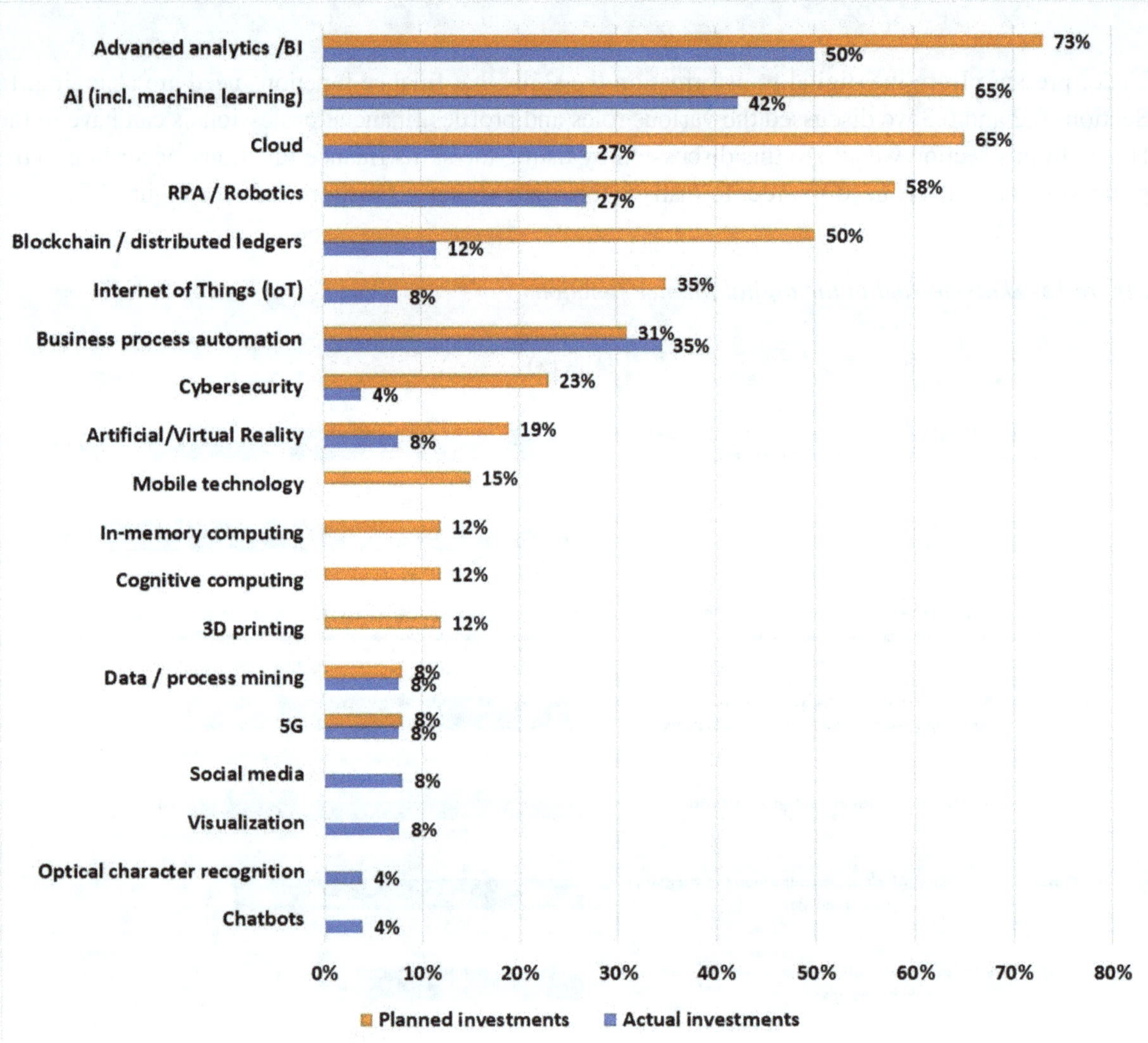

Figure 16 shows that actual investments are lagging planned investments, despite the surge in IT investment spawned by COVID-19. This could indicate that companies are still underestimating the urgency of the importance of digitalization and digital transformation of the organization and its finance function and thus are not allocating enough resources to the finance function (Reilly, 2018); that organizations are struggling to free up or find resources for a digital transformation; or that many resources are seized by updating and/or strengthening the current IT infrastructure (for example by implementing an ERP system) – often to catch up after the financial scandals and turmoil at the beginning of this century which caused many finance functions to go "back to the financial basics" and spend time on increasing the reliability of data, not leaving enough time for modernization of the finance function itself – leaving not enough funds for state-of-the-art digitalization. The latter could be indicated by the fact that actual investments for business process automation (which is the collective name for automating the current situation) exceed planned investments. Elaborating on this, Farrar (2019) makes a distinction between 'core modernisation' and 'exponential' technology tools. Core modernisation tools are those that focus on updating current financial systems and existing digital capability. Exponential tools deliver new capabilities to the finance function. It seems clear that the main focus of many finance functions is still on investing in core modernisation IT tools.[8] This finding is mirrored in recent international research among financials in Austria, Australia, Belgium, Finland and the Netherlands (CM: & Executive Finance, 2021) who stated that, although they are of the opinion that a digital transformation is vital for the professional growth of their finance fucntion, in practice they are mainly busy with getting the basis in order - as their ICT systems are not yet reliable enough – and that they have not spend time (yet) on developing a coherent digital strategy.

Obstacles on the Road to a Digital Finance Function and How to Deal with Them

As can be noticed so far there is a wealth of information available in the professional literature on the nature, content and especially benefits of digital transformations in finance functions. However, as the observation about two-thirds of surveyed organizations not being satisfied with the progress and results of their digital transformations and Figure 16 already forewarn, the actual picture of finance functions becoming digital finance functions in practice is not that rosy. When we summarize the status of digital transformation of finance functions worldwide[9], we get the following picture (see Figure 17):

Figure 17. Status of digital transformations in finance functions, worldwide

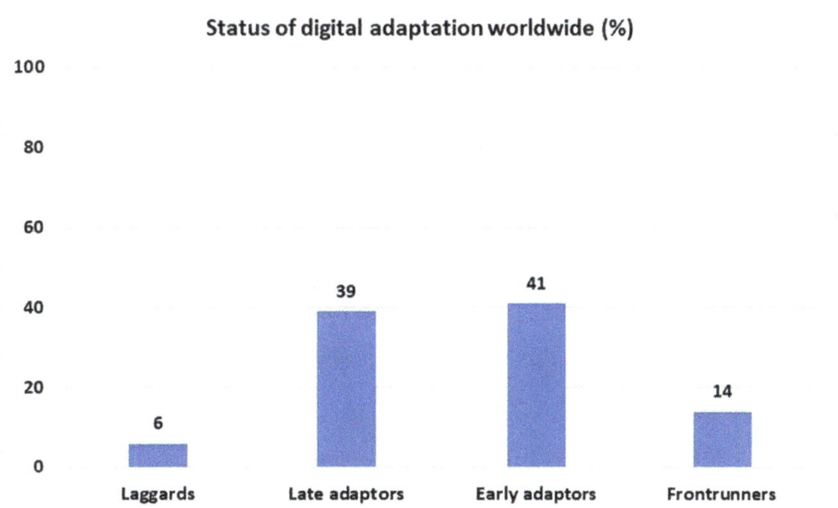

The delay in finance functions conducting a (successful) digital transformation might be explained by the obstacles on the road to creating a digital finance function, as reported by the professional literature (Figure 18).

Figure 18. Obstacles while creating a digital finance functions

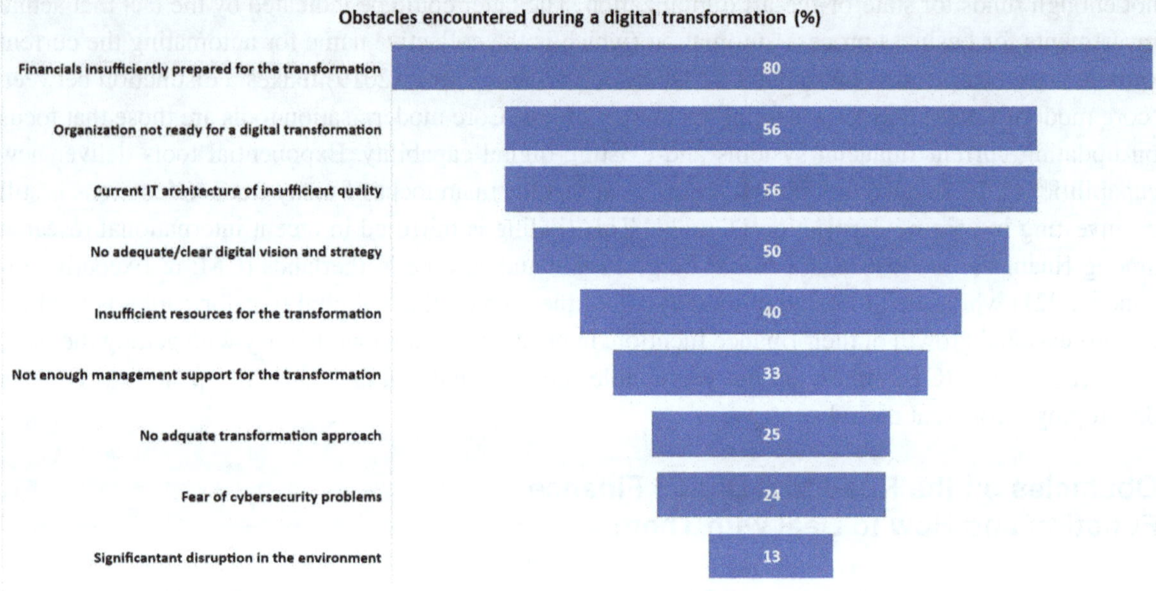

During the sessions with the experienced financial professionals a cautionary message was given to not focus too much on the current lagging status of digital transformations in finance functions. After all, every organization has its own circumstances (internally and externally) which dictate the resources available for a digital transformation and the tempo in which this transformation can take place. Thus the urgency placed on the speed of digital transformations – and the success stories – as communicated by the authors of the practice-driven management research reports might not (and often does not) match with the everyday practice and status of organizations. In that everyday practice the progress is much more step-by-step, because of the in general limited time available for improvement as it is always busy in the finance function, and also opportunistic in the sense that the finance function looks at what the business (which gets most resources to do this type of activity anyway) is doing and will join in when significant steps are made there. This modus of operating will naturally create finance functions as "late adopters". In addition, a digital transformation is not a goal in itself but a means to an end: the better servicing of customers, which does not depend solely on the IT architecture status of an organization but also – for a big part – on the attitude, professionalism and customer-focused attitude of the employees of the organization. Thus, both the "technical" side and the "human side" should at least get equal (change management) attention.

We then focused on discussing possible courses of action to deal with the four main obstacles (i.e. the top 4 in Figure 18).

Financial Professionals are Insufficiently Prepared for the Digital Transformation

This obstacle consists of two elements: 1. content – financials do not have enough knowledge about IT and/or there is too little internal training to make them more knowledgeable; 2. behavior – people are not motivated to change, uncertain about the change, (actively or passively) resist change, have fear for their position or job, are in general risk averse.

The participants of the various roundtable discussions made the following suggestions for courses of action to deal with this obstacle:

- Develop a "sober view" of the market. This means making sure that financial professionals regularly receive information about what is happening in the sector/industry the organization is operating, what the developments are in the digital technology space, what the current and desired digital state of their finance function is, what resources are available on the short and long term for digitization, and what is realistically possible and feasible to achieve in this respect. It helps to develop a clear vision and strategy for the digital transformation (see obstacle 4) as this gives people some security about what is going to happen.
- Encourage the "three C feelings" in people. These are: Compelling ("the digital transformation is needed to make our finance function and our organization stronger and better prepared for megatrends and disruptors in the environment, and it will increase your personal competency and add to your skills so you feel up-to-date and relevant to the organization and the clients"), Courage ("let us feel brave to start fearlessly with the transformation as soon as possible"), Confidence ("we will help you during the transformation by offering enough time and opportunity to develop yourself in the digital space, so you can feel confident that you are prepared and can contribute").
- Stress in the communication that the organization and its people have done this before. After all, the swift rollout and quick acceptance of for example home-work technology at the beginning of the COVID pandemic has shown that people are capable of more than they previously might have thought.
- Install a Finance Academy. With this academy financial professionals can be prepared for the digital transformation, by offering them courses and programs on, for example, how to use IT effectively, how to apply storytelling to construct a story from data, or the change management aspects of a digital transformations.
- Change the composition of the financial team. Make sure that newly hired people have strong IT and data analytics skills and affinity, and preferably have experience with digital transformations. This will foster the spread of digital skills in the finance function.
- Use cross-functional teams of finance and ICT in digital transformation projects. ICT professionals are used, during their whole career, to continuously update their skills and adjust to changing IT techniques, platforms and infrastructure. In fact, if they would rely on their way of working and tricks of 20 years ago, or even 3 years ago, they would have been out of a job. This attitude, willingness and mindset of constantly adapting and learning by ICT professionals will "rub off" on finance professionals when they work side-by-side in these project teams.
- Create regular interaction between ICT experts and the finance team. Invite ICT experts into finance team meetings to talk about developments in the IT and digital transformation areas so

people stay informed about what is happening around them. Let those IT experts also challenge current ways of working in and the current level of digitalization of the finance function.

- Be as a leader in Finance open to digital. As management of the finance function be open to the knowledge and ideas of the more digitally skilled people in the function. Regularly team up with digitally skilled people to gain knowledge. Visibly use new IT applications and be visibly involved in digital transformation activities, so people will know that IT is important to you as manager and therefore to them as team members.
- Reassure people. Make clear that there will always be people who will strictly perform operational tasks (probably between 20 to 30% of the finance professionals). These people will experience a change in their tasks though, for example no longer entering invoices but checking the automatic processing of those invoice. But it is okay that there are professionals working in the finance function with different levels of digital knowledge as a mix of skills is always needed. There will also be a group of experts with deep knowledge of non-digital issues, such as compliance and tax. These experts will often conduct the specialist conversation with for example the auditors. In addition, discuss with people who cannot or do not want to make the transformation about individual solutions, for example early retirement, finding another job inside or outside the organization, doing specialist work until their retirement.
- Use "seduction" techniques. Show and tell people how much time will be saved because many tedious tasks will now be done automatically without human intervention. And even those tedious tasks which cannot be fully automated will become much simpler and less time-consuming. Ask them whether they would want to miss their dishwasher and then point them at the parallels between what technology progress brought them in their home situation and what digital progress can bring them in their work situation. Also let people who have experience with working in a digital environment tell their colleagues about the benefits of such an environment, while managing expectations what it can and cannot offer.
- Involve people in the transformation process. Let the team talk and decide about what needs to be done during the transformation, with which priority, in what order, which particular activities, and who will do what. This will increase the commitment to the transformation of team members considerably.
- Appoint a Business Change Leader from inside the organization who is responsible for the communication regarding the digital transformation, spreading knowledge and information about the digital transformation, organizing and stimulating training sessions for financials, reflecting on behavior of people during the digital transformation, and in general be a coach to colleagues during the digital transformation.[10]
- Resistance can also originate from the feeling people have there is never enough time to do this type of activity. Therefore review the priorities of the finance function to see what can be postponed (or even stopped) to free up time for the digital transformation; make a realistic planning (a digital transformation will soon take a few years anyway); and do not make the digital transformation plan too big but break it down in small steps that are manageable for people.

The Organization is Not (yet) Ready for a Digital Transformation

Not being ready can be noticed by outdated ways of working, silos, lack of a data-driven culture, a bureaucratic and not innovative culture, and in general not seeing the need for the transformation. This unpreparedness severely hinders the transformation of the finance function.

The roundtable participants made the following suggestions for courses of action for this obstacle:

- Make clear to the people that external pressures create "a burning platform" for the organization to start a digital transformation, which increased competition and continuous pressure on budgets and revenue basically force the organization to go along with this trend of further digitalization and digital transformation.
- Develop the correct "tone at the top" regarding the importance of a digital transformation for the future well-being of the organization. Clearly visible management support will help people to become convinced of the need for the transformation. Also, management painting "the beckoning perspective" of a fully digitized organization and its benefits for clients and employees will help greatly.
- Incorporate the digital transformation in the organizational strategy – preferably develop on the basis of the organizational strategy a tailored digital vision and strategy–, this will make sure there is continuous attention for the topic of digital transformation throughout the organization.
- Deal with "old thinking" in the organization. Holding on to old ways of working (which come from old ways of thinking, e.g. "this is how we have always done it") prevents innovation and thus the adoption of new technologies (which bring with them new ways of working). In addition, there will be a tendency to, if new applications are implemented, to put old ways of thinking and working in those new environments causing them to be (much) less effective than they could have been. Courses of action to deal with this are to involving influencers (both internal and external ones) to entice people to start thinking differently ("thinking outside in"); involve external people in designing the new IT environment to prevent "tunnel vision" from internal people (who might hold on to the old ways of working); emphatically make time for improvement so people get the time to orientate themselves about what is happening in the organization's sector and in other organizations/competitors, and get knowledgeable about what is available in the market and what is possible IT-wise.
- Put much focus on development of communication skills of financial professionals. Many operational people derive their position and get respect because of their knowledge of current processes, procedures and systems. They know the short-cuts and can often take decisions on their experience and intuition. With a digital transformation the role of data analytics will become increasingly larger and more important in decision-making. This will create resistance with the operational people who feel that their "respect base" is crumbling because of the digitalization. Verbally skilled financials can help by explain the benefits, and thus removing the threat, of working together to combine human experience with systems' data to jointly provide even better advice to the business.
- Look carefully at the composition of cross-functional improvement teams. Make sure that in every improvement team not only multiple departments are represented but that there are people in there with good IT and data analytics skills. This will foster the spread of digital skills over the organization.

- Create discussion groups on various organizational levels in which management team members, financials and operational people together can develop a picture of the future digitalized organization and the way to get there. Also potential and foreseen bottlenecks, and how to deal with these, and the consequences of the digital transformation for teams and individuals can be discussed and dealt with. Core questions for the discussion are: what will our way of working be in the digital organization (i.e. agile), what IT architecture is needed, how will the customer benefit from it?
- Create a frontrunners team (consisting of financials, IT professionals and operational people with an innovative nature, and an enterprise architect) straight under the Board/management team and reporting directly to them, with the task to plan, communicate, coach and supervise the digital transformation in the organization.

The Current IT Architecture (Systems/Processes/Data) Is Of Insufficient Quality

It is too complex, not aligned, not integrated, and there is not enough knowledge in the organization about the (legacy) systems. The roundtable participants made the following suggestions for courses of action for this obstacle:

- Establish a innovation group in which all relevant functions are represented (CIO, financials, BU managers, program managers etc.) who develop a two to three year transformation plan to upgrade the current IT architecture, taking into account the digital vision of transforming to a digital finance function (and organization), and also dealing with the new ways of working required in a digital finance function (organization).
- Aim at standardizing IT systems as much as possible as this will make a digital transformation much easier.
- Start modest with small projects in the operation, aimed at increasing the quality and reliability of data, information and forecasts. Start issuing and discussing, as finance function with operational managers, updated management reports even if these are not yet fully filled with data. This will entice the operation to start collecting and delivering the missing data for these reports, and will generate support for further digitalization.

No Adequate and/or Clear Digital Vision and Strategy

An adequate and clear direction-setting digital vision and strategy has not been developed for the digital transformation of the finance function. “Inadequate” can be noticed for insufficiently alignment with the business strategy, and/or being insufficiently long-term oriented.

The roundtable participants made the following suggestions for courses of action for this obstacle:

- Assemble a separate group of frontrunners. Get a group of forward-thinking people together, to develop the digital vision and strategy; and let them discuss these with their colleagues in iterative sessions (meaning that after each session an update will be made of the vision and strategy).
- Use (small-scale) pilots. Test the developed vision and strategy in those pilots, involving rotating groups of financial professionals, and evaluate the relevance, feasibility and appeal of the digital vision and strategy.

- Look for a sponsor in the organization's management team. This person will keep a close eye on the alignment between the organizational vision/strategy and the digital vision/strategy (both for the organization and the finance function), and who will challenge the finance department on this alignment.
- Have a strong person in the finance function that has many connections in the organization and thus knows what is going on and what can be expected. This person can make sure that the finance function is prepared on what is coming and therefore will be able to join in, in a timely fashion. In this case when a digital vision and strategy is developed for the organization: the finance function will be part of this activity to influence the development with its expertise, and to take the results and tailor it to the finance function itself.
- Base the digital vision/strategy on previous experiences. Collect examples of effective digital application use in the organization and bundle these, to then discover the common thread in those examples on which to base the digital vision/strategy which can be successful in your organization.
- Hire new people with a different background and experience from the current people in the finance function. These people should be able to develop a digital vision and strategy for the finance function because of their different skills, previous experiences and because they are (relatively) new in the organization and thus still have an open mind.

There is some overlap between the various courses of action as suggested by the roundtable participants. Combining similar courses of action and categorizing them according to the core elements of the digital finance function yields Figure 19.

Figure 19. Courses of action to deal with the obstacles while creating a digital finance function

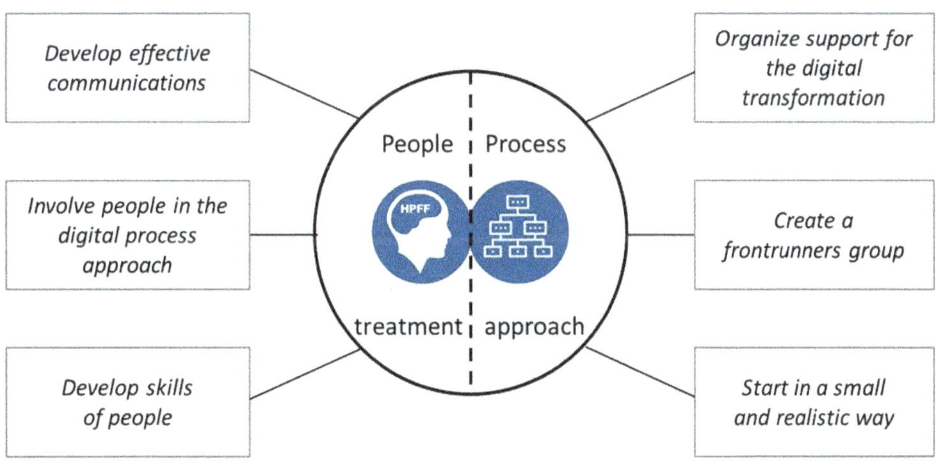

At the people side the four main obstacles can be addressed by:

- developing effective communications, which consists of providing financial professionals with timely and accurate information on the why, what and how of the digital transformation; reassuring people about what is going to happen; offering them a beckoning perspective of the future state of the finance function; and in general having the right tone at the top;

- emphatically involving financial professionals in the design, process approach and implementation of the digital finance function;
- developing the skills of current financial professionals so they can create and operate successfully in a digital finance function; and hiring new financial professionals with the right skills.

At the technical (or process approach) side the four main obstacles can be addressed by:

- organizing support for the digital finance function transformation by finding a sponsor for this in the organizational management team; developing a digital vision and strategy; and establishing good relations with the ICT function;
- creating a frontrunner group, consisting of people from various departments who will take the lead in the digital transformation, under guidance of a Business Change Leader;
- starting with small steps in a realistic timeframe.

REFERENCES

Accenture. (2014). *The CFO as architect of business value, delivering growth and managing complexity*. Accenture 2014 High Performance Finance Study. Accenture LLC.

Accenture. (2018). *From bottom line to front line*. CFO Reimagined. www.accenture.com

Agrawal, A., Eklund, S., Waite, J., & Woodcock, E. (2020). *Finance 2030: Four imperatives for the next decade*. McKinsey and Company.

APQC. (2018). *Ten characteristics shared among best-in-class finance functions*. American Productivity and Quality Center.

Association of International Certified Professional Accountants (2020). *Agile finance reimagined: building finance resiliency and returning the business to scale*. Association of International Certified Professional Accountants (AICPA).

BearingPoint. (2020). *CFO 4.0, Digital transformation in the financial function*. BearingPoint.

Beyer, M. (2011). *Gartner says solving 'big data' challenge involves more than just managing volumes of data.* Gartner Special Report. Gartner UK Limited.

Blackline. (2020). *The Future of Automation in the Finance Function, Global Survey 2020*. FSN The Modern Finance Forum, FSN Publishing Limited.

Campagna, C., Delawalla, A., & Peabody, A. (2021). *CFO Now: Breakthrough speed for breakout value*. Accenture LLC.

Caswell-LaPierre, A., Kracklauer, S., Essaides, N., Dorr, E., Hall, B., & Willman, T. (2020). *Transforming finance to prevail in the next normal*. The Hackett Group.

CFO Community & Unit 4. (2020). *Whitepaper digitale transformatie: De CFO is aan zet* [White paper digital transformation: it's the CFO's turn]. CFO Community/Unit 4/Alex van Groningen.

CM & Executive Finance. (2021). *Finance heeft mond vol van transformatie, maar is eigenlijk nog helemaal niet zo ver* [Finance is talking about transformation, but is actually not that far yet]. White paper. CM & Executive Finance.

Commissie Beroepsprofiel van de Vereniging van Registercontrollers [Professional Profile Committee of the Association of Registered Controllers]. (2021). *CFO of the Future*. VRC.

de Waal, A., Bilstra, E., & Bootsman, J. (2022), *Dealing with digital transformations in the finance function*. Paper submitted to the EURAM (European Academy of Management) 2022 Conference, ZHAW School of Management and Law, Winterthur/Zurich, Switzerland.

de Waal, A., & Linthorst, J. (2022). *Futurize! Dealing with megatrends and disruptors*. Routledge.

Eklund, S., Tam, M., & Woodcock, E. (2018). *New technology, new rules: Reimagining the modern finance workforce*. McKinsey and Company.

Ernst & Young. (2008). *The changing role of the financial controller*. Ernst & Young.

Essaides, N., Willman, T., & Dorr, E. (2019). *World-Class Finance: Redefining Performance in a Digital Era*. The Hackett Group Inc.

EY. (2021). *Digital disruption in finance Survey insights*. Ernst & Young Associates LLP.

Farrar, M. (2019). *Re-inventing finance for a digital world*. Chartered Global Management Accountant & Association of International Certified Professional Accountants.

Fourné, S., Guessow, D., & Schäffer, U. (2018). Controller roles: Scale development and validation. In Epstein, M.J., Verbeeten, F.H.M., and Widener, S.K. (Eds.), *Performance measurement and management control: The relevance of performance measurement and management control research*. Emerald Publishing Limited.

Gartner. (2021a). *Unlock your finance team's digital potential: 5 critical competencies*. Gartner for Finance, Gartner Inc.

Gartner. (2021b). *Top priorities for finance leaders in 2021*. Gartner for Finance, Gartner Inc.

Gartner. (2021c). *2021 Gartner CEO Survey: The CFO Perspective*. Gartner Inc.

Gartner. (2021d). *The Digital Future of Finance, 10 CFO Opportunities to Accelerate Digital Transformation*. Gartner Inc.

Gartner. (2021e). *The CFO's Guide to Enterprise Digital Strategy*. Gartner Inc.

Gartner for Finance. (2021). *Differentiators of Today's Personally Effective CFOs*. Gartner Inc.

Glader, M., & Strömsten, T. (2020). Digitalization of the Finance Function. *Controlling & Management Review*, *64*(6), 64–67.

Grant Halvorson, H., & Higgins, E. T. (2013a). Do you play to win—or to not lose? *Harvard Business Review*, *91*(3), 117–120. PMID:23451530

Grant Halvorson, H., & Higgins, E. T. (2013b). *Focus: use different ways of seeing the world to power success and influence*. Hudson Street Press.

Grund, T., Schmitz, J., Rodt, M., Pierer von Esch, S., Krühler, M., & Ponnath, F. (2020). *Bionic Finance Offers a Strategic Edge*. BCG and Siemens Healtineers.

Hope, J. (2006). *Reinventing the CFO: how financial managers can transform their roles and add greater value*. Harvard Business School Press.

Horváth & Partners. (2019). *Three routes into the digital future*. Horváth & Partners.

ICAEW & ISCA. (2019). Digital transformation in finance functions: ASEAN and UK perspectives. ICAEW thought leadership in partnership with The Institute of Singapore Chartered Accountants. ISCA.

Kaplan, B. (2021). *Develop Talent to Elevate Finance in a Digital World*. Deloitte Insights.

KPMG. (2014). *The view from the top. CEOs see a powerful future for the CFO, are CFOs ready for the challenge? An Asia Pacific survey*. KPMG International Cooperative.

KPMG. (2019). *De toekomst van Finance: impact op de personele bezetting, nieuwe talentstructuren en -strategieën* [The future of Finance: impact on staffing, new talent structures and strategies]. KPMG Advisory N.V.

Lawson, R., Hatch, T., & Desroches, D. (2019). *Achieving a Competitive Advantage in the Digital Age—The Value of Training and Certification*. IMA® (Institute of Management Accountants).

Liu-Lindberg, A. (2021). *Welcome To Finance Function 4.0*. BPI. https://www.linkedin.com/pulse/welcome-finance-function-40-anders-liu-lindberg/

McCaffry, R. (2020). *Finance transformation: the human perspective*. Association of International Certified Professional Accountants.

Mirvis, P. H., Albers Mohrman, S., & Worley, C. G. (2021). *How to do Relevant Research, From the Ivory Tower to the Real World*. Edward Elgar Publishing Limited. doi:10.4337/9781788119405

Moll, J., & Yigitbasioglu, O. (2019). The role of internet-related technologies in shaping the work of accountants: New directions for accounting research. *The British Accounting Review*, *51*(6), 100833. doi:10.1016/j.bar.2019.04.002

Morgan, B. (2020). Is COVID-19 Forcing Your Digital Transformation? 12 Steps To Move Faster. *Forbes*. https://www.forbes.com/sites/blakemorgan/2020/04/05/is-covid-19-forcing-your-digital-transformation-12-steps-to-move-faster/

NBA. (2019). *Maturiteitsmodel financieel professional 2022, profielen financieel professional: hoofdactiviteiten en primaire rollen* [Maturity model of financial professional 2022, profiles of financial professional: main activities and primary roles]. Koninklijke Nederlandse Beroepsorganisatie van Accountants.

Oesterreich, T. D., Teuteberg, F., Bensberg, F., & Buscher, G. (2019). The controlling profession in the digital age: Understanding the impact of digitisation on the controller's job roles, skills and competences. *International Journal of Accounting Information Systems*, *35*, 100432. doi:10.1016/j.accinf.2019.100432

Ramakrishnan, V. (2021). *How the CFO Can Be an Effective Partner to the CEO in Navigating the Pandemic's Economic Storm*. Tata Consultancy Services.

Reilly, A. (2018). *Accelerating the digital agenda in finance: Part 1 + Part 2*. Accenture.

Ryan, V. (2018). *A (Digital) Dream Deferred*. CFO, February/March.

Sablinskiene, R. (2021). *Digitalization of Corporate Finance: How Finance 4.0 is changing the role of Chief Financial Officer (CFO)?* [Master Thesis]. Jönköping University

Salesforce. (2018). *Perceptions of Digital Transformation, 2018 Survey Results*. Salesforce.com

EY Singapore & ACCA Singapore (2021). *Is digital culture the key to unlocking finance transformation?* Ernst & Young LLP.

Solutions, N. (2020). *State of Digital Transformation 2020*. Net Solutions.

Technologies, D. (2020). *Digital Transformation Index 2020*. Vanson Bourne Research Findings & Methodology, Dell Inc.

Ten Rouwelaar, J. A. (2015). *Business unit controller involvement in management*. H&G Uitgeverij.

The Enterprisers Project. (2021). *What is digital transformation? Your top questions answered*. EnterprisersProject.com

Thornton, G. (2021). *CFOs need to win the talent war but not at any cost, Balancing post-pandemic human capital costs and needs will define success*. Grant Thornton LLP.

Tjandra, J., Swaminthan, A., & Jing Yi, P. (2021). *Finance of the Future: Being a resilient CFO*. KPMG Services Pte Ltd.

Trianz. (2020). *State of digital transformation worldwide: 2020*. Trianz.

Verbeeten, F., & Heinen, J. (2019). *Finance transformation in the digital era, acquiring new skills to drive the digital transformation*. Finance on a Mission (University of Amsterdam/Workday/PLUC!/ Finance Transformation Forum).

Verhoef, P. C., Broekhuizen, T., Yakov, B., Bhattacharya, A., Qi Dong, J., Fabian, N., & Haenlein, M. (2021). Digital transformation: A multidisciplinary reflection and research agenda. *Journal of Business Research, 122*, 889–901. doi:10.1016/j.jbusres.2019.09.022

Webb, C., & Lawson, R. (2021). *The CFO of the Future*. ACCA and IMA.

Workday & Deloitte. (2021). *A More Effective CIO-CFO Partnership, Reinventing Finance Transformation*. Workday Inc.

Workday. (2020). *Finance Digital Transformation: How Finance Leaders Can Equip Their Team to Tackle Change, CFO Indicator Survey 2020*. Workday Inc.

Workday. (2021). *How Finance Can Build a Data Foundation to Fuel Frictionless Finance*. CFO Indicator Survey 2021, Workday Inc.

Wunsche, A. (2007). The CFO as strategist and catalyst in building a high-performance culture. *Ivey Business Journal, 71*(8), 1–10.

Yooz. (2019). *Finance Departments: what's your digital plan? AT LAST your user's manual!* Yooz France.

ENDNOTES

1 Being an information architect does not mean that the finance function "owns" the data, that stays with the different departments of the organization. But the finance function as information architect has a place at the decision-making table so it can ensure that the data are sound and can be trusted for informed decision-making.

2 In the code of conduct of the Dutch finance association NBA/VRC this is called: having a "moral compass."

3 This section is based on de Waal et al. (2022).

4 De Waal and Linthorst (2022) in their research into megatrends found that the *increasing speed* of technological developments has nowadays the most impact on organizations.

5 Calculated by dividing the number of literature sources in which the particular benefit was mentioned by the total number of literature sources in which the benefits were mentioned (= 18 in total) x 100%.

6 Calculation: number of literature sources in which the particular skill was mentioned divided by total number of sources that mentioned skills (= 26 in total) x 100%.

7 Calculation: number of literature sources in which the particular investment (e.g. IT application) was mentioned divided by total number of sources that mentioned investment areas (= 26 in total) x 100%.

8 According to Gartner (2021e) the average organization dedicates 37% of the digital financial budget on digital business optimization (i.e. core modernisation), 29% on digital business transformation (i.e. exponential) and 35% on digital enablement that builds a technology foundation necessary to achieve the other two.

9 In nine literature sources (Agarwal & Shroff, 2021; Campagne et al., 2021; Liu-Lindberg, 2021; Net Solutions, 2020; Reilly, 2018; Trianz, 2020; Verbeeten & Heinen, 2019; Workday, 2020, 2021) finance functions were asked how far they had progressed with their digital transformation (answering options: not started with the transformation, just started, underway, fully transformed). In five other sources (Blackline, 2020; CFO Community & Unit 4, 2020; Dell Technologies, 2020; Farrar, 2019; Ryan, 2018) finance functions were questioned about how they saw their digital status compared to other finance functions (answering options: laggard, late adaptor, early adaptor, frontrunner). We have combined these answering options into the categories as given in Figure 16.

10 In this regard the Business Change Leader looks similar to an HPFF Coach.

Chapter 7
The HPFF Diagnosis

ABSTRACT

The initial step in the transformation to an HPFF involves performing an HPFF diagnosis. The diagnosis is the starting point for initiating change, prioritizing topics, and taking steps for improvement. For a process in which improvements take root, after a diagnosis and discussion of the outcomes, a follow-up is needed to continue the movement that has been initiated. This translates into concrete actions and projects. The focus must be on small improvement steps, so that employees save time for further improvement steps. In this chapter, what the HPFF diagnosis looks like is discussed. In addition, the experience of a finance function that conducted the HPFF diagnosis is related.

7.1 SET-UP AND EXECUTION OF THE HPFF DIAGNOSIS

The HPFF diagnosis consists of three main steps, which are described below.

First Step: Preparation and Communication

It is important to create clarity about the why, how, and what of the HPFF diagnosis and subsequent transformation. Communication about the different steps and what is expected of the financial professionals is important, not only via e-mail but also verbally by the management team members. It is also nice to create a newsletter to communicate regularly. Another option is to conduct communication by means of a vlog (preferably from the CFO) indicating why this "HPFF business" is being initiated and what the next steps will be (such as the questionnaire that will be sent). It is also wise to give financial professionals the opportunity to respond to the intended process, for example, by reflecting on it in the work meetings of the various finance teams. It is crucial that everyone participates, not only by completing the survey and attending the HPFF workshop but also—especially—during the execution of the HPFF transformation actions.

DOI: 10.4018/978-1-7998-6929-0.ch007

Second Step: The HPFF Questionnaire

Step 2 consists of collecting the necessary data. All financial professionals complete the HPFF questionnaire which consists of questions based on the 28 HPFF characteristics, the five finance function performance characteristics, and the 10 obstacles. The financial professionals are asked to what extent their finance function meets the HPFF characteristics and the finance function performance characteristics, with possible answers on a scale from 1 (not at all) to 10 (completely). In addition, they assess to what extent the 10 obstacles in their organization can actually hinder the transformation to HPFF, with a rating scale from 1 (not at all) to 10 (very severe obstacle). After this, the scores for all characteristics and obstacles are calculated and displayed in graphs. The graphs indicate how far the finance function is on the road to HPFF and what obstacles it can expect on that road. Incidentally, in order to be called an HPFF, the mean score of each HPFF factor must be at least 8.5. The graphs show which factors (and underlying characteristics) need to be strengthened in order to improve the performance of the finance function as a whole, and which obstacles need to be tackled to make this happen.

The Stages on the Way to the HPFF

In practice, a finance function does not become an HPFF overnight. In general, four development stages can be distinguished that bring a finance function ever closer to the HPFF. We have summarized these four stages in Table 1.[1]

Table 1. The four development stages of the finance function

Development stage	Basic finance function	Effective finance function	Leading finance function	High-performance finance function
Criteria	Maintain and comply with financial regulations	Improve processes in the finance function	Improve organizational processes (touching adjacent finance processes)	Impact on the organization by helping to develop the organization
Focus	Execute core financial processes	Implement "point (= specific) improvements" in current processes	Implemented improvements in organizational processes and value chains	Act as a high-performing finance team on all fronts (focus on the HPFF factors).
Associated HPFF diagnosis score	Between 1.0 and 4.0	Between 4.1 and 7.0	Between 7.1 and 8.4	Between 8.5 and 10.0

In the HPFF graph, these stages are displayed such that, at a glance, the financial professionals can see (a) at which development stage their finance function is, and (b) what the strong points and the areas of improvement for their finance function are (see Figure 1 for an example).

Figure 1 shows that the finance function of Company XYZ has an average score of 6.2 for the five HPFF factors, which puts this finance function in the "effective" stage. This means that this finance function is essentially able to fulfill all its (internal and external) reporting and processing requirements, and also has some time left over for improving its own processes. The graph also shows an area where the finance function requires urgent improvement, i.e., 'Role Clarity' where the score of 5.4 indicates that there is still a lot to be gained by defining and communicating clear roles for the financial professionals.

Figure 1. HPFF graph with scores for the HPFF factors and the development stages

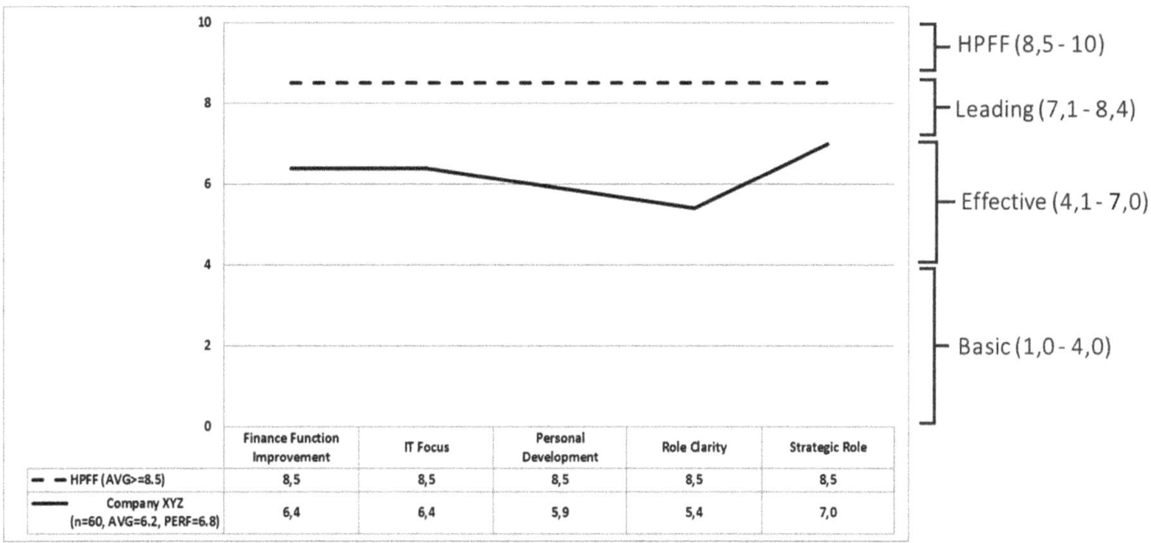

Third Step: the HPFF Workshop[2]

In step 3, a feedback and action workshop is held at which all people working in the finance function are in attendance. During the workshop, the scores on the HPFF factors, HPFF characteristics, and obstacles are discussed in a plenary session, and the HPFF points of attention are addressed. Subsequently, in groups, it is discussed whether the scores and HPFF points of attention are recognized and acknowledged, what the possible causes for the scores are, how the scores can be improved or how the obstacles can be tackled, and whether there may already be good examples of improvement of the finance function in certain areas. The outcome of the workshop is an HPFF transformation action plan consisting of two parts: actions for improvement that are necessary to address the HPFF concerns of the organization, and a prioritization of these actions.

The HPFF Workshop in Detail

The aim of the HPFF workshop is to introduce financial professionals to the HPFF philosophy. During the workshop, first of all, the theory of the HPFF framework is explained: how it was developed, what the HPFF factors and characteristics are, and what added value its use has for the finance function. Next, the results of the HPFF questionnaire are discussed so that everyone knows how far the function currently is on its way to high performance. The remainder of the workshop is then devoted to discussing the results in-depth, identifying points for attention, formulating actions, and choosing priorities. This takes place by means of three interactive break-outs in which groups of financial professionals discuss the HPFF diagnosis results: 1. Interpreting the diagnosis results (i.e., discussing the current situation of the finance function); 2. Describing the finance function when it is an HPFF (i.e., discussing the future of the finance function); and 3. Describing what was done to become an HPFF (i.e., discussing the period between now and then). The instructions that the workshop participants received for the break-out rounds are shown below.

Instruction Break-Out 1: Interpreting the Results of the HPFF Questionnaire

Each group of financial professionals looks at the scores for one HPFF factor. The purpose of this break-out is to describe together the story behind these scores. It is useful as a group to first briefly look individually at the scores. However, do not get stuck with that for too long: focus mainly on the assigned factor. You can give brief attention to scores on other HPFF characteristics and look for relationships with "your" HPFF factor, but focus mainly on your own factor. Describe examples of obstacles, especially if they are relevant to the scores on your HPFF factor. Also provide examples from practice that are illustrative of the scores. Questions to answer about your HPFF factor are: 1. What explains the scores? Describe the story behind the scores. Use examples from your own practice. 2. Which obstacles does your factor suffer most from (in other words, which obstacles need to be tackled)? The carousel starts after 30 minutes: your groups visit the other groups to hear what these have discussed. One group member stays behind with a flipchart to explain the discussion results of your group and to note the comments of the "visiting" groups. Each visit lasts a maximum of five minutes, after which you continue on to the next group.

Instruction Break-Out 2: Describing the Finance Function as an HPFF

Each group discusses the same HPFF factor as during break-out 1. The purpose of this break-out is to jointly describe what the shape and functioning of your finance function would look like if it scored on a high-performing level for your HPFF factor. What does the finance function look like when they come to film you? What words characterize the finance function? What would the internal customers say about the finance function? How do you treat each other in this finance function? How do your products/services look (different)? TIP: use the examples from the first break-out and describe how the same situations would turn out if, for example, you scored 3 points higher on the HPFF questionnaire. Please note: the temptation may be great to mention text similar to the HPFF characteristics in the answer, for example "The implementation of improvements is then tackled in a structured manner within our finance function." However, try to describe what that structured approach will look like. Check also whether the picture you are painting actually entices you to look forward to becoming an HPFF, whether the picture does feel like the start of "a bright shining future"? After 30 minutes, the carousel starts again.

Instruction Break-Out 3: Describing What Was Done to Become an HPFF

Each group again deals with the same HPFF factor as in break-outs 1 and 2. The purpose of this final break-out is to identify what you have done (or what you have stopped doing) as a finance function in order to arrive at the situation where you score highly on your HPFF factor. So you put yourself in the situation you described in break-out 2. That is now a given. Use all the discussion time to describe what has happened since the HPFF diagnosis and this workshop to arrive at this high-performing situation where you are an HPFF. Questions to answer are: What did you do or stop doing to make your factor high-performing? What resources and how much time did you need to become high-performing? How did you keep the rest of the organization informed and included? How did you successfully implement HPFF? The final carousel starts again after 30 minutes.

After the third carousel, all participants come together in a plenary session to jointly review the results of the three break-outs, to reflect on them, to identify the most urgent actions, and to agree on the next steps. The HPFF workshop is concluded with a drink to chat informally and have some additional group bonding.[3]

Fourth Step: Executing and Monitoring the Actions

In step 4, the actions from the HPFF transformation action plan are executed. A review/preview meeting takes place every quarter to review the progress of the implementation of the HPFF transformation action plan, and to discuss which actions will be taken in the coming quarter. To evaluate the progress made by the finance function toward becoming an HPFF, a second HPFF diagnosis is performed 18 to 24 months later. The activities within this step are the same as in the first steps. The purpose of this second diagnosis is not only to "officially" evaluate the progress that the implementation of the HPFF transformation action plan has resulted in, but also to provide additional and possibly new HPFF points for attention so that even more improvements can be made. In Chapter 9, we discuss the HPFF transformation process in more detail.

7.2 THE HPFF DIAGNOSIS IN PRACTICE

What does an HPFF diagnosis and workshop look like in practice? To illustrate them, we turn to the example of an organization that embarked on an HPFF transformation, which started with conducting an HPFF diagnosis. We describe their story on the basis of an interview that was conducted with the CFO of this organization.[4]

Introduction

As part of the process of becoming a high-performing organization (HPO), Vesteda's finance function decided to transform its finance department into an HPFF. According Vesteda's CFO: "Vesteda wants to be the best landlord in the Netherlands. This also includes a best-in-class finance organization."

Vesteda is a Dutch residential real estate investor focusing on the mid-rental segment in economically strong areas and metropolitan regions. The organization invests money from institutional investors, such as pension funds and insurers, into more than 27,000 homes. It employs approximately 240 people, 45 of whom work in the financial and business support function. In 2013 Vesteda embarked on the process of becoming an HPO. Since then, the finance function of Vesteda has become engaged in the transformation into an HPFF. Just before the COVID-19 lockdown, the complete Finance and Control department attended an HPFF workshop. Vesteda's CFO is quoted as saying "It takes quite a few years for an organization to transform into an HPO. For a few years now, we have been working on a number of processes that should lead to this. Ultimately, you have to score an 8.5 on all HPO factors for a number of years in a row. We are not yet at that, but we are making a move toward 8.5. And, if we ultimately want to become HPO, Finance and Control (F&C) must also achieve a higher score."

To One Location

Until 2016, Vesteda was operating from three locations, with its head office in Amsterdam-Zuidas; Property Management in Amsterdam Southeast; and Finance, IT, HR, and part of the Operations departments in the Dutch town of Maastricht. Vesteda's CFO: "In 2016, it was decided to close the Maastricht office and transfer all activities to Amsterdam. Only a very limited number of people made the transfer to the one office in Amsterdam, so a whole new Finance and Control department had to be set up. All processes were initially transferred one-to-one into the new finance organization. Ultimately, the whole of Vesteda was physically brought together in 2017. Apart from our employees in the various regions of the Netherlands, we now all work from Amsterdam. We are on the first floor in one of our own apartment complexes, so with our tenants living directly above us."

New ERP System

"With the move to Amsterdam, we also chose to implement a new ERP system. This took us about two years, including the choice of the package and all the preparations for the actual implementation. That took place in June 2020," the CFO outlines an important milestone in the run-up to the decision to become an HPFF. "It was a logical part of the transformation we already started in 2013 and a logical extension of a number of improvement processes, including the start of a completely new F&C organization. In recent years we have invested a lot in the organizational side, with new systems and processes. Now was the time to pay more attention to the employee side."

Improvement Initiatives Often Lose Momentum

Vesteda has gone through a number of improvement initiatives in recent years. At many companies, such initiatives get bogged down over time. There are always differing priorities and other day-to-day concerns. "The great thing about HPO and HPFF is that these give you frameworks to link those improvement initiatives," the CFO replies when asked why the choice to embark on an HPFF transformation was made. "HPFF is part of the HPO initiative within Vesteda, it is a logical part of it. Everyone understands that. In addition, André de Waal's team has conducted a lot of research at other organizations, so that you can compare yourself. That way you know how you are doing. And a lot of thought has gone into how you can implement the frameworks in an organization. With the five HPFF factors and a very clear methodology it is easy to assign actions to people within the organization. This gives you very concrete tools for improvement actions."

Workshop with the Complete Team

At the beginning of 2020, Vesteda and all its departments received an HPO score from the latest HPO diagnosis conducted at the organization. This score showed that Finance and Control strongly needed to

Figure 2. HPFF scores for Vesteda F&C

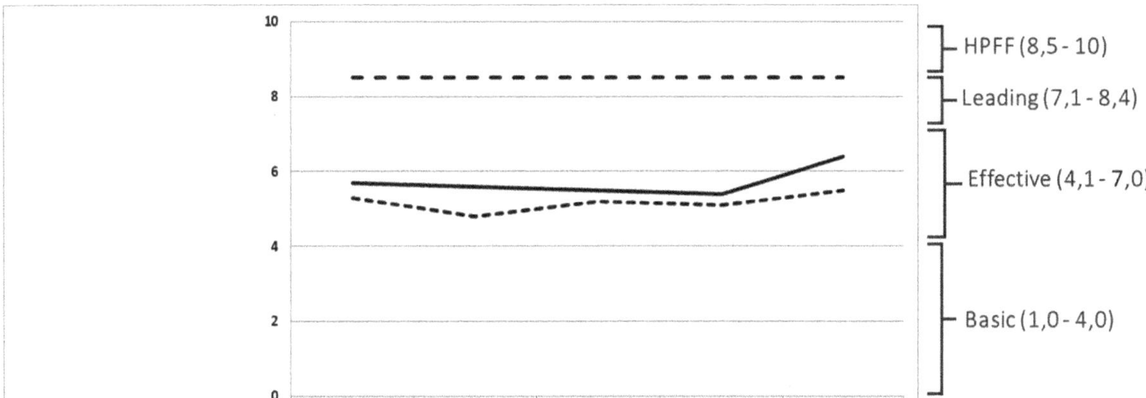

	Finance Function Improvement	IT Focus	Personal Development	Role Clarity	Strategic Role
HPFF (AVG=8.5)	8,5	8,5	8,5	8,5	8,5
Vesteda (n=47, AVG=5.2, PERF=5.7)	5,3	4,8	5,2	5,1	5,5
HPFF database Dutch financial functions (n=597, AVG=5.7, PERF=6.3)	5,7	5,6	5,5	5,4	6,4

make a change to its way of working to obtain a higher score. Vesteda's CFO said: "With a few senior managers we thought about how we could give substance to a workshop with the finance team. For this purpose, we used the HPFF framework and scored the department on the five HPFF factors." The workshop was then organized for the entire team at the beginning of March—just before the lockdown. The morning was spent discussing the results of the HPFF diagnosis (see Figure 2).

And then the team went to work in groups with the questions: 1. What do the results of the diagnosis mean? 2. What does our ideal finance function look like? 3. Which actions do we need to achieve this ideal? "The great added value of this workshop is that you have the whole group together," says the CFO. "And that everyone has a say about issues they encounter, areas for improvement they see and how we can ultimately become a better finance function. You see different people from the organization who stand up to tell their story, or who moderate parts of the workshop. That is very nice to see. You get a lot of dialogue. That alone is already a very good outcome of the day."

Getting Started on the Transformation

The team that prepared the HPFF workshop also took over the follow-up from the workshop. All outcomes for each HPFF factor were discussed and detailed and the team created a spreadsheet with all actions. "Then we drew up an action plan, per HPFF factor and with a time schedule," says the CFO. "At the beginning of July, the action plan was completed and we shared it with all finance employees in a virtual meeting via Teams. The presentation was very concrete: What are the results and what are we going to do with them? We invited people to participate in drafting the plans and a number of people actually signed up for this after the meeting. We also had good reactions to the presentations and the next steps we had identified. A follow-up meeting was held in October to provide feedback on which initiatives have been launched: What have we promised? What have we done? It is of course not the case that everything will be resolved next month. But we try to involve the group and give a lot of feedback about the actions we are taking. And hopefully as many people as possible want to get involved. Then they can also see that something is really happening with their input."

What Are the Improvements?

The improvement measures in the action plan are categorized for each HPFF factor. What kind of improvement measures does the plan deliver, in concrete terms? Vesteda's CFO: "There are still some short-term improvement points from the ERP implementation, things that are not going well yet and which need to be improved. Next to this, in the area of HR personal development is very important. We have already started a Real drives program. This helps teams member to get to know each other better by understanding their motivations. A person can be very much about structures, the other wants to speed things up, the third person focuses more on connecting in the team. If you know each other's motives, you can better assign certain tasks to individual team members and you can complement each other better. Continuous improvement is another important point of attention. We should definitely score better on that. There is now a Quality and Improvement team that will play a major role in this. For example, by creating specific performance dashboards with performance indicators and by implementing all kinds of improvement actions. And by ensuring that these improvements are actually implemented. Because many people see all kinds of improvement opportunities, you notice that again in the HPFF workshop, but those improvement initiatives are not always reflected in daily practice. Or they are limited to the department, while you want to implement them broadly in the organization, you really have to think beyond just your own department."

Awareness

A side effect is the awareness of the role of finance in the organization, says the CFO. "We want to ensure that people learn more about the processes across the organization. And also start to better understand the impact certain actions of one department have on other departments. This needs more training and knowledge sharing within the organization. And raising the profile of the finance function within the organization. There are also a number of plans for this to happen."

And What About the Business?

Until now the HPFF transformation has been a process of Finance and Control. Can you handle something like this without the business? Isn't there also a role for the operational managers? The CFO says: "We also asked ourselves that question when we started this. For optimization of F&C, shouldn't you also have a score on how the rest of the organization views F&C? We have decided that is the next step in the process. It would be good to do that in a year's time. What we did do, was to invite the Operations Director to the HPFF workshop. She was present all day and is also on the team to roll out the plans. In this way the business is very clearly represented."

Positive Vibe

"It still takes some blood, sweat, and tears," says Vesteda's CFO. "But the great thing is that there is a positive vibe noticeable after the HPFF workshop. We show that we take the improvements seriously.

And at the same time take the issue of, for example, the ERP implementation seriously. It is therefore also important that after presenting the plans in July, we continue to provide regular feedback on how we are doing. Involve people. And celebrate successes!"

Vesteda's Finance Function One Year Later[5]

Figure 3. Scores for the finance function of Vesteda, for the first and second HPFF diagnoses

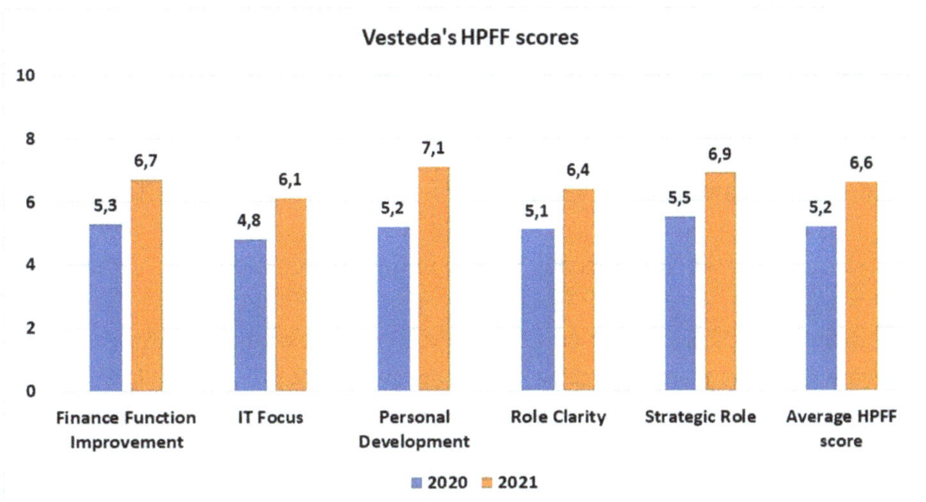

In order to evaluate the progress of the HPFF transformation after one year Vesteda's finance function decided to conduct an abbreviated HPFF diagnosis. For this the HPFF questionnaire was simplified to a limited number of questions which could be answered quickly by the team. These questions basically all had the same design: "To what extent do you think that we as Vesteda's finance function are on the right track in the area of <HPFF factor>? Team members could score this on a scale of 1 ("we are not well on our way") to 10 ("we are doing very well"). The resulting scores for the HPFF factors are given in Figure 3.

During a conversation with Vesteda's CFO and two staff members we discussed the considerable improvement (+27%)[6] in scores and the lessons learned. These are the highlights of that conversation:

- The improvement in HPFF scores can be directly attributed to the activities deployed after the workshop in 2020. Team members now feel ánd are more involved, they really want to know the results of the improvement activities undertaken by their colleagues, and they also want to be kept updated on the progress of HPFF improvement activities. The implementation of the new ERP system has helped considerably in this respect, although implementing the new system during the COVID pandemic (with most employees working from home) had been quite a challenge. Now most of the implementation issues have been resolved and many improvements were realized in the software, more cooperation across the finance teams and throughout the complete organization (which is required because of the use of an integrated system) can be noticed. Team members are also faster inclined to involve people from other non-finance departments so improvement activities are not restricted to just the finance function but affect and support the complete organization.

- Within the teams an awareness and feeling is growing that the finance function is indeed *one* function which should operate as an integrated team toward the other departments in Vesteda. Also pride is growing about what the finance function is achieving and how it contributes to the success of Vesteda. Movies were made in which one person of each team in the finance function talks about what the team has done regarding the HPFF transformation and what specific actions they are particularly proud of.
- Because of HPFF factor Personal Development team members realized the importance of their continued development. They are looking in the organization on what is on offer with respect to training programs. An attention point here is that there should be continued attention to aligning individual interests with the needs of Vesteda.
- After the HPFF workshop project leaders for each of the HPFF factors were appointed. These project leaders are responsible for the progress of the improvement of "their" factor. After the second HPFF diagnosis the results and remarks made were discussed with all team members, and successes were celebrated. Subsequently a more in-depth discussion took place among the project leaders about the suggestions for improvements and possible quick wins. From this discussion follow-on actions were formulated which were then shared with the team. Examples of follow-on actions are the daily team starts to which colleagues from other Vesteda teams are frequently welcomed, and an internal customer satisfaction survey where the F&C department entered into the dialogue with colleagues from other Vesteda departments to further improve the F&C activities. Also project leaders are developing knowledge sessions on the new ERP system to improve expertise of the system's functionalities throughout Vesteda.
- Once per month the project leaders get together to review the progress made regarding the HPFF improvement activities. Every quarter there is a plenary feedback with the complete team about the HPFF transformation progress. These meetings are increasingly interactive, in the sense that people are emphatically asked for their input, ideas and suggestions about current and future improvement activities, and how they feel they can contribute to these.
- Within each team of the finance function there have been workshops to increase the knowledge of the team members about HPFF and the improvement activities, and to help develop a high performance mindset within members. In these sessions team goals were jointly set, key performance indicators with which to track progress on the goals were developed, dashboards were created so the indicators could be made visually, and discussions took place on how to use the dashboards (for learning purposes, not for settling scores or giving people negative reviews). This new way of working has been very well received by the team.

Lessons learned were:

- Keep people informed, conduct regular update meetings, make sure that people know what everybody is doing, and make sure these meetings are interactive with lots of participation. This increases participation and commitment to the HPFF transformation.
- The five HPFF factors turn out to be a great umbrella for structuring and planning of improvement activities in the finance function, and for informing team members about what is going on in the function.

- Make sure as management to not impose improvement activities on the team, instead develop these together with team members. Also make the translation of HPFF to operational daily activities together with the team, so HPFF becomes very practical but also easy to understand for team members what it is and how it contributes to daily life in the organization.
- A difficult point is to keep making time for the improvement activities. Therefore try to incorporate these improvements as much a possible in daily activities. Also make sure that team member know they are "allowed" to spend time on improving.

CASE: The HPFF Diagnosis - Not a Judgement but a Development Tool

Telecom Ltd. is a subsidiary of a large telecom multinational operating worldwide with several thousand employees. The company has faced severe challenges over the past decade because of the increasing convergence between fixed and mobile networks and services, the arrival of international players such as Netflix and YouTube that have a significant impact on internet use and data traffic, and more fragmented and rapidly changing viewing behavior: the fierce competition in the telecom sector is undeniable. In the meantime, the market for television, internet, and (fixed and mobile) telephony is becoming more and more mature. Telecom companies are optimizing their products at an accelerated pace, for example by launching new and more extensive bundles and new services via various platforms. If Telecom Ltd. wants to grow and innovate even more, the company must look at new growth areas where it has traditionally been less strong. The chosen growth strategy has been, and will be in the foreseeable future, to take over smaller competitors and incorporate these into the existing organization.

In order to keep up with the rapidly expanding organization, the finance function of Telecom Ltd. several years ago initiated the program 'Staying ahead.' The goal of this program was to create a finance function that could better cope with changes in the organization and market (such as acquisitions, new tooling) and thus better fulfill the role of business partner. It was necessary to change the finance function from a position that monitors and consolidates financial data, i.e., a score keeper, into a proactive player: a position that was not only a business partner, but, above all, a business challenger who added value and was a source of practical insights and the guardian of processes. The plan was tailored to the roles that a financial function should fulfill: that of steward (audit and compliance), operator (transactional accounting), catalyst (providing analyses to the business), and strategist (looking forward to the future). Included in 'Staying ahead' was addressing systems in order to become more efficient and effective. Two initiatives in this respect were the implementation of a new ERP system and of an integrated planning system.

The HPFF Diagnosis

As part of the rollout of 'Staying ahead,' the finance function faced many operational challenges. For example, there were the acquisitions of the competitors and associated integrations of systems, and completely new and different reporting expectations as a result of the changing market and needs of management and shareholders. Not only did this delay the planning of system improvements and the implementation of the ERP system, it also put increased pressure on the finance function. In order to better understand where the priorities of the finance function should lie in the coming year and to gain insight into how far the function was on the way to the HPFF, the CFO decided to perform an HPFF diagnosis, whose results are given in Figure 4.

Figure 4. The HPO diagnosis results for Telecom Ltd.

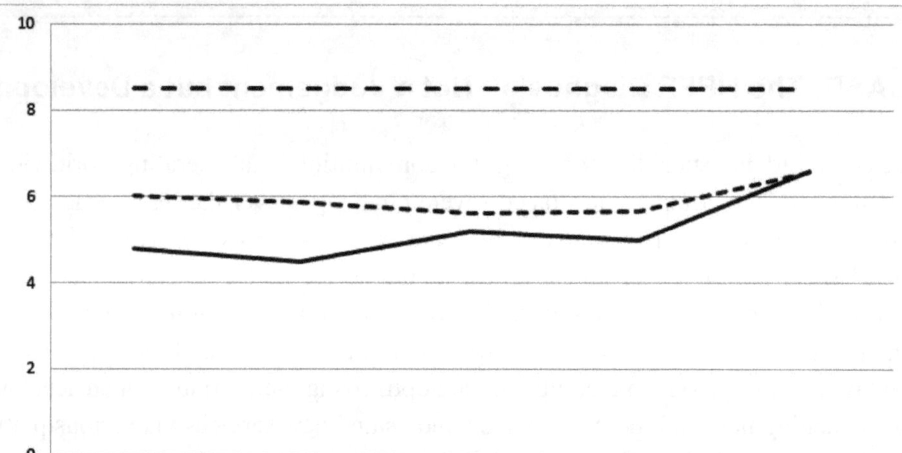

	Finance Function Improvement	IT Focus	Personal Development	Role Clarity	Strategic Role
HPFF (AVG>=8.5)	8,5	8,5	8,5	8,5	8,5
Telecom (n=148, AVG=5.2, PRES=6.01)	4,8	4,5	5,2	5,0	6,6
HPFF database (AVG=6.0, PERF=6.5)	6,0	5,9	5,6	5,7	6,6

Figure 4 shows that Telecom Ltd.'s scores are more or less in line with the scores in the HPFF database. However, steps still need to be taken in terms of efficiency and IT focus, mainly to be achieved by the next development phase in which system implementations and the introduction of clear processes will take place.

An Interesting HPFF Workshop

The results of the HPFF diagnosis were discussed during a workshop with representation of Telecom Ltd.'s finance function. An interesting thing happened during this workshop: after a brief introduction of both the HPO and HPFF frameworks and the HPFF diagnosis process, we presented the graph as depicted in Figure 4. At that very moment, the CFO, who had been delayed in a previous meeting, entered the room and saw the graph projected on the wall. Immediately he exploded into a loud objection against these results, demanding how we dared to label his finance function as "bad" with a score of 5.2; he added that, in fact, his people in the finance function were top-notch and very hard-working and did not deserve to be deemed a "weak department." After he had calmed down a bit, we replied that we were in total agreement with him. In fact, the diagnosis showed the extraordinary effort his financial professionals had put into, despite the rapid successive acquisitions in which procedures, systems, and reporting mechanism had to be integrated, still delivering the outputs (in the form of management reports and financial statements) in time and with sufficient quality. What the HPFF diagnosis also revealed, however, was that because of this "blood, sweat, and tears" way of operating, his financial professionals clearly had had no time whatsoever to spend on improving and strengthening the finance function toward a higher quality-level and a less stressful environment. Thus, the 5.2 did not denote an insufficient mark but the current status of his finance function: 52% on the way to HPFF. After all, the HPO diagnosis is not a judgment tool but a development tool as it indicates the areas of the finance function that need to be further developed and strengthened. The financial professionals present immediately agreed with us and took the opportunity to voice their strong desire to start working on an HPFF transformation as soon as possible.

In the discussion that followed, several attention points were agreed upon which the finance function had to take into account during the next phase of 'Staying ahead':

- The process improvement method had to be optimized. Because the new systems were not yet sufficiently implemented, the finance function continued to "put out bush fires," leaving too little time for structural improvement. More structured time therefore had to urgently be made available for improvement activities. Attention also had to be paid to training financial professionals in improvement management, and work should be done on the development of an improvement culture in which managers should take the lead ("lead by example").
- To accelerate automation, a good ICT architecture was needed that would be the basis from which to develop an HPFF. The full roll-out of the new ERP system was planned for the end of that year, which should already provide a significant improvement in this respect. Other priorities were the roll-out of the financial planning tool and further automation of the finance function.
- A third point was focused improvement of the processes. Every HPFF has a reliable foundation of good processes; and this is essential before automation can properly take place. The finance function had to rapidly achieve this before the ERP implementation could be commenced. In addition, achieving fluent processes would give financial employees more time to work on activities that provide added value to the business.
- More attention was also needed for the role of the finance function within the organization. In recent years, the focus had been mainly on absorbing the extra workload created by the acquisitions, and therefore less on creating an optimal structure for the financial function within the wider organization.
- The fifth and final point was to further increase the added value of the financial function for the business. The finance function could be even more proactive toward the business by creating added value together with the business in a structured way. This was important to continue to guarantee the satisfaction of the internal customer.

The result of the HPO diagnosis was in line with the vision of the financial professionals of Telecom Ltd. in regard to the structure of their finance function necessary to start the transformation into an HPFF first, and, second, the attention points for the (near) future. Telecom Ltd.'s finance function clearly was high-performing in terms of output, but, at the same time, had a fair way to go to better structure its efforts to achieve this output. Furthermore, because of the almost constantly changing regulations and tougher competition, the financial professionals realized that it was important to stay sharp both now and in the future. They therefore emphasize that if they could be given the necessary time and space, they could definitely fulfil the potential for further improvement.

CASE: Multinational - The HPFF Framework as Organizational Glue

A multinational had grown considerably in recent years through a large number of acquisitions, making it one of the largest companies in the industry. Integrating so many new organizations, each with their own working method and culture, required a lot of energy and caused quite a few "growing pains." The finance function was not immune to this. Because of the many different data and reporting systems, the reporting and consolidation process was a daunting task every month and quarter. What did not help in this respect was that the finance function was geographically dispersed, had a different maturity level in each country, and that language and cultural differences often led to misunderstandings. To deal with this, the management of the finance function in the holding company had organized a first meeting for the Top 50 of the financial professionals working in the multinational two years ago. This meeting turned out to be a success because these financial professionals got to know each other better. According to the CFO, it was now time for the next development step: setting a joint agenda for improvement.

To achieve this, the HPFF questionnaire was sent to all local finance functions with the request to have it completed by all financial professionals. Financial professionals at the holding also took part in the survey. The results were summarized in HPFF graphs for the total finance function, and by continent and country, and presented at a joint global meeting. Subsequently, the financial professionals present were divided into groups per continent to discuss the results and formulate improvement actions for the finance function located in that continent. These actions were presented to the other groups, after which a lively discussion arose about the usefulness and necessity of the various actions, and whether they should be taken locally or for the entire finance function. The result of the meeting was a joint improvement agenda in which joint priorities were set for all finance functions worldwide and for head office. This significantly strengthened the "bonding" in the multinational's finance team, which was important for the implementation of the ambitious improvement agenda.

Table 4. The four levels of operation al maturity of the finance function.

Development stage / Aspect	Stable *(foundational)*	Efficient *(automated)*	Predictive *(insight-driven)*	Future-ready *(intelligent)*
Technology	Foundational tools and technologies	Robotic automation with workflow capabilities	Advanced data science	AI, cloud and blockchain enabled
Talent	Human-only workforce	Machines augment humans for select processes	Machines augment humans for majority of processes	Knowledge workers focusing on judgement-based work; agile workforce at scale
Processes	Non-standardized and fragmented	Industry- and function-leading practices applied selectively	Industry- and function-leading practices applied widely	End-to-end digitized and transformed processes
Data	Siloed or incomplete	Aggregated at the organizational level	Leveraging analytics to drive data insights	AI at scale using divers data
← Transactional/incremental →			← Strategic / transformational →	

REFERENCES

Agarwal, S., & Shroff, M. (2021). *Elevate every decision with intelligent finance operations, fast-track to future-ready performance*. Accenture.

Jalink, A. (2020). Frits Vervoort, CFO Vesteda, over de weg naar HPFF: 'Je krijgt heel veel dialoog. Alleen dat is al winst'. *CM, 9*. https://cmweb.nl/2020/11/frits-vervoort-cfo-vesteda-over-de-weg-naar-hpff-je-krijgt-heel-veel-dialoog-alleen-dat-is-al-winst/

ENDNOTES

1 Agarwal and Shroff (2021) use an alternative model for the HPFF development stages which they call "the four levels of operational maturity" and which are depicted in Table 4.

2 The HPFF workshop can also take place virtually, by using virtual break-out rooms offered by most virtual meeting applications. The plenary parts of the workshop take place in a central virtual meeting.

3 This is of course post-COVID-19!

4 This interview was published in Jalink (2020) and translated and published in our book with kind permission of CM: and Mrs. Jalink.

5 This section is based on an interview we conducted with Vesteda's CFO and two staff members, held 1½ years after the initial HPFF diagnosis took place.

6 The interviewees stated that they are well aware that the adjusted measurement method (with the abbreviated questionnaire) may have influenced the figures positively, but they certainly see a positive trend in Vesteda's finance function. In addition, they remarked that the lower scores received in the first survey were due to the fact that the F&C department at that time had only just be created and a large number of new employees were not yet familiar with all processes.

Chapter 8
Current HPFF State of Finance Functions

ABSTRACT

Since the development of the HPFF framework, extensive data collection by means of the HPFF diagnosis has taken place. This makes it possible to discuss how far in general finance functions are on the road to high performance. In this chapter, the average HPFF scores of finance functions worldwide are given, and the reasons for these scores are discussed. Potential courses of action for improving and strengthening finance functions are described. This chapter concludes with a discussion of a specific improvement opportunity: measuring and increasing internal customer satisfaction with the finance function.

8.1 AVERAGE HPFF SCORES OF FINANCE

Figure 1 shows the mean scores for the HPFF factors as averaged from all the responses on the HPFF questionnaire collected in the HPFF database,[1] while Figure 2 depicts the average severity of the obstacles finance functions encounter while striving to become an HPFF. Table 1 shows the detailed scores for the HPFF characteristics and the finance function performance characteristics.

The total average score of 6.0 for the finance functions in the HPFF database (AVG in Figure 1) and a performance of 6.5 (PERF in Figure 1) show that the 1,094 respondents of the HPFF questionnaire consider their finance function to be 60% on the way to high performance. This score illustrates our earlier claim that many finance functions are (still) driven by "blood, sweat, and tears" to meet the information requirements of internal users, external stakeholders, and the (external) accountant. This is underscored by the fact that the highest scoring HPFF factor is 'Strategic Role' (5.6 in Figure 1), indicating that finance functions manage to provide their internal clients with at least satisfactory service. The business is very important to the finance function so it does its utmost to meet the wishes and requirements of the operation. But because the finance function is not efficient, which can be seen in the lower scores for the other four HPFF factors which are far from the high-performance level (yet), this tends to take a lot of effort. As a result, the financial professionals work hard to serve the internal and external customers, but that places a great deal of strain on them because the resources at their disposal are not optimal for

DOI: 10.4018/978-1-7998-6929-0.ch008

this. The total average score of 6.0 also determines that the average finance function is in the "effective" stage; this score indicates that this finance function is able to fulfill all its (internal and external) reporting and processing requirements and also has some time left for improving the processes in the function itself (but is not yet able to or has the time to help other departments to improve).

Figure 1. Average HPFF scores for the finance functions collected in the HPFF database

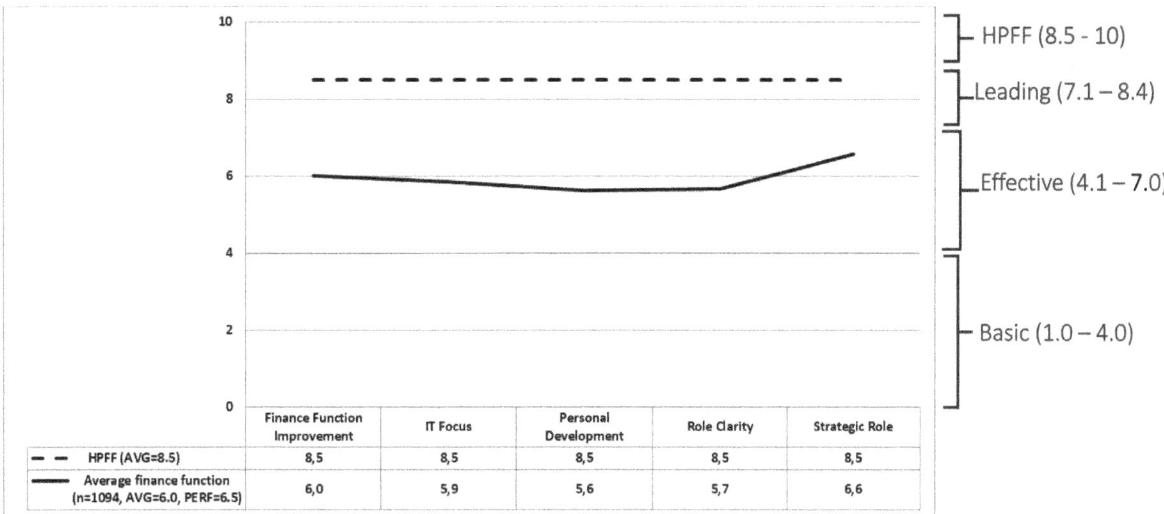

	Finance Function Improvement	IT Focus	Personal Development	Role Clarity	Strategic Role
HPFF (AVG=8.5)	8,5	8,5	8,5	8,5	8,5
Average finance function (n=1094, AVG=6.0, PERF=6.5)	6,0	5,9	5,6	5,7	6,6

Figure 2. Severity of the obstacles finance functions encounter

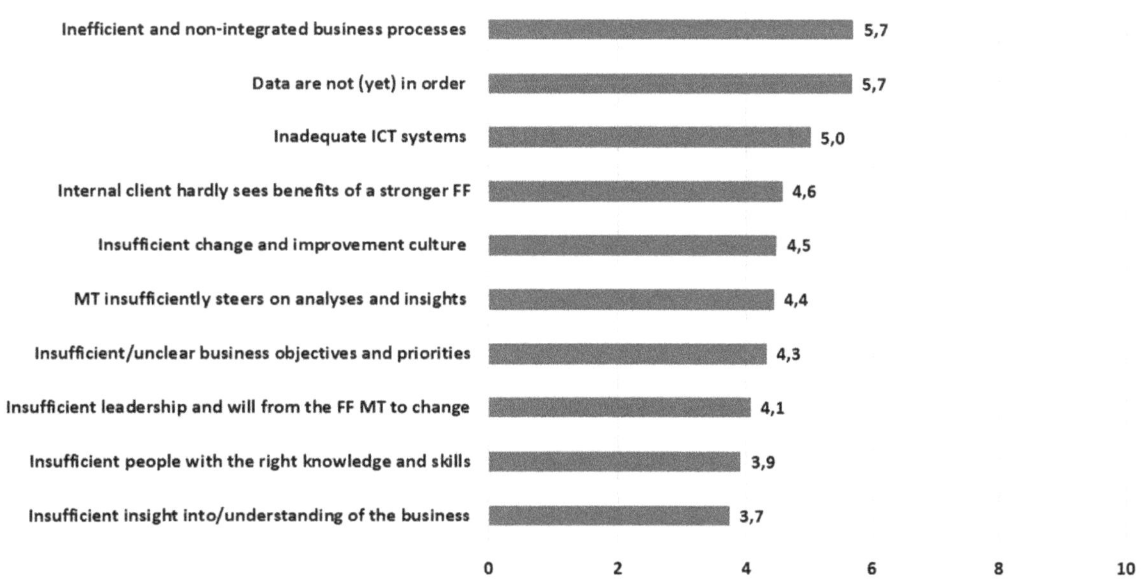

Table 1. Scores for the HPFF and Finance function Performance characteristics

HPFF factor	No.	HPFF characteristics	Score
Finance Function Improvement	1	In the finance function, improvement efforts are tracked and evaluated using performance indicators	5,4
Finance Function Improvement	2	In the finance function, improvements are implemented in a structured way	6,2
Finance Function Improvement	3	In the past year, financials have had enough time to make their work activities more efficient and effective	6,1
Finance Function Improvement	4	In the finance function, implementing improvements is actively encouraged	7,1
Finance Function Improvement	5	In the finance function, processes are executed as much as possible in a uniform way and in one place, so that expertise about these processes is bundled and centralized	6,3
Finance Function Improvement	6	In the organization, managers engage in financial self-service	5,1
IT Focus	7	The finance function is capable of implementing the latest IT software	5,6
IT Focus	8	In the finance function, all routine processes have been fully automated	5,4
IT Focus	9	The finance function has (a lot of) IT application knowledge	6,1
IT Focus	10	The finance function has sufficient budget at its disposal each year to accelerate automation and digitalization of the function	5,8
IT Focus	11	In the finance function, automation and digitalization have a high priority	6,7
IT Focus	12	The finance function is aware of the current and newest applications and possibilities of IT software	5,7
IT Focus	13	The finance function spends less and less time on routine activities	5,9
Personal Development	14	In the past year, financials have followed sufficient technical training to be able to excel in their work activities	5,7
Personal Development	15	In the past year, financials have followed sufficient personal development training to be able to excel in their work activities	5,9
Personal Development	16	In the finance function, everyone has a personal development plan	5,3
Role Clarity	17	In the finance function, there is a clear description of the behavioral requirements for each financial role	6,0
Role Clarity	18	In the finance function, there is a clear description of the technical requirements for each financial role	6,2
Role Clarity	19	In the finance function, there are specific development programs for each financial role	4,9
Strategic Role	20	The finance function is seen as an important partner during strategic discussions	6,7
Strategic Role	21	The finance function has important input in each decision of strategic importance	6,4
Strategic Role	22	Other departments regularly spontaneously ask the finance function for advice when taking important decisions	6,5
Strategic Role	23	The finance function is actively involved in all the important processes conducted in the organization	6,5
Strategic Role	24	The finance function actively searches for possibilities for cooperation and collaboration with the business	6,8
Strategic Role	25	The finance function performs more and more value-adding activities for the business	6,7

continues on following page

Table 1. Continued

HPFF factor	No.	HPFF characteristics	Score
Strategic Role	26	The finance function, together with the business, regularly examines possibilities to create more value-adding activities for operations	6,8
Strategic Role	27	The finance function proactively adapts prognoses on the basis of important developments	6,7
Strategic Role	28	The latest prognoses, as developed by the finance function, are given priority during important management decision-making	6,2
Finance Function Performance	a	The internal customer is very satisfied with the finance function.	6,7
Finance Function Performance	b	Financials themselves are very satisfied with the finance function.	6,7
Finance Function Performance	c	The finance function is very efficient.	6,2
Finance Function Performance	d	The finance function always has an important say in the decision-making process that takes place in the organization.	6,6
Finance Function Performance	e	The finance function is highly effective.	6,5

The Meaning of The HPFF Scoring Scale

Because the HPFF questionnaire uses a measurement scale of 1 to 10, one could be inclined to consider an average HPFF score below 6.0 to be relatively unsatisfactory. After all, if you get a 4.5 on your school report card this clearly is an unsatisfactory mark which does not earn you any plaudits. However, there is no good or bad in an HPO or HPFF, there just "is." This means that an average HPFF score of 4.5 is not an unsatisfactory or bad; rather it indicates that the finance function is 45% on its way to the high-performance level. You could and should have a discussion as to why this is not 60 or 70% and this discussion should lead you to the root causes of the score so you know what improvements to make. The discussion should not lead you to putting the blame at individuals or circumstances. It is a fact-finding mission, aimed at gathering information to make considered decisions about what to tackle first in order to raise the quality of the finance function to a high-performance level. Having said this, circumstances *in* the organization do matter, as Figure 2 highlights. Three obstacles score 5.0 or higher, indicating that the finance function has to deal with at least three severe obstacles on its way to becoming an HPFF. Another five obstacles score in the 4-point range, indicating that these also need attention.

There might be several reasons for the fact that the average finance function has not yet come close to achieving the high-performance level. The most probable reason is that in previous years there has been little time to improve, given that the finance function only came round to considering this after the aftermath of the financial and economic crises had been dealt with—a situation that has not really improved in recent times because of COVID-19! Moreover, the improvements that have been made might not have sufficiently borne fruit as of yet because they are so recent. Another reason may be that finance functions did not know exactly where to improve, given that, as stated earlier, there is no consensus on this in the literature. Because of this lack of focus ("the hope-and-hit something scattergun approach"), the implemented improvement actions have had little effect. It also has to be noted that, in recent years, insufficient attention has been paid to the development of financial professionals on a structural basis, as a result of which their capacity to improve has lagged. Finally, Figure 2 shows that finance functions have to deal with several significant obstacles on their journey to becoming HPFFs. This can divert extensive resources that could have been used to strengthen the HPFF factors. In the subsequent sections, we look closer at possible reasons by asking finance experts for their opinion on this.

Differences Between Sectors

When we look at the HPFF scores for the different sectors and sizes of finance functions, and their organizations, and whether a finance function is part of a larger whole (such as a consortium or a multinational company), we see that there are few differences.

Figure 3 shows that the differences in HPFF scores for each sector are within a one-point range. More importantly, the shape of the scoring graphs is basically the same for all three sectors, meaning that it does not really matter in which sector respondents work—they see the same areas to be strengthened. Figure 4 shows a slightly bigger difference in the severity of the obstacles, with nonprofits and governments "suffering" from obstacles that are more severe than in the for-profit sector. An explanation could be the continuing pressure on cost reductions and budget cuts, which causes the nonprofit and government sectors to be able to invest less in addressing the obstacles (De Waal & Linker, 2021).

Differences in Sizes

Figure 3 shows that the differences in HPFF scores by size of the finance function are basically marginal. The scores are similar and the graphs have the same shape. In principle, this means that most finance functions have the same strengths and attention points. The conclusion could be that finance functions struggle with the same generic problems. Of course, the underlying causes of the HPFF scores differ for each individual finance function, and, furthermore, the severity of the obstacles they encounter will be different (as Figure 5 shows, especially for finance function with a size between 26 and 50 FTEs). However, it can be concluded from all these scores that finance functions, regardless of the type or size of the organization they are part of, still have a significant task for improvement in their attempt to becoming an HPFF. It would be beneficial if they helped each other in this regard, in terms of learning from each other: this is something we discuss in the next section.

8.2 DISCUSSING THE HPFF SCORES

In several meetings with financial professionals, we discussed the outcomes presented in the previous section. The overall conclusion from those discussions is that the time has come, now that the COVID-19 pandemic is coming to an end, to start devoting structural attention to strengthening the finance function in order to transform it into an HPFF. Financial professionals will have to take the lead in this regard and be more assertive toward the rest of the organization in order to make it clear that a strong finance function is vital to the high-performing organization. Below is a summary, per HPFF factor, of the discussions about the HPFF scores, including possible improvement actions, as derived from the discussions.

HPFF Factor 'Finance Function Improvement' (score 6.0)

The financial professionals agree that, in general, too little time is made available to improve the finance function, and that deadlines are mainly met by "running hard". In addition, too little time is spent collecting information on what the business really needs from the finance function. This means there is a considerable risk that the finance function is spending too much time and effort on certain issues that operational managers may not be interested in at all. Another observation is that the "blood, sweat,

Figure 3. HPFF scores per sector (profit, nonprofit, government)

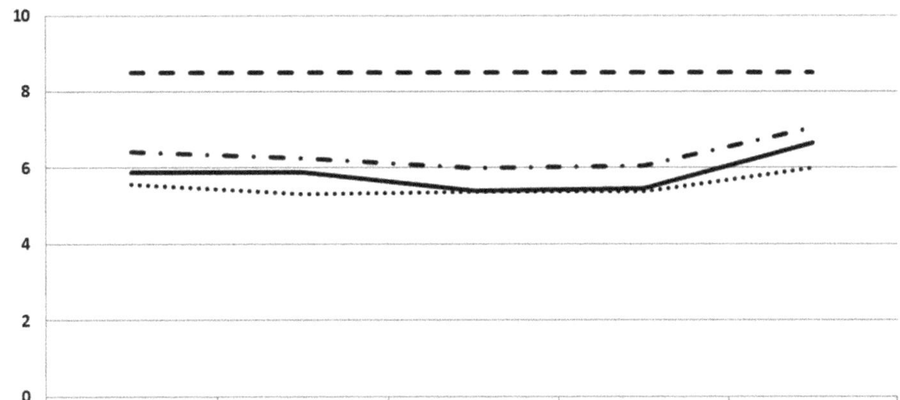

	Finance Function Improvement	IT Focus	Personal Development	Role Clarity	Strategic Role
HPFF (AVG=8.5)	8,5	8,5	8,5	8,5	8,5
Profit (n=460, AVG=6.4, PERF=6.9)	6,4	6,3	6,0	6,1	7,0
Nonprofit (n=262, AVG=5.9, PERF=6.5)	5,9	5,9	5,4	5,5	6,6
Government (n=354, AVG=5.5, PERF=6.1)	5,6	5,3	5,4	5,4	6,0

Figure 4. Severity of obstacles per sector (profit, nonprofit, government)

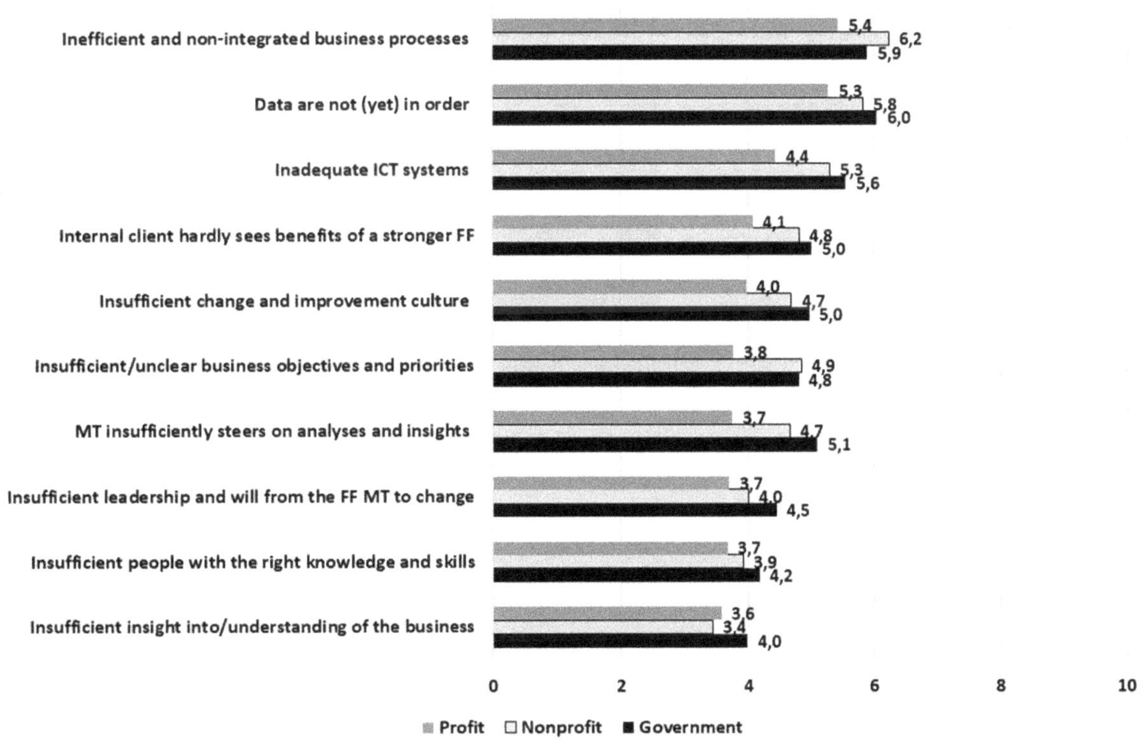

Figure 5. HPFF scores by finance function size (in FTE, full-time equivalents)

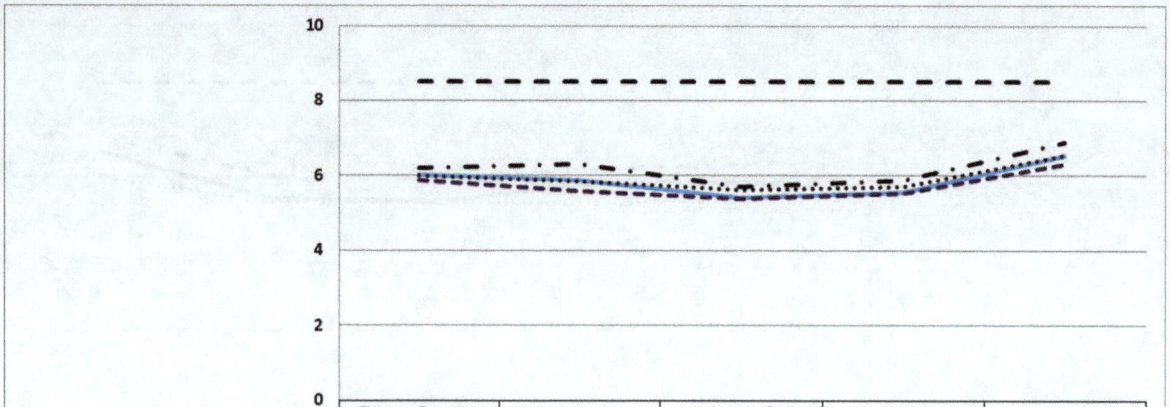

	Finance Function Improvement	IT Focus	Personal Development	Role Clarity	Strategic Role
HPFF (AVG=8.5)	8,5	8,5	8,5	8,5	8,5
<10 (n=167, AVG=6.2, PERF=6.9)	6,2	6,3	5,7	5,9	6,9
10-25 (n=197, AVG=5.9, PERF=6.6)	6,0	5,9	5,4	5,6	6,5
26-50 (n=106, AVG=5.7, PERF=6.4)	5,9	5,6	5,4	5,5	6,3
>50 (n=539, AVG=5.9, PERF=6.4)	6,0	5,8	5,6	5,7	6,6

Figure 6. Severity of obstacles by finance function size (in FTE, full-time equivalents)

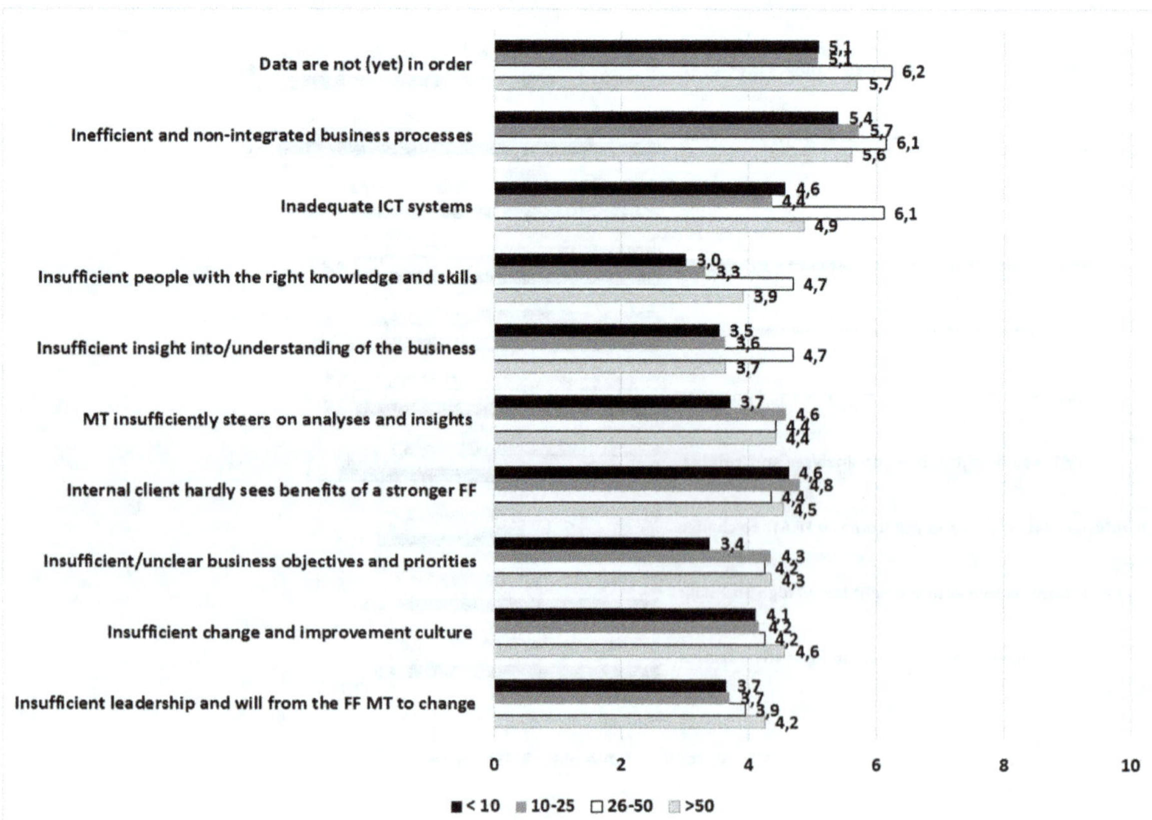

and tears" attitude is more or less ingrained in the DNA of financial professionals, which means that they will struggle through even if they have to drive with a "square wheel" (i.e., if they do not have the right tools to do their work efficiently). A suggestion for improvement is to measure internal customer satisfaction, discuss the results and identify improvements, make one financial responsible for each improvement, come to an agreement that there must be an improvement result within 90 days, and present progress each week during a "stand-up session." Another suggestion is to divide the improvement effort into small pieces of work and then improve one piece completely and ensure that the improvement is secured in the organization (for example by training the financial professionals in the new situation or working method). Only when this has been done satisfactorily should the next improvement be started. As a result, there will be slow but steady improvement in the finance function.

HPFF Factor 'IT Focus' (score 5.9)

The main reason that the IT situation of the finance function is so precarious, according to the financial professionals present, is that IT investment decisions mainly benefit the operation. So the operation automatically gets priority, which means that IT in the finance function receives relatively less attention and less budget. In addition, the aforementioned 'DNA' of the finance function ensures that, for example, if certain reports do not work with the current IT, the financial will set to work independently to produce those reports in a different way. As a result, the operation overlooks the limitations of the IT architecture of the finance function and logically pays little attention (and budget) to it. Add to this the fact that the IT department generally has little knowledge of what a finance function does and about the financial systems available on the market—again because the focus of the IT department is mainly on the operation—and it makes sense that the IT architecture of the finance function is lagging behind. The participants agreed that the way to change this situation is to talk to both the IT department and the operation about what is actually happening in the finance function and what role IT plays or should play in the function, in order to create more knowledge and understanding within the organization about the IT requirements of the finance function. For this, it is necessary that financial professionals strengthen their IT knowledge, so that they not only know "what is for sale on the IT market" but, above all, are also able to communicate with IT professionals.

HPFF Factors 'Personal Development' (score 5.6) and 'Role Clarity' (score 5.7)

During the discussion, an interesting distinction is made between managerial and operational financial professionals. According to the participating financial professionals, the first group often receives tailormade development programs for personal development, while the second group has to make do with training that is offered in a standardized way and often has to be taken only when this is necessary for the proper execution of the assigned tasks. There also seems to be a distinction between young new financial professionals who are offered and participate in a lot of training, while the older experienced financial professionals seem to be a little "forgotten" in this respect and therefore start lagging further behind in their development. In addition, the daily hustle and bustle and "issues of the day" play a big role, which means that too little time is spent on training. Often, financial professionals themselves do not feel like following training courses "because there is still so much to do, I have to focus on real work." The suggestion is that management of the finance function should structurally enter into dialogue with their people about what they need and what the organization needs from them. Managers must also regularly exert some pressure on their employees to ensure that they continue to develop themselves by following training courses and moving on to another position after a number of years. It helps to establish a "Finance Academy" aimed at developing the talents of employees, taking into account the organizational context in which they work.

For rotations within finance, one automotive company requires executives to have worked in a minimum of two divisions, two finance functions, and two countries before ascending to senior roles. Another automotive company requires senior finance leaders to rotate through non-finance roles. In both cases, the emphasis on building operational and leadership as well as technical finance capabilities is the important differentiating factor (Agrawal et al., 2020).

HPFF Factor 'Strategic Role' (score 6.6)

Concerning this HPFF factor, many questions are raised by the participating financial professionals, such as "We are increasingly being pushed toward the strategic role, but do we actually like that and are we actually really good at it?" and "What would happen if you, as a finance function, were no longer working hard and no longer produced all the reports, what would be the response of the operation?" The suggestion is to apply the "ESSA principle" to the latter: Eliminate reports, then Simplify reports and associated procedures, subsequently apply Standardization, and finally Automate the remaining situation. It is also noted that the influence of the CFO is important for the specific fulfillment of the strategic role and how active the finance function must be in it. This can be done by the CFO demonstrating exemplary behavior, propagating a vision of the HPFF, and aligning the vision of the finance function with that of the organization.

8.3 IMPROVEMENT OPPORTUNITIES

With the HPFF framework, it is possible, by examining the detailed scores of the HPFF characteristics in Table 1, to identify the main areas of focus for improvement. These are discussed below.

Make the Improvement Process Itself More Effective

In general, improvement is actively encouraged in the finance function, but financial professionals should be given more time to work on it. Improvement itself must also be tackled in a more structured way. The improvements should make it possible, among other things, for business managers to take care of their own financial information needs. This would make time for the finance function to undertake more improvement activities and to strengthen the strategic role, which will only increase satisfaction within the organization with the finance function.

> The finance function has activities with a regular rhythm of monthly, quarterly, and annual closings. It often turns out to be difficult to fit improvement initiatives into this annual agenda. To accommodate for the busy first months of the year, the finance function at one company shifted the work of the year-end closing process to November and December. A draft annual account and report are now being submitted to the board of directors at the beginning of December: "the Santa Claus version." In mid-December, the finance function will know which points for attention in the reporting still need to be addressed, so that accounting issues can be raised with the external auditor before Christmas. In this context, this company speaks of "peak shaving": activities are capped in busy periods and moved to quieter periods. By highlighting the workload, space is created for other activities and financial professionals can better manage their time throughout the year.

Strengthen IT Knowledge in the Finance Function

Advancing automation is already having major consequences for the work of the finance function, and this will only increase in the future. There is therefore an urgent need for the finance function to increase knowledge of software applications and new technologies that are available or soon to be released in the market that can support not only the finance function itself but also the rest of the organization. Knowledge about the applications and their effective use must also increase, which is important because the majority of IT implementations are still very difficult and not overly successful. More budget must be made available for ICT, among other things, to automate more routine activities.

> At this organization, the finance function always took a long time to provide information to management; moreover, it was information that was of little use to the operation. In addition, small inaccuracies often crept into the details of the reports, as a result of which conversations that should have actually been about decisions based on the figures degenerated into discussions about the correctness of those figures. The finance function at this company had little connection with the operation, thus creating a kind of "information black hole" in the company. To tackle this issue, the decision was made to hire a number of smart professionals who started working exclusively on increasing data quality. These professionals knew how to handle data well, delved into the systems to retrieve data from servers, linked them to other source systems, addressed questions, and made connections between sources to gain insight into the drivers of the business. In doing so, they combined business insight with data expertise, thus providing high-quality information that line managers were very happy with.

Increase the Quality of the Financial Professionals

The quality improvements necessary for the finance function to reach the HPFF level require structured development of the knowledge and skills of finance professionals. This means that every financial must develop a personal development plan, tailored to his or her role in the finance function. As long as there is structured and regular attention for the development of the employee, this plan does not necessarily have to be a written document. In addition, financial professionals must be given the time to actually follow training in technical and behavioral skills.

One of the organizations participating in the roundtable set up a development curriculum with a range of education and training courses, to facilitate its financial professionals in their learning and developing. This "Finance Academy," as it is called, contains many examples of activities that employees can learn from, but it is more than just a summary of training and education. It is a structured framework of learning interventions aimed at learning, developing, and improving, so that financial professionals will be better able to achieve the objectives of the finance function. The principles of the curriculum are: learning is something you do yourself, learning is different for everyone, the work environment is the best learning environment, and you learn from and with each other. The development curriculum includes, for example, learning interventions aimed at working together to achieve the goals of the finance function, growing in employee roles and management roles, and developing self-knowledge.

> The way an international banking group is building successful finance leaders of the future is by establishing a CFO Academy for mid-level and emerging talent, designed internally in partnership with a University. The focus of the CFO Academy is on developing within the finance function key skills needed for the future, such as leadership, communication, empathy, and collaboration. The program is designed to take people out of their comfort zones in areas where their experience is limited. The team found thinking like clients the most difficult. The purpose of the Academy is to help create a successful future finance function which is diverse, innovative, and a trusted partner that pursues the best interests of the bank and its stakeholders (IFAC, 2018).

8.4 A SPECIFIC IMPROVEMENT OPPORTUNITY: MEASURING AND INCREASING INTERNAL CUSTOMER SATISFACTION

One of the most important activities of the finance function is to provide the business and its management with the best possible support. In fact, 'internal customer satisfaction' is widely seen as a measure of the success of the finance function (as it also is in the HPFF framework). If the internal customer is served well, is satisfied, and is closely involved in financial processes, the strategic role of the finance function—one of the HPFF factors—will be fulfilled to a higher standard. In order to get a clear picture of what the internal customer thinks and needs of the finance function, a customer satisfaction survey must be conducted regularly among internal customers. A number of recent studies have shown that high customer satisfaction cannot be taken for granted. For example, in a study of the satisfaction with the effectiveness of staff departments, such as the finance function, less than 10% of the organizations surveyed were satisfied with that effectiveness. In addition, fewer than two out of 10 managers surveyed indicated that those staff departments added value to the organization (Kunisch et al., 2014). In another study, specifically into the contribution of the finance function to the efficient running of the logistics process in the organization, less than a quarter of the logistics managers interviewed were positive about this contribution (Kunisch et al., 2014). And a survey amongst more than 80 finance teams and interviews with more than 70 finance leaders showed that while 89% were of the opinion that they delivered effective governance (in the sense of enforcing accounting, auditing, statutory reporting and cash management policies, and providing management reporting, budgeting, forecasting, and planning services), only 35% agreed that they provided effective guidance (in the sense of supporting the business with analysis for operational and strategic decision-making, and translating business strategies into operational-level financial plans for example pricing and capital allocation) (Gartner, 2021).

It seems clear that there is work to be done for staff departments—work that starts with getting better insight into what makes those internal customers more satisfied. We therefore started a study with the aim of finding answers to two specific questions: "When the finance function asks its internal customers how satisfied they are, with which criteria should that assessment take place," and "How can the finance function promote and improve the relationship with its internal customers so that they become more satisfied with the finance function?" The study should yield so-called relationship-building actions that are about what both the finance function and the other departments can do in reciprocity to promote their relationship and collaborate more effectively together.[2]

The Delphi Study

After studying the literature, a number of things became clear: there was little to be found about the performance criteria against which finance functions could and/or should be assessed; little is known about what the internal client thinks of the finance function (and whether this matches with what financial professionals themselves think); and limited research has been conducted into how relationships between the finance function and the other organizational departments can be improved. We therefore decided to apply the Delphi technique to obtain answers to our research questions, from both financial professionals and the internal customers, namely the Board of Directors and line managers. The aim was to compare how both groups view the performance criteria that should be applied, the logistics of the customer satisfaction measurement process itself, and the relationship-building actions, and to assess whether a consensus could be reached on this between both groups. The Delphi study is described in the Frame in section 5.6.

In this Delphi study, 21 financial experts participated, who had, on average, 21 years of experience in finance of which 16 years were in a management capacity. The study was executed in three steps:

1. We made a list, based on a study of the academic and professional literature, of the (a) the performance criteria against which the internal client could assess the finance function; (b) the logistics related to measuring internal customer satisfaction (such as how often should measurements be taken, who should be questioned, and how); and (c) possible actions with which the relationships between the finance function and the other departments in the organization (= the internal customers) can be improved.
2. We submitted both lists to the panels of "Delphi financial professionals experts" and "Delphi manager experts." These experts then ranked the performance criteria, logistics, and relationship-building actions according to their preference, based on how effectively they had experienced them in practice. Each expert answered for himself, so the experts did not meet each other and therefore could not be influenced by each other. Their rankings were sent to us, and we rearranged the criteria, removing the criteria and actions with the lowest effectiveness. The updated list was again sent to the experts, who re-ranked the items on it.
3. After each round, we matched the results from the "Delphi financial professionals expert group" with those of the "Delphi manager expert group" to identify similarities. After two rounds, there appeared to be a high degree of consensus between both expert groups. This provided us with a list of performance criteria with which the finance function can measure its performance and the satisfaction experienced by its internal customers. In addition, it became clear how the internal customer satisfaction survey should be logistically approached and which actions are most effective to improve and promote the relationships between the finance function and the internal customers.

The Results

In Table 2, the 15 criteria on which the performance of the finance function—according to both the internal customers (the managers from the business) and the financial professionals—should be assessed are given and explained. The performance criteria are ranked in order of importance as indicated by the managers. For the sake of completeness, the ranking of the financial professionals is also mentioned to illustrate the high degree of consensus between both groups.

Table 2. The 15 internal customer satisfaction performance criteria of the finance function

Ranking managers	Performance criteria	Ranking financials
1	The finance function understands the business and its needs.	1
2	The finance function provides advice on the parts of the organization that should be given attention in order to create more value.	2
3	The finance function provides timely insight into how the organization is doing.	3
4	The finance function is explicitly involved in the strategic decision-making process of the organization.	5
5	The finance function makes an explicit contribution to the achievement of the objectives and targets of the organization.	4
6	The finance function brings financial expertise to the discussions that take place in the organization.	6
7	The finance function can explain financial matters well to operational managers.	7
8	The activities of the finance function are explicitly linked to the provision of added value to the organization and the achievement of organizational objectives.	8
9	The finance function responds quickly to the needs of the business.	11
10	The finance function is explicitly involved the operational decision-making in the organization.	10
11	The finance function supports management in propagating the leadership vision and how organizational performance can and should be achieved.	9
12	The control framework of the organization is well structured and maintained by the finance function.	12
13	The finance function helps to reach consensus in the organization about the most important risks, opportunities and priorities of the organization.	13
14	The finance function helps the organization to deal adequately with business challenges.	15
15	The finance function is part of and explicitly participates in the management team of the organization.	14

In regard to the logistical process of measuring internal customer satisfaction, there was consensus on all points between the financial professionals and the managers, except for one—the question of how often internal customer satisfaction should be measured. Financial professionals believe this should be done every six months. Perhaps unsurprisingly, managers are in favor of a lower frequency, i.e., annually. There was, however, full agreement that the measurement should consist of a combination of questions about a customer satisfaction rating figure and open questions. Thus, the measurement process should consist of a questionnaire and interviews. The performance criteria can then be measured by, for example, formulating questions as: "Can you indicate how satisfied you are, on a scale from 1 (very dissatisfied) to 10 (very satisfied), with how the finance function supports you in …" In interviews with (selected) managers, the finance function can then ask about the motivation for giving certain scores, and for examples that can then be explored in greater detail in order to learn from them.

Table 3 lists the 10 most effective relationship-building actions, again ranked in order of effectiveness as indicated by the managers. For the sake of completeness, the ranking of the financial professionals is mentioned in order to illustrate the high degree of consensus between both groups.

Table 3. The 10 most effective actions to promote the relationship between the finance function and its internal customers

Ranking managers	Relationship-building actions	Ranking financials
1	Develop and interpret performance indicators and management reports jointly, so that there is mutual understanding about what the important matters are within the organization that need to be managed.	1
2	Make sure that the business has a good understanding of finance, so that both the business and the finance function develop a common language. This prevents misunderstandings or lack of understanding and also ensures that management reports are better used within the organization.	2
3	Carry out important processes together, so that both financial and business expertise is present within these processes, and the business and the finance function get to know and complement each other better.	3
4	Clarify the added value of the finance function by explicitly linking its activities to where and how added value is created within the organization.	4
5	Implement joint improvement projects, programs and training courses so that both financial and business expertise is present within these projects and programs, and both groups get to know and complement each other better.	5
6	Regularly organize cross-business and cross-functional meetings with the finance function and the business to jointly discuss what is going well and what could be improved in the organization.	6
7	As a finance function and business, jointly discuss and manage the end-to-end processes in order to jointly monitor the "big picture."	7
8	As a finance function, decide together with the business the content of the business partner role of the finance function, to ensure that it closely matches the needs of the business.	8
9	Ensure that the finance function is present and actively participates in the decision-making process of the organization so that the finance function and the business are clearly jointly engaged at every step in that process.	10
10	As a finance function and business, create a shared understanding of the roles, responsibilities, challenges and needs of the finance function and the business.	9

From the Delphi study results, a number of conclusions can be drawn with regard to conducting a satisfaction survey among the internal customers of the finance function:

- Implement an internal customer satisfaction measurement process—based on the 10 performance criteria—that is conducted at least once a year with management.
- Link to the internal customer satisfaction questionnaire interviews with the most important internal customers and discuss with them what makes them satisfied and how the finance function can deliver (even) more added value.
- Reach consensus within the finance function and with the business on which issues to address first in order to increase internal customer satisfaction.
- "Do not be a stranger"; in other words, ensure as a finance function regular interaction with internal customers and explicitly involve them in the improvements that are part of the transition to the HPFF, which is after all also in their interest.

- Realize that a high internal customer satisfaction does not automatically mean that the finance function is doing well. It may well be that internal customers are a bit too "easy-going" and not very critical, or only think of their own business interests and less of organizational interest. In such situations, the finance function itself must take the initiative to initiate discussions and convince internal customers of the necessary changes to bring the organization to a higher level.

CASE: Healthcare Institution - Rebuilding After Difficult Years

A healthcare institution—a large care organization for the elderly and the vulnerable with services such as nursing home care, home care, and youth health care—had experienced a number of difficult years with cutbacks in budget and high turnover of employees. As a result there was "deferred maintenance" and thus the institution urgently needed to make improvements with regard to the quality and safety of care. All the attention of the institution was focused on this, and with success: after a number of years of improvement the Healthcare Inspectorate gave the institution "a clean bill of health." The institution could now focus on the future: "building a healthy organization in connection with its environment."

Reason For and Results of the HPFF Diagnosis

In recent years the entire institution, including the finance function, had been in turmoil. A "reconstruction" more or less had to take place in the function; because all attention had been paid to improving care ("the front line") the support functions had hardly received any attention. This meant that they—albeit necessarily, because of the circumstances—had been neglected to a certain degree. In addition, as is the case in most organizations today, the front line stated the need for financial professionals to transform into business partners. Finally, in the context of a reorganization, a number of financial professionals had been let go so there were fewer people to get the job done. In order to give the financial professionals new inspiration and also knowledge in these trying circumstances, management of the finance function decided to organize a workshop around the HPFF framework. The aim of the workshop was to introduce the finance function to the HPFF philosophy so that it could start to improve and strengthen itself to become a better business partner for management and colleagues in the primary care process.

The HPFF workshop consisted of the following parts:

- *Preparation*: All financial professionals received a link to the internet-based HPFF questionnaire, with the request to complete it for their own position.
- *During the meeting*: a lecture on the HPFF framework, followed by a discussion of the HPFF diagnosis scores; then an interactive break-out in groups about these scores on the basis of the following questions: Do you recognize and acknowledge the scores and what do they mean? What improvements are needed? Which improvement actions should be given priority? What does the HPFF action plan look like? Finally, a plenary discussion took place about the break-out outcomes, further roll-out of the identified improvements within the finance function, and the conditions needed to do this successfully.

All financial professionals completed the HPFF questionnaire. The resulting scores are shown in Figures 7 and 8.

Figure 7. The HPFF scores for the healthcare institution

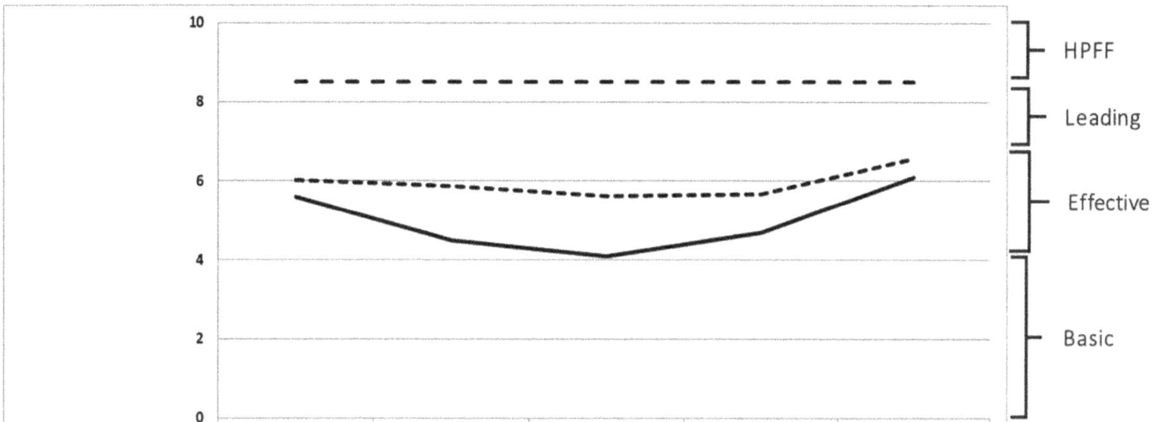

	Finance Function Improvement	IT Focus	Personal Development	Role Clarity	Strategic Role
HPFF (AVG>=8.5)	8,5	8,5	8,5	8,5	8,5
Healthcare institution (AVG=5.0; PERF=5.9)	5,6	4,5	4,1	4,7	6,1
HPFF database (AVG=6.0, PERF=6.5)	6,0	5,9	5,6	5,7	6,6

Figure 8. The obstacles encountered by the healthcare institution in its journey to becoming an HPFF

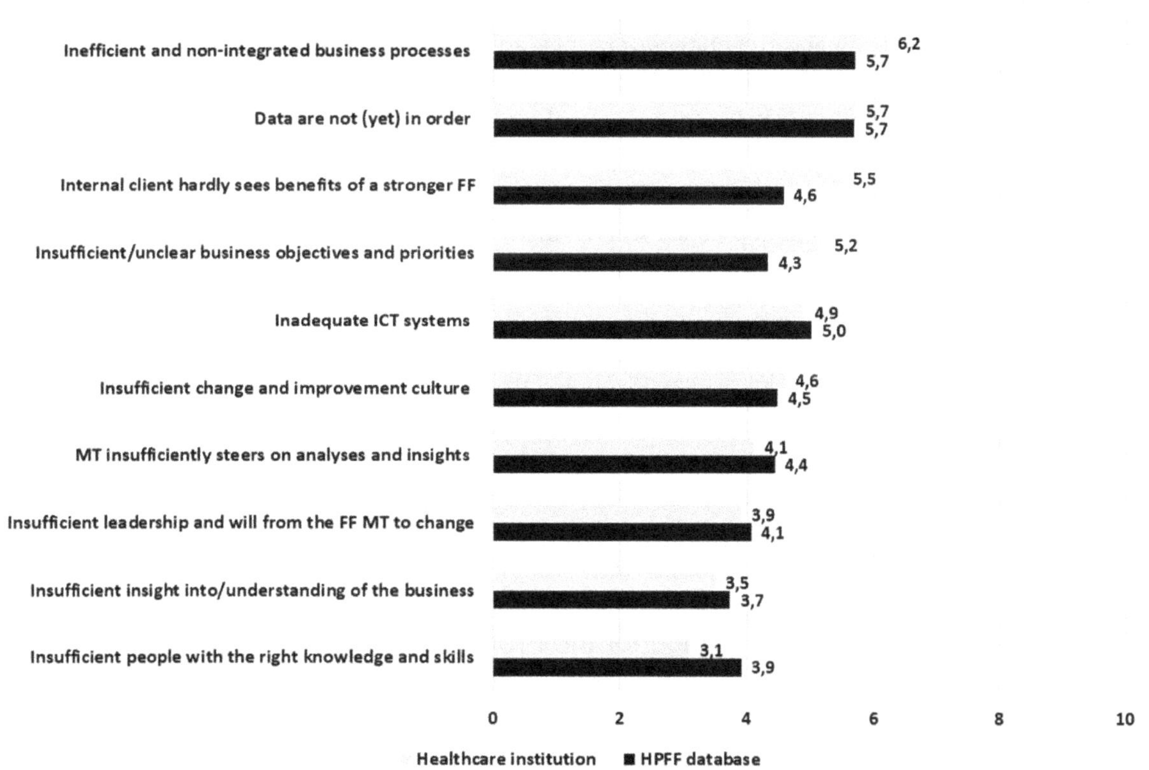

Figure 7 shows that the finance function of the healthcare institution did not differ much from the finance functions in the HPFF database because the shape of the score lines are almost identical. However, it should be noted that the healthcare institution had not made much progress on its way to attaining HPFF status, an outcome that was to be expected given that the financial professionals of the institution had mainly been busy supporting the front line in its improvement process. The realization that the finance function succeeded in supporting the front line with at least the minimum necessary information, but that this—because of all the obstacles that existed in the organization (see Figure 8)—was actually done through a "blood, sweat, and tears" approach by the financial professionals, given that they awarded a 5.9 to their performance level. During the workshop, it was clearly stated by the financial professionals that the time had now come to start working on the quality level of the finance function, because this was necessary to be able to support and serve the front line better without everybody running the risk of becoming burned out.

Results of the Break-Out

From the discussions in the break-out groups and the subsequent group discussion, a number of important issues that the finance function had to address in order to become an HPFF were identified.

Create More Role Clarity in the Organization

Because of the many changes in the past years, confusion had crept into the organization about who was responsible for what. The finance function was particularly bothered by this because it was not always clear who had to take action on a given task. Specific questions that therefore needed to be answered were as follows: What is the main role of the finance function within the organization (supporter, advisor, pioneer)? What is the role of the unit managers in the financial processes? Who is responsible for the design of the annual budgeting process? What is the role of the business controllers: do they have to support the units on paper, while in practice still having many central tasks?

Create a Common Goal

Financial professionals regularly felt isolated from the rest of the organization. This was partly due to the lack of a common goal for all functions and departments within the organization: What do we all want to achieve? The following options were suggested to promote collaboration: more integrality of actions in which the finance function should always be involved alongside the front line; seek each other out more and thus avoid the silos many functions/departments worked in; structurally work together on improvements more and achieve these jointly with discipline.

Increase the Added Value of Finance for the Front Line

Given the score for the performance of the finance function, the financial professionals felt a strong need to increase the contribution of their function, in terms of added value, to the front line. To this end, a range of actions emerged from the discussion:

- The HPFF workshop was the first time in a long while that the finance function had come together. Such a meeting should be held once a quarter to review the improvement actions and discuss new actions.
- The front line should be listened to in a structured way, and the insights should be explained from the perspective of the finance function to mutually come to structural solutions.
- At least one problem that has to be solved together with the front line should be included in the personal development plan of every financial employee.
- The finance function should take ownership of the quality of the management information.
- Structured evaluation and analysis of the quality of the financial processes, with explicit input from the front line, should be implemented. In the coming year, all teams in the finance function should evaluate two processes together with the front line, to get to "smart" outcomes.
- More should be invested in ICT resources, especially for reporting and repetitive activities.

Pay More Attention to the Development of the Financial Professionals

A variety of interesting ideas emerged, such as creating a better match between function and performance; visiting other healthcare institutions to see how they are doing; attending seminars regularly; celebrating joint successes with the front line; and allocating more of the budget for training and ensuring that financial professionals actually undertake this.

At the end of the workshop, priorities were immediately set for the first improvement actions to be taken and, on the spot, a working group was set up for each action:

- One working group with the aim to realize uniform roles and definitions within the healthcare institution. The following agreement was made: within three weeks, coordinate and compile an urgency list that will be followed.
- One working group for personnel and team development. The following agreement was made: arrange a session in which the financial professionals will discuss institution-wide cooperation and needed training on content and behavioral skills.
- One working group that examines how to increase the added value of the finance function to the front line. The following agreement was made: for each financial process, determine the needs and wishes of the front line and arrange a number of concrete consultations where there will be joint discussion on how to meet these.

REFERENCES

Agrawal, A., Eklund, S., Waite, J., & Woodcock, E. (2020). *Finance 2030: four imperatives for the next decade*. McKinsey and Company.

de Waal, A. A., & Linker, P. J. (2021). *The high performance government organization: a different approach to effective improvement*. In Blackman, D. (Ed), Handbook on Performance Management in the Public Sector. Elgar Handbooks in Public Administration and Management. doi:10.4337/9781789901207.00020

Gartner. (2019). *Hallmarks of Winning Finance Transformations*. Gartner, Inc.

IFAC. (2018). *Perspectives on the finance function journey*. International Federation of Accountants.

Kunisch, S., Müller-Stewens, G., & Campbell, A. (2014). Why corporate functions stumble. *Harvard Business Review*, *92*(12), 110–117.

ENDNOTES

1. Most data originates from Dutch and Belgian finance functions.
2. For the sake of clarity: the study was not about an interpretation of the frequently mentioned "business partnership" role of the finance function, because that role generally revolves around the things the finance function itself has to do towards the rest of the organization to fulfil that role adequately.

Chapter 9
Transformation Into the High-Performance Finance Function

ABSTRACT

In the literature to date, a generally accepted approach for the transformation into an HPFF cannot be found. Therefore, the approach for the transformation into an HPO was taken and adapted to an HPFF transformation. This approach, which encompasses a series of key steps and the use of so-called HPFF Coaches, is described in this chapter. In almost every organization, resources are scarce, which forces the finance function to compete for financial budget and people's time against the business (a battle often lost). Therefore, the issue of how to secure a sufficient proportion of an organization's resources for the HPFF transformation is tackled. In addition, ideas from experienced financials on how to realize the HPFF have been collected and are given in this chapter.

9.1 INTRODUCING THE HPFF TRANSFORMATION APPROACH

The approach to the HPFF transformation process consists of five key steps (see Figure 1): (1) develop a clear and compelling HPFF vision and HPFF transformation action plan, (2) execute the HPFF transformation actions, (3) sustain the momentum of the HPFF transformation, and (4) institutionalize the HPFF. We now describe each (sub)step and propose specific activities that you can undertake during each (sub) step. In Figure 1 there are several boxes (and lines), which are dotted; these denote sub-steps that directly address the change process individual people will go through during the HPFF transformation process.

> At least 75% of large change programs fail to achieve their objectives. Why? Because they start with technology rather than with people and behaviors. In contrast, 80% of programs with a clear people-centered change focus do achieve their benefit targets. Leading with a mindset shift that addresses what people do and how they can be part of the solution is critical. People adopt what they help to create. Mindsets are built over decades. Attempting to change mindsets in just a few months requires an element of unlearning. If employees are surrounded by others who are not changing, the challenge becomes harder.

DOI: 10.4018/978-1-7998-6929-0.ch009

Figure 1. The key and sub-steps of the HPFF transformation approach

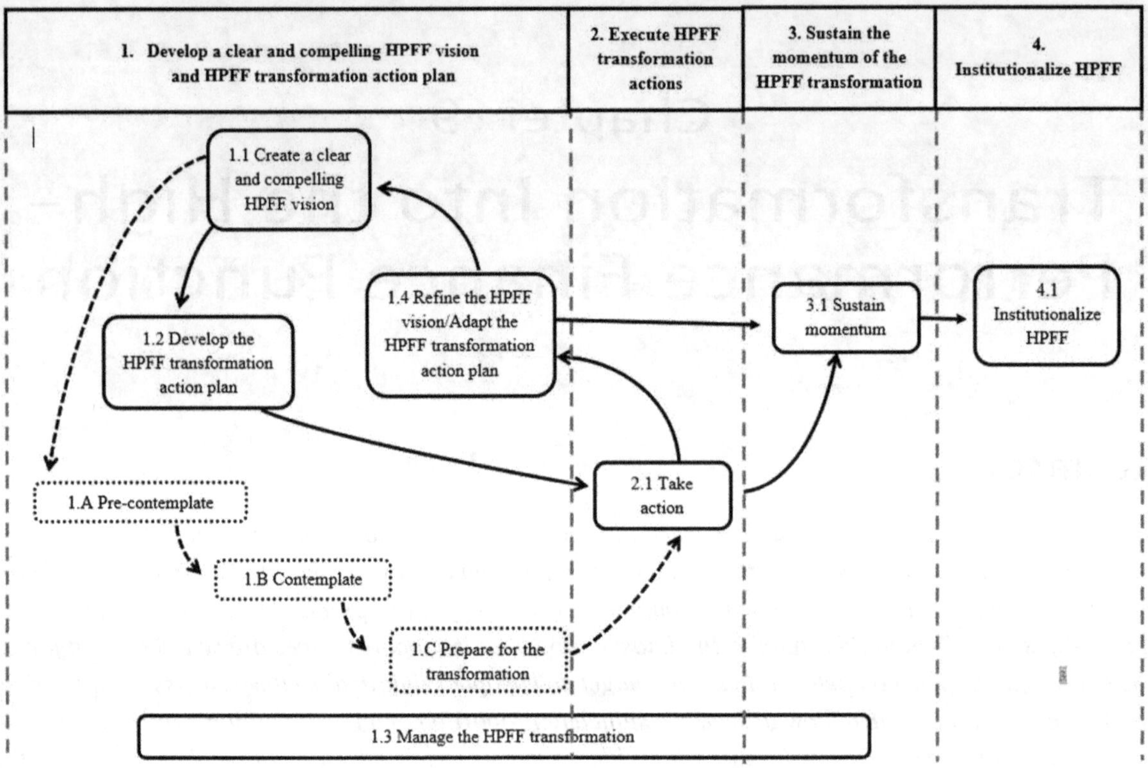

9.2 KEY STEP 1: DEVELOPING A CLEAR AND COMPELLING HPFF VISION AND HPFF TRANSFORMATION ACTION PLAN

Sub-Step 1.1

The first step in the HPFF transformation process consists of creating a clear and compelling HPFF vision (sub-step 1.1 in Figure 1). Every successful HPFF transformation has a vision that is both easy to communicate and attractive to all financial professionals as well as to the internal stakeholders of the finance function (such as the Board and line management). A clear and compelling HPFF vision should describe the aspects, characteristics, and outcomes of the desired state of the finance function as an HPFF. A positive and inspiring vision of HPFF is created by managers and financial staff together, which makes people enthusiastic and creates something they can believe in. The HPFF vision contains the purpose of the transformation and the reasons it is worth undertaking, and it describes the positive differences between the current and the desired state of the finance function. Emotional arguments are used in creating and conveying an appealing picture of HPFF by describing strong positive benefits of a successful transformation using words with an emotional and positive connotation and metaphors. The vision is made appealing by using alluring names, images, pictures, slogans, music, colors, and humor to create good feeling about the HPFF. Active language is used to convey the dynamics of the transformation. When presenting and discussing the vision, emotions are used to convey warmth and sincere commitment. Fears about the transformation are reduced by emphasizing the opportunities being an HPFF brings. The consequences of what HPFF will mean for the finance function and the financial professionals are made tangible by explaining the implications of becoming an HPFF for the structure, processes, and people of the finance function. What will or will not change is made clear, and assurance is given that good things, such as existing social security arrangements, will not be tampered with. The role that financial professionals can and will play in the HPFF transformation is also discussed. Thus, financial professionals can picture what HPFF will bring them, how they will personally benefit from it ("what's in it for me"), and how they can contribute to it. They may not necessarily understand all the ins and outs of HPFF and its implications, but they can certainly believe in it. The financial professionals can almost "smell" and "touch" HPFF. They can start the transformation with an image of the end goal in their minds.

Sub-Step 1.2

In sub-step 1.2, a clear strategy for the transformation, with short- and long-term objectives, is set so that it can be steadfastly guided. The HPFF transformation is visibly made the most important priority for the finance function for the coming years. Then, a flexible and adaptive transformation action plan is made that is not too elaborate. Priorities for the transition actions are set, based on the outcome of the HPFF Diagnosis, and resources are made available for those actions. Transformation goals and a timeline for achieving them are set to build momentum and show progress from day one. The function should not schedule giant leaps but take small steps—preferably with a maximum time span of three months—to keep the transformation actions manageable and adaptive to changing circumstances. Time should be taken to become an HPFF and build in some slack so that unexpected setbacks or delays can be dealt with without having to change the complete action plan, but the function should not falter in getting to the end result, which is not up for discussion. Current HPFF-like activities should be taken into account and used as starting points for the plan. Running and proposed projects are evaluated on their contribution to the HPFF transformation. Projects that have added value to HPFF are incorporated, and other projects are not commenced or discontinued to free up the function's time and resources. The HPFF transformation plan should be all about focus. It should not only deal with changes in the current finance function (with its current processes) but also anticipate (fundamental) changes in the environment and the organization that may affect the HPFF transformation. The financial professionals should closely be involved in deciding how to become an HPFF and should have a say in the setup of the transformation action plan and the starting time for the transformation. In this way, the collective knowledge of the finance function is mobilized and buy-in for the action plan is easily achieved. Finally, enough resources should be (made) available on a continuous basis to source the transformation into an HPFF.

Sub-Step 1.3

A special HPFF transformation support structure is used to manage the transformation process through all its steps (sub-step 1.3). Such a transformation management structure requires organizational members who are respected by their leaders, have the power to mobilize resources, and possess the political and interpersonal skills to guide the transformation process: the HPFF Champion and HPFF Coaches (see section 9.6 The HPFF Coaches). The HPFF Champion and HPFF Coaches support the financial professionals throughout the sub-steps of the transformation process to move forward with the adoption and implementation of the HPFF vision. The HPO Champion, who is the sponsor of the HPFF transformation and is one of the senior executives in the finance management team, supervises the HPFF transformation and takes responsibility for its success. The HPO Champion must make sure to spend enough time on HPFF so that the organization sees that the promoter, and therefore the finance management team, is taking the HPFF transformation seriously. Because the transformation takes up a lot of the attention of the finance function, active and visible support from the finance management team and a budget made available for the transition convey the importance of HPFF to the financial professionals. The HPO Champion regularly communicates progress and results of the transformation to the finance function and the larger organization. The finance management team visibly drives the transformation and helps people by creating the conditions that make it possible for them to participate in the transformation. By also guarding the tone at the top, there is always alignment between the pronouncements, statements, and declarations of the finance management team and its actual deeds and behavior. When management walks its talk, does what it says, shows the finance function that HPFF is really important by paying continuous attention to it, and gets its hands "dirty" by involving itself in some of the day-to-day transformation activities, the financial professionals will follow suit.

Sub-Step 1.4

It is possible that the HPFF vision and the HPFF transformation action plan have to be refined and adapted because of issues, challenges, or concerns that may arise as a result of the first actions executed (sub-step 1.4).

Sub-Steps 1.A+B+C

Regarding the change process of individual financial professionals, during the 'pre-contemplate' sub-step (sub-step 1.A), it is essential to start a dialogue with financial professionals about the reason for the HPFF transformation. This reason is based on a sense of urgency or a desire or aspiration. The most obvious reason is the burning platform caused by severe problems or a compelling event, for example, a change in strategy or in the execution of the current strategy because of dramatically changed circumstances or dramatically increased needs of the business. Reasons for change that can be given are showing how other finance functions have made successful transitions, talking about current bottlenecks and failed projects and the costs of these to the organization, or indicating that the finance function is not ready (enough) for the increasing dynamics of the economy and the environment. However, management should not focus only on "negative" reasons. A positive way to create commitment is to appeal to the ambition and pride of financial professionals to work toward becoming the best finance function in the sector. Aspiration, the desire to become a better finance function, is a great motivational force, and the concept of HPFF will certainly cater to this desire. An added benefit is that an appealing picture forms a vision, a dream that can push people further than they ever thought they could go. The gap between performance in the current state and performance in the desired HPFF state is quantified by the HPFF Diagnosis, which shows the potential and opportunities that exist within the finance function. This dialogue is especially important to entice and convince those financial professionals who are resisting changing into an HPFF or who are unaware, uninformed, underinformed, unconcerned, defensive, in denial, or demoralized about their own ability to make the changes involved. Therefore, consciousness raising is needed to increase awareness about the required behaviors, processes, and solutions to transform the finance function into an HPFF. In addition, financial professionals have to experience and express their feelings and emotions about these problems and solutions, because dramatic relief of strong emotional reactions to transformation processes can motivate them to change.

During the 'contemplate' sub-step (sub-step 1.B), financial professionals become aware of challenges of the HPFF transformation and start to think about how to deal with these upcoming challenges. At this time, they consider changing their behavior, for instance, by self-revaluation, in which they assess their feelings and emotions about themselves and define what exactly needs to be changed. During the 'prepare for the transformation' sub-step (sub-step 1.C), financial professionals become committed to taking action and are actually already taking several behavioral steps. They have a plan of action and are making preparations and devising actions to change their behavior and thinking (sub-step 1.D).

The transformation approach is focused on strengthening the belief that financial professionals can not only change but also have the commitment to act on that belief. They become aware of alternatives, realizing that they can create alternatives themselves and, thus, can be effective in making a successful HPFF transformation happen. In this respect, it helps to regularly train the finance function in HPFF—introduce so-called change-eager management training sessions to help financial professionals obtain the knowledge with which they can make the HPFF transformation. In these sessions, financial professionals begin to understand what becoming an HPFF means for their own activities, performance, and behavior. They start speaking the same language and adhering to the same performance-driven values. Also, celebrate the start of the HPFF transformation by celebrating the past before departing from it ("look at what we have achieved") and then introducing stimulating content ("and now we are going to become even better"). Establish and execute a tailored communication strategy to create shared expectations and report progress. Tailor the communication to the finance function: use words, images, and symbols that are aligned with the function's current culture and that resonate with the financial professionals. Convey the message that HPFF is definitely coming and that it is not just a flavor-of-the-month activity. Emphasize that HPFF will make the finance function the front-runner in its sector, and that the transformation into an HPFF is a joint voyage of discovery. Make sure the communication is not one-way but a real two-way dialogue followed by action. Set up a dedicated intranet site with a forum where financial professionals can actively discuss HPFF with management and the HPFF Coaches.

9.3 KEY STEP 2: EXECUTE THE HPFF TRANSFORMATION ACTIONS

In the second key step of the transformation process, financial professionals are engaged in the transformation and, as a result, adopt the required changes needed in the finance function (sub-step 2.1). The interventions in this key step provide support to financial professionals so that they can easily adopt the changes and modify their behaviors. Before they can change their work behaviors, the contingencies and causes that regulate behavior will first have to be changed and managed. Financial professionals need help from management and encouragement to change and to counter their less effective behaviors. Finger-pointing and unwanted work behaviors should be addressed and removed, and instead helpful behaviors should be introduced.

Carefully choose the sequence of attention points—originating from the HPFF Diagnosis—to be addressed. Although all attention points are important, it is best to stay practical and keep the transformation manageable; thus, choose the most logical order in which the finance function is going to address these points. Do this based on the life cycle of the finance function (what needs to be rejuvenated now); the current situation of the finance function (what needs to be fixed right away); HPFF-like projects that are currently going on (what can you piggyback on); and the culture of the finance function (the amount of change the finance function can handle stipulates the speed of the transformation process). Then start the transformation before everything is perfectly thought out and before everyone completely understands everything about the HPFF transformation. If you wait until every last detail of the transformation action plan is in place, the transformation will probably never start at all. Experience is the best teacher, so the sooner you start the transformation the more you will learn. Starting on time has the advantage in that the tempo of transition can be set a bit slower, if needed. It is better to have a steady pace that takes you to the finish line than to make a quick dash and collapse before reaching it.

During the transformation, there will be plenty of time to change and adapt activities and maybe even the HPFF transformation action plan and the HPFF vision (sub-step 1.4), if circumstances dictate this. But you need to get going; remember, you cannot steer a car that stands still. Also start creating a culture of dialogue and cooperation. During the transformation, financial professionals have, and take, the opportunity to question, challenge, interpret, and ultimately clarify the goals of the different actions that need to be performed in order to become an HPFF. They regularly engage in a dialogue to monitor behavior and ensure that it is aligned with the goals of the HPFF transformation. Take the lead to

The finance function of one of the world's largest and busiest container port undertook a successful finance transformation that entailed (IFAC, 2018):

- Providing a clear vision and expectation for the role of the finance function in supporting the organization's objectives, based on the finance function and its professionals moving beyond a support role to being co-pilots in the organization; being champions of customer-centricity and innovation
- A constant upgrade of the finance ERP systems architecture, and deploying specialist tools and applications for budgeting and business analytic
- Enabling effective business analytics delivered in real-time and in easily-consumable formats to mobile devices such as tablets
- Constant review of process and procedure design using process mapping, with the aim of reducing human touch points and replacing them with system processing, when possible. This reduces risk as checkpoints and verification become increasingly embedded in the system. It also allows more time for the finance function to identify and evolve key performance indicators and review performance with a sense-making capability. This requires close partnership with the business and wider skillsets and behaviors.
- Implementation of an enterprise risk management framework to provide a structured approach to determining challenges and risks confronting the organization, including finance-related risks, and subsequently adopting risk mitigation measures.

instigate the dialogue and guard the transition principles, and at the same time, be receptive to financial professionals' questions, objections, and ideas. Conduct regular discussions, for example, during finance management team meetings, in which progress of the transformation is openly discussed, including possible setbacks and suggestions for adapting the transformation approach.

9.4 KEY STEP 3: SUSTAIN THE MOMENTUM OF THE HPFF TRANSFORMATION

Sustaining the momentum of the transformation entails making sure that the transformation actions receive adequate attention and resources; if this is achieved, the transformation does not run the risk of failing because of the urgency of daily operations or a lack of attention (sub-step 3.1). Management makes sure to keep sharing information with the financial professionals about the importance of the transformation and the successes and challenges encountered during the ongoing transformation. This means discussing the current rate of transformation, the degree of organizational stability, the interference of the transformation with daily routine operations, the time spent on actions, and the possible damage from excessive change. Take appropriate follow-up action to either slow down or speed up the transformation process. Balance continued delivery of day-to-day services with transformation actions, making sure that the delivery of regular services is not disrupted by these actions. The internal clients need to be serviced regardless of the ongoing internal changes in the finance function. Celebrate when the finance function successfully completes a transformation action, then review the way forward for the next action. After completing an action, make sure its results and quality are maintained while the other actions are executed.

> Each department within the finance function creates a vision and roadmap to meet project objectives, but these plans must align with the function's vision. Each department must demonstrate how it will support the function's goals to have world-class processes, act as engaged business partners, and maintain the corporate culture. With these aligned roadmaps in hand, finance departments conduct periodic "vision checks" with partners on their team. Furthermore, they report each month to the CFO on roadmap progress. Several times a year, department leaders meet with managers and controllers to update the roadmap status on both completed and unfinished projects, as well as partner involvement. This helps to ensure both top-down and bottom-up alignment on organizational strategy (APQC, 2018).

9.5 KEY STEP 4: INSTITUTIONALIZE HPFF

The HPFF transformation and its outcomes have to be institutionalized, and being high-performing should become part of the finance function culture, ongoing operations, and processes (sub-step 4.1). In this key step, the organization regularly (once every 18 to 24 months) checks whether it has improved its scores on the HPFF factors and its results by conducting an HPFF Diagnosis. This diagnosis is executed by

In a recent survey, only one-third of respondents reported that capability-building programs often or always achieve their objectives and business impact. To improve this success rate, CFOs can help in the following ways (Abdelal et al., 2021):

1. Identify opportunities to invest in value-creating capabilities. CFOs have access to the required financial and operational data, as well as a cross-functional understanding of the business to help the organization identify the capabilities needed to differentiate from competitors.
2. Boost financial acumen at all levels. To reduce confusion and increase efficiency in the organization, CFOs must ensure that all managers use a common language to discuss finance. In this way, the CFO can build core functional capabilities for monitoring cash flows, establishing base and momentum cases, and using a range of scenarios in decision-making, all critical to understanding how an organization can unlock more value.
3. Support the company's talent-development efforts. CFOs have a critical opportunity to develop talent by systematically reviewing the talent profile, identifying the skills needed now and in the future, and working with HR leaders to map skill sets to strategic and operating plans. The CFO can also make the argument for preserving the organization's employee-training budgets.

the HPFF Coaches. From each diagnosis, additional or new attention points for the transformation are identified and then addressed with new actions. When the desired HPFF status is reached, the finance function takes time out to celebrate its achievements, to recuperate, and to enjoy its success. After the celebration, management takes stock and sets its sights on new objectives. In the spirit of continuous improvement, the new quality goals and targets are higher and more difficult than the old ones. It has to be remembered that an HPFF transformation is not a project but a process: it does have a starting point but not necessarily an ending point. After all, things can always be done better and quality requirements from internal and external clients increase all the time. In addition, circumstances change, to which the finance function has to continuously adapt.

CASE: Governmental Institution - Creating the HPFF Transformation Plan

The finance function of the government organization had undergone major changes in the recent past and faced many challenges, in particular the introduction of a new financing method. This entailed that the government organization was no longer funded from the overall government budget, but that from now on the organization had to, for the most part, provide from its own income. These changes put a lot of pressure on the organization and its people and forced many adjustments, including having to adapt internal processes and systems. The finance function of the organization also did not escape from these changes, but, despite the adjustments and the associated pressures, the function succeeded time and again in achieving the required basic performance. However, this was achieved through "blood, sweat, and tears" which put a lot of pressure on the function: it was only a matter of time before things would go wrong. This gave finance function management its first motive to want to become an HPFF: financial professionals should no longer have to work with a blood, sweat, and tears approach and constantly fire-fight. Instead, they would work in a thriving finance function where life would be a pleasure. The second motive was, now that the finance function had things reasonably under control, the ambition of management and financial professionals both to want to excel in the field, and thus to be able to contribute significantly to the further development of both the finance function and the entire organization.

How Far Along Was the Finance Function Toward Becoming an HPFF?

Figure 2 shows how far along the finance function of the government organization was with regard to the five HPFF factors.

According to the financial professionals who completed the HPFF questionnaire, their finance function scored, on a scale of 1 to 10 (with 8.5 indicating the high performance level) with regard to the

Figure 2. HPFF scores of the finance function

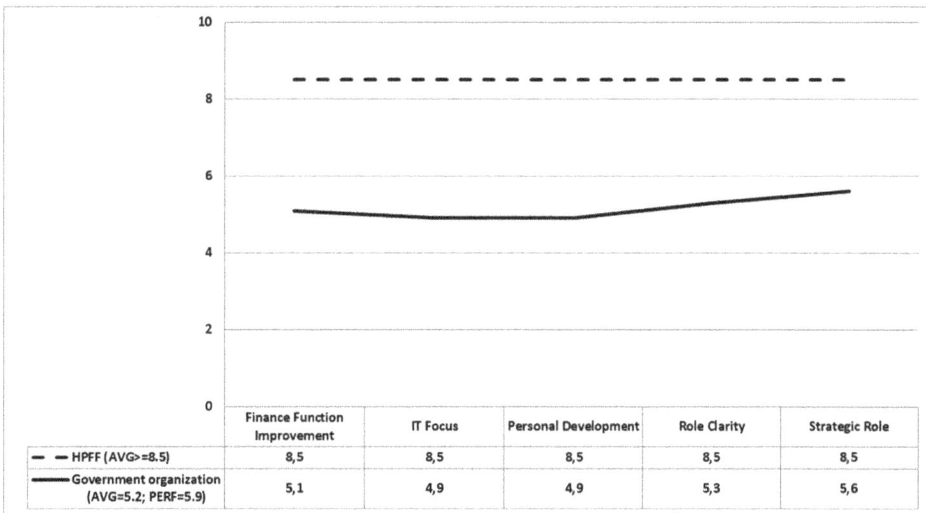

Figure 3. The obstacles within government organization on the way to the HPFF

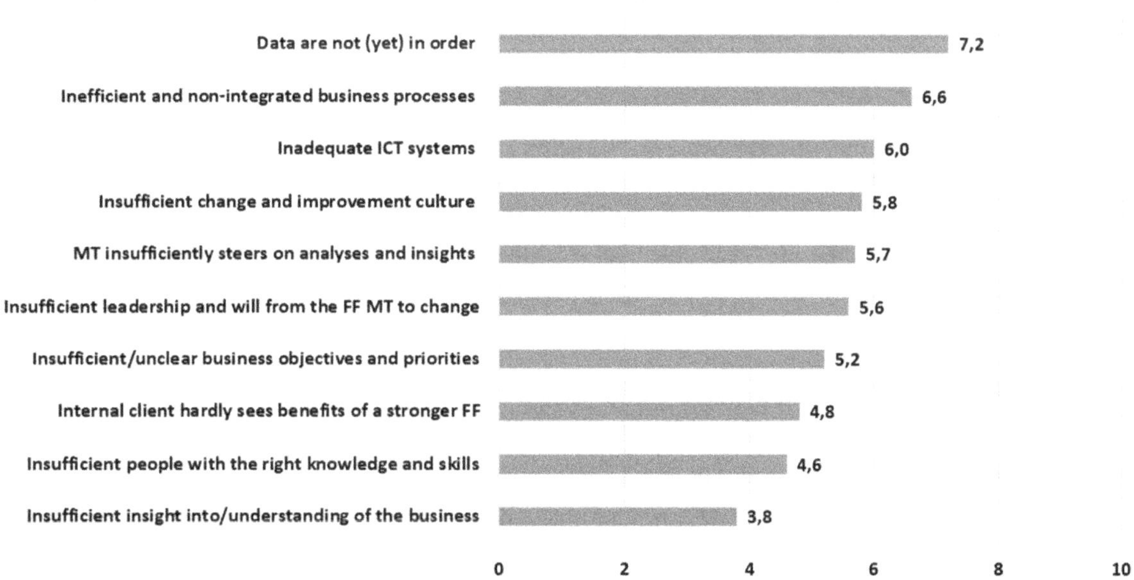

HPFF factors, an average of 5.2, while they estimated the performance of the function to be 5.9. This performance score substantiated the previously described reason for becoming an HPFF, namely that the finance function worked under great pressure (with blood, sweat, and tears) to meet the requirements set by the organization. Given that all HPFF factors were more or less at the same level, there were many opportunities for improvement. This meant that good, well-considered choices had to be made to prioritize the right transformation actions. The obstacles that existed within the government organization as a whole and in the finance function had to be taken into account (see Figure 3). This meant that the HPFF development plan also had to include actions that would tackle the most important obstacles (these are the obstacles that score above 5.0).

Approach of the HPFF Transformation Action Plan

Higher performance in organizations is promoted by involving employees in important changes. That is why the management of the finance function chose to organize a dialogue day attended by all the financial professionals. During this dialogue day, financial professionals and their managers were given the opportunity to discuss the results of the HPFF diagnosis with each other. In order to facilitate the dialogue, the following core questions were asked during three discussion rounds:

- *Round 1: Do you recognize and acknowledge the HPFF diagnosis results?* The participants were invited, in groups, to describe the story behind the diagnosis results, to indicate possible causes for the scores in their own focus area of the finance function, and to draw examples from their own practice. The aim of this round was to create a common basis for recognition and to reach consensus about underlying causes. This would increase the willingness of the participants to work together to improve their finance function. A carousel was organized where the groups visited each other briefly. One participant from each group was given a flipchart containing the results of the group discussion, to explain these results to the visiting groups. These groups in turn asked explanatory questions in order to create good understanding and recognition among the group participants.
- *Round 2: How would the finance function look like if it scored two points higher?* Participants were invited to describe the finance function when it would function at a higher level. It was explicitly asked to convert the examples from round 1 into "ideal situations." The aim of this round was, given the fact that people usually find it easier to say what they don't like and who is to blame for that, to let participants experience the magnetic effect of "the beckoning perspective." In other words: if one could get a good idea of what working in an HPFF would look like, one would become enthusiastic about it and be willing to participate in the creation of that HPFF. Moreover, the more concrete the future picture envisioned was, the easier it would become to come up with one's own contribution to it.
- *Round 3: What did you do to score those two points higher?* Participants were asked to think creatively about the actions they could take (and activities they could stop) in order to arrive at a situation where the finance function would score two points higher. In doing so, explicit account had to be taken of removing the most severe obstacles (as shown in Figure 3). The purpose of this round was to identify concrete transformation actions for the finance function.

Table 1. Part of the HPFF transformation action plan for the finance function of the government organization

Current situation	"Dream image"	Transformation actions
Accounts are deemed correct with unqualified auditor's approval.	Supporting management from the various finance roles in order to help them realize their intentions, goals and desired (financial and non-financial) performance.	- Review the mission, vision and strategic multi-year plan for the development of the finance function (with input from HPFF diagnosis results).
Individual expectations are sometimes discussed ad hoc by financials with internal clients or colleagues.	Images of current and desired performance are shared with internal clients and between parts of the finance function, mutual expectations are discussed, and work is done on increasing the quality of mutual relations.	- Organize formal and informal dialogues with important internal and external people.
The basic performance of the finance function is realized annually but through the blood, sweat, and tears approach. In addition, the performance of the finance function is not explicitly defined or monitored.	The performance of the finance function is explicitly defined, monitored, discussed internally and with internal clients, and successes are celebrated.	- Define, in interaction with the operation, the performance to be achieved by the finance function, monitor this and discuss the progress both internally and with internal clients.
Improvements in the FF are made ad hoc. Coherence, prioritization and structural monitoring of progress are largely lacking.	The finance function operates as one team, there is continuous improvement with a focus on the most important things to be improved, and actions are not only deployed, but also properly completed. There is sufficient time and resources for the agreed improvements.	- Create a challenging and feasible multi-year improvement plan. Accommodate space in this to continuously work on small daily improvements in line with the vision and strategy of the finance function.
There is a gray area between what the operation and what the finance function does or should do. The finance function, often to unburden the operation, sits too often in the operational chair (e.g. drawing up plans, making reports, adjusting forecasts).	A clear P&C cycle, and a clear allocation of TVA (Tasks, Responsibilities and Authorities) for both the finance function and the operation.	- Make the TVA explicit. - Set up together with the operation a clear P&C cycle.
Financials develop on their own initiative, job descriptions are mainly used for vacancies, there is little stimulus from management to develop, and managers do not take the responsibility to develop themselves either.	Roles within the finance function are described and assigned. There are competency profiles for each role. A good training program has been developed for each role for which financials can enroll themselves. Professional knowledge is up to standard and behavioral skills are being developed. Financials develop proactively (they also feel responsible for this), development is also monitored, assessed and valued.	- Prepare a multi-year strategic personnel planning for the finance function in which development efforts are incorporated in the workforce planning. - Describe and assign: roles, functions, and competency profiles. - Make an inventory of the gap between current and desired knowledge / competencies and develop a development program for the gaps, together with HRM. Look at how comparable government organizations have arranged this for their finance function. Think beyond just training, for example also apply job rotation, internships, and learning from other organizations.

The results of the three rounds were combined in a transformation action plan. As an example, a part of this plan is given in Table 1. The transformation action plan is currently being discussed by management and financial professionals and further refined. Subsequently, management will discuss the plan with the most important internal clients within the government organization to determine to what extent they agree with the described action. After that, the green light will be given to the final plan, which will then serve as a guideline in the coming years for the further development of the finance function into an HPFF.

9.6 THE HPFF COACHES

You cannot hire consultants to become high-performing: high-performing comes from within you as it is driven by intrinsic motivation. It is therefore imperative that people from within the organization take the lead in the HPFF transformation, so that they gain HPFF knowledge and experience that then will stay in the organization (in contrast to consultants doing the work and then leaving, taking the knowledge gained with them). Taking the lead will also increase the motivation of financial professionals to achieve HPFF because this is *their* transformation. To make it possible to take the lead, we recommend appointing finance managers as HPFF Coaches. Because it is the task of managers to develop their team and their people anyway, it is natural that they will take the lead in the HPFF transformation; after all, this transformation is all about developing the finance function, i.e., the team and its people. In addition, the main duty of managers in an HPO is to create the conditions under which employees can excel in their work, and that is precisely what HPFF Coaches will do for the people in the finance function.

The objectives of the HPFF Coaches are to:

- enable the finance function to grow into an HPFF from within
- spread HPFF knowledge throughout the finance function
- 'ignite the HPFF fire' among managers and employees in the finance function
- be the pioneer in HPFF transformation actions
- promote cooperation between the units in the finance function
- develop top talent into HPFF leaders that will help the finance function to grow into and remain an HPFF
- enable the finance function to perform future HPFF Diagnoses

The behavior of the HPFF Coach can be characterized as being active and enthusiastic and taking the initiative; having a unifying role and being a "people person"; being critical but always in a positive way, putting forward ideas and suggestions; being curious; visibly enjoying what he or she is doing; being results-oriented; taking responsibility; holding others accountable and not being afraid of criticism and resistance while doing so; and being quality-oriented and believing improvement is always possible.

> A number of companies had implemented the role of change champions who helped to encourage transformation and support staff amidst the changes at work. One company described these change champions as people who were not functional experts but focused on listening to their colleagues' concerns and issues, showing empathy and providing feedback to management (ICAEW/ISCA, 2019).

The HPFF Coaches play a plethora of roles during the HPFF transformation:

- *Advisory role*: Giving advice on the content, approach, and desired results in regard to the HPFF attention points and actions to management.

- *Supporting role*: Organizing and facilitating HPFF workshops, facilitating the dialogue required to clarify emerging results, and helping and motivating people in executing the HPFF actions.
- *Communication role*: Giving regular updates on progress, bottlenecks, results, and lessons learned in regard to the HPFF actions in the unit of the finance function they are coaching.
- *Ambassador role*: Propagating HPFF ideas in the finance function and being, in word and deed, an HPFF role model.
- *Unifying role*: Aligning and cooperating with colleague HPFF coaches in other units of the finance function and involving them in drafting HPFF advice, being the intermediary between the finance management team (including the CEO) and the financial professionals, and aligning current improvement activities with the HPFF actions.
- *Educational role*: Interacting with the financial professionals to discuss the HPFF Framework and HPFF behavior and obtain feedback on issues and progress.
- *Quality role:* Monitoring and evaluating the quality of the execution of the HPFF actions and the level of dialogue on HPFF, signaling possible problems, and identifying additional improvement opportunities.

There are several actions that will help to make the HPFF Coaches a success in the organization:

- *Regularly conducting meetings.* Conducting regular meetings in the finance function to discuss progress, experiences, and bottlenecks and using these meetings to increase the HPFF competency of financial professionals by discussing the HPFF attention points in-depth.
- *Creating a high-quality HPFF transformation action plan.* Making sure that the HPFF transformation action plan has clear improvement goals and activities, deadlines, and resources so that the HPFF Coaches can guide the HPFF transformation and hold people accountable for agreements made in regard to who does what, when, and with what result.
- *Instilling in-depth HPFF knowledge in the finance function.* Making sure HPFF Coaches have as much knowledge about the HPFF Framework and its working in practice as possible and letting them regularly exchange HPFF experiences gained in practice with each other and with HPFF Coaches of other organizations.

CASE: The Kitchen Table Sessions - Staying in Touch With the Financial Professionals

The Director of Finance and Control emphasizes that in an HPFF transition, it is important to just get started and then learn what works and what does not along the way. The main task of the management team must primarily be to provide facilitating and supportive leadership. The Director therefore mainly uses the following phrases to describe his own role and that of his management team: connecting, rewarding, offering support, and taking employees seriously. Connecting refers to continuous connection with the financial professionals, making sure they know the strategy of the organization and more importantly, the direction of their own finance function. If every financial professional knows what the finance function stands for, they can work much more independently. According to the Director of Finance and Control: "This way they don't have to keep coming back to you as a manager to ask what they should do or which choices to make. While finding answers together to important questions such as "Do we want to lead the way? and Do we want to be the best?" helps to tap into the intrinsic motivation of the financial professionals."

In an HPFF, remuneration of financial professionals must be clear and transparent. This means both positive rewards for good performance (promotion and development opportunities) and punishments for disappointing performance (demotion to another position with lower salary, no development opportunities). As the Director of Finance and Control explains: "The message in the organization must be clear: 'you get equal to what you achieve' and 'your reward will be in money and attention for your development.' It is also important that achieved results are transparent and visible to all financial professionals. We publish these results on the intranet. We work together with HR in this process, this department attends the planning and assessment interviews with financial professionals and monitors the quality of the process."

Offering support as their main task is reflected in the vision of the management team. "We want to be a management team that identifies problems earlier than the rest of the organization. Because then we can act on this faster and earlier as a team, thereby ensuring peace and space in the finance function," the Director of Finance and Control continues. "Everything must be about ensuring this peace and space; if not, we must reconsider our focus. In addition, we offer all employees a support structure for the development of their professional life within our organization. For this you have to make sure that there are agreements about the learning structure, dialogue structure, and collaboration structure. If you organize that well, you have less discussions, you have to organize less, and you have more trust in each other. Finally, taking this seriously starts with taking yourself seriously. I try at all times to be honest and have integrity and to let that resonate in my story. I have two commitments that show this to my people. Every day I block an hour in my diary, a kind of consultation hour. Nobody has to make an appointment for that period, everyone can drop by my office, the door is always open. Those five hours a week are a task to guard, but I think they are very important. A second commitment is that once every two weeks I spend an afternoon sitting at the kitchen table next to the department's coffee machine. We then have the most engaging conversations from person to person and with the group as a whole, which can be about the strategy of the company, our principles or the development of the function and the organization. It is not an obligation for employees, but it has increasingly become a natural moment in everybody's agendas to make sure to be there. Sometimes I am talking with 40 people. This works better for me than weblogs or e-mails in which I share my vision. Because this is purely two-way communication without obligations and that is hugely appreciated by the financial professionals."

How HPFF Can Be Realized: A Discussion With Finance Professionals

In the past two years, we conducted five sessions with a total of more than 100 finance professionals. In these sessions, the HPFF framework was explained and the attendees were then presented with the following situation: "You conducted the HPFF diagnosis three years ago, which resulted in a score of 5.7. Much has been done and changed in your finance position since then, and in the recent HPFF diagnosis you now score a 8.5 on average. What have you done to start the transformation into an HPFF? How did financial professionals become enthusiastic about this? And how did you maintain focus and discipline during the transformation?" Here are the most interesting results of the discussions, which were not about what the respondents would have done to improve their finance function but about how they would have handled the HPFF transformation.

How to begin

- Use the HPFF diagnosis as a common starting point so that everyone knows and agrees what that starting position is and what "the dot on the horizon," i.e., the shared ambition, should be. From there, create a joint vision and image of your finance function as an HPFF.
- Discuss "what's in it for you" with the financial professionals: give them perspective. Include the financial professionals in all facets of the transformation, and especially in determining the improvement actions to be implemented and their priority.
- Create an HPFF transformation plan with clearly defined actions, expected results, financial professionals responsible, resources needed, and deadlines.
- Map out the required and available budget and human capacity for improvement. From there consciously make time to work on improvements in a structured way. Assemble a transformation team and identify ambassadors for HPFF.
- Make a direct link between the HPFF transformation and the operation, by informing operational managers about HPFF, discussing the benefit of an HPFF for them, and identifying their wishes and needs and including these in the transformation plan.
- Provide visible approval and support for the HPFF transformation from the board of directors.
- "Think big, start small": steadily make small improvement steps towards the larger goal of the HPFF. For example, with regard to "Role Clarity," start by redistributing work, let financial professionals develop ownership of the assigned work, and then increasingly emphasize the importance of the roles and their proper execution.
- Create room for experimentation to try things out in a safe environment.

How to create and maintain enthusiasm among financial professionals

- Choose a metaphor for the HPFF transformation. For example the metaphor of a journey, or that of a caterpillar (now) via pupation (halfway) to a butterfly (in three years).
- Clearly recognize the different roles (along with the accompanying tasks) during the HPFF transformation. Then talk to financial professionals about their capacities, competencies, and ambitions in order to match these properly with the identified roles, and to consider where certain financial professionals need extra support or development. Provide these financial professionals with (extra) coaching.
- Ensure that sufficient time remains available for improvement activities.
- Discuss progress regularly and include financial professionals in these discussions.
- Regularly express appreciation and celebrate the successes of achieved milestones together. But also "celebrate" the failures, in the sense that they are recognized in order to learn from them.
- Regularly demonstrate relevance and impact, on both the finance function and the operation, of the HPFF transformation.
- Exchange many experiences in order to learn from each other and thereby grow both individually as a person and collectively as a finance function.
- Dedicate a lot of attention and create opportunities for the personal development of financial professionals during the transformation process.

How to Keep Focus and Discipline

- Install a steering committee that monitors progress and supports HPFF transformation activities.
- Regularly measure the progress and results of the transformation based on the HPFF transformation plan; provide information about this and discuss it with management and financial professionals, and then make adjustments (if necessary).
- Continue to make small improvement steps, keeping pace with the improvement projects and actions. Set priorities sequentially, not in parallel. Use an agile/scrum approach.
- Keep the operation well-informed about the transformation and also let the operation address/challenge the finance function on its progress and delivery of promised results.
- Have periodic discussions with the operation about (further) opportunities for improvement.
- Continue to hold regular dialogue sessions about HPFF with management and other stakeholders, and stay connected with the right forums with regard to decision-making at a strategic level.
- Keep emphasizing that the HPFF transformation is a process, a movement, and not a project.

9.7 OBTAINING RESOURCES FOR THE HPFF TRANSFORMATION

As has become quite clear in this book so far, it pays to become an HPFF. However, making continuous improvement and renewal possible requires time and a financial budget, and this is where unfortunately the problems start in many organizations. In general, the benefits of improving the finance function are clear to the finance professionals involved, and, based on the benefits available, securing resources for improvements should be easy. However, in practice it proves difficult to actually get these resources, and they are often obtained only partially or not at all. This is because, in most organizations, operations take precedence in the allocation of resources, not least because improvements in customer processes are immediately noticeable to external customers (Katchamart, 2013; Kraan, 2017). In addition, finance functions frequently have difficulties quantifying the quality improvement in internal processes, and consequently there may be 'gaps' in the justification offered for the required resources. This means that finance functions regularly do not receive (enough) resources for improvements even though they do urgently need these, especially if they aim to transform into an HPFF. To help finance functions overcome this hurdle of organizations not being inclined to provide resources for improvements to a supporting function, we studied the courses of action available to finance functions to obtain these necessary resources after all. In particular, we considered obtaining approval for significant improvements that generally require many resources, such as a training and education program for financial employees, the implementation of a new ICT system, or a transformation of the function to a higher-quality level (i.e., the creation of an HPFF).

Research Approach (De Waal et al., 2021)

The scientific and professional literature contains only limited information about how resources for improvements can be obtained by a finance function. Therefore, in order to determine which courses of

Figure 4. Schematic overview of the research approach

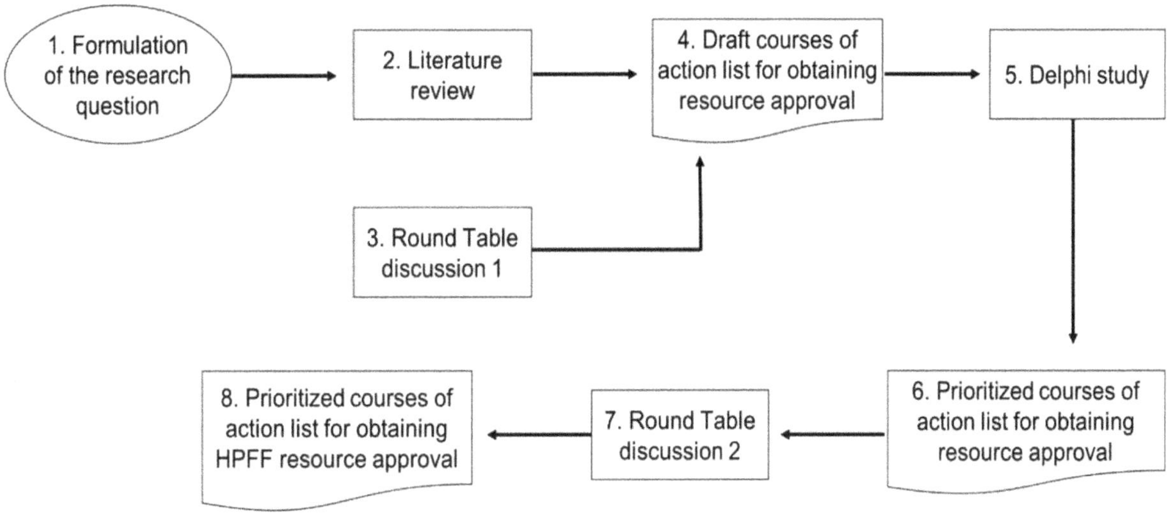

action are used in practice and how effective they are, our research largely relies on input from experienced finance experts. Figure 4 depicts our research approach schematically.

Step 1: Formulation of the Research Question

The research started with formulating the research question, which is as follows: 'How can a finance function get approval and resources for an improvement that is mainly internally oriented (within the finance function) and where the benefits are mainly indirect in nature?'

Step 2: Literature Review

We conducted a literature search of various academic databases. This search identified only four sources which featured 14 courses of actions. It was not clear from the four sources how effective these courses of action actually were in helping to obtain resources for improvements.

Steps 3 + 4: Roundtable Discussion 1

To identify other possible courses of action, we organized a virtual roundtable discussion in which 10 financial experts participated. They discussed the following questions: How did you get the topic of obtaining permission and resources for improvements on the management team's agenda? How did you approach obtaining the permission and the resources? Which objections did you anticipate, and which objections actually emerged? How did you structure your request? Do you have any other tips or strategies? During the session, each participant was given five minutes to introduce a real-life situation where they had asked resources for an improvement in the finance function, and then they explained how they went about this. After all participants had spoken, more tips and strategies were exchanged in an open discussion. This produced 15 courses of action, which were combined with the 14 courses of action identified in the literature review to yield (after removing duplications) a draft list of 25 courses of action.

Steps 5 + 6: Conducting a Delphi Study

To determine which of these 25 courses of action are most effective in obtaining resources for improvements and whether there is a particular order in which these courses should be used, we used the Delphi method to obtain the opinions of 24 financial experts. In Delphi Round 1, the list of 25 courses of action was sent to the experts, with a request to rate these courses according to effectiveness. The experts were advised that in this context, 'effectiveness' meant that the course of action would actually lead to the finance function acquiring the desired resources for the improvement. The experts were also asked to add courses of action that they had applied in the past and were not on the list. The feedback of the experts was summarized and courses of action were ranked according to initial effectiveness scores. The lowest-ranking courses of action were removed because these were deemed not to be sufficiently effective, and additional courses of action suggested by the experts were added to the new list. In Round 2, the experts were asked to rank the resulting 26 courses of action according to effectiveness, but this time without adding additional courses of action. Again, the experts' feedback was summarized and courses of action were ranked in order of effectiveness, with the lowest-scoring courses of action being removed from the list. For the remaining 10 courses of action, consensus about their effectiveness was achieved among the Delphi experts because they more or less placed these courses in the same order of effectiveness. In Round 3, the experts were asked the following question: "You know that you want to make a fairly large improvement in your finance function early next year. It will consist of three subprojects for which you need resources (in staffing and financial budget). Which courses of action are you going to use for this and in what chronological order, to get the necessary resource approval?" This yielded several different sequences of courses of action, which were ordered in an overall sequence and presented to the experts during Round 4. In this round, the experts were able to achieve consensus on the 'ideal' (i.e., most effective) courses of action in the 'ideal' chronological order.

Steps 7 + 8: Differentiating the Courses of Action for an HPFF Transformation

The Delphi experts indicated that the resulting 14 courses of action apply in principle to any improvement proposed for which resources are needed, but that the content of the steps will differ depending on the type and size of the proposed improvement and that every improvement requires customization. To find out how this customization could be achieved, we organized another (virtual) roundtable discussion around the question of how to tailor the courses of action to obtain resources (financial budget, staffing) for a specific improvement: a transformation to an HPFF. For this roundtable discussion, we invited another 10 financial experts who constructed a 'narrative' for each course of action: a story that the finance function can use when implementing the course of action to obtain resources for the HPFF transformation. In this way, the participants "translated" the general courses of action into specific actions to obtain resources for a scenario in which they wanted to implement an HPFF transformation.

Ten Courses of Action

The Delphi study yielded 10 effective courses of action, and the 24 Delphi experts emphasized that combining these courses of action makes them more effective in practice. There appeared to be two types of courses of action: process-based courses (six courses), which mainly concern the process of applying

Figure 5. Schematic overview of the process for obtaining resources for an HPFF transformation

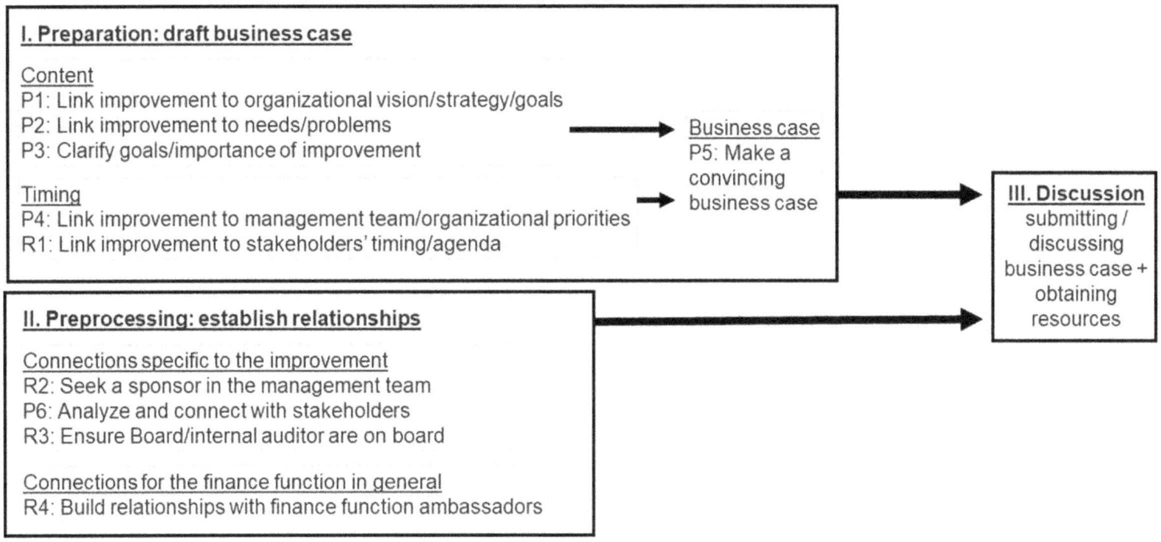

for the resources for improvements, and relational courses (four courses), which concern building and maintaining good relationships with stakeholders of the finance function so that they will support the resource request in due course. Figure 5 shows schematically how the Delphi experts ranked the selected courses of action.

Figure 5 shows that the proposed strategy for successfully obtaining resources for improvements takes place in two parallel steps. During step I, a business case for the improvement and the required resources are compiled. The Delphi experts emphasized that this is not just about putting together a financial business case, but specifically about building a qualitative business case that clearly shows the need for change. In step I, a distinction is made between the content of the improvement and the timeframe in which the improvement will be implemented. With regard to content, the Delphi experts state that the improvement requested by the finance function should benefit the organization by supporting the achievement of the vision, strategy or goals, and priorities of the organization and the management team (P1 and P4 in Figure 5), and/or it should address specific problems in the organization or specific needs relevant to the organization's operations (P2). In both cases, it is essential that the purpose of the improvement and its importance (not only for the finance function but for the entire organization) are properly clarified and explained (P3). Relationally, it is sensible to align the improvement with the agendas of the most important stakeholders in the organization (R1). By matching both the content and the timing of the improvement to the other things happening in the organization, a strong business case is obtained (P5).

Step II actually commences before step I and continues after the business case has been presented. In this step, relationships are built and maintained with the organization's most important stakeholders so that they can (start to) act as ambassadors for the finance function and support its resource requests (P6 + R4). In addition, support can be sought for specific improvements by, for example, identifying within the management team the person who could benefit most from the improvement and is therefore most likely to support the resources request (R2). Another course of action is to inform the Board and/or the internal auditor about the improvement and make it clear to them that implementing this improvement will afford the organization more control, i.e., less vulnerability to risks and exposure (R3). Only when

Step 1 and Step II have been properly executed, according to the Delphi experts, is it time to present the business case to the management team in order to obtain the resources for the proposed improvement (Step III).

The second roundtable discussion addressed how to customize the steps in Figure 5 to the actual case of obtaining resources for the transformation of the finance function to a HPFF. The results of this discussion are presented below.

Preparation: Create a Business Case for the HPFF - Content

The business case to be drawn up must contain convincing substantive arguments for the proposal and make clear its advantages. The participants in the roundtable discussion had the following suggestions for achieving this:

- Make the role of the finance function clear within the organization and also explain how the organization can be better supported when the finance function becomes an HPFF. Make clear that creating an HPFF is a 'must have' for the entire organization because the finance function can provide critical insights into the organization's strategy and achievement of its goals, thus offering more targeted support and recommendations to the organization.
- Highlight that because every department needs to improve in order to improve the organization as a whole, the finance function intends to support this effort by becoming an HPFF.
- Emphasize that because an important part of steering the organization is provision of management information, becoming an HPFF will ensure that a better information supply (more relevant, more timely, and more to the point) with more reliable underlying data is guaranteed.
- Show that the HPFF will unburden managers and employees by providing them with a better and more easily accessible supply of information, and will help them to become more proactive by providing better support for scenario planning and making forecasts.
- Identify the concrete problems facing the organization and show how an HPFF can help deal with them.
- Explain the specific benefits of the HPFF for each department in the organization.
- Help stakeholders visualize what the HPFF might look like and what it will do for the organization.
- Show the current status of the finance function (e.g., 'blood, sweat, and tears') and how this limits what can be done for the organization at present.
- Show how difficult it is to recruit good new staff members, and that doing so is crucial to the success of the finance function and the organization, and show that an HPFF will attract good people much more easily than a low-performing finance function ('everybody wants to be on a winning team').

Preparation: Create a Business Case for the HPFF - Timing

Concrete courses of action regarding the timing of the improvement project and the wording of the proposal can also be formulated. The participants suggested the following:

- Maintain frequent contact with the management team and stakeholders in order to be aware of their priorities and agenda.

- Speak the language of the management team and stakeholders, and then translate the HPFF (benefits) to their 'world.'
- Emphasize that the priorities of the management team and stakeholders are also those of the finance function, and that being an HPFF will help better support these priorities.
- Meet with the management team and the stakeholders to identify a connection between their plans and those of the finance function (with regard to becoming a HPFF).
- Show that the HPFF will ease the administrative burden on the organization.

Preparation: Establishing Relationships - Connections of the Finance Function

In regard to establishing relationships to guarantee support from specific stakeholders for the transformation into an HPFF, the participants gave these ideas:

- Identify the main stakeholders of the finance function. Map out their mutual relationships and their (informal/external) influencers. Determine their (possible) interest in the creation of the HPFF.
- Consider which of the stakeholders can and want to become a sponsor of the HPFF. Start with the most positive stakeholder. Introduce the HPFF philosophy to this stakeholder by means of a case study from his/her own practice in order to demonstrate the benefits of an HPFF for the stakeholder.
- Connect the HPFF with issues such as compliance and risk management, thus creating alignment with the priorities of the Board and internal auditor.
- Involve critics so they know their voices are being heard. This also allows the finance function to better prepare for any counter-arguments during the discussions about the required resources.
- Involve sponsors in the HPFF transformation after resource approval; keep them regularly informed of the progress and results achieved.

Preparation: Making Relationships - Other Connections in the Organization

Finally, the participants discussed how to establish general relationships with key stakeholders of the finance function, and suggested the following:

- Identify possible ambassadors of the finance function, such as members of the Supervisory Board (especially those with audit and finance in their portfolio), the external auditor (especially if they prescribe improvements to the finance function), operational budget owners (with a focus on provision of information to them by the finance function), and operations/shared service center (with regard to data quality).
- 'Plant the finance function ambassadorship seed' outside the budget period; share the HPFF vision, announce improvements in the finance function, create enthusiasm, and ask for feedback.

Of course, following steps I, II, and III will not always lead to successfully obtaining resources for improvements. However, based on the extensive experience of the finance experts we consulted, we are confident that the chances of success will be significantly improved, and that therefore the importance of and value added by the finance function for the organization will increase.

Financial Transformations: What Works and Doesn't Work.[2]

Gartner surveyed more than 80 finance teams and conducted interviews with more than 70 finance leaders to identify what does and doesn't work during the transformation of a financial function, and made the nice overview below of this (see Table 2).

Table 2.

Transformation aspect	Successful transformations	Unsuccessful transformations
Vision and strategy	Identify future business needs and the services the finance function needs to offer so these business needs can be satisfied	Base the transformation on hitting cost targets
Target setting	Base targets on how the finance function will support achievement of the targets	Base targets on finance function cost as percentage of revenue and on internal customer satisfaction
Service offering	Eliminate low-value services, enhance/add high-value services	Keep adding services while taking out costs
Resource allocation	Spend resources in areas of highest return	Spread resources (and resource cuts) evenly over the function
Role design	Differentiate roles (in guidance/support and governance ones)	Change reporting structure but do not redesign roles or performance measures
Centralization	Centralize services while maintaining alignment with business needs	Focus on finding synergies and gaining economies of scale across all non-business facing finance processes
Processes	Focus on making processes more effective by using a continuous, collaborative productivity improvement approach	Focus on making processes more standardized and scalable
Automation	Focus on technology governance and end-user adoption	Focus on IT functionality and capability
Data	Make the correct trade-off between data accuracy and speed of the decision-making process	Aim for the "perfect data" in every process
Employees	Capitalize on human-centered and strategic skills	Develop technical and analytical skills in all the financials
Internal customers	Manage customer expectations (based on budget realities)	Delight the customers

CASE: HPFF - Can A Finance Function Become "Too Good"?

The finance function of the multinational had come a long way in the past decade. Ten years ago, the function was structured along hierarchical and national structures with many legacy systems inherited from the many companies that had been taken over in that period. It was no wonder that the monthly closing was a cumbersome operation that took more than 10 days; it took the Finance team a lot of time and effort to come up with the correct figures on time. Moreover, there was a corporate culture in which the focus was mainly on the performance of operations, while the focus on customers was rather limited. It was clear that the finance function had to evolve in a way that would benefit the entire organization. It decided to reformulate its roles, activities, and priorities. The first priority was re-establishing the roles of the finance function, as being:

- Analysts: analyzing and interpreting financial information efficiently and accurately
- Trusted advisors: competent and credible partners who provide effective solutions
- Future-ready: anticipating, adapting, and responding to the changes and needs that arise

Next was the redefinition of the main activities of the finance function:

- secure funding, create the best business structures and help investors understand the organization and its value
- advise and support internal teams to get the most value from their activities
- ensure compliance to protect the organization's reputation
- create a strategic focus and "connect the dots" by seeing and interpreting connection within the organization and the outside world
- stimulate optimal resource allocation and measure performance
- provide more insight into what really lies behind the numbers and use advanced analysis methods and new technologies to do so
- propose solutions and measure their impact
- getting things done by creating an efficient, flexible, and compliant "backbone," thus creating a positive user experience.

Finally, the priorities of the finance function were, in consultation with the business, reformulated to be as follows:

- with costs under pressure, a lean and more responsive back office function must be created,
- the decision-making process in the organization must be better supported in order to promote the performance of the organization
- the focus must shift from purely transactional activities to business partnering activities that can create higher added value
- time must be set aside to create opportunities for the organization, in the form of developing and delivering meaningful insights that contribute to business activities.

The HPFF Diagnosis

After having been busy for several years with this finance transformation, the management of the finance function wanted to assess how they were doing. They decide to conduct the HPFF diagnosis as that would map the strengths and weaknesses of their function on a scientific basis. The results of the HPFF questionnaire, after completion by the financial professionals of the function, are given in Figures 6 and 7.

The curve of the HPFF graph for the finance function is similar in shape to that for the population collected so far in our HPFF database. The areas in which other companies typically score the lowest, namely clarity of roles and staff development, are also lower scoring points at the finance function.

However, we note that the finance function's scores are, on average, higher (+1.2) than those for the rest of the database population, indicating that this is a leading finance function. If we consider the scores for the individual HPFF characteristics, it turns out that the finance function is already at HPFF level for a number of those. The detailed scores on the HPFF characteristics also show what the finance function should focus on advancing from being a leading finance function to becoming a high-performance one, through the following actions:

- Paying more attention to personnel development; in particular, providing more technical and training courses to support the financial professionals in becoming high-performing in their particular roles.
- More attention should be paid to the use of IT. Despite the priority given to automation, the results of this focus do not seem to convince the financial professionals. For instance, routine processes are not yet fully automated. This means that there should still be more time potentially available for financial professionals to initiate value-adding activities, such as creating a self-service facility for managers. A process and IT improvement effort must be made at the organizational level

Figure 6. The HPFF scores for the finance function after the finance transformation

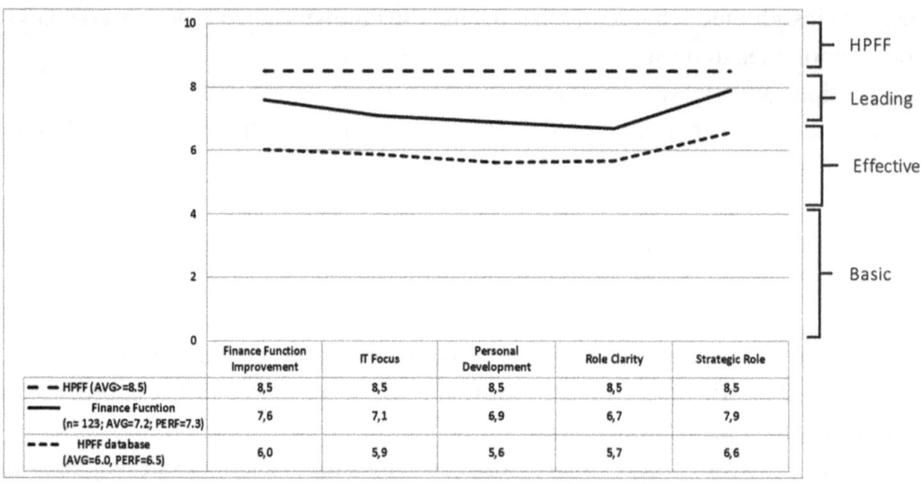

	Finance Function Improvement	IT Focus	Personal Development	Role Clarity	Strategic Role
HPFF (AVG>=8.5)	8,5	8,5	8,5	8,5	8,5
Finance Fucntion (n= 123; AVG=7.2; PERF=7.3)	7,6	7,1	6,9	6,7	7,9
HPFF database (AVG=6.0, PERF=6.5)	6,0	5,9	5,6	5,7	6,6

because the biggest obstacle—inefficient and non-integrated business processes—in the organization is not limited to just the finance function.

- Examine the difference in score between "performing the strategic role" and "internal customer satisfaction." It is noteworthy that the highest scores are given for the way the finance function fulfills its strategic role. However, the same financial professionals that gave this score believe that internal customers are only reasonably satisfied with the support they receive from the function: these two notions seem at odds with each other.

Figure 7. The obstacles faced by the finance function after the finance transformation

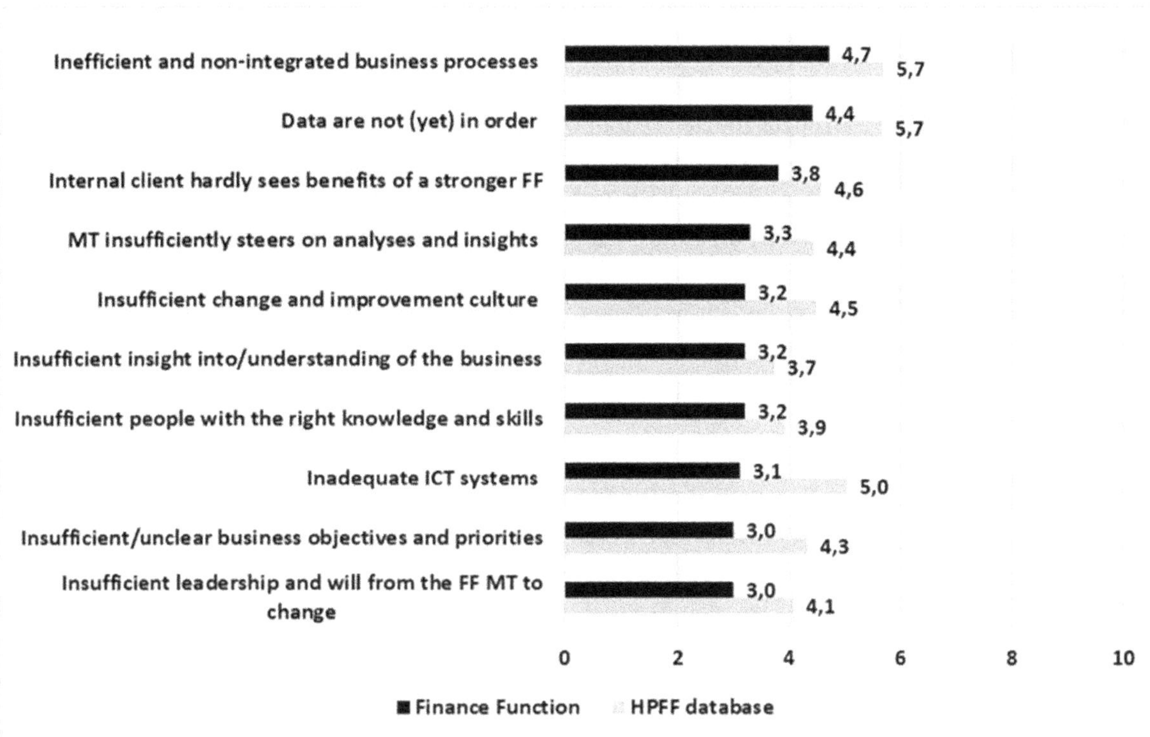

Discussing the HPFF Analysis: Can You Be "Too Good"?

We presented our analysis to the CFO of the finance function. He was pleasantly surprised to find that his team scored better than average on the factors "Personnel development" and "Role clarity." As he told us: "Since our sector is changing rapidly, we have to make constant adjustments. As a result, an important part of the job descriptions and roles within the finance function changes every two years. So I am not surprised that our colleagues score lower on role clarity. We have worked continuously for the past 10 years and we are still making progress, we strongly believe in continuous improvement. I am very happy with what the team has achieved through hard work and a very resilient attitude over the years. In my view, HPFF is more of an "evolutionary" process than a fixed end goal anyway."

The CFO also commented on the HPFF framework and diagnosis: "It is exciting to gain insights through the HPFF diagnosis, especially since this analysis specifically focuses on the performance of the finance function. In general, it is not easy to distinguish the performance of the finance function from that of the company as a whole, precisely because the financial processes are related to all business processes. For example, we recently organized a NPS survey to measure the satisfaction of internal customers with certain financial processes. Five percent of the points identified as problematic by internal customers turned out to have nothing to do with the finance function. This concerned, for example, problems related to interaction between different levels and communication within the company itself. Another 20% was not directly related to the processes of the finance function, but did concern areas in which we can take the initiative and help solve the problem. Only 25% of all problems cited were directly related to the financial processes. This shows that we really need to work very well with our business partners to create the right understanding and impact."

When considering which factors can hinder the ambition to realize the full HPFF potential, the outlook for the finance function looks promising. It is noteworthy, however, that the obstacle "the internal client hardly sees benefits from a stronger finance function" scores as the second-highest obstacle, something that is not observed very often at finance functions in other organizations. However, the CFO did not react to this outcome with much surprise: "The Business wants a strong business partner. But if you are strong and capable in that role, you sometimes end up in areas where people prefer not to see you. Not everyone feels equally good when he or she is critically questioned. Sometimes managers rather want things to stay hidden, like secret budget nest eggs for eventualities which is still fairly innocent. But sometimes it goes to more serious issues and then a finance function that cannot be put off is not that convenient. In this sense you could say that yes, as finance function you can become too good .. in the eyes of weak managers!"

As a last point, despite the good score, our attention was drawn by something remarkable: There is a strong focus on IT in this finance function; the CFO stresses the importance of automation and digitization. However, the financial professionals gave a comparatively lower score to the HPFF factor 'IT focus'. "To me this does make sense," the CFO reacted. "Yes, we are working diligently on further automation, but we are far from finished. Besides, you can look at this score positively: now that we are busy with further automation we see more and more opportunities and we have a better understanding of what can still be automated. So we are not easily satisfied in this area. And let's not forget that automation cannot solve everything. A worthless process that you digitize remains a worthless process, so more work needs to be done there. In addition, the need for clean, usable data is great when you start working with advanced analysis methods and AI. That also takes time. As I said, it is an evolution and since we believe in continuous improvement, chances are we will succeed in becoming a full-fledged HPFF."

REFERENCES

Abdelal, R., Carmody, K., Hill, M., & Pearson, W. J. (2021). *The CFO's role in capability building*. McKinsey & Company.

APQC. (2018). *Ten characteristics shared among best-in-class finance functions*. American Productivity and Quality Center.

de Waal, A., Bilstra, E., Bootsman, J., & Linthorst, J. (2021). Future-proofing the finance function: An empirical approach. *International Journal of Management and Applied Research*, *8*(2), 122–140. doi:10.18646/2056.82.21-008

de Waal, A. A. (2020). *High Performance Managerial Leadership*. Praeger.

de Waal, A. A., & Heijtel, I. (2016). Searching for effective change interventions for the transformation into a high performance organization. *Management Research Review*, *39*(9), 1080–1104. doi:10.1108/MRR-04-2015-0094

Gartner. (2019). *Hallmarks of Winning Finance Transformations*. Gartner, Inc.

ICAEW/ISCA. (2019). *Digital transformation in finance functions: ASEAN and UK perspectives*. ICAEW thought leadership in partnership with The Institute of Singapore Chartered Accountants. ISCA.

IFAC. (2018). *Perspectives on the finance function journey*. International Federation of Accountants.

Katchamart, A. (2013). Mapping value added positions in facilities management by using a product-process matrix. *Journal of Facilities Management, 11*(3), 226–252. doi:10.1108/JFM-10-2012-0045

Kraan, D. (2017). Enhancing the finance function in line ministries. *OECD Journal on Budgeting*, *16*(2), 75–92. doi:10.1787/budget-16-5jg30cchbf5k

ENDNOTES

1 The reason to do this is twofold: (1) the HPO transformation approach has been developed in a scientific manner, as described in de Waal and Heijtel (2016); and (2) the HPFF framework is strongly related to the HPO framework, so it makes sense that a transformation approach for HPO will also work for HPFF (with some possible adaptations). The text for this Chapter has been derived and adapted for HPFF from Chapter 5 of de Waal (2020).

2 See Gartner (2021); the Table has been slightly adapted and abbreviated.

Chapter 10
Best Ideas

ABSTRACT

During the research into the HPFF, many fine ideas that finance functions have implemented to strengthen themselves in order to become high performing were collected. These ideas that all can be tied to the HPFF factors and are thus useful to know about when undertaking an HPFF transformation were gathered during interviews with financial professionals and many case studies conducted at finance functions. In this chapter, 50 of those best ideas are discuss. They are categorized according to the HPFF factor they most support and strengthen (some of the ideas can target multiple factors) and serve as inspiration for further strengthening finance functions.

Best Idea vs Best Practice
A best idea is a working idea in practice in a certain context, and may be of value when experimented with in the relevant context. A best idea cannot and should not simply be copied as a best practice; what works in one context does not necessarily work in another. We ask you to read a best idea and then contemplate whether it would be relevant, useful, and helpful in the context of your own finance function: maybe the best idea has to be tailored to fit that context, or maybe it has to be discarded as not applicable in the particular context of your finance function.

10.1 BEST IDEAS FOR HPFF FACTOR "FINANCE FUNCTION IMPROVEMENT"

The "Finance Function Improvement" factor concerns how able financials are at improving their finance function. HPFFs follow improvement actions and evaluate their progress using performance indicators. Implementation of improvements is actively stimulated and tackled in a structured manner. In addition, HPFFs conduct processes uniformly and in one place to the greatest possible extent, so that expertise on these processes is bundled. HPFFs use financial self-service through which managers can make their own reports without needing the finance function. In this section, we discuss 17 best ideas concerning the ability to improve finance processes and the processes of adjacent organizational departments.

DOI: 10.4018/978-1-7998-6929-0.ch010

Best Ideas

Table 1.

No.	Best idea	Key point of this best idea
FFI1	Taskforces: tackle cross-departmental problems	Using multidisciplinary teams, focused on addressing one specific issue, leads to cross-organizational collaboration with a dedicated focus on improvement.
FFI2	Standardize reporting: develop a "language" for the same version of the (numerical) truth	A single front end and alignment of operational and financial systems are key to getting one version of the truth.
FFI3	Principles of organizing: give direction to cooperation and leadership	Creating an open culture requires knowledge sharing, autonomous decision-making, putting trust in craftsmanship, giving feedback, focusing on action, and taking time for dialogue asking "what and why" questions.
FFI4	Lean reporting: bundle expertise in reporting	Silo-busting between finance teams, introducing self-service BI, and discouraging the use of spreadsheets is crucial for a 'lean' reporting process.
FFI5	Shared services: centralize processes and work more efficiently	The quality of execution of finance processes is boosted by bringing services and knowledge together and through digitization, standardizing invoice handling, and closer cooperation between teams.
FFI6	Team cooperation: collaborate more effectively in and across teams	Knowledge transfer to colleague financial professionals, weekly stand-ups, peer-to-peer coaching, a joint skills development program, and mutually following courses given by colleagues with specific expertise stimulates collaboration in and between finance teams and professionals.
FFI7	'Peak shaving': close early as a symbol of progress	Bringing work to the fore ensures peace of mind among financial professionals, increases the quality of their output, and provides room for real continuous improvement.
FFI8	Self-service: the foundation for better support of the management processes	Giving operational managers ownership of their reporting process increases their involvement in and knowledge of finance.
FFI9	Chain management: stimulate collaboration across business units	Focusing more on discussing chain management and less on technical implementation of changes in administrative processes and discussion of internal figures creates smoother-running finance processes.
FFI10	'Agile' decision-making: more strategic impact in a data-driven market	Decision-making that has an agile rhythm of "measure, decide quickly, anticipate" is especially of value in data-driven organizations where IT and finance have to be closely connected.
FFI11	Improve processes: simplicity in integrated processes with motivated employees	When processes are simplified and integrated, the satisfaction of financial professionals will increase and thus the quality of their service will improve, leading to more satisfied customers.
FFI12	Integrated performance management: connect few financial and many business indicators to the corporate strategy	Steering based on a set of a limited number of financial indicators combined with lots of 'close to management' KPIs connects better with the priorities and worldview of management.
FFI13	Horizontal and vertical finance: a 360° finance view on the organization	Changing the organizational model in the finance function so that it provides three perspectives (business controlling, operational controlling, strategic controlling) leads to more communication and cooperation.
FFI14	Integration of the planning processes in one platform: higher-quality processes by structuring and automating data translation activities.	Working towards one platform forces finance functions to structure data processing, opens possibilities to align different data-driven processes (budgeting, reporting, forecasting), and eliminates data translation activities, thus generating higher data quality.
FFI15	Outsource on the basis of result, not assignment: organize win-win in an outsourcing relationship	When in an outsourcing relationship the interests of both parties head in the same direction, the speed and quality of the processes increase considerably and provide mutual benefits.
FFI16	Increased quality of management information: cause-effect relationships are the link between strategy and execution	Effective use of management information is dependent on a complex set of factors (tooling, data quality, culture, management style), but should always be based on insight in the (cascading set of) leading indicators that support the strategy of the organization.
FFI17	Regular self-assessment: monitor high performance	Regular self-assessment creates a common language, stimulates dialogue and creates more knowledge of continuous improvement in the finance function.

10.1.1 Best Idea FFI1: Taskforces - Tackle Cross-Departmental Problems

The professionalism of the finance function depends on good cooperation between the shared service center, the financial professionals from the head office, and the finance function professionals in a given country. The Director of Finance of a multinational indicates that when the organization is set up in a specific country, the operational processes are well-organized up to a certain point, but that each country still applies its own customization in managing the local business. "That was in itself not surprising. The control processes and systems could not sufficiently keep up with the growth of the organization. We therefore tackled a number of problems and worked on them in a small committee. Then we put together a number of task forces with participants from commerce, the shared services center, IT, and the central Finance department of the European head office. In each task force, a financial professional was given the lead and was made responsible for solving the problem. It was the responsibility of each task force to come up with proposals for process and system improvements, which were then reported to senior finance leadership. The purpose of the task forces was to bring the processes and systems to a higher level, to learn from colleagues from different environments within the finance function, to encourage working with best practices, but above all to follow-up the own finance function mission: continuous work on improvement."

The Director of Finance explains how this works: "For every topic, whether it concerns the process from ordering to payment (procure-to-pay), strategic sourcing, or the monthly closing process, we ask three questions: Where are we now?, Where do we want to go?, and How do we arrive at the next phase? The topics can be standardized fairly well, with the 'one size fits all' approach working fine for 80 percent of the topics. When we reach that percentage, we dissolve the task force and then organize a new task force for the next topic. In this way we have been able to quickly improve a large number of processes in a short period of time. The advantage of working with task forces is that the prioritization of issues within the different environments in the finance function becomes explicit, and tackling the issues together provides insight and understanding of each other's activities."

10.1.2 Best Idea FFI2: Standardize Reporting: Develop a "Language" For the Same Version of the (Numerical) Truth

An important precondition for conducting a planning or review discussion properly is that there is one version of the financial truth. The Director of Finance of a pharmaceutical company emphasizes that ease of access to information is very important in becoming a business partner: "In the early years we had a lot of discussion about the differences between financial and commercial figures. An important reason was that we used different tools, but we also reported the results in different ways. We had already taken the first step towards a lasting solution by standardizing reports within the finance function. Our monthly report, created in a spreadsheet and distributed in PDF format, over time largely covered the information required by internal customers. This report included revenue, cost, margin, analysis, and head count. Due to the growth in the number of countries in which we operate, but also due to changes in the organizational structure, reporting became too complex to continue to generate from a spreadsheet. We could no longer guarantee reliability." The next step was therefore to invest in specialized management reporting software. The Director of Finance, together with the central IT department, opted for a package to be used by the commercial departments: "We wanted one system for the complete financial management reporting. We knew what our internal customers wanted, but lacked the facilities to satisfy those needs in Excel. We were looking for flexibility, reliability, and an automated process built on solid data sources with a single front end."

Through the new system, the process of creating management reports has been greatly simplified and accelerated and the reports, offered via the web, are also more flexible for users: they can now independently make selections and analyses. A major advantage is that in the current reporting, the sales and the financial reports are combined so that there is no discussion about the figures during reviews. The Director of Finance comments: "The sales and financial data come from two different sources. The tricky point is then to use the same data definitions. The commercial teams are busy with sales figures on a daily basis. The difficulty is to reconcile that daily sales data with the financial figures that are updated monthly. But we succeeded through standardization. The uniformity of the reports has yielded a lot for us, in time and in quality. In the old situation we made all reports for all countries, we now have standard reports and the other reports are provided by the local financial professionals in the countries themselves. The countries are positive about this, and their confidence in the figures has increased considerably. If we now look at the daily sales, we know those numbers are accurate. In addition, we created a shared language with the visual presentation of the information. You can make presentations in a thousand ways, but we nowadays do it all the same way. In presentations, for example, you now see the same graphs for 27 countries, with the same look and feel. This allows us to make quick decisions during a business review based on the business drivers, because it all compares very easily. Our reporting system facilitates both the manager who looks at the figures at a higher level and the financial professional in the country who makes more detailed analyses and delves deeper into the figures. Furthermore, during the implementation of the system, numerous opportunities for improvement in operational financial processes came to the fore, so that we could also implement improvements there."

Reporting reliable figures is "core business" for the finance function—a hygiene factor that only sticks out when the data are questioned. The transparent formulation of data and the use of unambiguous data definitions is a process that every finance function must have in order; according to the Director of Finance: "Thanks to the transparent connection between financial and operational systems, we can now see faster than before whether a region is doing well or not and we can spend more time in collaboration with the business."

10.1.3 Best Idea FFI3: Principles of Organizing - Give Direction to Cooperation and Leadership

An important step in realizing the transformation of a finance function is to create a culture of continuous improvement. This requires that all employees and managers actively use their craftsmanship, share their knowledge and experience with colleagues, and have room to make their own choices in order to achieve goals. The finance function of a governmental service organization applies three "principles of organizing" that every financial professional can fall back on (see Figure FFI1). These principles apply to all financial professionals, and every financial professional can hold a colleague accountable for working according to these principles.

1. *From control and rules to trust.* Clear goals and frameworks enable professionals to determine for themselves how they accomplish their task. This means that rules and agreements that limit the completion of tasks should be avoided as much as possible. It also means that professionals must be able to make their own choices in achieving (organizational) goals. One of the financial profes-

sionals indicates: "You can assume that all professionals perform their tasks. You do not have to check each other if you have made agreements about who will perform which task. If you think things are not going well, give feedback and address these issues immediately."

2. *From craftsmanship to professionalism*. It is important that financial professionals share and transfer their professional knowledge and practical experience with each other. This is done during the regular working relationships that people have with each other, but also through workshops; for example, in a Finance Academy. The Director of Finance and Control comments: "Being a professional means that you understand your profession and are good at it. And that you also transfer your expertise to colleagues. In this way you help each other and the organization further along."
3. *From attending to contributing*. Everyone has to contribute and if there are discussions, partnerships, or working relationships that are not productive, financial professionals are expected to do something about them. The Director of Finance and Control explains: "If you are interested in each other and in the organization, you will understand each other better. If you understand each other better, you work together better. The result of this principle is that financial professionals now indicate themselves that they will not attend a particular meeting because they do not believe they will contribute to it. That saves a lot of wasted time."

Figure 1. The organizational principles of the finance function

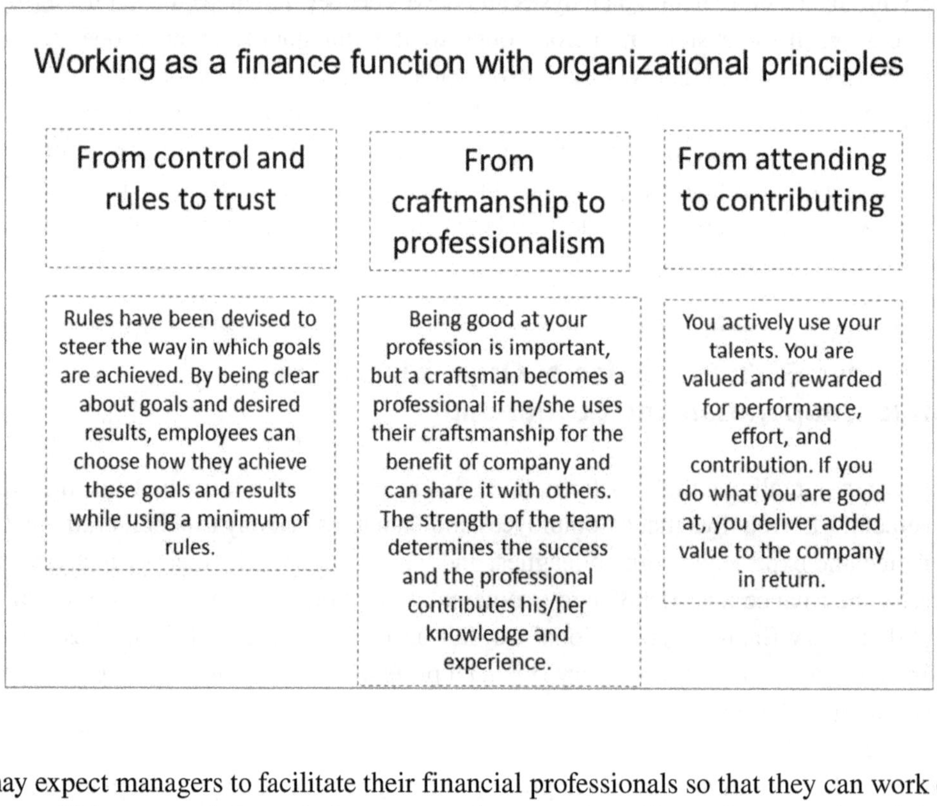

You may expect managers to facilitate their financial professionals so that they can work optimally. The Director of Finance and Control also wants to increase the self-steering capacity of the financial professionals: "In the past, 'manager' was a position whose main activity is to manage and control employees. Now we expect managers to facilitate and support financial professionals in their development.

We expect managers to get started with our four principles of leadership. If they apply these properly, their financial professionals become more self-managing and productive." The finance function uses the following leadership principles:

1. *Set a clear framework.* Managers must indicate what they expect from their financial professionals and why they expect this. It is important that the manager is strict about goals, the performance criteria, and the desired tasks, and that financial professionals are enabled to learn during the transformation. Using this clear framework, it is helpful if the manager inspires the financial professionals regularly so that they understand what is expected of them. But managers should not undertake the transformation themselves: financial professionals should be able to discover for themselves what works and what does not.
2. *Promote good and desirable behavior.* Managers must intervene during the transformation to stimulate and promote desired behavior; the finance function calls this "changing from A to B according to the principles of B." This can become difficult if an employee does not do what is expected in the new situation because of an ill-considered course of action. The Director of Finance and Control states: "It is especially important that managers do not immediately disapprove of the outcome, but above all emphasize that the initiative is very good, but that this particular outcome cannot be the intention. Appreciate good behavior and correct bad behavior."
3. *Establish a clear dialogue and learning structure.* The Director of Finance and Control says: "We want managers to offer financial professionals a structure to promote learning. You cannot force financial professionals to learn but you can certainly encourage them to do so. A good dialogue structure is important so that financial professionals have the opportunity to discuss their task and receive feedback on their behavior. Not only from managers, but also from colleagues. It is important that financial professionals provide short, cyclical feedback on each other's behavior. An employee satisfaction survey often has too large a gap between the time of the survey and the time of feedback. A Finance Academy is another example of a structure that provides support when financial professionals want to gain knowledge and experience."
4. *Create ownership and take employees seriously.* Managers must encourage financial professionals to take action by responding to their motivations. Financial professionals can choose their current role as well as a future role in which they want to develop. The Director of Finance and Control states: "You can then tell financial professionals: hé, you want this, you take action. The intrinsic motivation of the financial professional must come first. If they execute the tasks they themselves aspired, commitment to the future situation of the finance function is ensured. If however financial professionals do not act on the developments they themselves want, then they do not fit within the framework of organizational principles, even though they have said 'yes' to them. You then need to conduct a good dialogue with these financial professionals about their performance. Conversely, management must of course set a good example by making time for dialogue and by not filling in every detail for the financial professionals. You need to give financial professionals direction by mainly asking 'what' and 'why' questions, for example 'what do we want' and 'why do we want that.' 'How' and 'who' questions, such as 'how are we going to tackle this' and 'who is going to do it,' should be passed back to the financial professionals. As professionals they often already have very good ideas about this."

The organizational and leadership principles interact. The Director of Finance and Control explains: "The organizational principles give direction to the activities, the from-to movement. The leadership principles indicate the actions needed and have a facilitating effect. Incidentally, the principles recur at various times. In planning and progress meetings, which every financial professional has every year, it is discussed what they have done to their development, but also how they have worked according to the organizational principles. We regularly organize workshops that everyone can participate in, to learn how to deal with the organizational principles. In our daily conversations about work, we often test against the principles. And that process always continues, it is never finished."

10.1.4 Best Idea FFI4: Lean Reporting - Bundle Expertise in Reporting

An HPFF requires processes of information provision that are in tip-top order. The Director of Finance and Control of the service organization elaborates: "One problem we had was the separation between Management Control and Business Control. Business Control made many of its own reports or changed the reports they received from Management Control. This regularly led to discussions about the correctness of data between the report makers of Management Control and Business Control, but also between Business Control and the operational teams it serviced. We decided to approach the reporting process differently. The core idea in improving the information provision is to put operational managers in the lead with regard to purchasing the financial services they need. This means that operational managers carry out as many financial activities as possible - which are not too complex and do not have too much organizational impact - themselves, such as requesting reports in the form and at the time they want" (see Figure 2).

Figure 2. Information provision at the government organization

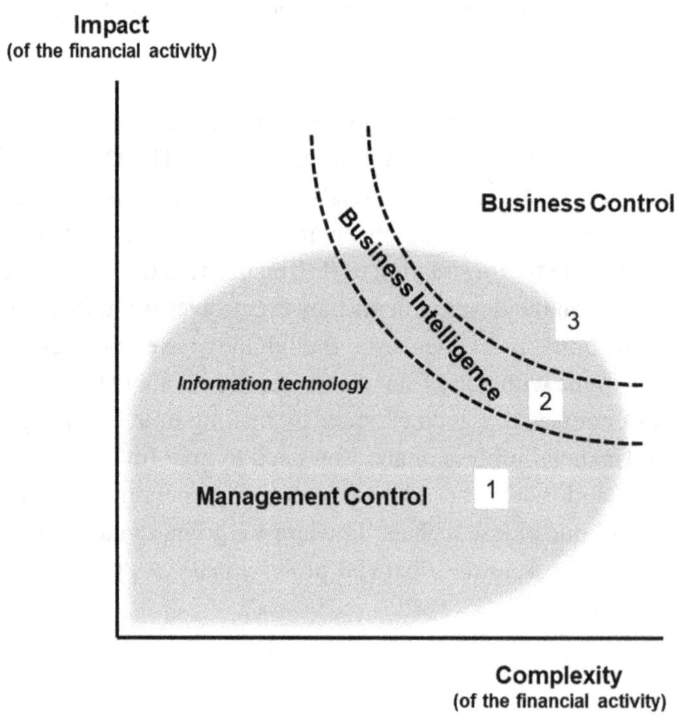

To make this possible, routine transactional activities and standard data processes have been automated as much as possible, wherein Management Control ensures that the data and information in these systems have high reliability (area 1 in Figure 2). This information can be accessed by the operational managers via a business intelligence layer (area 2) that shifts increasingly to the top right as more financial activities are automated and operational managers become more financially skilled. Business intelligence is the collection of IT instruments that makes management information accessible to decision-makers, wherein the decision-maker can compile his own information for the benefit of their own advice. Business Control then focuses on more complex financial activities and/or on activities that have a high organizational impact (area 3). Those activities require specialist knowledge that operational managers do not have; additionally operational managers need those services less continuously and more on demand.

This set-up ensures that operational managers are not forced to use financial products that they often do little with in practice. They themselves determine what they need and when they need it, and they are also better financially educated at the same time. Business Control can concentrate on the really difficult and thus value-adding activities and can develop into a real business partner. New financial services will first end up in area 3 of Figure 2 because of their relatively great complexity for the organization. As experience with the new service grows and options for automating the service are explored, the service will move into area 2 or even area 1. The Director of Finance and Control states: "We call this movement 'operational Excellence of information provision.' We try to discourage Business Control from structurally using spreadsheets when reporting to the internal customer. They can use a spreadsheet for new questions, but they must be able to push these information needs back into the information chain and thus transfer it to Management Control when these types of questions appear to be becoming structural." Combining the expertise of reporting was in line with the lean approach to process improvement in vogue throughout the organization. The Director of Finance and Control says: "We already use lean as a method in a large number of processes. Almost all our financial professionals have been trained to Orange Belt, some to Green Belt, and some even to Black Belt, as a result of which we have achieved numerous improvements. Think of the implementation of formats for fixed reports, the provision of more compact monthly reports, the discontinuation of some reports, and the introduction of standardized risk management for group and board levels."

10.1.5 Best Idea FFI5: Shared Services - Centralize Processes and Work More Efficiently

One of the first steps in the transition of the finance function of an energy network cooperative was to centralize the transactional financial processes. "By organizing well you can make enormous progress," says the Corporate Control manager. "As an organization we work a lot with contractors. We used to receive a total of 135,000 invoices per year, which involved quite a bit of handling. We have digitized and automated this process considerably. We introduced "self-billing" in which we ourselves provides the invoice for the contractors. We are now on 85,000 invoices per year. With ongoing IT developments in process automation, the number of invoices can be reduced even further, to about 50,000 per year."

The organization consciously chose to place operational purchasing activities in the Shared Service Center. In doing so, the company extended the purchasing processes with the administrative processes, creating a chain across departments. The Corporate Control manager explains: "From operational purchasing to accounts payable is a logical synergistic chain. Operational purchasing involves a lot of repetitive work. In the Shared Service Center, we can do this efficiently and therefore cheaply through the concentration of activities. Our buyers are thus free to develop a purchasing strategy, enter into and finalize large contracts, and develop purchasing policies. They now have the time to talk about rates and cooperation, instead of only delivery terms." The same approach was also applied when adding operational facility and HR processes to the Shared Service Center.

The Corporate Control manager insists on a good process design: "Shared services is primarily about organizing the processes in a customer-friendly manner. You have to arrange your purchasing process well at the front, so you will have fewer problems at the back. Some employees only purchase once or twice a year. Then you need accessible and manageable processes so that little "waste"—a term from the Lean philosophy that the organization uses in process design—is created. We measure our processes against the yardstick of four questions: can we do it without that process, can it be simpler, can we standardize it, and when all other steps have been completed do we want to automate this process? An example: hiring external staff was a problem. The Shared Service Center received the invoices for this, the line management the timesheets, and HR managed the contracts, so that was asking for problems in aligning and matching. In addition, various officials had made individual agreements about, for example, the reimbursement of costs. With a tight Purchase-to-Pay process we now have the purchasing chain in one place. We do this by digitally entering and approving hours and automating more tasks, which reduces ambiguities and creates stronger coordination."

10.1.6 Best Idea FFI6: Team Cooperation - Collaborate More Effectively In and Across Teams

During the transition of the finance function of the energy network cooperative, the emphasis was squarely put on collaboration, both within teams as well as across teams. The management team of the finance function deployed various new working methods and tools to promote this collaboration, as the Director of Finance tells:

- *Agreements about knowledge transfer*. "The result of the first phase of the transition resulted in many job changes in the finance function. We had foreseen that inevitably some knowledge would disappear in the transition from the old to the new organization. That is why we asked the financial professionals to document their knowledge and pass it on to their successors. Those successors were obliged to accept the transfer. We wanted to complete this knowledge transfer process in six months. In reality, the functions were not all transferred at the same time, which caused some delays. But after nine months we had transferred as much knowledge as possible. Our check point was the maxim that a process was not successfully transferred if the successor had not signed for receipt."
- *The look at the week*. "We introduced "the look at the week" across all teams in the finance function. This is a brief meeting reviewing operations from the previous week and looking ahead to the coming week. In the beginning we had a coach there to keep structure in the meeting. The great thing is that this meeting structure still works in most teams. We have noticed that the more homogeneous the team and the closer the team is to the operational activities, the better this type of meeting works."
- *Deployment of coaches*. "We have 12 teams in our finance function, and each team was assigned a coach. These coaches came from our own organization and received a short training of three to four days on intervention and dialogue techniques. They attended the team meetings and afterwards

evaluated how these meetings were conducted and what they had noticed could be improved. We did this for a year, and each team decided for themselves whether to proceed with their coach."

- *Team assessments*. "We conducted team assessments with the aim of working together more effectively and becoming a high performing team. Each team assessed itself. In this way, the financial professionals gained insight into the team composition and their own contribution to the team."
- *Intervision*. "We put a lot of energy into peer meetings between teams. With an exercise such as "put yourself in the shoes of," you learn to gain insight into the processes of other departments. It has helped enormously in reducing the perceived distance between for instance the shared service center and the other departments of the finance function. We use this method to understand each other's work, because we really need each other for creating an effective information chain in the finance function."
- *Knowledge and skills development program*. "We set up a knowledge and skills development program that was largely designed by the financial professionals themselves. We sometimes work with external experts, but 80 percent of the program is taught by colleagues. In total we have about 20 to 25 training courses. The knowledge program deals with topics such as IFRS, regulations, and balance sheet files. An example: a few colleagues provide a short course in which they discuss a self-devised method to provide better insight into the 30 to 40 balance sheet files we have in our company. Another example is the two-day training Business Model Canvasing that we did with all business controllers to understand how you can look at the business model of the various parts within the organization, thus giving controllers better knowledge for their work in their organizational unit. We have recently been certified by the professional association of accountants and controllers, allowing our financial professionals to earn permanent education points in our own knowledge and skills program they need to keep their license to practice."

10.1.7 Best Idea FFI7: 'Peak Shaving' - Close Early as a Symbol of Progress

Every finance function has activities that follow the regular rhythm of monthly, quarterly, and annual closings. Improvement initiatives or project-based work does not relate well to this regular rhythm. The Corporate Control manager of the wholesaler states: "During the first phase of the transition of the finance function, we sat together as a management team and agreed that everyone would formulate individually how we would determine the effects of the transition. For this I wrote a story about the finance function three years on and in which I look back with satisfaction at the developments which have resulted of the transition. The story began like this: *It's February 21 and I can already smell spring when I get in the car to drive to the office. Today is the day that we will publish the annual report. We have achieved something together that even I did not expect. Because wasn't it just three years ago that we only managed to publish our annual report no earlier than April 25? What has changed since then?*

After sharing our visions of the future, we set ourselves the goal of bringing the publication of the annual report forward by two months from the end of April to the second half of February, and to do so within three years. To create space in the busy first months of the year, we shifted activities from the year-end process to November and December. For example, at the beginning of December we are already preparing a draft annual account and report that will be submitted to the Board of Directors for assessment. We call this our 'Santa Claus' version. We thus know which bottlenecks there are in mid-December, so we already discuss accounting issues with the external auditor before Christmas. We do this by means of so-called position papers, documents of only a few pages in which a position on a certain subject is laid-out, which we send beforehand to the accountant for review. I call this "peak shaving," capping activities during busy periods and moving them to quieter periods. By bringing forward the workload, space is created for other activities and you can better manage your time throughout the year. We also built in more checks in the process, so that the quality visibly improved resulting in much less issues raised by our accountant.

After the first year we already managed to bring forward the publication date by three weeks, the second year another three weeks were shaven off, and in the third year we managed to get a publication date of February 20th. One day earlier than we had aimed for three years earlier. At one point the publication date fell during spring break, so I asked the team: 'Guys, what are we going to do: move back a week or finish before the holidays?' The whole team, no one exempt, went for the latter, and we made it. That created an incredible amount of pride and satisfaction among the team. This result was also a nice symbol for making the results of the finance function transition visible because everyone within the function is involved in the annual report in one way or another. And the nice thing is that we scored high in the benchmark for the most transparent annual report and our annual report was nominated for an award for companies that distinguish themselves in their financial reporting. This indicates that the quality of our financial processes has improved considerably because of our peak shaving."

10.1.8 Best Idea FFI8: Self-Service - The Foundation for Better Support of the Management Processes

A bank provides services related to mortgages, payment and savings, and consumer financing ("retail banking"), and also serves large- and medium-sized companies ("wholesale banking") by offering all kinds of financial services. The banking sector is under pressure due to the crisis in the financial sector in the past decade, discussions about bonuses among bankers, and new entrants to market segments (the so-called fintech companies). Lowering the cost level of the bank is therefore a recurring topic. The bank seeks a balance between local (regional offices close to the customer) and central (head office and staff functions with centralization of activities), and thus between customer focus and efficiency. Information provision throughout the organization is crucial in order to be able to manage that balance. The bank uses self-service to improve the reporting process as well as to reduce the costs ("total cost of ownership") of the entire chain of management and control information.

The business change manager who is responsible at head office for integrating the management information of head office with that of the local branches picks up the story: "It is clear that our costs have to be reduced. This applies to the costs of information and communication technology as well as those of Finance. We have to work smarter with fewer people. A few years ago we came to the conclusion that we deliver a homogeneous service but do not report homogeneously. Although we initially focused on just improving reporting, nowadays it is about supporting the management of the organization. This has accelerated the thinking process about a number of other dilemmas in the organization and the finance function, such as: 'how does the right control information reach the right user at the right time,' and 'what is the role of financial controllers and business controllers?' What we discovered was that many organizational units reported from their own silo, we had to get the data for the reports from a huge number of systems, and we had too many different tools in-house to access that data in an efficient manner. A second observation was that the customers of our bank can arrange their financial affairs via apps on their mobile phone and via the internet, but that internal customers of the finance function do it all with their own tools. A third observation was that our strategy of more management of chains of processes was not sufficiently supported by information. By organizing the provision of information integrally across chains, personnel costs become lower. After all, the current number of reporting flows is decreasing and the number of employees who spend time creating reports is decreasing. IT costs will also be lower because the number of reporting tools will decrease."

These observations have a major impact on the finance function because business controllers' roles become much less about reporting and far more about providing advice. This forces a large group of controllers to consider whether this advisory role is their future. The business change manager states: "As a business controller you are responsible for the smooth running of operational financial and reporting processes. If not, then you have to take action and solve the problem with your fellow data specialists and financial controllers. The quality of the data turned out to be an important precondition for the success of the self-service concept. The business change manager: "We had to improve the quality of the data from the systems. An important starting point was that when we change numbers, we always adjust the numbers in the source systems, never outside the system. We also spent a lot of time on data definitions. Due to differences in definitions, we could not always add up the data to the highest level, which meant that we could not make cross-sections. In addition, we made sure that we moved to one platform and one front-end as much as possible, which means that a number of systems and tools had to be phased out. We also introduced standardized sections in all reports: customer and market information, HR information, hours information, financial information, and project information. In addition, we introduced four levels that you can easily click through: level 1 a start screen with organization information; level 2 a diagram with dashboards that show the coherence of KPIs; level 3 the KPI level of the own business unit; and level 4 in-depth reports in which users can drill-down to the invoice. The outcome of our project is a series of cockpits that make it possible at a glance to see what the organization is steering towards, how you as a manager and your team contribute to this, and which buttons you have to turn to make adjustments."

The introduction of self-service is certainly not merely a technical adjustment: a lot changes for both the manager in the business and the controller. The business change manager states: "An important change in the provision of information is that in management team meetings the manager gives the explanation and not the controller. The controller used to make a report, write the explanatory notes, and speak at management team meetings. Nowadays reports are not sent in advance, the figures are viewed live during the management team meetings, and the controller only discusses the realization up to and including the current month and does not give explanations. The controller must ensure that managers provide explanations themselves and has to occasionally stimulate the discussion with probing questions. At the highest level management level we still have an old-fashioned report, but we use screenshots of the application there. At the lower management levels, the figures are discussed in the meeting by opening the application and zooming in on your own business unit."

The move towards self-service was significant and has not yet been fully completed. It is a process of several years to involve the organization in a different way of steering and to organize support accordingly. The business change manager: "In order for the move to self-service to succeed, we had to deal with a multitude of factors: a complex system landscape, many different types of users, and changing work processes. It has helped to consistently adhere to the starting point of the project: the data must be of good quality, unambiguously interpretable, and contribute to achieving the goals of the organization. During the move this means above all clear communication and facilitation. We are not there yet; it is a continuous process to improve and renew the information provision. We have a good idea of the concept of self-service, but we will have to keep innovating. In the short term, we will make the data accessible for tablets and smartphones. Furthermore, we continue to look closely at smart access possibilities to the data and the making of analyses: the developments in big data and smart data are going fast and we want to embed these in our information process. Lastly, a big turnaround has been the other way of steering. A solid foundation has been laid with self-service for information provision, you could say: the C of the PDCA cycle. We are now looking more ahead, the P of the PDCA cycle is receiving more attention: there will be faster feedback in reviews, and planning and budgeting will become more short-cycle in nature. The self-service provision of information makes that possible."

10.1.9 Best Idea FFI9: Chain Management - Stimulating Collaboration Across Business Units

Within the bank, the move from separate operational processes to chain processes was in full swing. The bank had many front and back office processes that were functionally separated in individual business units and departments. By putting the focus on working in process chains, sub-optimal processes became evident. One of those sub-optimal processes was internal charging. The correctness of the allocations of costs and revenues was often questioned. Managers and controllers felt that these allocated charges did not help in managing their organizational unit. For example, as a result of the charging, several budget-holders were actually responsible for the same costs, which created a lot of confusion and irritation. This prompted a closer look at the process of internal charging. The project leader, whose goal it was to turn the internal charge process into a process with which the organization could steer the chain more effectively, explains: "We conducted various analyses over the years. The business case for allocation costs could not be found in reducing the administrative burden, the administration itself had become reasonably efficient over the years. The problem was that the system grew by itself, as it were. New product specifications, organizational changes, and the urge for more and more details, caused the number of allocation rules, despite a few tidying-up efforts, to get larger and larger over the years. It was wrongly argued that more detail is needed to manage properly, cost management does not require a very high level of detail. Another disadvantage of the current process was that the cost allocations distracted from the true intention of cost control. Because of the charging, the budget holders steered towards reducing these allocated costs instead of focusing on lowering the costs created by their own unit. The budget holders de facto managed costs that were largely caused by other organizational units. Another issue was that it was difficult in our organization to record costs in a structured and disciplined manner at every organizational level in the correct level of detail, which led to a lot of discussion about numbers, descriptions, and quality levels of the cost data. What we wanted was a focus on controlling operational chain processes and thereby create a complete and good overview and coherence in the organization, so that decision-making could be supported on the basis of cost data of the chain."

The project manager continues: "We tried to preserve the good, the budget holders controlling their own activities and costs, while trying to overcome the disadvantage of the limited focus on the chain by no longer passing on allocated costs, but only allocating costs in a separate model. In the management information we no longer shown allocated costs. We do still include some of the charged costs in some parts of the administration, but much less extensive than before. Because of the charging, controlling costs actually took place "too deep" in the organization. At every organizational level, we pretended to be cost-driven, while at the operational level the focus should be on managing operational indicators and process improvements rather than financial indicators. Provide managers with the operational information they need to do their jobs, and only provide them with the financial information they can influence, and then at a lower level of detail. At higher management levels, we make the allocated costs visible in the reports, which is also the management level at which decisions are made about (groups of) costs."

The project was about more than just stopping the charging. The project manager states: "We as finance function included many operational managers in the developments of the allocation project and coached them in the idea that management information without allocated internal costs was good enough to manage their departments with. Furthermore, we have not given much publicity to the end of the charging process itself. At a certain point we literally changed the project name from "stop charging" to "manage differently." Not a large-scale project and no extensive newsletters about what was no longer reported, but a focus on conducting conversations about "what information is needed if we work in the chain," "what is already working well," and "how do we want start monitoring." Parallel to the project we developed the cost allocation model which made it possible to show managers the alternative management information. By paying a lot of attention to "manage differently," the main project activity was consistently discussing chain management and much less the technical implementation of changes in administration and processes."

10.1.10 Best Idea FFI10: 'Agile' Decision-Making - More Strategic Impact in a Data-Driven Market

An online travel company with a large number of brands and websites wants to become the market leader in various countries and grow on all continents. With sales offices, customer operations, and the financial Shared Service Center in different parts of the world, the orientation is clearly global. The finance function is relatively large because the organization works with three platforms for its brands for online ticketing. The CFO explains what the organization is all about: "We are mainly a Business-To-Consumer company where our market is very competitive, we are a real 'high volume, low margin' organization. If there is price pressure, we can only cope with that through increased sales. We have to keep a constant eye on prices and quantities. We therefore monitor sales and financial figures on a daily basis. So we are also a real data-driven organization. The competition in the market means that at the back-office standardization is needed to keep costs as low as possible. Therefore we are working on migrating the three platforms in the back-office to a single platform. We also achieve standardization by working with protocols in processes, so that 95 percent of all actions automatically end up in the general ledger. We still have to manually process the other five percent. We are of course trying to reduce that five percent. The extent to which we have to match suspense accounts often indicates to what extent the processes are in order. At the front-office, online marketing and R&D is important. We earn money from the flight business, but we also want to earn through so-called up-sell, (offering services in the higher price segment, and cross-sell, offering additional services such as online hotel bookings and online car bookings. Two indicators on which we steer are the conversion, the number of customers per number of website visitors, and the cost per acquisition, the advertising costs to turn a web page visitor into a customer. In order to increase the conversion, we are constantly working to improve the IT technology behind the websites. We develop the software ourselves and that is one continuous big optimization issue. We use an agile/scrum like way of software development for this. We have so-called sprints of two weeks to quickly arrive at a product which satisfies the requirements of the business."

In addition to improving IT in the operational processes, the company continuously tries to increase insight into consumer behavior. A specialized Finance Business Intelligence (BI) team links files, enriches data, and performs analyses on databases to answer questions such as: Why do visitors come to our site? Where and how do they click and in how many clicks do they book a flight, trip, or hotel? How do consumers make decisions? How do we attract traffic to our sites? The CFO states: "These are questions that not only the BI team but actually everyone in the organization deals with on a daily basis. Every employee knows that we are a 'run-rate business with a seasonal pattern': we can extrapolate sales reasonably well, taking into account the pattern that consumers generally book trips in January, May, and September. But we do need to act quickly to respond to the daily numbers. Strategy and execution are therefore closely linked, it actually feels as if the execution is the strategy. And that is also reflected in our decision-making process: measure, decide quickly, and anticipate."

Once a week, management meets in the so-called progress team, which consists of the CEO, CFO, Head of Sales, Head of Marketing, CTO (chief technology officer), and the HR director. The CFO explains: "We then briefly look back ('what did last week look like') and reflect longer on the coming week ('what are we going to do based on the available information'). If the figures go in a certain direction (over- or underperformance), we immediately decide whether we are going to conduct additional marketing campaigns or, for example, improve the search engine. It's not putting your feet on the table and reflecting, but doing it right away. There is therefore only one scorecard for the entire company so everybody is focused on the same things. In addition, it is important as a progress team to find a good rhythm and to maintain discipline to make these kinds of decisions. Otherwise, the issues of the day reign which creates constant fire-fighting. That is why we meet every Monday and then have a compact meeting, discuss the figures, briefly discuss the alternative actions, and then make decisions and put these immediately into action."

10.1.11 Best Idea FFI11: Improve Processes - Simplicity in Integrated Processes With Motivated Employees

An insurance company with a number of well-known brands operates in a fast changing market. Consumers increasingly want more value for their money; they become more price-conscious, more self-reliant (via the internet) in their choices, and can switch to other insurers relatively easily. The diversity in customers and the changing customer needs force the insurer to offer different service concepts: the so-called multi-brand strategy. Behind the brands are a large number of administrative processes, and the competition and price pressure create cost pressure in these processes. Simplicity and uniformity are thus crucial. The insurer also wants to increase the financial self-reliance of consumers by organizing the administrative processes in a transparent and clear manner. A few years ago, this led to a clear choice to set up a financial shared service center (FSSC) for the brands. This FSSC is part of the finance function, of which half of the financial professionals work in the FSSC, while the other half mainly works on internal reporting, business control, external reporting, and some specialist finance functions. The FSSC takes care of the financial tasks across the full range of the company's services: all incoming and outgoing payment transactions, the entire general ledger administration, and the administrative handling of intermediaries.

The manager of the FSSC, who has been involved in the set-up since the beginning, explains the working method within the FSSC: "With the establishment of the FSSC, administrative processes came together in one place. This has helped enormously to implement process improvements. We use the Lean method and we do this as integrally as possible. So not only on sub-processes but on all processes within the FSSC. We work on continuous improvement on three fronts: leadership & behavior, simplicity in processes, and KPI management. In this integrated approach, we base ourselves on a pyramid of three pillars (see Figure FFI3). At the bottom of the pyramid, the three pillars are still separate from each other, at the top of the pyramid they are integrated. The approach works in steps from bottom to top, from giving direction through internally putting things in order, to integrated working on and ultimately steering customer processes. The philosophy is: increase employee satisfaction and improve quality of service which will lead to more satisfied customers. This philosophy in combination with good quality processes, good professionals, and result measurement leads to a truly integrated focus on the customer. Our experience with working with this philosophy of continuous improvement has told us that this takes several years. Especially if the mindset in the organization is not yet focused on continuous improvement meaning the organization is still at the bottom of the pyramid."

Figure 3. The pillars leadership & behavior, processes, and key performance indicator (KPI) management

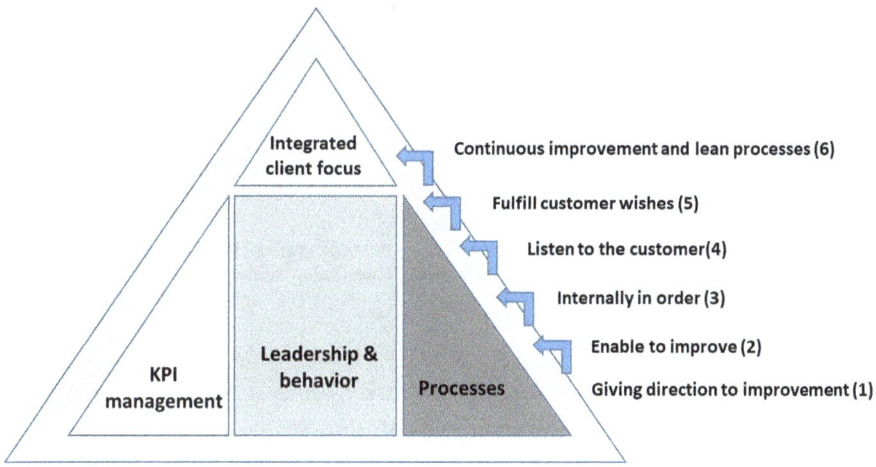

Leadership and Behavior

In order to raise the pillar "Leadership & behavior" to a higher level, the finance function has developed several initiatives. For example, the management team and the financial professionals have mapped out the preferred styles and resistance of the teams using the Profile Dynamics method (an instrument that makes the motives of people, teams, and organizations clear and transparent). This insight has been taken into account in the recruitment and selection of new employees and in determining the composition of the management team. Another tool used was the "golden circle" model.[1] The finance function kept the "why" of the organization intact: increasing the self-reliance of customers remains at the top of the list of priorities. The objective of the FSSC was ultimately in line with the "how" of the "golden circle": to be a professional and customer-oriented Financial Shared Services Center through cost leadership and with committed employees. The FSSC manager states: "An important learning point in the process was that we as managers had to give our people space. Financial professionals often have enough ideas about how things can be done differently. As a manager you have to stimulate this, not tell them how to do it, but give them a platform to turn ideas into reality, and free up their time to execute these ideas."

Processes

The pillar "Processes" entails analyzing, together with all employees, what the value-adding activities are, i.e., identifying which activities add value to the business and which do not (see Figure FFI4). Although business value-adding activities are not always visible to the customer and do not add value from that perspective, they are necessary for the organization: activities such as setting up a segregation of duties or maintaining a business control framework cannot be eliminated.

Figure 4. Lean and focus in continuous improvement

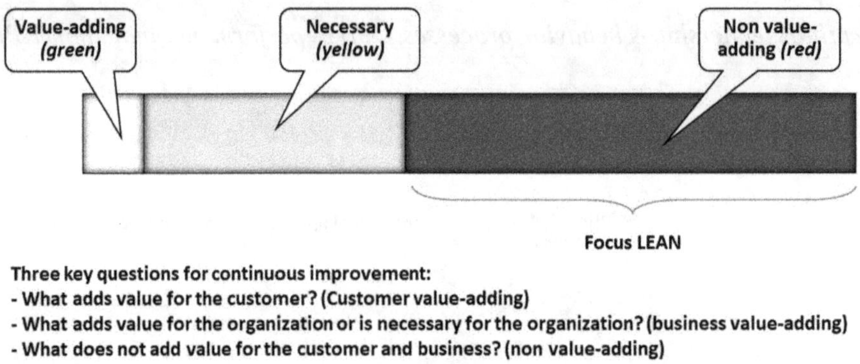

The FSSC manager explains: "We want to apply simplicity, unravel and reduce complexity as much as possible. We take processes from start to finish; we call that "value stream trajectories." We try to implement the Lean philosophy as well as possible. For us it is lean if three inefficiencies do not apply to a process: activities that do not add value for the customer, unequal workload for financial professionals, or unreasonable workload for financial professionals. We want to eliminate these inefficiencies from our processes. An example of a value stream process is the collective value transfers of pensions (for example, the conversion of accrued pension entitlements from one administrator to another administrator because employees have a new job) that we carry out for intermediaries. The turnaround time was far too long, with peaks of up to one year. You cannot do this to an intermediary: wait more than a year for the service to be arranged. Our goal was to reduce that period to a maximum of 60 days. At the start, this was the case for only 11 percent of the transfers. We started a value stream process in which the whole team mapped out and improved the process. Results was that we went from seven to three process steps, solving 27 forms of waste. Then we started optimizing, the result was that we went to 76 percent of transfers within the time target. This result gave a huge boost to the self-confidence of the financial professionals and subsequently led to more initiatives for improvement from the team itself. That is great to see, because continuous improvement does not stop after a project has been completed."

KPI Management

The third pillar is the measurement of results, namely KPI management. Key performance indicators (KPIs) are useful to assess whether goals are being achieved. Furthermore, the finance function uses the OGSM method (Objectives, Goals, Strategies, Measures)[2] so that it is clear on one A4-page how the various indicators of the FSSC are interrelated and how they are linked to the objective of the FSSC. The KPIs are a means of monitoring progress and focus, and are reflected in dashboards. The most important KPIs are those concerned with how the teams are doing. Each financial professional needs a maximum of five minutes per day to complete the spreadsheet with their KPIs, while the supervisor takes 15-20 minutes. The update is processed at night and the dashboard is available the next day. In addition, employees complete a barometer once a week: they give a score on how things are going at work as well as in their private lives. Within the team, the results are discussed and, if necessary, help is offered by colleagues.

The FSSC manager assesses the results achieved so far: "The FSSC has existed for three years now and a lot has been achieved. More than 20 percent lower costs than at the start, the delivery reliability is above 95 percent, with shortened lead times for customers. We have agreements with all operational units about the quality of our services, one third of our financial professionals went to Lean training and are highly self-managing and committed. We have been able to create time to take up innovations such as robotics. Looking back, we can conclude that we have taken two major steps. Firstly, we put work stocks in order. These were very high at the start of the FSSC. If you bring this down structurally, you secondly have room to increase delivery reliability. The outcome of the two steps is a reduction in costs, more satisfied customers and more motivated employees. The latter was symbolized when another large insurer paid us a reference visit and one of our junior employees beamed with pride when she related the story of the process improvement to our guests."

10.1.12 Best Idea FFI12: Integrated Performance Management - Connect Few Financial and Many Business Indicators to the Corporate Strategy (De Boysere, 2021)[3]

The manager Controlling of a retailer recounts why and how the finance function of this organization introduced integrated performance management: "Two years ago, we switched from typical reporting to integrated performance management. We wanted to help steer the organization with simplicity and insight. Therefore, amongst other things, our reporting had to become more strategy-supporting. We already had the advantage of having a huge mountain of data available. But we also looked for and found an external partner to help develop integrated performance management. As Controlling we had a coordinating role for the company in this development process. We now have 25 key performance indicators (KPIs), of which only four are financial. The other KPIs are linked to the company's strategic priorities and objectives: sustainable growth, targeted transition, resilience, and quality of core processes. In the finance function we opted for relatively simple KPIs, such as EBITDA. That sounds logical, but is not as straightforward as it seems. Before introducing the KPIs, we looked mainly at the net result. But steering on net result is quite difficult for us, as management has little control over it, it is difficult for us to support them. By focusing on EBITDA, finance can come much closer to the organization and thus to management. During the year, we may adjust and update the plan in light of events. In the long run, we want to be predictable because we know that we must incur financial debt to finance our investments. Therefore we look at the debt-EBITDA ratio. Today that might not be too alarming, but in the multi-year planning we see the ratio increasing which incites us to make relevant forecasts of it. Another KPI we use is the CAPEX realization rate. Everything you include in your portfolio of investments, to what extent does that become reality? There is a lot of ambition and passion in the organization, but the list of investments is also very long. In terms of predictability, it is important that you know to what extent you can effectively realize those investments in the set deadlines. We aim to realize at least 80 percent of our annual investment portfolio. With those KPIs we can steer adequately and thus connect better with the priorities and world view of management."

10.1.13 Best Idea FFI13: Horizontal and Vertical Finance - A 360° Finance View of the Organization

A manufacturing company divides its finance function into three parts. While most companies have a vertical finance function headed by a director or manager, this organization has an organizational model in which the finance function is "woven" horizontally and vertically like a loom. In this model, business controlling looks at the most important departments and is mainly responsible for the processes of realizing and reporting operating income and gross margins. Then there is operational controlling, which analyzes the customer service and operational departments and calculates the investments. The third cell is strategic controlling, which oversees the multi-year plan and the rolling forecast.

These three cells together provide a consolidation with a 360° view of the organization. In order to achieve more end-to-end coordination between BI (business intelligence), controlling, and the business offices (these are analytical departments working specifically on customer behaviors and developments within the business departments themselves), the finance function worked on the harmonization of definitions with the goal of using the same language internally. In addition, the finance function places a special focus on analysis and working with big data. A specific BI team distills a number of value drivers from the data warehouse that can be used by controlling to estimate the financial future of the organization even more accurately. The BI team thus forms an important source that provides data input for controlling and thus for the rolling forecast. To round off the new structure, the BI team consists of two parts: a BI business center and a BI solutions center. The BI business center, which co-operates with the business, falls under the finance function, while the BI solutions center reports to IT.

10.1.14 Best Idea FFI14: Integration of the Planning Processes in One Platform - Higher-Quality Processes by Structuring and Automating Data Translation Activities

Recently, the finance function team of a retailer finalized the complete renewal of its PBFC (Planning, Budgeting, Forecasting, and Consolidation) system and associated processes. By integrating systems and processes, the team significantly increased the effectiveness and efficiency of the planning, budgeting, and forecasting activities and deliverables, both for the finance function itself and its stakeholders. The planning processes now run according to two fully integrated systems. Parallel to this, the existing consolidation tool was replaced with a new system, to which a solution for tax reporting was linked. Now that both planning data and actual data are on the same platform, it is much easier for the finance function to report on both data series without having to copy data from one system to another. In addition to the IT platform, the PBFC processes were also revised to establish a fast and integrated feedback system between strategic planning, budgeting, and forecasting processes.

10.1.15 Best Idea FFI15: Outsource on the Basis of Result, Not Assignment - Organize Win-Win in an Outsourcing Relationship

The finance function of a consultancy firm renewed its contract with its outsourcing partner. The main objective of the renewal was to evolve from an assignment-oriented model into a result-oriented model. To achieve this, the focus was put on two implementation pillars: a clarification of the integral responsibilities for the outsourced processes ("end-to-end") and a business process outsourcing (BPO) reward system based on results. As a consequence, it was no longer only transactional activities that were outsourced. The BPO partner moved up the finance value chain and became fully responsible for preparing the financial reporting of the subsidiaries of this multinational. Headquarters intervention and input stayed limited to the overall supervision of the process, and tax responsibility still rested with the organization itself. To enable such a change, the operational model was transformed into a model with local front-offices in the subsidiaries (focused on compliance and support of the local activities), a joint middle-office (focused on general accounting and control of the back-office), and a BPO back-office (performing standardized, routine, and transaction-related activities).

The design of the BPO model was aimed at achieving specific results: strengthening the focus on core activities (i.e., compliance and local business partnering); clarifying roles and responsibilities and giving the BPO partner the space to integrally manage transactional activities; making better use of tools, systems, and the BPO partner; and strengthening the organization with capabilities and skills according to the needs of the company. This shift led to a significant change of mindset among the (local) finance teams. The positive impact on the speed and quality of the monthly closings as well as on the timely and correct payment of suppliers quickly became apparent.

10.1.16 Best Idea FFI16: Increased Quality of Management Information - Cause-Effect Relationships are the Link Between Strategy and Execution (Paterson & Vermaas, 2013)

The finance function of a retail company reports management information and this must be of good quality. This seems quite self-evident but is not always easy to realize in practice. Good quality management information consists of data of high quality and of correct, clear, and relevant relationships between the control variables with which managers steer their organizational unit. In this particular organization, an interim controller helped his fellow controllers to determine what the quality of management information should be. To this end, business controllers teamed up with their business colleagues in the management team. They started with setting clear and tangible quality standards for the management information, such as relevance, accuracy, and timeliness. These standards are quite obvious but difficult to make concrete, which is why they jointly came up with the following specific standards:

- focus on the realization of strategic goals: the management information provides insight into the extent to which the set strategic goals are being realized.
- insight into result-determining factors: the management information provides insight into the financial and non-financial factors that determine the realized and expected financial result.
- supporting and monitoring actions aimed at performance improvement: actions to improve results are followed up in the management information.

Subsequently, the factors that influence the standards were identified: strategic fit; design of the management information; and preconditions (see Figure FFI5). Strategic fit entails that the management information must contain indicators aimed at measuring the value proposition (elaboration on how the organization attracts customers for its services and products) and the earnings model (elaboration on the way an organization makes its revenue), and must be of both a financial and non-financial nature. Cause-effect relationships must be made explicit in order to understand the manner in which results are achieved. Understanding the distinction between "leading" indicators (performance indicators that closely follow and measure the process) and "lagging" indicators (result-oriented performance indicators that provide insights when things have happened) is crucial. When designing the management information, the requirements for the level of detail the management information should contain are put center-stage. Think of the translation of key performance indicators (KPIs) to departments and managers, the visibility of the "drivers" in the management information, and the "drill down" of KPIs to underlying control variables such as the customer or product.

The preconditions are that the finance function has a controlling and directing role in the definitions and data needed to put together the management information, and a controller that is relieved of the day-to-day workload of creating management information reports. Apart from these factors that the finance function can actively influence, other factors such as management style, technology, the interaction between CEO and CFO, and corporate culture also play a role. Insufficient quality of management information mainly lies in limited compliance with the preconditions. A well-known limitation is that controllers spend a relatively large amount of time creating reports, with causes being a lack of available detailed non-financial data, no discussion with the business about the value proposition and accompanying earnings model, the inability to drill down to control dimensions, the finance function not controlling data definitions, and/or the ICT architecture being too complex and fragmented.

Figure 5. Nine influencing factors for the quality of management information (Paterson & Vermaas, 2013)

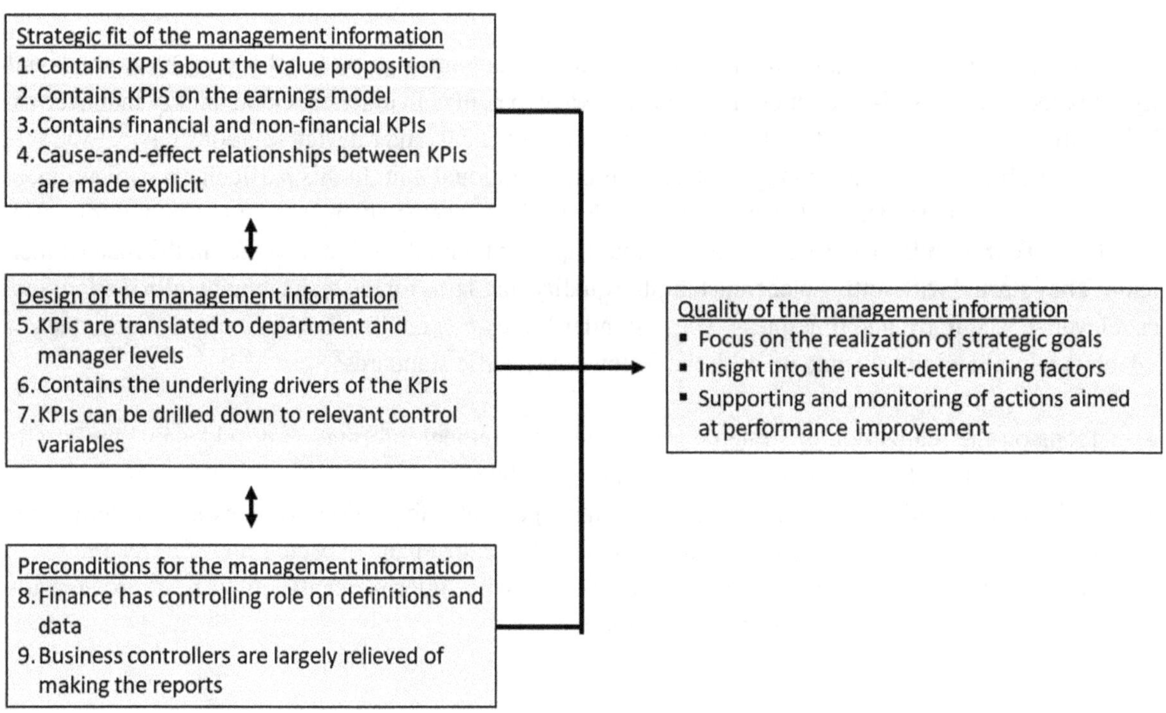

Despite the considerable effort that often has to be made to arrive at good management information, it is still important to work on the quality of that information. After all, managers rely on management information in their decision-making and to test their expectations with results achieved. In addition, management information (partly) removes managers' uncertainty about the success of the chosen strategy and the decisions taken. The management information thus puts the facts on the table. Furthermore, managers see management information as an important resource for making business decisions (for example in relation to investments or new customer contracts). The non-financial, often leading, KPIs provide managers with insight into the development of future business results and necessary corrective actions. Management information is also a communication tool to convey the strategic goals and to focus employees on the realization of these goals. A final remark is that improving the quality of management information does require a multi-year effort on all factors and a sustained focus on working towards high quality. Thus, a leading role for the CFO and CEO is indispensable in this respect.

10.1.17 Best Idea FFI17: Regular Self-Assessment - Monitor High Performance

A government organization and its finance manager are strong proponents of performing self-assessments in order to be able to continuously improve the function on the basis of the results. In the past, the organization used all kinds of self-assessment; however, recently, the HPO framework has become the preferred tool. The Director of Finance and Control explains how she uses the HPO framework in the finance function: "In our finance function, we basically have two types of activities: operational activities and activities aimed at steering and managing the function. The two are connected with each other. We therefore have to be in constant dialogue with each other and continuously improve operations. I connect the five HPO factors to this cycle. For both the operation and the steering of the finance function it is important to have good management in order to be able to manage and realize the improvement of the quality of transactional and control processes (quality of management). For both the operational and the steering side of the finance function, it is also important to have high-quality employees who can get and keep the execution of the financial processes at an excellent level (quality of employees). This also requires interactive internal communication ("an open dialogue") between the financial professionals so that free and continuous vertical and horizontal information exchanges take place (open- and action-orientation). Because dialogue with the line is of great importance for a finance function, the finance function must work on its skills in this area (continuous improvement and renewal). Continuity always comes before making a profit in the short term. This is anchored in the strategic objectives and the right to exist (the "why") of the finance function (long-term orientation)."

The Director of Finance and Control explains that the organization, and thus the finance function, carries out an HPO diagnosis every two years: "The first diagnosis three years ago was a baseline measurement, which was the starting signal for change. The second diagnosis, two years later, showed an increase in scores. We had expected this because we had devoted a lot of attention to improvement in that period. We recently made a third diagnosis. We scored slightly lower than during the second diagnosis for continuous improvement; the other four HPO factors remained more or less the same. In hindsight, the timing of the third HPO diagnosis was somewhat difficult as it was performed just a few months after the introduction of working with roles in the finance function. The new working method led to a sense of uneasiness among employees and this was reflected in the results. Still, the HPO diagnosis results alerted us that we should still pay more attention to this issue. And in order to achieve more improvements, we are planning to start an HPFF diagnosis in the intermediate years between the HPO diagnoses."

10.2 BEST IDEAS FOR HPFF FACTOR "IT FOCUS"

Automation and digitization have a high priority in HPFFs. The finance function has a sufficient annual budget for automation and digitization at its disposal; in addition to this, it is important that the financial professionals have knowledge of IT applications suitable for the finance function and the organization as a whole. The HPFF is up to date with the latest applications and possibilities of IT programs and is able to use the most recent IT applications. Focus on IT means that all routine financial processes are fully automated and that less time on routine activities is spent. In this section, 12 best ideas concerned with the application of ICT in the finance function are discussed.

Table 2.

No.	Best idea	Key point of this best idea
IF1	Data management: work on future capabilities	Key for the future of organizations is data and how to embrace it; therefore creating a vision of data management will be the foundation of the support that the finance function provides the organization in this respect.
IF2	Business analytics: hire IT professionals with business sense	Hiring IT professionals with business sense is an important step towards bridging the gap between the current situation of departments that do not understand each other and a more desired data-driven and collaborative future.
IF3	Robotics: make space for tasks in which human intervention has more added value	With robotics, finance functions can automate manual, simple, and repetitive tasks to relieve the (manual) workload of financial professionals and provide them with time to perform more value-adding activities.
IF4	Process mining: proactively prevent problems and bottlenecks	Process-mining techniques can be used to simulate processes leading to insights that enable opportunities to improve the processes of the finance function itself or other organizational processes.
IF5	Artificial intelligence: make better predictions	Machine learning is an Artificial Intelligence (AI) technique that can be used to make more accurate predictions than traditional prediction techniques can, especially when large quantities of data are involved.
IF6	Robotics: start small and in an accessible manner	Robotics are often the start to a digital transformation in the finance function, and can, for instance, be used to add extra control steps for a higher-quality process.
IF7	Flexible IT architecture: be adaptive to new tooling	Focusing on replacement of unnecessary or outdated tools and on a quick integration of new tools is the approach to having a flexible IT architecture.
IF8	Robotics: do not forget the people aspect	An obstacle to introducing robotics can be that financial professionals may feel 'unneeded' and resist the new tools; integrating and treating robots as a virtual colleague in the finance function will help acceptance.
IF9	Robotics: using a robot to free up people	Robotics can be of great help in accounting processes, maintenance of master data, intragroup transactions, and eliminating differences between group companies.
IF10	Artificial intelligence: Questions? Ask ARIA!	With a chat-based user interface, any financial question can be asked, which saves time for the finance function.
IF11	Lean Robot Process Automation (RPA): combine lean and robotics	By combining both Lean and RPA, finance functions can increase effectiveness by optimally automating lean processes that do not have waste anymore.
IF12	Data quality: reporting data reflects the level of correctness of underlying data	Varying the coloring brightness of reported data according to the quality (correctness, completeness, and a couple of other criteria of data from sources) of the data gives managers advanced warning.

10.2.1 Best Idea IF1: Data Management - Work on Future Capabilities

The management team of the finance function of an energy company realizes that data are becoming increasingly important to the organization. The Corporate Control manager says: "The possibilities of IT are constantly increasing. The finance function is pre-eminently a function that works with data and thus should have a leading role in this respect in the organization. We are increasingly aware that we actually reside on an enormous mountain of data and that the future is to derive value from it for the company. In addition, the finance function has a broad view of the organization and is ideally suited to link data files from, for example, HR, Purchasing and the operation and to look for the essential connections. With current IT developments, large amounts of data can be combined with each other. The ability to generate new insights from that data will help the organization further. Professionals with an IT affinity and understanding of finance, so-called data scientists, will increasingly become part of the finance function."

The Corporate Control manager continues: "An important task is therefore managing data and generating information from that data. We want to renew the management information so that more is combined with different types of data—operational and financial, internal and external, structured and unstructured—and forward-looking information is generated. We are conducting a pilot to play around with the data, make extractions, combine files, and generate new insights. We are conducting these pilots with a specialized external company where we let our own people work with them so that the knowledge and experience also ends up within the finance function. Our vision is that ultimately the entire organization will become "data-driven." And excellent data management will be the foundation of the finance function!"

Figure 6. Vision of data management

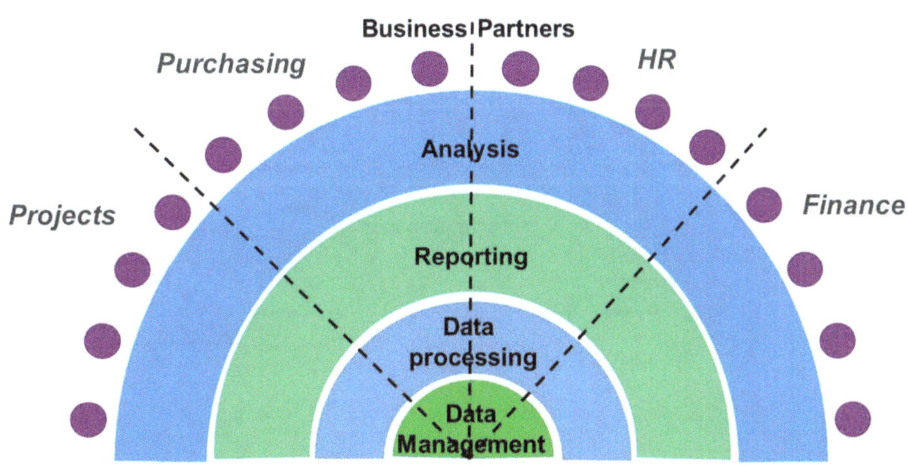

Figure 6 represents the finance function's view. Four information chains, leading to HR, Procurement, Finance, and Projects, provide management information through various stages (processing, reporting, analysis). The added value of the data from these functions is generated when these data are analyzed in combination. Furthermore, optimization becomes possible if, for example, data processing by these functions is not performed independently but in an integrated manner. The business partner becomes the central pivot in this information chain. Appropriate translation of the results of the analysis to the business ensures that added value is realized and that the finance function has a significant impact on the business.

10.2.2 Best idea IF2: Business Analysis - Hire IT Professionals With Business Sense

An internationally operating document management specialist sells and distributes high-, medium-, and low-volume copiers and printers of leading global brands. Thanks to its extensive range and high-quality service, the company offers a tailor-made solution for a diverse range of companies and industries. There is a direct sales channel to customers and an indirect sales channel with a dealer network that in turn serves the end customer. Market prices are falling and competition in the industry is fierce. The company is constantly looking for the latest "state-of-the-art" technology and new avenues for an even better quality of service, so that the current strong market position can be maintained. The Finance Director's task was to revive the indirect sales channel with dealers: "The focus was on compliance and control, there was no attention for business opportunities. Although the turnover was good, in retrospect, the organization lost a lot of turnover due to a lack of insight into profitability." The provision of information from the finance function to stakeholders took a long time, and the information provided was not sufficiently helpful to the business. In addition, the reports often contained inaccuracies, as a result of which conversations that should have been focused on the meaning of the data turned into discussions about the correctness of that data. The finance function also had and made little connection with the

Figure 7. Before and after the information gap

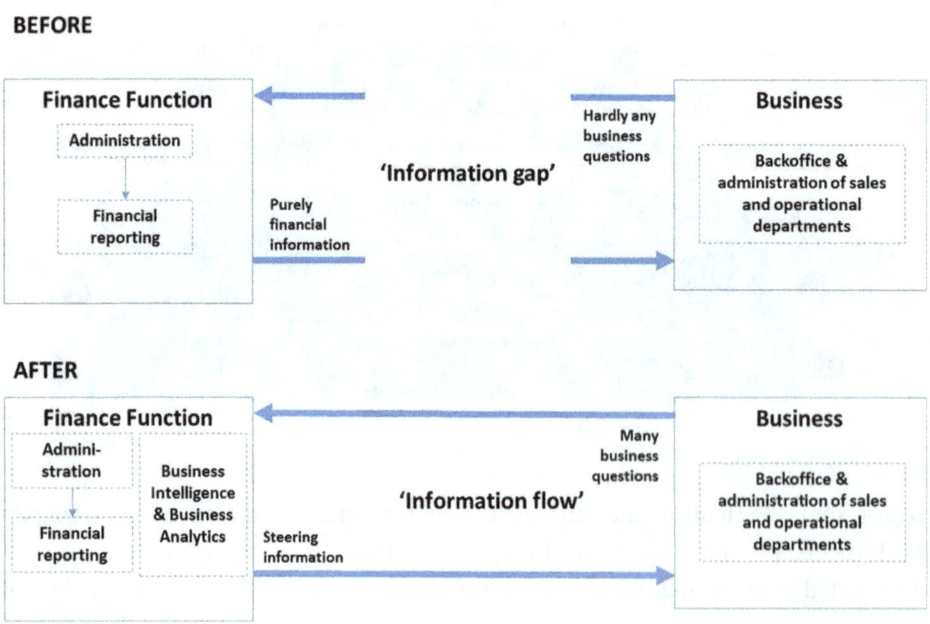

business, which caused a kind of "information gap": financial information was reported, but the business created and steered on a parallel flow of information. In addition, the finance function usually gave a brief explanation of the information, with the business hardly asking any questions because it relied on its own information flow instead (see Figure 7).

The Finance Director says: "The first thing we did was hire a number of smart professionals. These professionals set to work on the data quality so that we could at least properly deliver the important business information. Actually, I didn't have a budget for this and it made the department results negative at first, but it quickly paid for itself. These professionals were people who could handle data well, who actually went into the systems, did not hesitate to retrieve data from servers and link it to other source systems, started with queries, were eager to learn, and who made connections between various sources of data to gain insight into the drivers of the business. They linked business insight with data expertise. These professionals had an IT profile rather than a financial profile. They were also the people to whom you entrust the testing of a new financial system. My role was mainly to ensure that we created the right insights and to hold up a mirror to these professionals if that insight was insufficient and ask them: 'What would you really want to know if this was your own business?'"

The first round of analysis of the data from various source systems showed that the ratios per country differed enormously. The Finance Director states: "In some cases we sold at cost price of which the local sales teams was unaware. In a few months we created this valuable insight which we then made available through real-time online web reporting. Now the local sales teams have transparent insight into current results." After achieving a transparent and consistent information provision, the next step was making an actual physical connection with the sales teams. Both the CEO and the CFO made room in their agendas to get on a plane and then with a local sales team go to a local customer. This created a certain chemistry between finance and the sales teams. The Finance Director picks up again: "In addition, we gave the back office financial professionals, the data specialists, more freedom. I encouraged them to get on the plane themselves to go visit the branches and obtain and understand the story behind the numbers." After the first series of insights into efficiency, this quickly turned to tackling customer opportunities. The operating company's profitability increased. The data specialists had a serious impact on the organization with their knowledge of the business. The Finance Director: "The most interesting thing was that at international sales meetings the local sales teams were often present a day earlier and then did not visit me but went directly to the data specialists to look at the conclusions of the data work and to jointly find opportunities."

10.2.3 Best Idea IF3-Robotics: Make Space for Tasks in Which Human Intervention Has More Added Value

A Financial Shared Service Center (FSSC) of an insurance company has a lot of routine work. In the case of this FSSC, there are several systems in which a customer must be registered: for example, a customer can have more than one customer number; as a result, the customer registration process must be adjusted before the move to one back-office system can be made. There are also differences in input: for example, in one system, the customer name is written with a capital letter followed by a comma and the initial; in the other system, it is written as the first name and then the last name. The differences arise because of a lack of agreements about uniformity, but are also due to human errors during input. As a result, over time, different customer names for the same customer are present in the systems. To rectify this in all systems is not only a considerable task, but also a tedious manual job. Robotics offers a solution.

How does that work? The FSSC manager states: "The robot is a fictitious staff member, with a password and a staff number. He logs in as an employee, he gets signals of double counting in the customer files, opens a source file, enters a password to gain access, searches for the field to be changed and corrects it if necessary, saves, closes the file, and goes to next record or file. The robot can tirelessly adjust a stock of unwanted redundant registrations. If an employee does that, it is quite labor-intensive. The robot in itself is not faster than an employee, but it is never sick and of course does not take a break. Upscaling and downscaling of activities is of course also no problem. Normally we need 15 to 20 temporary workers per year, now we got rid of this workload within one year by means of robotics. And that at a significantly lower price, approximately one third of the price of hired staff, so that quickly turned out to be a positive business case. In addition, we had the robots operational in 8 to 10 weeks. Most attention in that process went into undertaking the last standardization efforts, so that the robot has minimal downtime. In an FSSC you want to standardize and automate as much as possible. Properly recorded data is important in this regard. Contaminated data is created quite easily with different systems. We still have a relatively large number of legacy systems and then the use of a robot is a nice tool. The alternative to a robot is outsourcing or offshoring. But that is not actually a comparison: robotics literally takes place in the own organization (the control over the processes is in your own hands, the knowledge of the processes remains in the organization) and it creates significantly cost-savings (no management organization required) for these types of clearly demarcated processes.

A robot has about 10 percent failure, the other 90 percent is executed flawlessly. And if a robot crashes (the 10 percent category), it is clear via a log file where it crashes and then you are quickly at the core to analyze the failure. In our industry, Straight Through Processing to the customer, the execution of the operational business processes that can be processed automatically without human intervention and in which the shortening of lead times and the prevention of errors, is an important development. For example, the process from requesting insurance by a customer to a confirmation in an email to that customer, and all intermediate steps and checks that have to be made in systems. In this process, robotics can help to properly implement the process logic of the system.

The use of robots also has limitations in practice. A disadvantage of robotics is that you are less inclined to keep improving processes: quickly deploy a robot and the goal of quality improvement has been achieved. However, the root cause of the problem will not be addressed. And speaking in lean terms, an organization should also not start robotizing "waste": that is not effective. However, in my mind the disadvantages do not outweigh the advantage that robotics force an organization to rethink and reorient the existing work of employees. What is the organization's view of the quality of work for employees? Does an organization want professionals to correct incorrect data entry, while they could better concentrate on the tasks that require human analysis, they and insight? We believe that we should primarily utilize the talents of our financial professionals and that employees should continue to think about the better running of processes. Correcting data in the various systems does not fit in with this philosophy. Moreover, we foresee that this type of work has no future anyway."

10.2.4 Best Idea IF4: Process Mining - Proactively Prevent Problems and Bottlenecks (Notten, 2020)

More and more companies are introducing and using process mining. Process mining is a method by which business processes are analyzed based on stored data in the entire application landscape. Using a system leaves traces in a database. For example, when an IT service employee "closes" an incident or a warehouse employee books a receipt, a system registers at what time which user took which action. The tool creates "event logs" from these digital footprints. The power of process mining is that it presents all of these event logs in such a way that they can be used for numerous analyses and improvement initiatives. For example, deviations and risks can be analyzed, addressed, and mitigated. The basic idea of process mining is that the data contained in information systems is used to automatically construct process models that describe what actually happens. For example, data from the information system of a hospital, an airport, or how people use Facebook show that something has happened; when a person checks in a suitcase at an airport, it is registered as event; similarly, every time the suitcase goes through the next gate, it is registered as an event; and if one places an order on bol.com, it is also an event.

This kind of data is present in every system. However, process mining shows what is actually happening, and a process model is generated. These models can automatically indicate where bottlenecks are. For example, if suitcases arrive late at the airport because a delay often occurs at a specific point, then—without anyone actively modeling anything—the automatically generated model shows where the problem exists. These models mainly have to do with performance: how fast or how cheaply, and with what quality, are things done? Process mining can also be used to automatically detect fraud or things that are very different from what the finance function thinks is happening. These deviations then show how the organization could do better. A more advanced use of process mining is to predict how a process will run. For example: although a production process may run smoothly today, process-mining techniques can be used to predict whether that process is likely to have problems tomorrow. If the process is observed for a long time, then patterns in the behaviors of people, machines, and products become clear —patterns that may cause a problem at a later point in time. The finance function can then proactively warn the organization about these expected problems and deal with them in time.

10.2.5 Best Idea IF5: Artificial Intelligence - Make Better Predictions (Ham & Becker, 2021)

Organizations are increasingly starting to use machine learning to make better predictions about, for example, the turnover per product or product group. These predictions are compared with predictions made in the traditional way. Machine learning often yields better predictions, and thus results in more advanced analytics.

A supermarket chain is a frontrunner in the use of data science and machine-learning techniques and organized a recruitment competition on Kaggle, a well-known platform among data scientists. The participants with the most accurate revenue predictions were offered a job. Students of the minor subject Data Science for business improvement at a University of Applied Sciences participated in this competition. They were provided with a dataset with more than 400,000 lines. Based on information on inflation, unemployment, weather, and marketing, they were able to accurately predict the weekly turnover of the divisions of 40 stores of the supermarket chain. One student group finished in the top 35% of all participants, which is remarkable as they first came into contact with data science only eight weeks earlier. The competition is a good example of integrating external data and internal data: historical sales and marketing data are combined with external data such as employment, temperature, and inflation to arrive, through the use of machine learning, at accurate predictions.

10.2.6 Best Idea IF6: Robotics - Start Small and in an Accessible Manner (Buist, 2021)

Robotization of processes is an accessible way to introduce an organization to digital transformation. Rather than working with complex technology projects, robots are very simple tools that assist and improve existing processes.

When an advisory firm digitized its internal declaration process, it encountered an unexpected challenge. With the introduction of a travel and expense management software system, paper claims were converted to digital claims, resulting in a stack of digital instead of physical receipts. The submission process became a lot easier with digitization, which increased the amount of receipts but unfortunately also the errors. At the same time, this new "mountain of receipts" had to be compliant with the retention and other obligations as determined by the Tax and Customs Administration. The organization noticed that occasionally receipts were submitted twice, not with malicious intent but because users made mistakes with the app with which the receipt was scanned or because the receipt was accidentally submitted again at a different time. A process was required by the Tax and Customs Administration in which the organization could demonstrate that double submission of receipts was checked.

The control process that had to be set up for this turned out to be just the task for robotic process automation (RPA). The basic idea of RPA is as follows: take a repetitive process that a financial professional has to go through time and again, analyze that process to an abstract level, and then build a software tool that takes over that process. In other words, RPA is simply the automation of labor-intensive tasks that always strictly run from A to B and nothing more complex beyond that. Basically, when talking about a robot, it is about software that performs a task based on the simple specifications: "do this" and "don't do that." If faced with "ifs and buts"; in other words, with more intelligent processes, cognitive intelligence needs to be used to further automate. Robots do not like "sometimes," "now and then," and "maybe," they require "always" or "never." Thus, especially in the initial phase of RPA, it is a matter of keeping the process and its decision points as simple as possible. Technically, this boiled down to a process that recognized duplicate receipts after which these were manually examined by the back office. The billing robot running at the back of the system took the receipts from the travel and expense management system, compared images with each other to deduplicate, performed additional checks with optical character recognition, performed "fuzzy matching" with what was already in the database, and finally threw out the receipts that might have been doubly submitted. Where this would have been an impossible task for a person, individual receipts can be checked by the robot against the entire digital database of receipts that the robot reads every day. The system was presented to the tax authorities and they approved the RPA check. Thus, a relatively small process that offered huge time benefits was introduced in the company, which fostered the acceptance of robotics in no small way among both financial professionals and the people submitting their declarations.

10.2.7 Best Idea IF7: Flexible IT Architecture - Be Adaptive to New Tooling (Cassauwers, 2019)

A fast-growing marketing company has more than 100 employees, yet the finance function only consists of two people. This is possible because the finance function is designed in a specific way and many processes have been digitized. The CFO explains: "We really have to work as efficiently as possible and deliver figures as quickly as possible. Like the rest of the company, we have to work lean and agile so we can respond efficiently and agile to the questions that arise from the company. We do this, amongst other things, by questioning ourself with everything we do during our day-to-day operational tasks: "Is it really necessary that we do this?" We have a philosophy of constant improvement. Just because we work in a certain way does not mean we should continue to do so. You have to constantly question yourself. In addition, our digital tools are extremely important. They are cloud-based and they can be easily integrated with other tools so data flows easily between tools and thus departments. The philosophy behind our digitization is that we can quickly integrate our tools with each other, but also quickly eliminate or replace them if they are no longer useful. We use a cloud based accounting system, a specialized invoicing tool and a front-end tool for reporting. Our approval flow tool will also flow to the accounting system. All this is based on our self-developed intranet, on which the data from the time tracking converges with financial data. They, in turn, provide feedback to our finance tools. We also use cloud software to create dashboards. So we have a whole range of tools that easily work on our own intranet. We are also constantly looking for new tools, which is possible thanks to our flexible approach. We can switch tools without the rest of our ecosystem falling apart. You often see that with other companies: they forget to regularly question the usefulness of the programs they use. We in contrast check often whether something is optimal and then act quickly. We are constantly reinventing ourselves."

The finance function also automates many traditional finance tasks through these types of tools. "We report to the teams via dashboards," the CFO continues. "So we don't have to tell managers how their team performed. They simply get their data real-time from their dashboard, and they have insight into it at any time. So we reversed the traditional way of working. We do not report to the teams how they are performing: they have the data available and they have the responsibility to analyze their performance based on those figures. Reporting to top management is mainly done via the front-end tool, which works more accountancy-based. The data from our accounting system flows through to our front-end tool where we draw up a managerial P&L, followed by additional financial analyses that provide insights into the state of affairs. We are thinking of also fully automating this reporting. That would allow top management to immediately consult these figures and analyses from the moment we close a month. Finally, we use a combination of tools for forecasting, in which teams plan themselves for specific projects. That ends up in a dashboard, so we immediately see how many billable days have been planned in the following months which is how we determine our forecasted revenue."

The finance function uses all of the above described tools to support their organization. "We are not completely separate in some corner of the office," according to the CFO. "We are very approachable as a finance team and we regularly attend operational meetings. These meetings are often about how teams work with customers, or what difficulties they had in delivering their product. As finance, this information is very interesting, because that way we gain insights into why a team will achieve a better or lesser financial performance that month. Being approachable is crucial, you should not always be perceived as "those angry finance people." Teams can come to us with anything, and then we offer advice from our finance perspective. With the figures in mind, you sometimes come to different conclusions. Sometimes a team says they are overworked, for example, but the figures show that their billable hours are actually low. So that indicates a deeper problem. There is often a narrative within a team, the figures enrich or sharpen that story. Our task mainly consists of stimulating the teams to also put on those finance glasses when looking at their figures. And that is very useful, because they can also use that mentality in meetings with their team or customers."

10.2.8 Best Idea IF8: Robotics - Do Not Forget the People Aspect (Vandamme, 2020)

Despite the 30% growth the company experienced in the past five years, the finance function continued to work with the same number of FTEs. Moreover, the finance function was assigned more tasks over that same period. This meant the function had to focus strongly on efficiency and quality improvement. One of the actions taken in this respect was to start a project around RPA, and more specifically, databots. These are small tools that enable different software tools to "talk" to each other; they are essentially algorithms that take over administrative tasks. The people installing the databots sat down next to the financial professionals and employees of the operational departments to see exactly what work they did and discuss how it could be made more efficient. Then, the databots were taught those work processes step by step, by actually copying the work of the financial professional/employee, which took a few weeks. In the first phase, a number of processes that were mainly manual and repetitive in nature were targeted. By then, thanks to RPA, the finance function had already identified many opportunities to save time and costs, make data more reliable, make processes more efficient, and use the qualities of its financial professionals in a different way. For instance, in the old system, small actions such as changing a customer's account number required financial professionals to go through many steps. Our databot took over, resulting in enormous time savings: this task often took a financial professional half an hour to complete, while a databot only required three minutes—this may not seem a lot but when multiplied with the number of changes happening in a year, it becomes quickly apparent that a lot of precious time is saved that financial professionals can use for performing more value-adding activities.

The implementation of the databots took a matter of weeks, including testing. However, at the same time, the organization was acutely aware that acceptance of the databots was a major step for the financial professionals. As a result, a large amount of attention was paid to the human aspect. For instance, even though a databot is an algorithm and not a physical robot, it was given a name: Adèle. As a result, the databot was better accepted by the finance team and not perceived to be a threat. Adèle did not steal jobs but took over part of the tasks so that financial professionals got more time to deliver added value and better use their competencies. The arrival of Adèle was also announced in a lighthearted way, not with an email but with a real birth announcement and accompanying sweets.

10.2.9 Best Idea IF9: Robotics - Using a Robot to Free Up People

Strongly believing that the use of robotics and automation technology would enable the finance function to achieve its compliance, productivity, reliability, and real-time information ambitions, the function implemented a full Robotic Process Automation roadmap (RPA) in which RPA solutions are implemented to take over manual and repetitive processes in a consistent and error-free manner. Several robots have already been fully integrated into the finance function and have taken over more than 90% of the manual booking processes. Internally, these robots are called JERI, short for Journal Entry Robots Intelligence. The entry of journal entries, a previously time-consuming and cumbersome task, is now no longer done by people. JERI can also send email messages and answer questions so that financial professionals can communicate with "him" in a simple, interactive way. Outside of accounting, the creation and maintenance of master data (suppliers, customers, and cost accounting) has become a process in which robots and financial professionals work together. The finance function also automated the generation of financial planning and analysis reports for day-to-day operations. Another time-consuming process that benefited from automation was handling intragroup transactions. By making better use of the ERP system and installing a small extension, the finance function was able to create "mirror entries" for transactions between group companies. As soon as a transaction is triggered at the sending company, a booking, to which all necessary documents are linked, is automatically generated at the receiving company. In addition to the consolidation tool, a system was implemented that links the data of the different companies of the group to each other, creating an environment in which discrepancies between companies of the group are something of the past.

10.2.10 Best Idea IF10: Artificial Intelligence - Questions? Ask ARIA!

The workload of the finance function of a bank, despite all the advances that automation has made in the function, remained significant. Artificial intelligence (AI) offered the potential to reduce this workload, freeing up time for value-adding processes and activities. The finance function had gradually built the required foundation to understand the true value of AI: the technology, the data, and—last, but not least—the acquired data literacy skills needed within the function. This eventually led to the implementation of ARIA (Artificial Intelligence Analyst), which covered the entire finance process and, if it turned out to be successful, would also be applied to other parts of the organization. Via a chat-based user interface, ARIA can now be asked any financial question, ranging from " How much is the net sales in Japan?" to " Why have I exceeded my budget? " In three months' time, ARIA taught itself to answer over 39 billion answer questions about the complete data archive of the finance function.

ARIA is now also used in another area. Every year, the strategic plans and the priorities of the company are converted into a financial 10-year plan, the implementation of which is translated into annual budgets. In addition, a more detailed rolling forecast over two years (current and next fiscal year) provides insight into the organization's performance and the possibilities for flexible resource allocation. Thanks to the AI algorithms on which its forecasting skills are based, ARIA can automatically make a new prediction for the next period with greater accuracy and detail than ever before — not just at the level of the group, but at the levels of each P&L post and any organizational unit (with the exception of one-time expenses). Moreover, this can be done almost in real time. Using these forecasting models, the finance function can detect dependencies, dissect variances down to the level of their root causes, explore in detail the underlying reasons for the variances, and use these insights to improve predictions and opportunities for resource allocation. Because the forecasts take into account past events, trends, seasonal factors, and outliers, it is also possible to incorporate new assumptions into the forecast. This is the point where people still play an important role in the process and create added value.

10.2.11 Best Idea IF11: Lean Robot Process Automation (RPA) - Combine Lean and Robotics

Robotization and Lean are powerful in combination (Maes & Schijns, 2020). Robot process automation (RPA) is the automation of mainly repetitive tasks with robot scripts that can simulate the human actions behind the computer. Lean is a commonly used method aimed at continuous improvement of processes. Lean is not just about automating those processes, but about eliminating inefficiencies and highlighting tasks that really add value. RPA as an integral part of lean ensures greater savings and more satisfied employees.

A retail and corporate bank used robotics to robotize simple tasks. However, this only yielded small time savings and no real cost savings; the latter savings were nevertheless achieved by using robotics in combination with the lean method. The robotization project started with analyzing processes and selecting tasks and processes that were suitable for automation by RPA. This analysis identified the potential savings and what other benefits—for example, error reduction or shortening the throughput time of processes—could be achieved. The analysis also assesses whether a process is stable or whether it is necessary to optimize the process first. After all, it is not effective to robotize a ramshackle process; although doing so may make the process potentially more efficient, opportunities are missed to increase its effectiveness and thus obtain more added value from it. If you integrate robotizing with lean, you need to answer not only the question "what can be robotized" but also "what does not need to be robotized?" However, within the lean philosophy, it is customary to keep technological/ICT-related process improvements separate from the step-by-step improvement. The application of new technology or the development of new ICT functionalities did not really fit within the short cycle of improvement. These more complex changes frequently take more than one month to complete, and financial professionals often have little to do with them. However, this view on lean is changing and the bank realized that robotization offered the possibility to quickly create better functionality in the change process. As a result, including RPA made it possible to realize the desired functionality in the bank within two to four weeks. By cleverly combining both methods, processes in the bank were optimized in such a way that no unnecessary work was done anymore and relevant work streams were automated as much as possible. This freed up time for financial professionals, allowing them to spend time on more challenging and varied tasks. In addition, not only were time and costs saved, but the continuity of processes was guaranteed, errors were reduced, and turnaround times of changes shortened.

10.2.12 Best Idea IF12: Data Quality - Reporting Data Reflect the Level of Correctness of Underlying Data

High-quality data are the foundation of high-quality management information. High-quality management information consists of clear insights on cause-effect relationships between control variables that managers use for steering purposes. The finance function of an energy network company started a project to map the relationships between control variables. During this project, it emerged that the data quality on which the control variables are built was not always sufficient, i.e., not complete, incorrect, or with duplicated information. The idea arose to express the underlying data quality in the reported figures—not in a separate key performance indicator (KPI), but in the brightness of the color of the reported numbers: for example, an indicator that is green can be bright green (meaning good data quality), medium green (meaning less good or average data quality), or light green (meaning poor data quality). The signal that this coloring sends to management is that if the indicator is medium green, the KPI itself is in order (e.g., has a good result), but the underlying data quality has to be improved. Therefore, full reliance on this KPI is not wise, and it is clear that an action point is to work on improving this data quality. The coloring also prevents discussions about "the figures not being correct." After all, this has already been indicated with the color brightness. Thus, the discussion can focus on what is really important: designing actions to improve the KPIs.

The question was, though: how can the quality of data and data sources be measured? To answer this, the project developed business rules on a number of quality aspects: correctness, completeness, layout, and no duplicates. This resulted in a score per quality aspect, which in turn resulted in a total quality score per KPI. Finally, this score was expressed in the "brightness" of the color of the reported KPI figure. If data are not maintained, their quality decreases. As a result, users can start using their own data sources. This not only means more work, both for the managers (maintaining an extra data source) and for the finance function (aligning with other sources, resolving inconsistencies in reporting), but also more uncertainty among other users about the correctness of the reported data. By integrating the data quality into the management reporting, it was actively ensured that the quality of data was maintained in good order in the organization.

10.3 BEST IDEAS FOR HPFF FACTOR "STRATEGIC ROLE"

The strategic role is predominantly about the way non-finance departments view the finance function. It is important that the finance function is a full discussion partner at the strategic organization level and

Table 3. -

No.	Best idea	Key point of this best idea
SR1	Mission and vision: create a link with the business strategy	A mission and vision that are aligned with the organizational mission and vision and that are supported by financial professionals will enable the finance function to add more value to the organization.
SR2	Internal customer satisfaction survey: measure and then increase added value	Understanding the business is fundamental for business partners. The customer satisfaction survey is an instrument to obtain feedback from the partners in the operation on the quality of the finance function and to also identify their expectations; with this, better business understanding and better quality can be offered and delivered.
SR3	'Top Impact Files': jointly prioritize for effect	In organizations, there exist different interests between the various business units, hierarchical levels, and regions, and by rating the big topics the focus of the finance function is directed towards the most important and urgent matters.
SR4	Training "Finance for non-financials": make operational managers better aware of the link between operations and finance	Educating the business in financial matters in a positive way will increase understanding of financial matters by operational managers, and help improve the dialogue between them and the finance function.
SR5	Forecasting and long-term planning: create a "lean" strategic business model in addition to a forecasting model	A top-down model of forecasting with a small set of parameters is useful for fast analysis with a relative short lead time and quick input into the planning process.
SR6	Business forecasting: keep focus through a compact process	Business forecasting is the connection between the strategic planning (at corporate level) and the operational planning (in countries), and an intensive, compact process is needed to keep focus on future business.
SR7	Trusted advisor: obtain a seat at the management table	Developing the important skills for a trusted advisor (working on your expertise; being able to look at the whole issue and its context; being a reliable discussion partner; providing proactive advice) will help financial professionals to be taken seriously by management.
SR8	Sensitivity analysis: determine the effects of events and megatrends	Changes in the environment of the organization, translated into effects for both the long-term year plan and annual budgets, will help to develop a coherent, challenging, and organization-wide integrated plan.
SR9	Measuring success: get things done or achieve progress?	Becoming and staying an HPFF or a good business partner is not a project with an end date but a continuous evolution based on progress.
SR10	Transform the traditional PDCA cycle: more emphasis on learning and acting quickly	With an accelerating plan-do-check-act (PDCA) cycle with more focus on the future, 'soft' information, and with feedback mechanisms, the cycle becomes a plan-do-learn-act (PDLA) cycle.

has an important voice during strategic decision-making. The finance function is actively involved in significant projects and processes of the organization and always delivers added value to the business. The emphasis is on great collaboration with the business as a common goal to improve the quality of the organization. An important part of fulfilling the strategic role means looking ahead: the finance function proactively revises its forecasts based on important events, and the latest adjusted forecast is always leading during important management decisions. The strategic role of the finance function is often expressed in the ambition to be a "business partner" to management. Business partnering is the development of successful, long-term, strategic relationships between the finance function and internal customers, in order for the organization to be able to achieve high quality and sustainable competitive advantage. In business partnering, financial professionals work closely with business leaders and operational managers to achieve the organizational objectives. In this section, 10 best ideas are discussed that help the finance function to become (more) recognized and appreciated as a business partner, thus increasing the strategic role of the finance function in the organization.

10.3.1 Best Idea SR1: Mission and Vision - Create a Link With the Business Strategy

The finance function must support the organization; therefore, the financial vision must not be at odds with the organizational mission, but rather strengthen it. The first action of the finance function of an international pharmaceutical company was therefore to formulate a vision that is in line with the mission of this healthcare organization. In several sessions and in collaboration with the organization's management team, the new vision of the finance function was refined in a vision document, to read as follows: "Being a trusted business partner for our internal customers in providing added-value services, tools and information with professional and sustained performance, by providing timely and accurate analyses, conclusions and recommendations in the operational and strategic decision-making processes." The vision was then presented at the biannual meeting where more than 80 percent of all financial professionals in the worldwide finance function were shown the vision. To reinforce the vision, it was regularly referred to through posters and other communications. The Finance Director commented: "We also made a promotional mouse pad with the mission and vision printed on it. We still come across those mouse pads, now a few years later, when we visit the countries or are in the head office."

To strengthen the mission of the healthcare organization, it adopted four values: passion for the patient, dignity and respect in word and deed, excellent execution to achieve excellent results, and courage

Table 4. The top three topics per quadrant for the finance function

Customer > Passion for the internal customer	Organization > Dignity and respect for each other
- High degree of business partnership - High scores on customer satisfaction surveys - The lowest possible number of negative remarks in internal and external audits of the finance function	- Personal growth for each employee, supported by a development plan - A feedback culture in which every employee feels at home - A well-functioning performance management process
Financial > Excellent execution of own processes	**Learning and growth > Courage to innovate**
- A well-balanced result of sales and costs - High forecast reliability - Execution of accounts receivable as flawlessly as possible	- Management reports at the highest possible quality level - Continuing to strive for the right person in the right place ("strategic sourcing") - Business analyses that help the organization further along

to face challenges. In order to measure these values for the finance function, the mission of the function was linked to four scorecard quadrants, with the focus on the internal customer. For example, in the scorecard quadrant "customer," the value "passion for the customer" was converted into "passion for the internal customer." Then, the finance function decided on the top three topics on which the function wanted to measure itself in the quadrants. The resulting scorecard is depicted in Table 4.

10.3.2 Best Idea SR2: Internal Customer Satisfaction Survey - Measure and Then Increase Added Value

In order to improve in a focused manner, the finance function must know to what extent internal customers experience the function as being a business partner. This means that the finance function must regularly ask internal customers what they think of the services offered. In a multinational organization, the finance function introduced an internal customer satisfaction questionnaire in order to do just that. This questionnaire first of all asks the internal customers their opinion of the current service provision: does the finance function add value for them and if so, by how much? Subsequently, the contribution that the finance function makes, in the view of the internal customers, to the values of the company (dignity and respect, courage, passion for the patient, and excellent execution) is evaluated. After that, the internal customers are asked about the satisfaction of the individual financial professional who serves them. Aspects on which satisfaction is measured, via a score on the scale of 1–10, are as follows: the quality of contact moments, accessibility of the financial professional, expertise offered, willingness to help, use of clear language, understanding of the needs of the business, solutions offered, record of keeping appointments, response time, quality of reporting (on time, consistent, reliable, clear, up to date, with explanations given), and quality of budgeting and forecasting (good support, transparent, explanations given, ease of use). Finally, internal customers are asked to suggest improvements that would increase their satisfaction (further) and to define what they see as particular strengths in the current service delivery of finance function.

This customer satisfaction questionnaire is digitally distributed, once every two to three years, among the two largest internal customer groups of the finance function: the general and commercial managers in the countries the multinational operates and its head office. The results of the customer satisfaction questionnaire are discussed in the management team of each country and in the finance team at head office. The financial professionals in each country draw up an action plan that they discuss with the country's management team, thus following up on the customer satisfaction questionnaire. The CFO uses the results of the questionnaire to interview country managers and selected managers at head office: "Collecting face-to-face feedback often provides additional valuable input for ourselves to improve. I also use those interviews to have a dialogue about the things the finance function looks at during assessment of the results of the countries. In addition, I check whether there is a decent budget that facilitates growth in the country, whether the right investments are being made to capitalize on the opportunities in their market, and whether the resource allocation, deploying the right employees at the right time, is going well. In this way I try to keep the discussions in the planning and review cycle focused on the important issues."

In addition, the CFO tests the results of the business partnership, because country managers can differ in their expectations: "One manager can say: 'I know exactly what to do and only want to hear from my financial professional if he thinks something isn't going well.' Another manager will say: 'I would like to know what will happen if we continue in the current way,' and asks her financial professional to enter into a dialogue. Knowing your internal customer and finding the right fit between your financial professional and the country manager is therefore important. The internal customer satisfaction questionnaire has really become an instrument for entering into discussions with our internal customers about the expectations of added value from the finance function."

10.3.3 Best Idea SR3: 'Top Impact Files' - Jointly Prioritize for Effect

In addition to regular activities, there are important and urgent matters that require the attention of the finance function. It is therefore important for the finance function to prioritize organizational improvement processes and its own improvement projects appropriately. The Corporate Control manager of an energy network firm explains: "The business controllers and the management team meet monthly to discuss all current business projects and important deliverables. All kinds of topics that are business-driven and have a clear financial component get discussed. Regularly among these topics there are some that we, as financial experts, find important for a broader application in the organization as they will have a lot of impact, either positive or negative. These topics we call Top Impact Files. The "business control framework," the combination of processes and internal control measures that must ensure that the risks of a company are known and are managed, is an example of this. That is a topic that did not arise in the business, but that we put on the agenda ourselves by declaring it a Top Impact File. Each business controller can submit a topic and the group checks whether the topic is worth being a Top Impact File and thus should be included in the Top Impact Files overview." The overview in Figure SR1 is a graphical representation of the topics that play a role in the finance function, based on their impact and urgency. The arrows indicate the focus from the previous month.

Figure 8. Example of a Top Impact Files overview

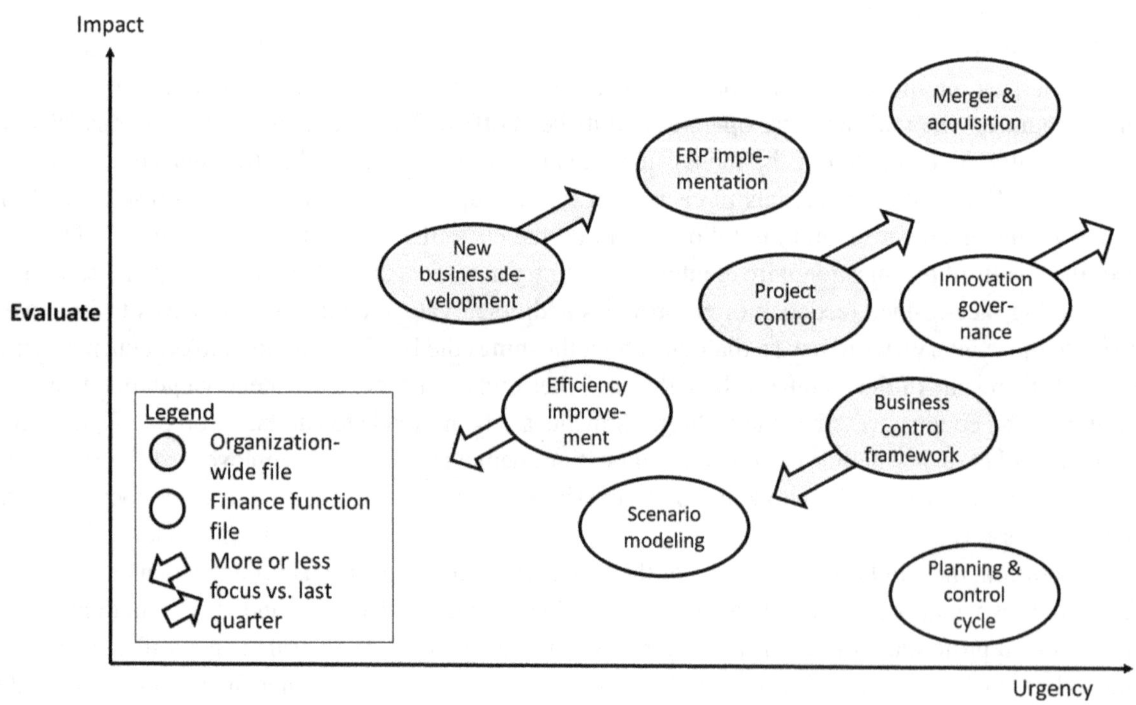

The Corporate Control manager continues: "Through this discussion and the Top Impact Files overview we learn to prioritize as a group, but in passing we also learn from each other's work and we know better what is going on in the organization. This provides insight into what we should give priority in the coming months and we learn to apply focus to our own activities. If there are now many Top Impact Files on the plate of one person, then we can quickly help each other. We will partner and work with more people on a Top Impact File. We can then deliver more than one controller in the business can do alone. The great thing is that we really make a difference with this. In some areas we have helped the business further and that is how we deliver added value. Another example that emerged from these discussions is that we are able to "challenge" and sometimes even change analyses made by strategic management consultancy organizations hired by the organization. For example, the analysis of a consultancy firm on the future investment in certain assets which has been recalculated by us. We created a sensitivity model with an interdisciplinary team of technicians, planning specialists, and financial professionals. By calculating it more precisely and not starting from preset notions and assumptions, we arrived millions of euros lower investment forecasts. As a result, capital allocation could be done in a much more informed way and unnecessary investments were avoided. The business really appreciated that."

10.3.4 Best Idea SR4: Training "Finance for Non-Financials" - Make Operational Managers Better Aware of the Link Between Operations and Finance

In the annual planning cycle and the regular progress review, the focus is on how an organization is managed and controlled. It helps if the discussion partners understand how the mechanisms of this control work. In order to increase the financial understanding of the managers of a biopharmaceutical company, the Director of Finance developed a training course titled "Finance for non-financials." In a day and a half, the local management team is trained in the "ins and outs" of finance. The training focuses on the activities of the finance function and specific attention points for the pharmaceutical industry. The basic administrative processes are explained, the balance sheet and profit and loss account are discussed, and the accounting principles are briefly elucidated. Then, the points for attention when reading financial statements and their relationship with the organizational strategy are discussed.

Over the past few years, training has been given in six regions, with more than 125 participants, by the financial professionals themselves. The training is highly rated, with a score of eight or higher, and has increased financial awareness in the organization considerably. Management has gained insight into how the financial figures come about, how they relate to non-financial figures, and how results can be interpreted. Discussions about how to achieve organizational goals are now also much more effective.

10.3.5 Best Idea SR5: Forecasting and Long-Term Planning - Create a Lean Strategic Business Model in Addition to a Forecasting Model

A high-tech listed company that supplies products worldwide has an R&D portfolio with a planning horizon of 10 to 20 years. The demand for the products fluctuates on the basis of economic and technological developments and therefore the company also experiences considerable fluctuations in sales revenue and profit development. The Corporate Controller described the company as follows: "We operate in a global ecosystem of partners and customers. It is actually a network in which knowledge institutions, suppliers, and customers work together on innovation in a multidisciplinary manner. Continuous technological development is the success factor of this ecosystem, and requires long-term investments and cooperation. Our own developers and engineers and those of our partners are the "heart of the ship." A functional organizational structure fits best with this. This structure enables us to bring together and continuously develop unique expertise in each of our business processes. But, as with any organizational structure, there are also challenges. In our functional organization not all revenue, costs, and investments are matched with and within every organizational unit. The planning horizon in our business model also differs per business process. The management of efficiency and the coordination thereof in the short and long term cannot be done in every functional unit in the same manner. For the finance function this creates a continuous challenge to create and guarantee profit-oriented thinking in every organizational unit. We pay a lot of attention to coordinating short and long term decision-making."

The Corporate Controller continues: "We have set up two processes for this: short-term forecasting and long-term planning. For the short term, we make an 18-month rolling forecast with each budget holder, in which detailed 6-month budgets are updated monthly. Every budget holder is supported by business controllers in updating the forecasts with the latest business insights. With this we safeguard the commitment of all budget holders to managing their own costs, margins, and cash flow. This detailed approach enables us to present reliable financial forecasts every quarter."

The long term is very important to the organization because of the large investment in new technology that is required. "In our long-term planning with a time horizon of 20 years, we dispense with a lot of the financial details. We use simplified, normalized profit and loss accounts to focus on company-wide, strategic topics such as development and availability of new technologies, development of existing and new customers, and long-term profit and cash flow development. In this long term, scenarios play an important role. We do this planning with far fewer players, the Board of Directors and senior management of Technology, Sales and Operations are the main participants."

With these two instruments, there are actually two planning processes that coexist in the organization and both are aimed at looking ahead. The Corporate Controller explains: "The fact that we have put two planning processes next to each other offers us important advantages. It enables us to realize the further desired improvements of our planning and forecasting process in a very focused and fast manner. In our rolling forecast process we pay more attention to the development of our sales pipeline. And we introduce the concept of "affordable cost": a cost standard based on market development and available resources. In this way, budget holders can better achieve market-based and affordable cost levels, as opposed to using up agreed budgets as we did in the past. We also pay more attention to the financing of our partners and customers in our long-term planning. That is why we want to develop our scenarios in a structured way to identify and monitor strategic actions. Because we have two processes, improvements in them can be implemented independently of each other. This means these can be realized faster. Still, there is no danger of the two levels losing their connection. That is because the finance function has a controlling role in both planning processes. Therefore we can make sure that innovations in one process will reinforce the other process: we include pipeline and cost development from the forecast model in the long-term planning, and we translate strategic actions from the scenario planning into our rolling forecasts."

10.3.6 Best Idea SR6: Business Forecasting - Keep Focus Through a Compact Process

Business partnering mainly involves supporting the business by estimating future developments in financial and organizational terms. An internationally oriented pharmaceutical company operating in many countries with multiple business units uses a business forecast for the short term (one to three years) and strategic plans for the medium (three to five years) and long term (10 years). The Finance Director states: "Our business is one of the long term. The lead time for medicines, from start in R&D to marketing, is around ten years. After approval to market the drug until the patent expires, the yields of medicines are very predictable. These factors determine that our planning horizon is long." This is also the reason that a strategic planning model is maintained at group level that includes the terms of patents, since patents differ per product and per country. The long-term plan is made stand-alone by top management and then coordinated with the business units. The results are input for the medium-term plan. The Finance Director: "Then we come into the picture. We update the medium-term plan each year and compare it with the forecasts. This process is part of the budgeting process. If the medium-term plan shows a gap between revenue and current costs, we include that in the business forecasting, so that we can start thinking about how to close that gap. Closing can be done by keeping the pipeline well-filled, and by thinking about strategic actions for example focusing more on R&D, making acquisitions, concluding additional partner deals, or making tax agreements with authorities in specific countries. We call this strategic P&L management."

Business forecasting needs to be performed in order to make the connection between the strategic planning and the operational planning that takes place in the countries where the company operates. Figure 9 shows the relationship between the types of planning and the drivers that are input.

Figure 9. Three types of plans at the pharmaceutical company (Morlidge & Player, 2010)

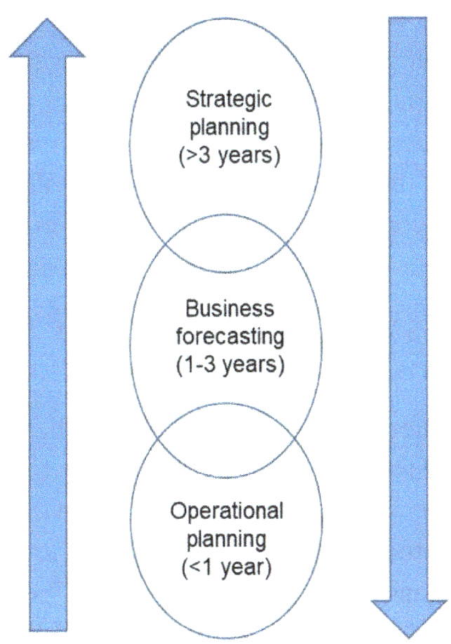

Planning level	Key drivers
Corporate	Patents R&D Competition
Business unit	Revenue Costs Margin
Country	Volumes Price setting Operational costs Margin Tax

The Director of Finance explains: "Financial target setting is relatively easy because plans can easily be calculated. The confrontation between top-down targets and bottom-up forecasts makes it difficult. Internal politics will play a role, because ultimately the management of a country is evaluated on the forecasts it issued. Forecast accuracy is extremely important to manage internal and external expectations, as we are a listed company. The trick is to keep the forecasting process compact, because otherwise you drive each other crazy in the process. We want to make the process short and fast and focused on decision-making. We therefore only forecast on revenue. If the "topline" (revenue) is known, then the costs of sales are known as the operational costs are stable (largely personnel costs), so that the "bottom line" (profit) can easily be calculated. Although our market is stable, it is a conservative market with major barriers to new entrants, the challenge lies in making decisions when R&D slows down, or when local market entry requirements increase, or when the healthcare structure in certain countries changes. Every forecasting process we ask ourselves "Should we change our distribution, marketing, and sales choices in a country now that circumstances have changed?" Every quarter, we complete this intensive process in two to three weeks. It is always a puzzle, but it is necessary to keep focus."

10.3.7 Best Idea SR7: Trusted Advisor - Obtain a Seat at the Management Table (Hagen & Willemsen, 2020)

In addition to financial expertise, being able to give advice is essential for the finance function to bring about changes in the organization. After all, it is not only about the quality of the figures, but also about the added value that the finance function can contribute to the organization on the basis of those figures. To this end, the finance function must act as a discussion partner to management in order to be able to give solicited as well as unsolicited advice. Here are six tips to make this happen, and become a trusted advisor.

1. Work on Your Expertise and Get Good At It

By specializing in and being aware of the latest developments in your field, you gain authority. For example, if you keep a close eye on newsletters and trade journals, you can answer the management team's question about a new ICT system with up-to-date information. Make sure you regularly consult with colleagues from other disciplines. Your role becomes (even) more interesting if you work at the interface of your job and those of your colleagues; this enables you to enrich the expertise of colleagues through your own expertise, and vice versa.

2. Know the Business, Your Management, and the Target Group

The playing field in your advisory role consists of the interaction with your internal client and the people in (or sometimes outside) the organization to whom the issue relates, i.e., the target group. For example, if an investment is made for the acquisition of a new purchasing system, it is important that, in addition to management, the employees who will be working with that system are also involved in its choice. Make sure you know them, know what their experiences are, and what interests are at play. Your advisory role as a financial professional is reinforced if you know what is going on in the organization and how things are progressing. You learn to understand the business by getting out of your ivory tower and talking to the employees in the organization. You often hear more in the canteen than when you eat your sandwich at your desk. Moreover, you can then directly ask questions at the lunch table about employees' ideas on topics such as absenteeism or an IT investment. This would give you access to information with which you can enrich reported figures and add greater value through the advice you provide. If you build a good network inside and outside the organization, you will quickly have information about, for example, the effect of investments that have been made. Did they deliver what you had hoped for or not? Why?

Was there sufficient support from those who have to work with the new system? And what could be better next time? With this information, you can give additional, better informed advice to management.

3. Look at the Whole Issue and Its Context

As a financial expert, your opinion is often asked for on a smaller, demarcated part of a larger issue. The trick is to link the broader issue or the organizational objectives and strategy to this sub-question. Learn to observe from a distance: what's going on, what interests are at play? As a financial professional, you are often the first to see trends. For example, if the costs for employee absenteeism have gone up in recent months, your work does not stop at just flagging this issue. In this case you should, together with management and HR, analyze the causes and financial consequences and place the issue in a broader perspective.

4. Be a Reliable Discussion Partner

As a financial professional you have two functions. First, the functional responsibility for guaranteeing factual and correct figures so that you support management in making the right decisions. Second, being a discussion partner. Digitization and robotization ensure that numerical matters take less and less time, leaving more space for interpretation and recommendations: your advisory role. You make the most impact with words, not numbers. The role of the financial professional is increasingly becoming that of a discussion partner who provides both solicited and unsolicited advice to management. This requires focus on and development of other competencies such as being able to have good discussions, being able to give feedback in a positive and constructive way, having a good feel for the different interests in the organization that are at play, and being able to connect with people. Make sure you skill yourself to a great extent in this.

5. Provide Proactive Advice

If you know what is going on in the organization and in the external world, you can link your expertise to internal and external developments. See which problems and improvements you can spot and get started with these yourself: advise proactively. Of course, this is also about getting your message across the stage: being right is not the same as being seen to be right. Is management open to receiving unsolicited advice? For answering this you have to think along with management, and have a feel for what is happening in the organization. In addition, you need to have the courage to speak up with a dissenting voice. This way, you are seen as someone who makes a valuable contribution to the organization.

6. Reflect on Situations and Work on Bettering Yourself

Investigate your own views and actions and the effect of these on others. Reflect on situations that went well or not. Use others to spot and reduce your own "blind spot." You know the saying: you go faster on your own, you get further together with others." Build a professional network of colleagues inside and outside your organization with whom you can discuss case histories and learn together. By continuously developing yourself, together with others, you will become better at your work. Know yourself and your qualities, but also your weak points and work on these. Finally, make sure that you remain vital in your work and thus continue to grow.

10.3.8 Best Idea SR8: Sensitivity Analysis - Determine the Effects of Events and Megatrends

In the light of capital-intensive investments, increased competition, the arrival of new players, increasing regulation and a rapidly changing landscape in the sector, for many organizations an annual budget based on a long term strategic plan is no longer sufficient. This particular organization had an LRP (long-term plan) that was insufficiently linked to current trends and insufficiently discussed by the finance function with the business. In other words, there was a missing link between what was expected on the basis of the LRP and its translation into the annual budget, and what could ultimately be achieved as actual results. The finance function therefore introduced a mid-term three-year plan with the aim of more closely intertwining the LRP with the annual budget process in order to make the latter more accurate and thus relevant.

This three-year plan effectively controls the budget, starting from a well-defined fact base in order to perform more accurate forecasting. This fact base consists of operational data and financial parameters at an aggregated, high level with a number of drivers that are relevant to the business. This enables the organization to perform sensitivity analyses and determine what effect an event will have on the three-year plan, and ultimately on the annual budget. To keep the three-year plan up to date, the finance function has put together a "strategic controlling cell." This cell integrates the input of the controllers in the various business units after they have collected, analyzed, and challenged that input data in consultation with the business leaders. The entire process is bottom-up driven and the plan is challenged top-down from the strategy and investor relations departments in order to arrive at an accurate plan and finally an accurate annual budget.

10.3.9 Best Idea SR9: Measuring Success - Get Things Done *or* Achieve Progress?

To every finance function, feedback from stakeholders inside and outside the organization should be very important because it is a great source of inspiration to implement change. This particular finance function used the so-called Net Promotor Score (NPS)[4] to regularly measure satisfaction among its internal clients. The CFO explains: "The NPS results have made it clear to us what the driving forces are behind what is perceived by our business partners as good performance by the finance function and what they think of us. Nevertheless, we must bear in mind that these NPS scores, just like benchmarks—and especially in times of change and changing value propositions—only offer exploratory insights. Let me clarify with an example. Everyone is after strong business partnering and thus wants the finance function to play the role of an independent and helpful challenger. In reality, however, it is still often the case that NPS scores are highest when the finance function is strongly focused on offering service and giving people what they ask for, while the scores drop when the finance function indeed acts as a strong business partner and challenger. I always stress the difference between "getting something done" and "making progress" when talking about performance with my team. There is a difference between training until you can run a marathon within a certain time—getting things done, and getting others to want to help create an impact together—making progress. Running a marathon is an objective which I can easily measure the realization of and for which I can take responsibility myself. But if I want to gain impact with the finance function and in collaboration with the business, then I have to get something moving within the function and the wider organization. That is a completely different story and it is much more complex than running a marathon on your own, because now you depend on a lot of others to move forward. That's why I look at and focus on progress in situations like that. I want to improve, change, evolve. For me, an HPFF is not a realization but a continuous evolution based on progress."

10.3.10 Best Idea SR10: Transform the Traditional PDCA Cycle - More Emphasis on Learning and Acting Quickly[5]

The standard plan-do-check-act (PDCA) cycle is often conducted (if at all!) only monthly, whereas in these quick changing times it should be a permanent and ongoing process that constantly forces the finance function to look ahead and to translate information directly into action and subsequent learning.

The traditional PDCA cycle was developed to manage and adjust activities in fairly stable and predictable environments. However, in today's VUCA (volatile, uncertain, complex, ambiguous) world, it is reasonable to doubt whether the pace of this cycle is adequate to keep up with changes. In addition, in many organizations, the PDCA cycle is not, or not completely, followed, which could be because it (no longer) is relevant for steering purposes. This best idea is therefore about a reset of the PDCA cycle and thus of concern to the way management control is practiced in the modern finance function. What first needs to be done is that the cycle must be radically accelerated. It can no longer have a monthly rhythm; instead, a daily cycle is needed, based on making adjustments on the basis of a continuous feedback loop. Second, the cycle must focus far more on the future than it does today, and not be just based on comparing budget against actuals, but on forecasts and scenarios. Third, the cycle should contain more "soft" information instead of exclusively focusing on "hard" management control data. With "soft" data, more emphasis can be placed on the underlying drivers of factual information—more on the *why* than strictly on the *how much*.

In order to achieve this renewed cycle, three things need to happen:

1. Management control needs to shift from the hierarchical top to the entire organization. Many organizations are moving in the direction of self-governance, networking, and other types of agile concepts, which all have in common a (partial) breakdown of the hierarchy in favor of a flatter, more empowered organization. This unavoidably means that management control can no longer reside centrally with one management layer but is a task that should be performed throughout the complete organization (whatever shape it has).
2. The pyramid in the finance function must be inverted. Logically following from the first point, the finance function will no longer be at the heart of the management control cycle. With digital technology, the tools to install do-it-yourself options are already available to the users of information within the entire organization. The finance function will be centralized and will only facilitate DIY management control and focus on added value activities such as providing real-time and predictive insights that make immediate action-taking possible.
3. The focus should be put on learning instead of checking, i.e., PD*L*A instead of PD*C*A. Over time, the PDCA cycle has transformed into a typical "in control" tool with a strong internal focus, which only suffices in a business-as-usual environment. In today's world, organizations need to be in control of rapid external changes, which calls for good feedback mechanisms to translate develop-

ments into corrective measures. The PDCA cycle can provide this feedback mechanism if the C of "check" is interpreted to mean the ability to *learn* rather than simply to *check*.

10.4 BEST IDEAS FOR HPFF FACTORS "PERSONAL DEVELOPMENT" AND "ROLE CLARITY"

"Personal development" relates to the development of sufficient professional skills by financial professionals through regular attendance of courses in order to excel in their role. Financial professionals also

Table 5.

No.	Best idea	Key point of this best idea
PR/RC1	Financial professionals' development: develop business partner skills	Offering a program in which the skills needed to become a business partner, combined with knowledge transfer of organizational experts, helps financial professionals to become effective and appreciated business partners.
PR/RC2	Talent development: develop skills based on own motivation and personal responsibility	Being responsible for one's own development means that financial professionals have to take talent management into their own hands and start investing in themselves regularly.
PR/RC3	Role portfolio: work with roles	When the job classification system is set in stone because of a collective labor agreement and salary structure, and thus difficult to work with in practice, a role portfolio can help create a common language about how to organize the workload internally in the finance function.
PR/RC4	Finance Academy: facilitate learning	A finance academy is an environment that facilitates financial professionals in their learning and development by offering various learning methods and interventions.
PR/RC5	Trainee program: allow new impetus and ideas to flow in	Working on the right team composition in the finance function also creates room for new financial professionals, bringing in new ideas from outside the company and stimulating other financial professionals to be pro-active. This can be achieved through a thoughtful trainee program.
PR/RC6	Skill pool management: organize career coaching and succession	Skill pool management strategically manages the pool of skills of the financial professionals by rotating them to certain positions, evaluating them regularly, and creating successors for the finance function's management team members.
PR/RC7	'Talent management': close the competency gap	During the course of talent management, the current and future competency gap in the finance function is periodically evaluated, and strategies are devised to close this gap (such as policies for retaining and retraining current financial professionals and attracting new financial professionals).
PR/RC8	Anticipating change: emphasize working together to deal with change effectively	It is neither the financial strategy of an organization nor its technology that ultimately determine its success, but the way people work together; accordingly, financial professionals should help and support each other to deal with changes.
PR/RC9	Career landscape and career paths: further development of finance professionals	'A career landscape' of possible roles and positions in the finance function provides guidance to financial professionals in planning and steering their ambitions and the competencies to be acquired to fulfill these ambitions.
PR/RC10	Remove resistance: get colleagues involved	People are more easily convinced about the need for a change when they discover the arguments for that change themselves rather than hearing those arguments from others; accordingly, get them thinking about the change in the context of their finance function.
PR/RC11	Team composition: optimize the strength of the finance function team	Creating a pro-active, well-balanced team of financial professionals working well together is hard work and requires dealing with the paradox control-mindset versus the need for transformation, different ambitions and expectations between current staff versus a new generation, and job security versus the expectation to develop oneself continuously.

receive adequate personal development training and all have a personal development plan stipulating their future development needs and wishes. "Role clarity" clarifies the various roles that exist within the finance function. After all, "the typical financial professional" does not exist, there are many different roles that they can have in the finance function. And there are different demands which are placed on the different roles, which should be reflected in clear descriptions of the technical job requirements and the desired behaviors of each role a finance professional can have. There are also specific development programs defined for each finance role. Given that these two HPFF factors are so closely related, we deal with the best ideas for these factors—in total 11 of them—in one section.

10.4.1 Best Idea PD/RC1:Financial Professionals' Development - Develop Business Partner Skills

Financial professionals must be given the opportunity to continue to develop towards business partnership. The Director of Finance of a pharmaceutical company took the initiative to invest in a development program for financial professionals. Sessions were organized in two waves of two years each, in which insight into the team composition was central so that employees could make better agreements about their way of working together. After two years, these sessions were followed by a course aimed at developing personal leadership among the financial professionals. This program taught them to increase their own productivity and to deal effectively with all the distractions that occur during the frenzy of the day. The entire finance function attended this course.

The starting point of the training was: "work continuously on yourself." Learning from colleagues in other disciplines in the organization ("cross-learning") was promoted by the Director of Finance by setting up a program in which financial professionals gained more insight into and understanding of syndromes and the effect of medical products. To this end, an intensive five-day program was developed specifically for financial professionals without a medical background. The program explored in detail the syndromes in hematology, oncology, and immunology; the treatment options available; the medicines and their effects; and developments in R&D. The Director of Finance wanted to use the training courses to create a culture of continuous learning: "If we want managers in the organization to understand finance and provide them with a "Finance for non-financial" training, then we must in turn also want to learn from the business. You gain more understanding and respect from your colleagues if you know and understand what they do, and what the challenges are that they face. And we have achieved that with this program."

10.4.2 Best Idea PD/RC2: Talent Development - Develop Skills Based on Own Motivation and Personal Responsibility

The Director of Finance and Control of a government organization indicates that in her view the motivation of employees is paramount: "Everyone has talent. For me it is therefore mainly about the motives; what drives someone largely determines the results of their behavior. That is why we firstly focus on what someone wants and secondly on what someone can or should be able to do. We do not want to offer expensive, often content-oriented training to develop talents. People can learn a lot from each other and from the work itself. We have agreed to have 70 percent of learning-oriented activities take place internally."

Developing talents is now central to the organization. But talent development is not a one-way street from manager to employee, employees are also expected to take action in this respect. The Director of

Finance and Control wants to give employees a boost in the further development of their talents, but indicates that employees themselves are at the helm of their career: "The development of an employee is his or her own responsibility, the manager has at most a facilitating role. In the evaluation interview, it is ultimately determined whether you have grown as a professional in a specific role. Following a learning intervention, as we call any structured activity from which you can learn something, is not a condition for this, at most an accelerator. The reverse also applies: following a learning intervention is no guarantee that you have grown into a role. Being responsible means that you take your own development into your own hands and take the initiative yourself. That is what is expected of you. The organization helps you with this, although that support certainly does not have to be covering everything in-house. If employees feel that another (external) training or experience supports them better, we advise them to take action themselves, in consultation with their manager, to ensure that they then actually follow that training."

10.4.3 Best Idea PD/RC3: Role Portfolio - Work With Roles

The Director of Finance and Control states: "We had made agreements about what we expected from financial professionals in their daily work. However, the split up of functions that we used provided little guidance. Of course we also had a job classification system, the positions in which are strongly interwoven with our collective labor agreement and salary structure. But functions mainly zoom in on

Table 6. Example of a role portfolio

General role *Knowledge carrier* How can I keep my professional knowledge up to date and use it for the benefit of the organization, its customers, and its clients?	
Based on events and processing of data *Service provider* How do I ensure correct, timely, and complete financial settlement of invoices, payments and all benefits? *Producer* How do I produce useful records in the general ledger, supplementing and correcting the submitted transactions myself? *Controller* How do I determine that the data are usable so that they are suitable for further information processing?	**Based on fixed methods and rules/generating information** *Analyst* How do I structure data into quantitative information so that it provides adequate insights? *Reporter* How do I report on observed deviations so that the management of the organization can justify and correct/redirect? *Scout* How do I identify policy standards that deviate from trends within and outside the organization, so that they can be adjusted?
Supporting roles *Process improver* How can I improve processes so that they become more efficient and effective? *Director* How do I know what is needed at any point in the process so that I can give direction to it? *Functional administrator* How do I keep the financial systems working and appropriate and suitable on a permanent basis? *Developer* How do I provide automated reporting and analysis options that make the work of my internal customer easier? *Information manager* How do I simplify information provision for steering and accountability purposes?	**Based on judgement/working with information** *Advisor* How do I help management make decisions based on the available information? *Connector* How do I bring people or information from different parts of the organization and external parties together so that the strategic goals of the organization are realized? *Change agent* How can I help realize the desired change in the organization such that the strategic goals of the organization are realized?

what someone should ideally be able to do. We wanted to start from what someone wants to do and encourage the person to actually do so. In addition to the existing job classification system, we therefore introduced working with roles."

The roles were inventoried and developed jointly with all financial professionals during a series of workshops. Financial professionals themselves indicated which role they play now and which roles they think will be better suited to them in the future or into which they would like to grow. The choice of role determines the environment within the finance function in which the financial professionals do most of the work, i.e., their so-called "home base." Because of their explicit involvement in the definition and clustering of the roles, the financial professionals gradually became more enthusiastic about these roles. A total of nine roles were defined, as follows: the service provider, the producer, the controller, the analyst, the reporter, the scout, the consultant, the connector, and the change agent. In addition, the following five supporting roles were defined: the process improver, the director, the developer, the functional administrator, and the information manager. The general role of "the knowledge carrier" would apply to every financial professional: everybody was expected to keep their knowledge up to date. Table 6 provides an overview of the roles, with the core question indicating what a financial professional mainly focuses on in that role.

The development of the financial professionals starts with their roles and their corresponding competencies. Every financial professional focuses on three roles per year. Of these three roles, one is core, one is supporting to the core role, and the third is a development role in which the financial professional wants to improve. The Director of Finance and Control explained: "We link the talents of financial professionals to the working method in the financial processes. The roles have become a common language in the cooperation among the financial professionals."

The introduction of the role portfolio enables the Director of Finance and Control to place emphasis for the financial professionals on working in (a chain of) processes in a temporary team, instead of working in a permanent department. These temporary teams have been dubbed "virtual teams." As mentioned before, although financial professionals have a maximum of three roles, they can work in multiple virtual teams and processes. From the clustering of roles based on content and result, three "home bases" emerged:

- A home base for administration and data processing. This was the base for Administration and Financial Control and concerned the activities in the administration, general ledger management, and the administration of funds. IT support and functional management were also part of the activities.
- A home base for methods and rules and the generation of information. This base was called Management Control and contained all the activities required to generate reports from the available internal and external data. The Business Intelligence Competence center was also part of this home port.
- A home base for judgment, connection, exploration of external developments, and working with information. This home base, aimed at interpreting figures based on information from the Management Control environment and advising the internal customer, was named Business Control.

The Director of Finance and Control commented: "Due to the clustering of roles, financial professionals are no longer 100 percent in a fixed department in the finance function. In practice, about 70 percent of them work from a home base and 30 percent work in a virtual team. We have eleven financial professionals who have the director's role: they put together the virtual teams and are responsible for the processes and substantive in those teams. The directors know through the roles which financial professionals they should have for their teams and the financial professionals from the home bases know from which role they come to strengthen a virtual team. If you know which number you have, then you know what your role is in the team. In this way we try to bundle the appropriate knowledge and experience in the teams to tackle issues that cover the entire finance function."

10.4.4 Best Idea PD/RC4:- Finance Academy - Facilitate Learning

In order to facilitate learning and development in financial professionals, the Director of Finance set up a development curriculum, consisting of a range of education and training courses, in collaboration with HR and a specialized financial recruiting company. This curriculum was named the Finance Academy. The Director of Finance states: "I know from experience that developing talents requires a lot of practice and effort. Within Finance we want to ensure that every financial professional takes the time to do this. How the financial professionals will do that depends on themselves. Your own development is too important to leave to someone else. We have therefore urged every financial professional to take matters into their own hands and think about their own development, but above all to take action." The Finance development curriculum describes how financial professionals can further train themselves in their roles. All financial professionals have their own learning goals; these learning objectives are part of the personal curriculum and are discussed by management in development planning meetings with the financial professionals. The curriculum is a dynamic document that financial professionals collectively supplement and improve on an ongoing basis. If a financial professional wants to follow a training or education goal that is not in the curriculum, this course can be included in the curriculum in consultation with the manager.

The curriculum contains many examples of activities from which the financial professional can learn—the so-called learning interventions—but is more than simply an overview of training and education: it is a structured framework of learning interventions aimed at learning, developing, and improving so that financial professionals are better able to achieve the goals of the organization. The principles of the curriculum are as follows: learning is done by yourself, learning is different for every individual, the work environment is the most powerful learning environment, and learning is done from and with each other. The development curriculum comprises the following types of learning interventions:

- Learning interventions aimed at working together to achieve the goals of the finance function. These interventions deal with the three organizational principles that the organization has and that are also used within the finance function ("go from control and rules to trust; go from craftsmanship to professionalism; go from attending to contributing"). The training "Working together on Finance and Control" has been developed for this purpose, it is for everyone and is mandatory.
- Learning interventions aimed at growing in employee roles and management roles. In these interventions, the role of the financial professional is central and the goal is that the financial professional becomes more effective in performing that role.
- Learning interventions aimed at understanding one's strengths and weaknesses. In these interventions, a financial professionals' own role is combined with working on a concrete improvement theme in the organization. Several financial professionals with different roles work and learn to-

gether. Activities that involve working on developing one's role also fall into this type of learning intervention. The learning objectives are thus aimed at the personal development of the financial professional her/himself.

- Learning interventions aimed at outward growth. As the Director of Finance explains: "You can grow within the organization, but it can also be a financial professional' s choice to want to grow outside the organization. To help the financial professional with this, we offer outplacement as part of the curriculum. With this we want to break the taboo around growing outwards and make looking on opportunities elsewhere normal. Because financial professionals will not work solely in our organization all their lives."

Everyone learns in their own way, which is why various learning methods are offered in the curriculum. The professionals can choose from:

- Mentoring. Anyone who is skilled in a role is expected to make time to help less-skilled colleagues develop in this role. For example, a skilled reporter can help colleagues to grow in the role of reporter. The mentor focuses on the task and less on the person. The mentor shares his approach and experiences and shows people the way to achieve growth and development in the profession.
- Intervision, team coaching, and individual coaching. These are work forms that closely resemble each other. Intervision is a way of discussing with colleagues and understanding issues that a professional may encounter during work. In team coaching, a team is guided by a coach in taking joint ownership for team results. In individual coaching, a coach guides a financial professional in achieving his or her learning goals.
- Masterclasses, reference visits, and network meetings. These are methods of learning from the knowledge and experience of external experts. This could take the form of a lecture on a specific topic, a visit to another organization, or attendance of a network meeting.
- Education and training. There is also space for the usual forms of learning: education and training aimed at specific professional knowledge and/or specific skills such as 'written communication.'

The Director of Finance states: "The development curriculum is aimed at increasing knowledge and skills through learning in practice. A financial professional learns about 70 percent in the workplace through new challenging assignments, 20 percent of the learning experience come from feedback from colleagues and by looking at exemplary behavior from others, and 10 percent of the learning experience is gained by a financial professional in formal settings such as training workshops and courses."

10.4.5 Best Idea PD/RC5: Trainee Program - Allow New Impetus and Ideas To Flow In

The advancement of financial professionals is an important point of attention for every finance function. One of the ways to ensure adequate advancement is to organize a good quality intake. The Corporate Control manager says: "Regularly introducing new impetus into the organization helps the development of all financial professionals. That is why we introduced a trainee program and I am happy to say it has worked very well so far. We recruit two trainees every year with the aim of preparing them to become future leaders in the finance function and the larger organization. These trainees have a one-year training program, under the supervision of a recognized training institute. In two periods of five months they must work in a corporate control or business control function and a back office function. This gives them experience with the different teams within the finance function. Then they can go into the operation and, together with operational managers, look where they can best start their career."

The Corporate Control manager continues: "Of course, feedback during the process plays an important role. Every six weeks I evaluate with the trainees their development and progress. It is important to know that we also encourage the trainees to complete their academic development with a postgraduate training. They must experience what it is like to do a study next to work, which provides self-insight and experience in planning their own activities. We also encourage them to collect information outside of our company and to develop a "helicopter view" on matters and issues. We assess the trainees up to three to four years after the trainee period. After that period they are expected to be able to continue on their own and they leave the program. If, for whatever reason, a trainee no longer meets the trainee criteria, he or she will leave the company. It is not a good signal to the other financial professionals to keep them in the organization if a trainee does not meet the requirements. It is nice to see that in practice the trainees come up with a lot of fresh ideas. We encourage them to take initiative and come up with proposals to realize these ideas. For example, one of the things they developed is the "top impact file" (see best idea SR3), an instrument that we now use in the finance function to prioritize important and urgent files."

10.4.6 Best Idea PD/RC6: Skill Pool Management - Organize Career Coaching and Succession

Strategic personnel management is a spearhead of this finance function. The Corporate Control manager explains: "In order to support the development of our professionals, we as management team look at the inflow and through-flow in the finance function. The inflow is supported with an intensive recruitment and selection process and a trainee program, in order to be able to select well at the gate. For promotion, we have an active policy to rotate people to certain positions. We call that "skill pool management." Once a year, we set aside time with the management team to estimate the throughput of our people for the coming years, for trainees we do this every six months. We start from the desired population of the finance function in 10 years' time and then look at which financial professionals are suitable for which positions now, which financial professionals could be given a leadership role in the near future, and when financial professionals should gain experience in a different financial environment. We want to be able to fill all senior management positions in this way. For the trainees, we go a step further by also estimating their ultimate potential. We do this on the basis of four criteria: capacity, their intelligence and expertise; achievement, their drive to achieve success; relationships, their ability to communicate with colleagues at lower, equal and higher levels; and social involvement, their degree of involvement and interest in societal issue. Based on these criteria, we estimate the job level that the trainees can ultimately achieve in their career."

The appropriate deployment of financial professionals also ensures that the knowledge level of these financial professionals corresponds to their positions, as the Corporate Control manager elaborates: "We have estimated for each position what knowledge you need in a position, what essential knowledge components are, and what knowledge is nice-to-have. All financial professionals, together with their supervisors, filled in their status in relation to the requirements as set by the management team. We then created a kind of "heat map," a two-dimensional representation of data in which the values are displayed in colors, which gave us a good idea of where knowledge and skills need to be improved in the organization and with which courses and training we have to do this. Agreements about this are then made with the financial professionals in review meetings."

The management team then assesses the employees from a career development perspective. The Director of Finance elaborates: "Thinking about advancement forces us to organize the succession of the finance function management team. Advancement is the link to guarantee continuity in the finance function. I inform our people that they roughly need eight steps of experience in order to arrive at the position they aspire. Each of these steps will take approximately three to four years so the financial professionals have to carefully consider which step is best for them to get where they want to go. Making choices is therefore important. For example, if an employee has the ambition to become CFO, he or she will need different experience steps than if he or she wants to become a Treasurer. For a CFO role, the financial professional needs at least experience with leading a team, managing executives, working as a business controller, working in a treasury environment, working on mergers and acquisitions projects, and working on external and internal reports. The managerial experience zooms in on skills such as cooperating, having opinions, convincing, involving people and dealing with issues between top management and the work floor. The experience in the areas of Treasury, M&A, and reports sharpens the professional knowledge. The financial professional does not have to become a specialist in these fields, but a good understanding of the activities in these areas is important. Financial professionals can gain these experiences in the finance function, but also outside in the wider organization. Above all, we want to inform the financial professionals that they have to think about their career, how they can shape it, and how they can deal with the dilemmas that come with progressing up the career ladder.

A "job-for-life" no longer exists. For every financial professional there may come a time when the next step is to leave the company. We want to be able to indicate to financial professionals at an early stage whether their knowledge and skills are sufficient for the next step in their career in our finance function. We coach them in this, so that they have sufficient time and space to get started with the competencies required for the next step. It is sometimes confronting when the expectations between financial professional and management team differ, but honesty works best. A senior financial professional had become redundant a few years ago—and became a successful one at another company—is a good example of our way of coaching. He gave our financial professionals a presentation about his career and what he would do differently with today's knowledge. He was still pleased that he had been able to develop himself in our finance function and he clearly conveyed his feelings."

The management team together with the HR department introduced skill pool management alongside new working methods. As the Corporate Control manager describes: "HR support is well organized within our organization, but we have noticed that on some fronts we as a finance function go beyond HR. We have done all the steps together with HR, but we have not waited for them. Fortunately, our HR business partner is very proactive and wants to participate in the development of this spearhead. Some parts of the skill pool management—such as dealing with promotions, the "plotting" of positions of financial professionals, and working with a panel of managers that assess the financial professionals—work so well that other organizational units are now also starting to work with skill pool management!"

10.4.7 Best Idea PD/RC7: 'Talent Management' - Close the Competency Gap (Cleton, 2020)

The foundation for a well thought-out approach to talent management consists of periodically assessing the current and future competency gap based on the desired fulfillment of the positions in the finance function. CFOs see talent management as a top priority for investment in the finance function, whilst at the same time regarding it as a relative weakness. Below, we list six steps and three strategies to address talent management sequentially and effectively.

Step 1. Translate the Organization's Strategic Objectives Into a Vision of the Finance Function

This vision consists of a clear role and responsibility for the finance function to contribute to the achievement of the organization's strategic objectives. This role has to be translated into clear objectives for the finance function. When deploying a growth strategy, the finance function could play an important role in assessing new investments or integrating new acquisitions. In an alternative situation, the finance function may be involved in cost or working capital savings projects. Another aspect to be taken into account when developing the vision of the finance function is the degree of influence the finance function desires for itself within the organization. This can vary between a proactive role in which the finance function is involved in important decisions at an early stage or a more reactive role as the ultimate solver of (financial) problems that arise.

Step 2. Map the Structure of the Finance Function

The structure of the finance function can be mapped out according to the role and the formulated objectives. This entails determining the number of positions and their content. When the finance function has a relatively high level of involvement in day-to-day operational activities, the number of business control positions will be relatively higher than when the finance function is more distant.

Step 3. Determine the Required Competencies

Based on the defined positions, the required competencies can be determined. These competencies can be broken down into required financial knowledge, training, and experience; required skills, such as communication and influencing skills; and behavioral aspects, such as perseverance, cooperation, and flexibility. It is important to specify the desired level per competency component so that the financial professionals' performance in this respect can be appropriately assessed.

Step 4. Map Current Competencies and Their Development

Start by mapping the existing competencies of the financial professionals currently working within the finance function. It is also important to map the expected development of the available competencies, taking into account the fact that financial professionals will progress to other positions inside and outside the finance function or may leave the organization altogether (to join another employer or due to retirement).

Step 5. Identify the Gap Between Current and Future Competencies

Compare the existing and future competencies with the required competencies, both existing ones and those in the future. In this way, determine where the greatest competency gaps exist.

Step 6. Determine the Strategy for Closing the Competency Gap

There are basically three strategies aimed at closing this competency gap:

1. Retain Current Financial Professionals

Financial professionals are actively encouraged to stay within the organization. It is important to strengthen the connection between the organization and the financial professionals by attending to the wishes of these financial professionals. Aim to meet their needs by offering career prospects, rewards, or specific training; and by involving them in important decisions (also concerning new recruits).

2. Train Current Financial Professionals

Financial professionals are offered training courses that are specifically linked to developing skills in the currently non-existent or insufficiently available competencies that are required now and in the (near) future. This has to be done well, otherwise the investments in training may be wasted. Currently, in many finance functions, training needs are determined ad hoc, without a clear relationship to the competency gaps, and usually the individual wishes of financial professionals are decisive (which can of course promote the retention of the financial professional concerned, but may not be beneficial to closing the competency gap in the finance function). It also appears that the added value of training is rarely or never measured. The appropriate way is to establish a clear link between current and required competencies and the way in which training courses are selected and evaluated. A choice can be made between the standard training offer that is available in the market or the development of tailormade training courses that are well suited to addressing the missing competencies. Figure PD/RC1 shows the relationship between the determination of the competency gap and the determination of the training program.

Figure 10. A structured approach to talent management[6]

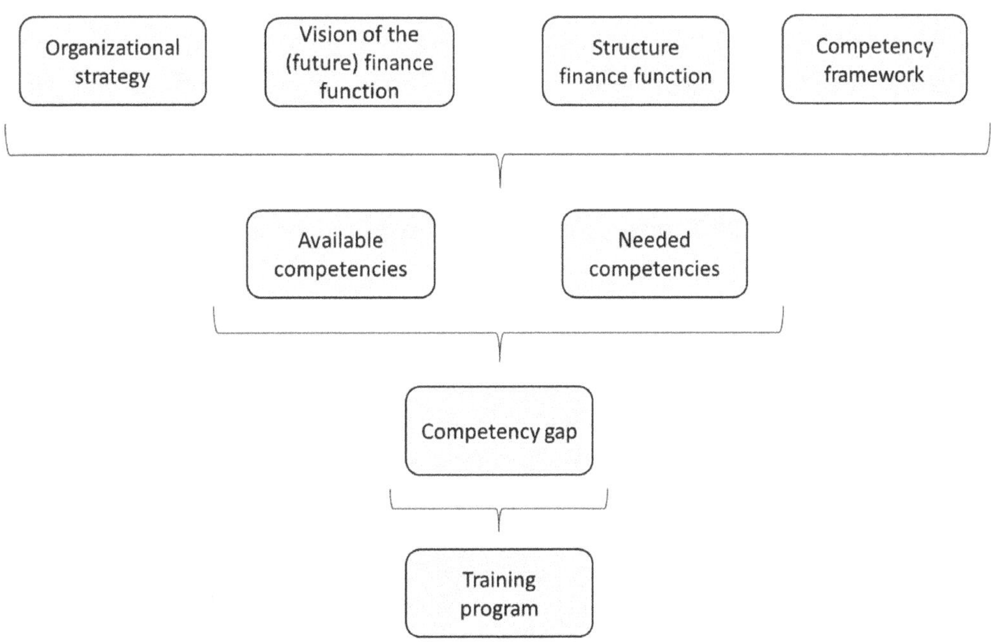

3. Attract New Financial Professionals

Attract financial professionals with the competencies that match the established profiles. It is important to also look for potential talent outside the finance function when seeking to fill the more business-oriented competency gaps.

10.4.8 Best Idea PD/RC8: Anticipating Change - Emphasize Working Together to Deal With Change Effectively

The "hobbyhorse" of the CFO is leadership based on a (at least for many finance functions) relatively new way of working. She explains this way of working: "As a manager, I think it is very important to consider the way in which we work together. Every year I discuss with my team what our goals are in terms of way of working and dealing with change. I always emphasize that change is something we have to deal with on a daily basis as change is a given. Yet people often find it difficult to deal with change, and it is then up to you as manager to ensure that change becomes part of the daily routine. Everyone should spend part of their time on change and they should spend this time together, helping and supporting each other to deal with this change. I am convinced that it is not the financial strategy of a company, nor the technology—although these things certainly contribute—that ultimately determine its success. I think it is the way people work together that determines whether an organization is successful. The difference is made by the team. That is why I have formulated with my team a mission statement for the finance function that we update and validate every year. Keywords in this mission statement are business partnering, reliability, pro-activity, and passion. In addition, I always emphasize a number of points: giving feedback—in all directions—is a must; give and take responsibility; have confidence in each other; and if you do something do it really well with full passion and focus. These are things that are often labeled "soft" but to me they deserve as much attention as the "hard stuff" such as processes and tools. Building the team is building the future. Optimal collaboration requires work. Optimizing the operation of the team is extremely important. In the future, I want to further stimulate my employees to work even more as one team and to step out of silo-thinking completely. For example, we now have the habit of making "activity reports" for all teams. These show what the teams got ready in the previous two weeks and what do they plan to do in the next two weeks, and how they have worked and are going to work together to achieve their agreed-upon results."

10.4.9 Best Idea PD/RC9: Career Landscape and Career Paths - Further Development of Finance Professionals

The CFO wanted to focus structural attention to the development of his financial professionals. To that end, he freed up 40% of the time of one of the managers in the finance function so that she could translate his vision on financial professionals' development into practice and make sure it would receive structural attention. The vision was based on the idea that working on professional development is primarily the financial professional's own responsibility. At the same time, the management of the finance function is responsible for actively guiding and supporting the financial professional in this development to ensure that it is in line with the objectives of the organization. The reason for developing and implementing a new vision was that financial professionals remained in their position for a long time and, according to the CFO's opinion, were experiencing too little personal growth. In addition, advancement in the finance function and in the greater organization was not really promoted, and thus hardly took place. Development agreements were sparingly made with financial professionals and if made they were not very concrete; often, job requirements and career opportunities remained unclear.

One of the tools that the manager developed was the "career landscape." For each position, role, and job scale in the finance function, the required professional, business, and IT knowledge; the behavioral competencies; and the required training level were mapped out in detail. The career landscape offered insight into what the financial professional must know and be able to do in his/her current and future position. Thus, the career landscape acted as an instrument for the financial professionals to shape their personal development and career path. With the career landscape, there was more consistency in the structure of competencies, order of follow-up positions—career paths—and required training levels with accompanying training program content. After introduction and simulation workshops were held with the financial professionals and their managers, the career paths were linked to existing HR processes and used in the cycle of annual review and development interviews. The current position and role of the financial professional are discussed in relation to higher, the same, or even lower level positions and roles, and the training and learning steps required when a financial professional wants to move into one of those positions and roles. The financial professional does not have to focus only on the next step in the finance function—a position outside Finance is also possible (for example, to gain operational or management skills).

The finance function developed career paths in close collaboration with the HR department as this department felt these to be a valuable addition to the existing HR processes. The managers from the finance function added practical experience to the evaluation process and raised awareness and prepared financial professionals for their next career step. During this process, it was strongly emphasized that every financial professional was free to choose his or her individual career path; there was no obligation to move to the next position.

10.4.10 Best Idea PD/RC10: Remove Resistance - Get Colleagues Involved (Bosch, 2021)

According to a well-known saying, it is not about being right, but about being seen to be right. Many financial professionals confuse the two and often wonder why operational managers do not listen to them. According to them, these managers ask silly questions and, in general, waste a lot of time discussing the numbers instead of taking decisions, despite having been prepared so well for these meetings with nice slides based on solid BI data that directly focus on the conclusions: no time to waste, after all!

The French mathematician and philosopher Blaise Pascal (17th century) was a great advocate of the scientific method and of facts and logic. But at the same time he was also a realist. He stated: "People are usually more likely to be convinced by reasons they have discovered themselves than the arguments of others." The essence of this remark is: help your colleagues to reach the correct conclusions themselves. A good example of this is a financial professional who once invited operational managers to "walk through his story." That this was not meant only figuratively became clear when the colleagues walked into the meeting room. All the data tables were taped in order to the wall of the room. The colleagues were given the opportunity to annotate the slides with post-its and were asked to explain what they thought they saw in the data. Because the colleagues were standing and actively walking around the room, people were more open than if they had slouched down in their chairs with their arms folded. They were now utterly involved.

This approach even works when people are working remotely at home. For example, start working with mini quizzes in your story: don't start with the slides, but start with a few fun questions that will make your colleagues think. Ask the questions that will help them reach the correct conclusion. This is possible with tools such as Mentimeter, Kahoot, or the quiz tools in Teams, but asking questions in advance also works. Both neurological and didactic research has shown that questions engage people's brains, causing the retention of your story to increase considerably. If you then also invite them to "walk you through the data" in search of the answers to these questions, you will see that resistance disappears and is replaced by energy and enthusiasm.

10.4.11 Best Idea PD/RC11: Team Composition - Optimize the Strength of the Finance Function Team[7]

The finance function of many organizations is understaffed and not always equally balanced in the sense that the right competencies, mindsets, and attitudes are absent. It is therefore important that the management of the function invests strategically in the development of the finance team. Ideally, this ensures that every professional in the team functions and contributes optimally and that they also keep developing themselves in order to remain or become of value on the labor market. In this way, it is possible to avoid value destruction and (even worse) the scenario of the better performing professionals looking for other challenges, leaving the finance function with the less flexible people supplemented with interim financial professionals.

Management can take the following steps to achieve an optimized finance team:

- Recognize that the context of the organization and the finance function puts people under pressure, so emphatically give them time and space to work on increasing their personal potential, so they are more prepared in times of change. Take their development seriously, do not pay "lip service" to it by conducting a few simple HR tests: objectively examine, together with them, their level of subject content (or the lack thereof) and reflect on the factors that need to be addressed to improve it.
- Increase your knowledge and skills in the field of conscious and unconscious behavioral patterns and dynamics in teams and organizations.
- Dare to set priorities in order to protect the team from wasting time on issues of limited or fleeting importance.
- Recognize the major differences in nature and strength between the various roles in the finance function and the financial professionals who fulfill these roles.
- Move tasks to the finance function that are well suited to binding and captivating people and allowing them to add value, not only at the back (control measures, risk management) but especially at the front: focus on business improvements that make the operation happy. Add value to the organization by exploiting everything that is available for adding value instead of running away from business opportunities. Think of tasks such as complaint follow-up, analysis and prevention of credit notes, stock problems, and aging in debtors: who or what goes wrong, how do we tackle that?
- Put digital finance on the agenda, preferably by involving the financial professionals in the change process. Finally start optimizing the IT architecture or start working on process optimization with the talents in the finance team.

- Identify the true potential of the financial professionals in the finance team and make clear how this potential could be exploited through specific exposure, training, or coaching of financial professionals. It is sometimes shocking how little management really understands their financial professionals. Who are potentially the business controllers and financial controllers who help the organization forward, and which people act as pencil pushers, show resistance, and throw sand in the engine that you are trying to get going? Deal with the "bad apples." But remember: every manager gets the financial professional he or she deserves. So reflect also on your possible shortcomings in managing these "bad apples."
- Dare to make mistakes and, for once, not meet deadlines. Many financial professionals are still of the old school. They focus on output, deadlines, and correctness and, if necessary, continue to work at night to complete the report instead of empowering and challenging colleagues. Try stopping this behavior and see how it feels.
- Understand millennials' truly different lifestyle. You have to manage them differently. Old methods no longer work.
- In addition to financial and business controllers, the finance team needs digital finance experts not only to "ignite" the others with the digital development fire, but also to stay in charge of IT developments yourself within the finance function. An HPFF has a good grip on data, the data master, reporting tools, and the ERP system and the data warehouse.
- Stop blindly giving education and training to financial professionals just to placate them. Take the time to really understand, motivate, and help people get started on their way to true personal development.
- Make sure that no one is overloaded with routine work and becoming burned out and apathetic. Motivate people by devoting part of their time to personal development and participation in, for example, digital finance matters. Let this development or participation not be a thing that "also" comes on top of the regular work: let it be the icing on the cake of working in the finance function. Accordingly, give financial professionals time and space for involvement in (the design of) digitization and systems, and to walk around and talk to other people to investigate matters and issues.
- Ensure diversity and rotation in the finance team. To serve as a "breath of fresh air" and keep everyone sharp. Ensure sufficient influx of talent into the finance function.

REFERENCES

Bouker, M., Geelen, F., & Wielaard, N. (2020). *The CFO in Pole Position, leading next-generation decision-making in a data-driven organization*. Boom uitgevers.

Buist, H. J. (2021). Begin aan digitale transformatie met simpele robots [Start digital transformation with simple robots]. *Controllers Magazine*. https://cmweb.nl/2021/04/digitale-transformatie-begint-met-rpa/

Cassauwers, T. (2019). In The Pocket gaat volluit voor 'lean en digital finance' [In The Pocket is fully committed to "lean and digital finance"]. *CFO Magazine*, (222), 41–43.

Cleton, F. (2020). Talentmanagement in zes stappen [Talent management in six steps]. *Controllers Magazine*. https://cmweb.nl/2020/07/talentmanagement-in-zes-stappen/

De Boysere, N. (2021). Controlling modelleert voorspelbaarheid van Port of Antwerp [Controlling models predictability of the Port of Antwerp]. *CFO Magazine*, (235), 55–57.

Gerritsen, E., & Kramer, P. (2020). Zo optimaliseert u de kracht van uw finance team [In this way you optimize the strength of your finance team]. *Executive Finance*. https://executivefinance.nl/2020/05/zo-optimaliseert-u-de-kracht-van-uw-finance-team/

Hagen, N., & van der Willemsen, M. (2020). De business controller in positie: Hoe kom je aan tafel?" [The business controller in position: How do you get to the table?] *Controllers Magazine*. https://cmweb.nl/2020/08/de-business-controller-in-positie-hoe-kom-je-aan-tafel/

Holvoet, M. (2021). Manier waarop mensen samenwerken, bepaalt succes van finance [The way people work together determines the success of finance]. *CFO Magazine*, (235), 31–34.

Maes, J., & Schijns, J. (2020). *Lean Robotics - Lean & RPA, de winnende combinatie* [Lean Robotics - Lean & RPA, the winning combination]. NUBIZ.

Morlidge, S., & Player, S. (2010). *Future Ready: how to master business forecasting*. John Wiley & Sons.

Notten, M. (2020). Wat is de toegevoegde waarde van process mining? [What is the added value of process mining?]. *Controllers Magazine*. https://cmweb.nl/2020/08/wat-is-de-toegevoegde-waarde-van-process-mining/

Paterson, R., & Vermaas, B. (2013). De business wil betere management informatie [The business wants better management information]. *Tijdschrift Controlling*, (January/February), 22–26.

Sinek, S. (2009). *Start with why, how great leaders inspire everyone to take action*. Penguin Group.

ten Bosch, J. (2021). Weerstand wegnemen bij een presentatie: zo doet u dat [Remove resistance from a presentation: this is how you do it]. *Controllers Magazine*, 4. https://cmweb.nl/2021/05/weerstand-wegnemen-bij-een-presentatie-zo-doet-u-dat/

van den Ham, E., & Becker, P. (2021). Data science en AI: wat betekent het nu echt voor controllers? [Data science and AI: what does it really mean for controllers?]. *Controllers Magazine*. https://cmweb.nl/2021/03/data-science-en-ai-wat-betekent-het-nu-echt-voor-controllers/

Vandamme, M. (2020). Robotisatie via databots [Robotization via databots]. *CFO Magazine*, (230), 52–54.

ENDNOTES

1 "The golden circle" is a conceptual thinking model developed by Sinek (2009). The model consists of three layers, from the inside to the outside: why, how and what. The outer shell ("what") are the products or services of a company. The "how" explains how companies do what they do. The "why" is about what drives companies. Inspired companies, regardless of size or industry, think, act, and communicate from the inside out.

2 See for an explanation of the OGSM method: https://en.wikipedia.org/wiki/OGSM.

3 Integrated performance management is sometimes also called corporate performance management, see for a definition https://www.gartner.com/en/information-technology/glossary/cpm-corporate-performance-management.

4 The net promoter score can be calculated by asking the customer the question: How likely are you to recommend us to a friend or colleague? To answer the question, the respondent can enter a score from 0 to 10. The scores are then divided into three groups: (a) Promoters: respondents who gave a score of 9 or 10; (b) Neutrals: respondents who gave a score of 7 or 8; and (c) Critics: respondents who gave a score from 0 to 6. The NPS score is subsequently calculated as follows: NPS =% promoters -% critics, which gives a number between -100 and +100 (Wikipedia).

5 This best idea is derived from and based on Bouker et al. (2020).

6 Figure derived from Cleton (2020).

7 Based on and adapted from Gerritsen & Kramer (2020).

Chapter 11
Future-Proofing the Finance Function

ABSTRACT

The last task remaining for finance functions is to become 'future-ready' to deal with all kinds of changes in the environment. Such changes consist of threats caused by (worldwide) disruptors and megatrends or opportunities provided by (mainly) megatrends. Unfortunately, there is limited literature on making the finance function future-ready, which limits the ability of the finance function to prepare itself for the future. This is illustrated by the COVID pandemic of 2020, which has shown that many organizations and their finance functions were not ready for the havoc it caused, resulting in considerable negative consequences. In this chapter, the 14 most important megatrends and disruptors are described, and courses of actions that finance functions should apply, in order to adapt to these megatrends and disruptors in such a way that they can remain high-performing, are discussed.

A future-ready finance function is an agile, integrated, and customer-led function that supports the organization in dealing with uncertainty and the challenges of a multi-faceted world (IFAC, 2018).

To help finance functions to prepare for the future, we extended a previous study we conducted into megatrends and disruptors (Linthorst & de Waal, 2020) to focus specifically on the finance function. Our goal was to identify how finance functions should adapt to megatrends and disruptors in such a way that they can become and remain high-performing. In the previous study, based on an extensive literature review, 14 megatrends and disruptors were identified that are expected to have the most influence on organizations over the next decade. In this chapter, we match these megatrends/disruptors with the characteristics of the HPFF to specifically identify their effects on this function.

DOI: 10.4018/978-1-7998-6929-0.ch011

11.1 MEGATRENDS AND DISRUPTORS

Megatrends are large social, economic, political, and technological changes that are slow to form and, once in place, exert an influence for a considerable amount of time (Naisbitt & Aburdene, 1990). Disruptors are defined as 'someone or something that prevents something, especially a system, process or event, from continuing as usual or as expected' (Cambridge Dictionary). The main differences between megatrends and disruptors are the speed with which they appear and the effects they have. Megatrends are changes that take place gradually over a longer period of time, whereas disruptors are short-term, seemingly unexpected changes with high impact. Our previous study yielded the following thirteen megatrends and one disruptor:

- *Megatrend 1: Speed of technological advancement.* Technological advancement is the collective term for the progress in the development of technological and digital tools, such as automation, big data, and advanced analytics, that increase productivity and provide better access to information and ideas. Organizations have been automating their work for decades, but it is specifically the increasing speed of change in the technological field that makes technological advancement so disruptive.
- *Megatrend 2: Flexible employment.* Flexible employment refers to an increasing variety in working arrangements and work practices, including variation in working time/hours, working locations, amount and types of work contracts, and forms of employment contract. It is expected that traditional nine-to-five jobs will increasingly be replaced by mobile and on-demand employment, and that due to mobile technology and the Internet, teams of employees will not need to work in the same location anymore. There will also be a rise in 'fluid' positions and jobs where people have multiple roles within one organization or work as independent contractors. A gig economy will emerge, which is a labor market in which temporary positions are common and organizations have contracts with independent workers for short-term engagements rather than long-term employment contracts.
- *Megatrend 3: Skills mismatch.* This refers to the expected gap between the skills of the existing/current workforce and the skills needed for jobs in the future. Learning new skills to adapt to the changing work environment is not a new phenomenon but, with the increasing speed of change, it is a challenge to prepare organizations, employees, and educational systems in time for these changes. In addition, it is becoming increasingly difficult to assess exactly what changes will occur and what new skills will consequently be required.
- *Megatrend 4: Sustainable employment.* Sustainable employment refers to the extent to which workers are willing and able to remain working now and in the future. It is about offering work and working conditions that keep workers happy, healthy, and motivated. There is rising interest and concern around sustainable employment among management because in many (Western) countries there will be an imminent shortage of workers because of the aging working population. This is coupled with a growing awareness of sustainability issues in general among the population (and thus among the organization's clients).
- *Megatrend 5: Continued globalization.* Globalization is the process by which businesses or other organizations develop international influence or start operating on an international scale. Alternatively, it can refer to the growing interaction and integration among people, companies, and governments worldwide. Although globalization is not new, it is increasingly being seen as a

similar force to the megatrends of 'technical advancement' and 'flexible employment.' In the wake of the COVID-19 pandemic, which caused global problems in production and logistics, there seems to be an upcoming trend of deglobalization for critical products, wherein countries aim to start producing these products themselves instead of relying on imports.

- *Megatrend 6: Changing workforce composition.* Both the aging of the worldwide population and generational shifts are expected to cause changes in the future of work. Not only do older employees represent an increasing proportion of the workplace, but they are also working until an older age than previous generations did. In addition to the aging of the world's population, generational shifts from baby boomers (generation X, 1950s to 1970s) to millennials (generation Y, 1980s to 1990s), followed by generation Z (2000s, 2010s) are occurring. In the future, generation A will cause major changes to the composition of the workforce, and, by 2025, millennials (generation Y) will make up the majority of the workforce.

The World Economic Forum projects a net increase of 58 million jobs across 20 major economies by 2022 as a result of technological advancements. Their research also finds that the majority of workers will need "reskilling and upskilling." As a result of these trends, businesses must outpace their competitors in their efforts to find, train, and retain employees who possess expanded skill sets (World Economic Forum, 2018).

- *Megatrend 7: Increasing inequality.* There is a growing concern about increasing wage and income inequality. Although employment rates have gone up globally, many categories of workers are not benefiting equally from this change, and their economic situation seems to be deteriorating. At particularly high risk of worsening economic conditions are low-skilled employees, employees with jobs that are likely to be replaced by automation, self-employed workers (gig-workers), and employees with a migrant background; in addition, the gender pay gap (which also creates differences in pay between workers) is not expected to disappear in the near future. Thus, there is an increasing need for social protection of vulnerable employees, with possible measures ranging from legal protection for individuals with flexible working arrangements to the introduction of a universal income.
- *Megatrend 8: Environmental issues.* This megatrend refers to changes in the world's climate—caused by human activity—and its consequences. Flooding, the rising sea level, extreme weather conditions, and natural disasters caused by climate change result in major impacts on daily life. These environmental issues are expected to have a huge negative impact on future economic growth because large-scale investment must be made to reduce the ecological footprint of people and businesses, foster sustainability, protect the environment, and deal with the expected migration of people from countries that are at risk of rising sea levels and flooding.
- *Megatrend 9: Economic powershifts.* Economic powershifts denote the shift in economic power from the developed West to the upcoming East. Countries in Asia, for example China and India, are becoming economically stronger, including globally, due, amongst other reasons, to the increasing consumption in these and neighboring developing countries. This has affected the competitive position of commercial organizations in developed countries, making them more vulnerable to competitors but at the same time creating opportunities for growth in Asian countries.

- *Megatrend 10: Urbanization.* This refers to the worldwide population shift from rural to urban areas, as a consequence of which more people are becoming permanently concentrated in relatively small areas (cities or metropolitan areas). This has an impact on organizations in rural as well as urban areas. In rural areas, there may be a drain in qualified workers leading to organizational bottlenecks, whereas urban areas are becoming overcrowded, leading to higher cost of living, increasing competition for jobs, and a more hectic or less balanced life, with negative consequences for health.
- *Megatrend 11: Cross-border migration.* Cross-border migration refers to employees moving to another country with the aim of finding (better) work. It occurs as a consequence of people being unable to find attractive work opportunities in their country of origin at the same time as other countries are unable to adequately fill their skills gaps. Cross-border migration changes the workforce composition and can create social problems. In addition, cross-border migrants are more vulnerable to poor economic conditions than native employees and they have a higher unemployment rate—especially those with a non-Western background.
- *Megatrend 12: Resource scarcity.* This refers to the problem of increasing demand for resources such as water, food, energy, land, and minerals, which is causing a scarcity of natural resources and inherent cost increases. Organizations increasingly need to address and reconsider their dependence on raw materials and resources. Finding new ways of working, innovation, and the use of alternative resources will be key to their future survival. Even if organizations are failing to respond to such issues because of the lack of intrinsic motivation, public pressure and government intervention will force them to minimize their negative impacts on society and the environment.
- *Megatrend 13: Individualism.* This is the trend for people to seek to distinguish themselves from others, which is causing a shift from a collectivist society to a focus on the individual. People and organizations are increasingly expected to offer tailored and personalized products, services, and solutions. Organizations need to address the increasing demand for individual attention. Client and employee experiences have become key performance indicators that require close monitoring. Corporate approaches to training and mentoring are becoming more bespoke and tailored to individual career ambitions.

- *Disruptor 1: Pandemics.* The term pandemic refers to the worldwide spread of an infectious diseases. Notable pandemics include the 1918 Spanish flu, HIV/AIDS, and COVID-19. Although pandemics have not been studied as either a megatrend or disruptor in the literature on the future of work, the recent COVID-19 outbreak is clear evidence that pandemics do have a significant and pervasive impact on societies and organizations globally, and thus much more attention should be paid to them. Consequences range from increased working from home and social distancing to economic crisis and increased illness and mortality within the workforce.

> Sixty-six percent of finance leaders believe the digital competency gap in their finance function is widening relative to the speed of evolving technology, increasing the disparity between digitally skilled and unskilled financial professionals and worsening the finance function's inability to take advantage of digital investments (Gartner, 2021a).

11.2 MATCHING THE MEGATRENDS/DISRUPTOR WITH THE HPFF FACTORS

To evaluate how the megatrends and disruptor impact the HPFF framework, we constructed an impact matrix in which we combined them with the factors and characteristics of the HPFF framework (de Waal et al., 2021). For each of the 13 megatrends and one disruptor, we analyzed whether and how they could impact each of the five HPFF factors and its underlying characteristics.[1] Table 1 summarizes the results. The Table shows that although the HPFF factors can be affected in both positive and negative ways by the megatrends, they are mostly negatively affected by the disruptor. In other words, some of the megatrends explored create opportunities, whereas other megatrends and the disruptor create threats to finance functions.

Table 1. The impact matrix depicting the effects of the megatrends and disruptor on the HPFF characteristics

			HPFF factors		
Megatrends/ disruptor	**Finance function improvement**	**IT focus**	**Personnel development**	**Role clarity**	**Strategic role**
M1. Speed of technological advancement	New technologies enable many improvements in the FF.	■ New technologies require continuous updating of knowledge in the FF. ■ New technologies make it possible to automate routine processes so that the FF has more time for other tasks.	New technologies require continuous updating of knowledge by finance personnel, who should be given sufficient time for this.	New technologies require new descriptions of current roles and also the creation of new roles.	The FF must contribute knowledge about the possibilities of new technologies during strategic discussions and important projects and processes.
M2. Flexible employment	The increasing number of flexible employees/workers makes it more difficult to structure and work on improvements with sufficient speed.	■ It is becoming more difficult to develop IT expertise and retain this knowledge in the company with employees who only work part-time or on an on-call basis. ■ Routine financial processes must be fully automated so that flexible workers can mainly be used for specialist tasks.	■ The FF is less able to influence the development of flexible workers. ■ The FF should pay more attention to the development of the skills needed for remote working.	■ Flexible workers bring in specialist knowledge and act as innovators/drivers for change. ■ The FF will have to invest in the development of flexible workers.	Flexible workers may not work at the FF for long enough to become strategic partners and to enter into partnerships with other parts of the organization.
M3. Skills mismatch	The FF must train its professionals the skills to work on improvements in a structured way.	The FF must use a (large) part of its budget to increase the knowledge and skill levels of its professionals.	The FF must give its professionals time to work on their knowledge and skills.	Role descriptions and development programs must ensure that the gaps between desired and available skills are closed.	The FF must ensure that the strategic partnership skills of its professionals are developed to the desired level.
M4. Sustainable employment	Actions must be taken to improve working conditions within the FF.	The FF's budget should be used for automation that promotes sustainable employment.	The development of employees must be given importance so that they feel confident and good about themselves.	Development programs must take into account the promotion of sustainable employment ('one size does not fit all').	
M5. Continued globalization	A globally operating organization must find a good balance between standardization and customization of its financial processes.	The FF must be able to implement ICT applications in many different (regional) settings.		Role descriptions and development programs must take into account local circumstances.	The FF will have to develop an international outlook to be a good discussion partner in a globally operating organization, and at the same time must have knowledge of local conditions.
M6. Changing workforce composition	The increasing proportion of millennials in the workforce will accelerate the use of digital applications.	The increasing proportion of millennials in the workforce leads to an increase in available IT knowledge.	Training courses will have to be more precisely tailored and differentiated for the different generations working in the FF.		
M7. Increasing inequality			The FF's management must ensure that all personnel have equal development opportunities.		The FF must be aware of growing inequality and its consequences for the organization, and of the financial and social impacts of the organization's actions in relation to inequality.

continues on following page

Table 1. Continued

			HPFF factors		
Megatrends/ disruptor	**Finance function improvement**	**IT focus**	**Personnel development**	**Role clarity**	**Strategic role**
M8. Environmental issues	There will be an explicit need to make improvements that better prepare the FF (and the organization) for the consequences of environmental issues.	Standardization is given high priority because it makes the FF (and the organization) less vulnerable to the consequences of environmental issues.			■ The FF must have knowledge of environmental issues and their consequences and risks for the organization, and of the financial and social effects of the organization's activities. ■ Financial forecasts (short and long term) must explicitly take into account developments and consequences of environmental issues.
M9. Economic powershifts	Shifts in economic power can encourage the FF's management to make quicker decisions around relocating the FF's processes.	The FF must be able to implement IT applications in different international settings.	Training courses must take into account the new markets and stakeholders that the FF will have to deal with.		■ The FF must have knowledge of the consequences, risks, and opportunities for the organization of economic power shifts. ■ Financial forecasts (short and long term) must explicitly take economic power shifts into account.
M10. Urbanization					■ The FF must have knowledge of the consequences and risks of urbanization for the organization. ■ Financial forecasts (short and long term) must explicitly take into account the consequences of urbanization for the organization.
M11. Cross-border migration			Personal development plans must explicitly take into account the migration background of employees.	The FF may have to provide specific training to new employees with a migrant background on the desired behaviors in the organization.	■ The FF must have knowledge of the consequences of migration for the organization. ■ Financial forecasts (short and long term) must explicitly take into account the consequences of migration for the organization.
M12. Resource scarcity	Improvement actions must explicitly take into account the scarcity of particular resources.	Digitization must be given high priority if it ensures that the organization will use lower amounts of scarce resources.			■ The FF must be aware of the consequences and risks of resource scarcity for the organization. ■ The FF must acquire knowledge about alternative scarce resources in order to advise the operation. ■ Financial forecasts (short and long term) will have to explicitly take into account the consequences of resource scarcity for the organization.
M13. Individualism			The FF will increasingly have to take the wishes of individual employees into account and tailor training programs to them.		The FF must have knowledge of the consequences, risks, and opportunities of individualism for the organization.
D1. Pandemics	Improvements must primarily be aimed at better protecting the FF against pandemics, or better dealing with the consequences thereof.	■ Standardization and centralization must be given high priority in order to make the FF more resilient to increased sick leave during a pandemic. ■ Automation should make remote working/working from home possible and efficient.			■ The FF must have knowledge of the consequences and risks of pandemics for the organization. ■ Financial forecasts (short and long term) must explicitly take into account the consequences of pandemics for the organization.

Developing the "Futurize!" Process
In order to evaluate the robustness of the impact matrix and to develop a process through which the finance function can apply it to develop actions to make itself future-ready, we organized two roundtable discussions with experienced finance professionals. We asked them the following discussion question: "Given the influences of the megatrends/disruptor on the finance function, how are you going to approach making your finance function future-ready; what are you going to do in practice?" We intended that the answers to this question would yield a generalized approach for making the finance function future-ready. Each roundtable started with a review of the impact matrix. The participants broadly agreed with the matching results, and, in general, the participants were quite satisfied with having such a matrix available to them. The first roundtable yielded a first draft of the process for making the finance function future-ready—this process which was termed the 'Futurize! process of the finance function.' During the second roundtable, this process was refined and optimized.

The key to success is to create a blueprint for how the finance organization can turn disruptors into opportunities (KPMG, 2019).

11.3 THE FUTURIZE! PROCESS

Figure 1 depicts the process in which the finance function uses the impact matrix to develop the actions that will help it become future-ready.[2]

Figure 1. Schematic depiction of the future-readiness process of the finance function

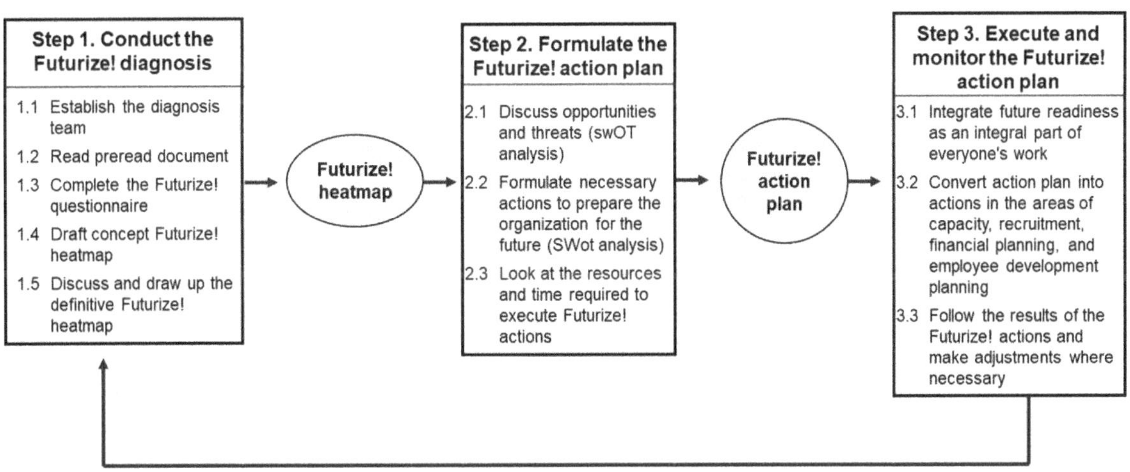

Step 1: Conduct the Futurize! Diagnosis

Step 1 starts with selecting the people in the finance function who have a good overview of the work processes and what is going on in the function. These are often the members of the finance function management team, supplemented with other knowledgeable financial professionals. Each of the participants in the diagnosis receives a preread document in which they will find the following information that is necessary before they start filling out the Futurize! questionnaire: a description of the megatrends and disruptor to be scored, a definition of the terms used, and a description of the various activities that take place during the Futurize! diagnosis.

The participants then complete the Futurize! questionnaire. In this questionnaire, the participants are asked to score each megatrend/disruptor on the estimated impact on the finance function, the degree to which the finance function is preparing itself for the impact of this megatrend/disruptor, and the estimated degree of preparedness or how prepared the organization actually is for this megatrend/disruptor. "Estimated impact" is defined as the participant's estimate of how great the impact of a megatrend or disruptor will be on the functioning and results of the finance function: this impact is generally negative but may also be positive. "Estimated degree of preparedness" is the participant's estimate of how well the organization is actually prepared for the megatrend/disruptor; in other words, an estimate by the participant of how effective the actions are that the finance function has taken to mitigate the impact of the megatrend/disruptor. The participants do this not only for the 14 megatrends and disruptor, but also for sector trends. They can add these sector trends during the diagnosis as they see them develop in the industry in which their organization operates.

A concept Futurize! heatmap is compiled based on the summarized score given by the participants. A heatmap is a two-dimensional graph with the estimated impact of the megatrend/disruptor on the y-axis and the estimated degree of preparedness for this megatrend/disruptor on the x-axis; see Figure 2.

Figure 2. Example of a Futurize! heatmap

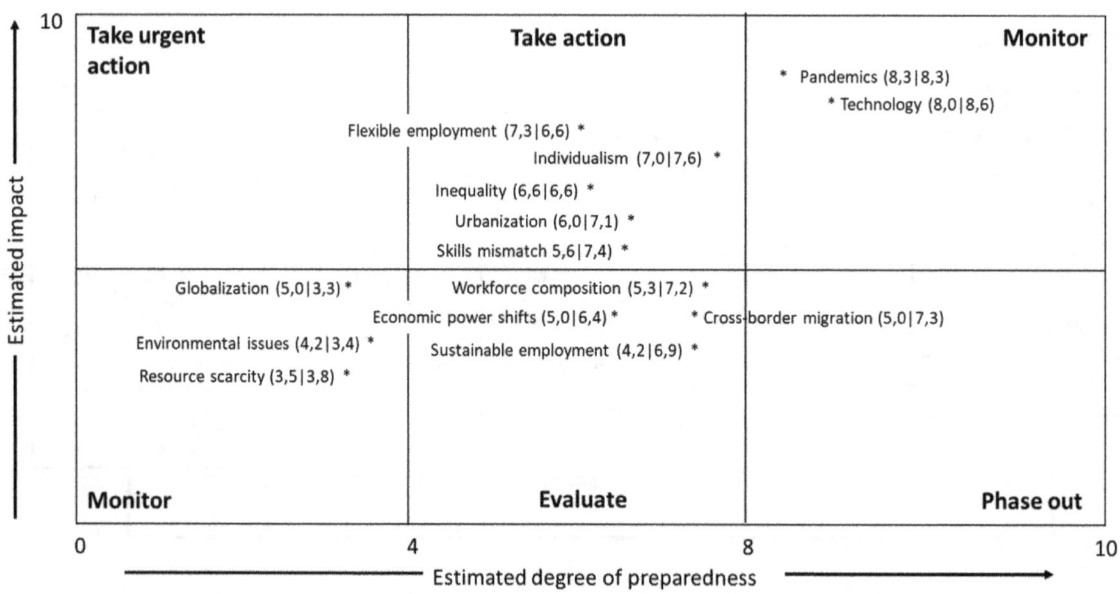

Based on the average scores for impact and preparedness, each megatrend/disruptor is placed in one of the six areas in the concept Futurize! heatmap. Each area differs in terms of the urgency with which the finance function must prepare for a particular megatrend or disruptor. If, according to the participants, a megatrend/disruptor has a low impact on the finance function while preparedness for this megatrend/

disruptor is also low ("monitor" area in the lower left corner in Figure 2), then the finance function only needs to track the megatrend/disruptor to see if it might become more urgent with regard to a growing impact; until then, no further action is needed. At the other end of the spectrum, the finance function should also monitor a megatrend/disruptor that is having a high impact and for which it is well-prepared ("monitor" area in the top right corner). In this case, it is necessary to track how well the actions that the finance function is taking to address the specific megatrend/disruptor are working. When a megatrend/disruptor has a low impact and the finance function is very well-prepared for it, it can be concluded that there is an excessive effort for this specific megatrend/disruptor. The finance function can then tone down or even stop some of its actions for this particular megatrend/disruptor ("phase out" area in the lower right corner). In contrast, when a megatrend/disruptor has a high impact but the finance function is not well prepared for it, the organization should take immediate and urgent action to prepare for it in the shortest possible time ("take urgent action" area in the top left corner). When the finance function's preparation is average (between 4 and 8 on the x-axis) for a megatrend/disruptor and this megatrend/disruptor has a low impact, the finance function may consider reducing the efforts it expends in dealing with this megatrend/disruptor ("evaluate" at the bottom center area). Conversely, if this megatrend/disruptor has a high impact, the finance function must take action to address it in the near future ("take action" area at the top center).

The concept heatmap forms the input for a discussion among a larger group of people from the finance function. During this discussion, each megatrend and disruptor is evaluated for its impact, which can be both positive and negative ("Opportunity" and "Threat" in a SWOT analysis), and degree of preparedness, until the discussants agree on the correct place of the megatrend/disruptor in the heatmap. The definitive Futurize! heatmap then indicates the priority with which the megatrends and disruptor must be tackled by the finance function.

Step 2: Formulate the Futurize! Action Plan

Once a joint picture of the current situation emerges, in step 2, an action plan is formulated. The Futurize! action plan provides an overview of the actions that must be carried out to prepare the finance function for the future, to defend itself against threats or to seize opportunities for the benefit of the organization. When preparing the action plan, the finance function takes into account the current status of the function, in terms of resources, budget, and time available to implement the actions, so that the resulting action plan is realistic.

One organization uses the situation-complication-question (SCQ) framework to address key issues and challenges for finance leaders and business partners. This framework includes eight steps for addressing organizational challenges (APQC, 2018):

1. Ensure the organization selects the right issue for improvement.
2. Analyze and prioritize the issue under consideration for improvement.
3. Build insights and conduct root-cause analysis.
4. Brainstorm and generate ideas for solving the problems identified.
5. Design solutions and analyze potential implications/impact.
6. Iteratively prototype solutions and gather feedback.
7. Reverse-engineer solutions and assumptions.
8. Create a storyboard and present the findings.

Step 3: Execute and Monitor the Futurize! Action Plan

In step 3, the action plan is implemented by integrating the Futurize! actions into the daily practices of the finance function at a realistic pace based on the function's capacity, recruitment, and financial and employee development plans. During the execution of the action plan, it will be updated regularly based on current conditions and events.

> Financial professionals need to be future-ready and they can develop this skill. The lack of time that professionals have cannot be the excuse for not doing the important work of becoming future-ready. Disruption will continue to happen and their lives will continue to become more complex as a result. Given the fact that clients, customers, and employers want financial professionals to be future-ready, it might in fact be one of the most important skills to be developed. To be a future-ready professional is the way to survive in an ever-changing world (Sheridan, 2017).

Using the Heatmap to Conduct Professional Discussions

The Futurize! diagnosis can be used as a tool for professional discussion among finance professionals. Recently, we organized a roundtable for finance professionals on the topic of making the finance function future-ready. We asked the participants to fill in the Futurize! questionnaire for their own finance function. Subsequently, we consolidated their responses into one Futurize! Heatmap, which is depicted in Figure 3.

Figure 3. The consolidated Futurize! heatmap derived from the finance professionals' roundtable

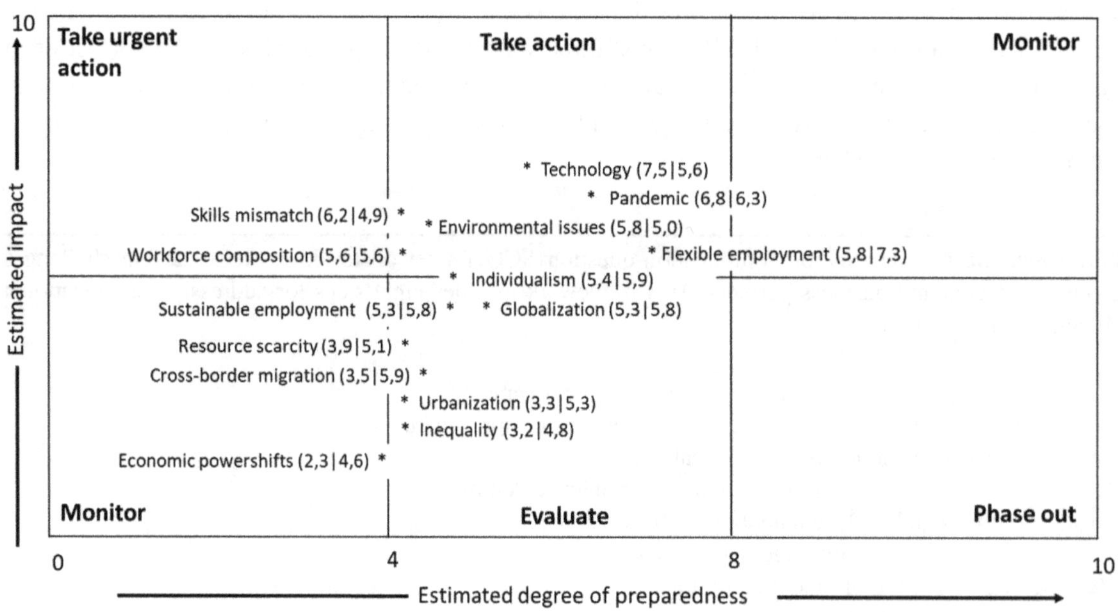

During the roundtable, we presented this heatmap as mirroring the future-readiness of an average finance function, and then asked the professionals whether they recognized this heatmap as also being representative for their finance function future-readiness, and especially the degree of preparedness finance functions generally have in regard to the megatrends and disruptor. At the end of this discussion, we asked the professionals if they had any comments or ideas on how to use the Futurize! diagnosis process at their own finance functions. Here is a selection of their responses:

- "This should be part of the risk thinking at the Board of Directors, the Supervisory Board, and possibly even the Works Council. It helps structure our risk management process."
- "Look for 4 to 5 concrete steps to be taken per megatrend; otherwise you will get stuck in high-over conversations and generalities."
- "Initially take a top-down approach, keep the "think tank on the impact estimation of megatrends" small to get an efficient and informed discussion. Broaden the scope of participants when discussing the actions to be taken to make the finance function future-ready."
- "Just thinking about this is already an advantage and increases anticipation and future-readiness in the organization."
- "It would be useful to incorporate the dimension of "long vs. short term" in the discussion, so that people get a feel for how urgent dealing with the megatrend/disruptor is."
- "Larger organizations, especially multinationals, should prepare a separate heatmap for each region they operate in."

11.4 THE FINANCE FUNCTION AND COVID-19

> "In just a few months' time, the COVID-19 crisis has brought about years of change in the way companies in all sectors and regions do business. Companies have accelerated the digitization of their internal operations and customer and supply-chain interactions by three to four years. And the share of digital or digitally enabled products in their portfolios has accelerated by a shocking seven years. Nearly all respondents say that their companies have stood up at least temporary solutions to meet many of the new demands on them, and much more quickly than they had thought possible before the crisis. What's more, respondents expect most of these changes to be long lasting and are already making the kinds of investments that all but ensure they will stick" (McKinsey Digital and Strategy & Corporate Finance Practices (2020).
>
> "As aptly stated by Microsoft CEO Satya Nadella in a 2020 quarterly earnings call, "We've seen two years' worth of digital transformation in two months" (Blackburn et al., 2021).

Introduction

As the aforementioned quotes illustrate, the COVID-10 pandemic has been an occurrence with a lot of impact on organizations and thus on finance functions. In this section we look at the impact the pandemic has (had) on finance functions, how finance functions dealt with it, what the lessons learned are, and what is still in store for the (near) future.

Research Approach
For our research we had to turn to the managerial literature. The main reason is that the COVID-10 pandemic was so recent that there was hardly any academic literature on its effect on the finance function nor on how the finance function dealt with its consequences. Therefore we needed to turn to so-called practice-driven management research as, according to Mirvis et al. (2021) this type of research – which is generally reported in white papers and research reports by consultancy and professional associations – identifies real-life phenomena much quicker than theory-driven management research which is generated in "university-time" – and which is reported in academic journals. Thus we selected professional literature about COVID-19 and its impact on the finance function. All sources reported on empirical research done in the past two years. In total 38 sources were used.

Impact of COVID-19 on the Finance Function

From the literature we first collected the impacts finance functions reported COVID-19 had on their operations and functioning (Accenture, 2021; Access, 2020; ADP, 2021; Blackline, 2020; Chakraborty et al., 2020; Davis & Trace, 2020; Essaides & Willman, 2020; Euler Hermes, 2020; EY, 2021; Financial Director & ADP (2021); Lapinskiene, 2020; Lawson, 2021; Magaro, 2021; Ramakrishnan, 2021; Slot, 2021; Totum, 2021; Webb & Lawson, 2021; Workday, 2021). These impacts are summarized in Figure 4.

Figure 4. Main impact of COVID-19 on the finance function[3]

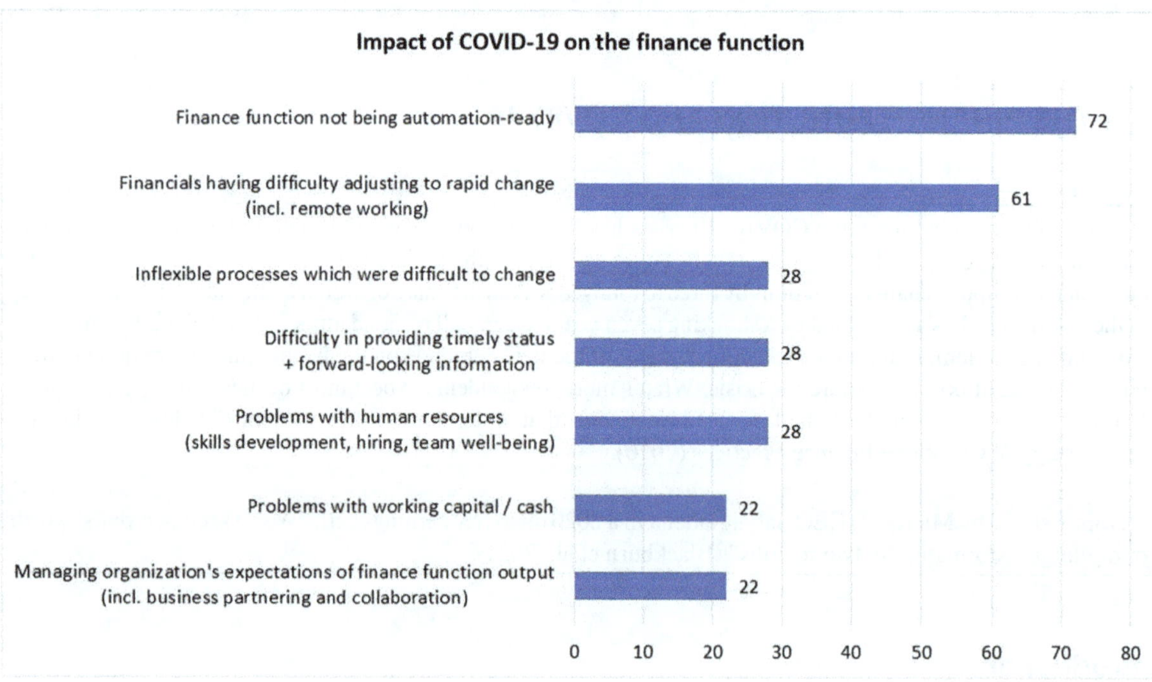

As can be seen from Figure 4 the biggest impact of COVID-19 was that, in general, the finance function found itself not ready for a big disruption, both on the technical (IT) and on the human side. Regarding the technical side, finance functions that stated that they were partly or completely digitalized before the pandemic hit, reported that their increased agility made it much easier for them to deal with the impact of COVID-19, they experienced less or no delays or budget cuts regarding improvement projects, they had hardly any problems switching quickly to widespread remote working and they experienced a positive impact on the growth of the business (despite the pandemic) (Accenture, 2021; Blackline, 2020; Euler Hermes, 2020; Filev, 2020; Harvard Business Review Analytic Services, 2021; Magaro, 2021; Verbeeten, 2020).

It was not only gloom and doom however, the pandemic did also bring several opportunities for finance functions. The following were reported (starting with most frequently mentioned opportunity/benefit) (CFO, 2021; Financial Director & Workday, 2021; Gartner, 2021b; Harvard Business Review Analytic Services, 2021; Oracle, 2021; Robert Walters, 2021; Ronan, 2020; Twilio, 2020):

- made changes that were previously considered too difficult to do and/or to be accepted by people (such as remote working or digitalizing internal customer services)
- redesigned and modernized the finance function (i.e. transformed how finance creates value for the business)
- accelerated the digitization of the finance function
- introduced other than the traditional goals (such as service continuity, finance function resilience and agility)
- accelerated transformation efforts already underway
- improved lines of accountability
- removed the red tape/bureaucracy (to speed up decision-making).

What Will Come After the Pandemic?

A majority of the finance functions is planning to free up resources for a multiple of activities to make sure they will be more ready for the next disruptors and be able to deal with them much better than they did now. Figure 5 provides an overview of these activities (Access, 2020; ADP, 2021; Agrawal et al., 2020; Blackline, 2020; Blackburn et al., 2020; Caswell-LaPierre et al., 2020; Chakraborty et al., 2020; Davis & Trace, 2020; Essaides & Willman, 2020; Euler Hermes, 2020; EY, 2021; Financial Director & Workday, 2021; Grant Thornton, 2021; Lapinskiene, 2020; Magaro, 2021; Proxima, 2021; Robert Walters, 2021; Slot, 2021).

Among the activities that the financial function wants to take up after COVID-19 are quite a few that could be expected: making the finance function more agile, resilient and digitalized (i.e. create a digital finance function), with better processes and more skilled people. In addition there are "newer" activities as changing the key performance indicators (the KPI dashboard) of the finance function – and thereby probably also of the organization –, better workforce planning, more attention for cyber-security and – typically a COVID-19 consequence – better and easier remote working in a hybrid environment. Regarding the latter, the combination of working at home and at the office creates the challenge of looking after the well-being of the Finance team (i.e. monitoring team spirit, paying more attention to personal situations). The conclusion from Figure 3 is quite clear: it is not going to become quieter in the finance function which means at the same time that this is a very exciting time to be working in the finance function, especially when it transforms to a high-performance digital finance function!

Figure 5. The activities that the financial function wants to take up after COVID-19

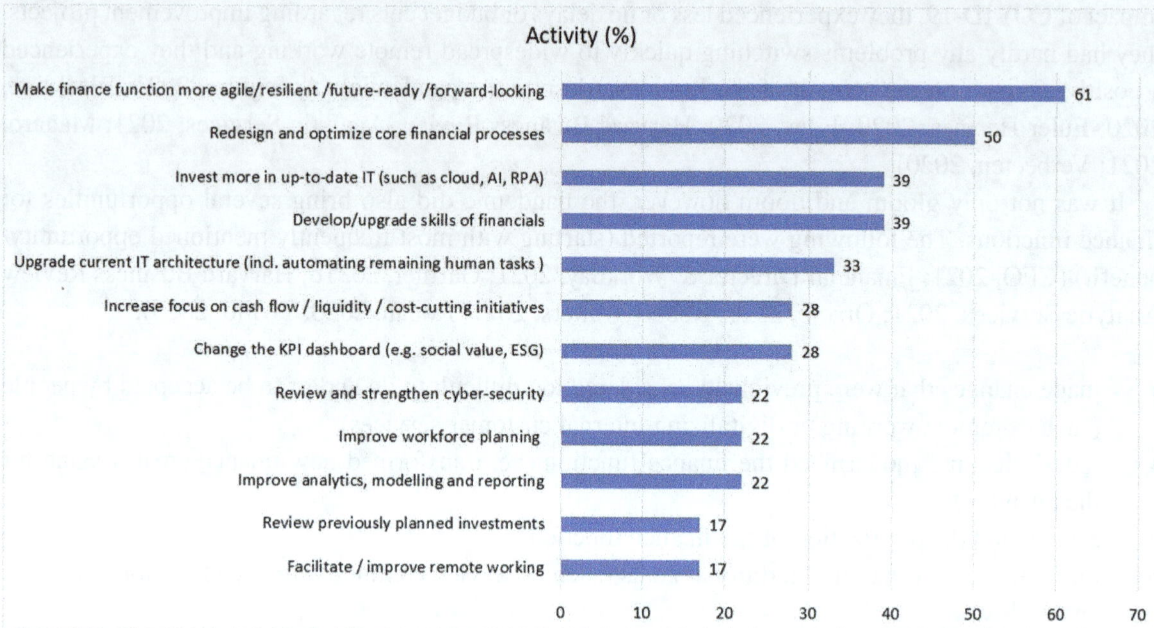

Final Observation: The Need for a High-Performance Digital Finance Function is Now!
A survey among 2,000 managers across the UK, France, Germany, Italy, Spain, Benelux, the Nordics and the Middle East, shows that since the COPVID-19 pandemic organizations have started to rely more on intuition and experience than on data (Oracle NetSuite, 2021). This in itself is not that surprising as organizations found it difficult to steer on historical data as these were not that relevant in the extraordinary circumstances created by the pandemic. However, after two years of COVID-19 organizations now have access to better and more relevant data but the inclination to relapse into steering on gut feeling remains with many of them. This is a problem because the survey shows that steering on intuition produces *less* growth compared to organizations that manage on data: organizations that focus less on data are more likely to fall short of their growth goals. Of the surveyed organizations who steer on data 41% met growth targets even during the pandemic, but in the case of organizations that do not manage with data it was only 22%. The latter organizations also tend to invest less in the core elements of a high-performance digital finance function, such as IT architecture, data analytics, and skills of the financials. And as the research study shows, this course of action does not benefit these organizations at all. In fact, the opposite can be stated: to recover from the impact of the pandemic and to thrive in the coming years there is an urgent need to transform to the digital HPFF: the time to do this is NOW!

REFERENCES

Accenture. (2021). *Leaders Wanted, Experts at Change at a Moment of Truth*. Technology Vision 2021, Accenture.

Access. (2020). *Covid-19 in Business: A Guide for Finance Department Leaders*. The Access Group.

ADP. (2021). *The potential of payroll: global payroll survey 2021*. ADP.

Agrawal, A., Bradley, C., & Uhlaner, R. (2020). *No longer on autopilot: Lessons for CFOs from COVID-19*. McKinsey & Company.

APQC. (2018). *Ten characteristics shared among best-in-class finance functions*. American Productivity and Quality Center.

Blackburn, S., Galvin, J., LaBerge, L., & Williams, E. (2021, Oct.). Strategy for a digital world. *McKinsey Quarterly*, October.

Blackline. (2020). *The Future of Automation in the Finance Function, Global Survey 2020*. FSN The Modern Finance Forum, FSN Publishing Limited.

Caswell-LaPierre, A., Kracklauer, S., Essaides, N., Dorr, E., Hall, B., & Willman, T. (2020). *Transforming finance to prevail in the next normal*. The Hackett Group.

CFO. (2021). *Getting Back to Growth (Perspectives from CFO Research)*. CFO Publishing LLC.

Chakraborty, S., Charanya, T., de Laubier, R., & Mahesh, A. (2020). *The Evolving State of Digital Transformation*. BCG.

Davis, N., & Trace, P. (2020). *Finance evolution: Insights from Australian CFOs and finance leaders on the impact of COVID–19 and their new reality*. KPMG.

de Waal, A., Bilstra, E., Bootsman, J., & Linthorst, J. (2021). Future-proofing the finance function: An empirical approach. *International Journal of Management and Applied Research*, *8*(2), 122–140. doi:10.18646/2056.82.21-008

de Waal, A., & Linthorst, J. (2022). *Futurize! Dealing with megatrends and disruptors*. Routledge.

Eagar, R., Teixeira, T., Taga, K., & Caldani, S. (2020). *Leading businesses through the COVID-19 crisis, first learnings from Hong Kong, Italy and Singapore*. Arthur D. Little PRISM Special Report, Arthur D. Little.

Essaides, N., & Willman, T. (2020). *Looking Past Covid-19: Five Critical Messages for CFOs*. The Hackett Group.

Euler Hermes. (2020). *The finance leader of tomorrow 2020 survey, how finance leaders view the world: Before and after COVID-19*. Euler Hermes.

EY. (2021). *Will you recognize your Finance function five years from now?* EY CFO Flash Survey, EYGM Limited.

Filev, A. (2020). COVID-19 Is A Before-And-After Moment In The Digital Transformation. *Forbes*. https://www.forbes.com/sites/andrewfilev/2020/03/30/covid-19-is-a-before-and-after-moment-in-the-digital-transformation/#b09c20bd4223

Financial Director & ADP. (2021). *Digitalisation and the pandemic: adoption accelerates to cope with challenges*. ADP.

Financial Director & Workday. (2021). *The future of finance 2021 and beyond*. Financial Director and Workday.

Gartner. (2021a). *Unlock your finance team's digital potential: 5 critical competencies.* Gartner for Finance, Gartner Inc.

Gartner. (2021b). *2021 Gartner CEO Survey: The CFO Perspective.* Gartner Inc.

Grant Thornton. (2021). *Values driving value, CFOs looking to lead on ESG.* Grant Thornton LLP.

Harvard Business Review Analytic Services. (2021). *Accelerating Transformation for a Post-Covid-19 World.* Harvard Business School Publishing.

IFAC. (2018). *Perspectives on the finance function journey.* International Federation of Accountants.

Kniffin, K. M., Narayanan, J., Anseel, A. J., Ashford, S. P., ... Van Vugt, M. (2020). COVID-19 in the workplace: Implications, issues, and insights for future research and action. *The American Psychologist*, (August). PMID:32772537

Koonin, L. M. (2020). Novel coronavirus disease (COVID-19) outbreak: Now is the time to refresh pandemic plans. *Journal of Business Continuity & Emergency Planning*, *13*(4), 298–312. PMID:32438951

KPMG. (2019). *Finance disrupted, how should the CFO respond to a business environment in turmoil?* Future of Finance, KPMG LLC.

Lapinskiene, V. (2020). *Lessons learnt from COVID-19: Building a resilient finance function.* ITR.

Lawson, R. (2021). *The Impact Of Covid-19 On The Finance Function.* IMA (Institute of Management Accountants).

Linthorst, J., & de Waal, A. (2020). *Disruptive forces and their postulated impact on organizations.* Sustainability, 12(20).

Magaro, M. (2021, Jan. 28). Turning Crisis into Opportunity: COVID-19 as Accelerant in Finance Digital Transformation. *FEI Daily.*

McKinsey Digital and Strategy & Corporate Finance Practices. (2020). *How COVID-19 has pushed companies over the technology tipping point—and transformed business forever.* McKinsey & Company.

Mirvis, P. H., Albers Mohrman, S., & Worley, C. G. (2021). *How to do Relevant Research, From the Ivory Tower to the Real World.* Edward Elgar Publishing Limited. doi:10.4337/9781788119405

Naisbitt, J., & Aburdene, P. (1990). *Megatrends 2000: ten new directions for the 1990s.* Morrow.

Oracle. (2021). *Four Big Moves Finance Should Make Right Now, Recapture growth and thrive in an unpredictable future.* Oracle.

Oracle NetSuite. (2021). *The State of Growth Part 2: Confident Decision-Making for Business Growth.* Oracle NetSuite.

Paliokaitė, A., Pačėsa, N., & Sarpong, D. (2014). Conceptualizing strategic foresight: An integrated framework. *Strategic Change*, *23*(3-4), 161–169. doi:10.1002/jsc.1968

Proxima. (2021). *Finance Leaders Outlook 2021.* Proxima.

Ramakrishnan, V. (2021). *How the CFO Can Be an Effective Partner to the CEO in Navigating the Pandemic's Economic Storm*. Tata Consultancy Services.

Robert Walters. (2021). *The Future of the Finance Function*. Robert Walters Group.

Ronan, S. (2020). *How COVID-19 Changed the Finance Function, Building a Finance Function for a Post-COVID World Series*. CitrinCooperman.

Sheridan, B. (2017). *Five steps for building a future-ready finance team, human work in the age of machines*. Maryland Association of CPAs and Business Learning Institute.

Slot, M. (2021). Covid-19 als versneller van digitale transformative [Covid-19 as accelerator of digital transformation]. *Executive Finance*. https://executivefinance.nl/2021/04/covid-19-als-versneller-van-digitale-transformatie/

Totum. (2021). *Future Finance: Developments in the legal finance function*. Totum report 2021, Totum Partners.

Twilio. (2020). *COVID-19 Digital Engagement Report*. Twilio Inc.

Verbeeten, F. (2020). *De impact van het Corona-virus* [The impact of the Corona virus]. Koninklijke NBA en de Universiteit van Amsterdam.

Webb, C., & Lawson, R. (2021). *The CFO of the Future*. ACCA and IMA.

Workday. (2021). *How Finance Can Build a Data Foundation to Fuel Frictionless Finance*. CFO Indicator Survey 2021, Workday Inc.

World Economic Forum. (2018). *The Future of Jobs Report: 2018*. World Economic Forum's Centre for the New Economy and Society. https://www.weforum.org/reports/the-future-of-jobs-report-2018

ENDNOTES

1 This approach resembles the strategic foresight method: the futurist begins with the megatrend or disruptor and thinks of possible direct consequences of that megatrend/disruptor (Paliokaitė et al., 2014).

2 The text for this section has been derived from de Waal and Linthorst (2022).

3 Calculated by dividing the number of literature sources in which the particular impact was mentioned by the total number of literature sources in which impacts were mentioned (= 12 in total) x 100%.

Appendix A: Benefits of the High Performance Finance Function

This appendix gives the benefits of creating a high performing finance function as found in several studies conducted during the last decade by consultancy firms and benchmark organizations.

Criteria/ Studies	Hackett Group (O'Conner et al., 2014)	PWC (2014)	Accenture (2014)	Oxford Economics (2018)	Accenture (2018)	Hackett Group (Essaides et al., 2019)	KPMG (2019d)	Hackett Group (Caswell-LaPierre et al., 2020)	Ferrin and Wong (2021)
Comparison of	Best-performing vs. average-performing FF	Best-performing vs. average-performing FF	HPOs vs. non-HPOs on their finance function	Finance Leaders vs. Finance non-leaders	High-growth vs. average growth organizations	World-class vs. average finance functions	Exemplary vs. average finance functions	World-class vs. average finance functions	Trans-formed vs. not trans-formed finance function
Results for the finance function									
Internal client satisfaction			More satisfied	More satisfied because of more cooperation		65% / 21% more likely to meet / exceed stakeholder expectations			
Influence of CFO			Higher	Higher	Higher				
Influence of FF			Higher	Higher		Higher			
Time spent collecting vs. analyzing info		50% less						22% less	
Time spent on added value activities		47% vs. 36%					More time spent		More informed decision-making
Business partnering		40% more FTEs in business partner role						41% more likely to be seen as valued business partner	Better answers to queries
Number of FF personnel (FTE)	52% less					23% less		45% less	
Average cost level	46% lower	60% lower		Lower		17% lower		59% lower	
Productivity improvement	1.4% vs. 2.7% of invoices to be corrected			More automation	More automation	34% higher; 60% less invoices corrected; 17% faster completion of budget cycle	More automation	23% less cost but more automation	Reduced reporting timelines + improved workflow through automation
Self-service for managers	50% of FF vs. 35% of FF							47% more self-service	

continues on following page

Appendix A: Benefits of the High Performance Finance Function

Criteria/ Studies	Hackett Group (O'Conner et al., 2014)	PWC (2014)	Accenture (2014)	Oxford Economics (2018)	Accenture (2018)	Hackett Group (Essaides et al., 2019)	KPMG (2019d)	Hackett Group (Caswell-LaPierre et al., 2020)	Ferrin and Wong (2021)
Capabilities of financials					Seen as more innovative, operational, agile and commercial	Seen as more innovative, operational, agile and commercial	Seen as more innovative, operational, agile and commercial	Seen as more innovative, operational, agile, pro-active and commercial	
Focus on talent							Greater focus, resulting in 61% vs. 43% more retention	24% more hours devoted to training	
Projects						3x more projects with high ROI	50% more successful projects	3x more projects with high ROI	
Results for the organization									
Organizational revenue / market share				Higher				20% more	
Organizational net margin								6.7% higher	
Organizational EBITDA								4.0% higher	
Organizational return on equity								5.9% higher	
Organizational total shareholder return								10.7% higher	

REFERENCES

Accenture (2014), *The CFO as architect of business value, delivering growth and managing complexity,* Accenture 2014 High Performance Finance Study, Accenture LLC, Chicago.

Accenture (2018), *From bottom line to front line*, CFO Reimagined, www.accenture.com

Caswell-LaPierre, A., Kracklauer, S., Essaides, N., Dorr, E., Hall, B., & Willman, T. (2020). *Transforming finance to prevail in the next normal.* The Hackett Group.

Essaides, N., Willman, T., & Dorr, E. (2019). *World-class finance: redefining performance in a digital era.* The Hackett Group.

Ferrin, M., & Wong, W. (2021). *Winning finance, Transformation harnessing the full value of the finance function.* Renoir Consulting.

KPMG International. (2019). *Future ready finance survey 2019.* KPMG International Cooperative.

O'Connor, J., Schneider, L., & Willman, T. (2014). *The world-class performance advantage: how leading finance organizations outperform their peers.* Finance Executive Insight, The Hackett Group.

Oxford Economics. (2018), *How finance leadership pays off, six ways CFOs stay ahead of the pack,* www.oxfordeconomics.com

PWC. (2014), *Finance matters, finance function of the future*, PricewaterhouseCoopers LLP, www.pwc.co.us/finance

Appendix B: Overview Ideas for Creating the High-Performance Finance Function

In this appendix, the ideas collected from the literature for creating a high-performance finance function are collected and categorized, and arranged in order of the most frequent suggested ideas.

Idea	Literature sources	Total
Increase the efficiency and effectiveness of the finance function *(this includes simplification and standardization of processes, better management reporting, higher agility of the finance function, better performance management, lean finance)*	1, 2, 3, 5, 6, 7, 8, 10, 11, 12, 13, 14, 15, 16, 17, 18, 20, 21, 23, 24, 25, 26, 27, 28, 29, 31	26
Apply even more IT to automate processes *(this includes automating financial processes, achieving process alignment and elimination where possible, creating a 'finance factory')*	4, 8, 9, 10, 12, 13, 16, 18, 20, 21, 22, 23, 24, 25, 26, 27, 28, 29, 30, 34, 37	21
Creating closer cooperation with the business by being a business partner *(making the financial operation of processes and issues easier for operational management, and more integration of processes across the business)*	7, 10, 11, 12, 14, 19, 20, 21, 23, 25, 28, 29, 31, 32, 33, 35, 37	17
1. Place greater focus on the execution of added value activities *(this includes applying added value technologies and techniques)*	1, 2, 3, 4, 7, 8, 9, 10, 14, 16, 17, 22, 23, 25, 27, 37	16
Develop a specific behavioral profile for each financial role *(this includes financials becoming more communicative, daring, flexible and innovative)*	3, 7, 12, 16, 17, 21, 22, 23, 25, 26, 27, 28, 30, 32, 34, 37	16
Pay more attention to the personal development of financial professionals	3, 6, 9, 10, 14, 21, 22, 23, 24, 26, 27, 28, 29, 30, 37	15
Place greater focus on looking ahead and forecasting *(this includes scenario planning)*	2, 4, 5, 6, 11, 12, 25, 29, 30, 31	11
Achieve greater involvement in the strategy and decision-making processes	4, 5, 10, 16, 17, 18, 20, 27, 28, 33	10
Apply more outsourcing and shared services	2, 5, 9,13, 16, 21, 26, 31, 37	9
Create financial self-reliance in the line *(this includes the shift from routine financial processes to the operation and financial self-service)*	7, 11, 12, 15, 18, 21, 25, 26	9
Gain deeper knowledge of IT	1, 8, 9, 10, 19, 22, 25, 30, 37	9
Implement better risk management	1, 3, 6, 8, 18	5
Create more flexibility/agility	7, 19, 25, 28, 29	5
Develop a data-driven analytic decision culture	22, 23, 26, 27, 28	5
Have more focus on effective controls *(with KPIs, automated controls cyber security)*	2, 24, 28	3
Focus more on growth	18, 20, 31	3
Put sustainability, ethics, environmental, health and safety on the agenda	1, 12, 36	3
Focus on better supplier collaboration	26, 34	2
Create more focus on innovation	7, 22	2
Have a stronger focus on compliance	14	1
Optimize working capital	28	1

Appendix B: Overview Ideas for Creating the High-Performance Finance Function

Legend

1 = Kelder, P., van Lindenberg, P.W., and Ghijsen Cohen, O. (2010), *Een moderne CFO stelt de juiste prioriteiten* [A modern CFO sets the right priorities], SDU Uitgevers, Den Haag.

2 = PWC (2012), *Putting your business on the front foot: finance effectiveness benchmark study 2012*, PricewaterhouseCoopers LLP, www.pwc.co.us/finance

3 = Chartered Global Management Accountant (2013), *Managing innovation, harnessing the power of finance*, Chartered Institute of Management Accountants, London

4 = CFO Research (2013), *Shaping the finance function of tomorrow: finance's strategic mandate - and the innovations that will help them meet it*, CFO Publishing LLC, Boston

5 = Lawson, R. (2013), *Rising to the challenge, achieving real-time visibility across the organization*, IMA® the association of accountants and financial professionals in business

6 = KPMG (2013), *Being the best: inside the intelligent finance function*, KPMG International Cooperative

7 = Tillema, K. (2013), *Van cijfers naar waarden, de nieuwe realiteit voor management accounting & control* [From numbers to values, the new reality for management accounting & control], Kluwer, Deventer

8 = Chang, H., Ittner, C.D., and Paz, M.T. (2014), "The multiple roles of the finance organization: determinants, effectiveness, and the moderating influence of information system integration", *Journal of Management Accounting Research*, Vol. 26 Issue 2, pp. 1-32

9 = O'Connor, J., Schneider, L., and Willman, T. (2014), *The world-class performance advantage: how leading finance organizations outperform their peers*, Finance Executive Insight, The Hackett Group, Miami

10 = Accenture (2014), *The CFO as architect of business value, delivering growth and managing complexity,* Accenture 2014 High Performance Finance Study, Accenture LLC, Chicago

11 = CFO Research (2014), *The next stage in creating the value-added finance function: turning data into insight and business actions*, CFO Publishing LLC, Boston

12 = PWC (2014), *Marktstudie financiële functie, goed voorbereid op de toekomst* [Market study of finance function, well prepared for the future], PricewaterhouseCoopers Advisory N.V.

13 = CFO Research and SAP (2014), *Building high-performing finance functions*, CFO Publishing LLC, Boston

14 = USG Finance and Tijdschrift Controlling (2014), *Samenvatting finance monitor* [Finance monitor summary], Research report, www.usg.nl

15 = PWC (2014b), *Finance matters, finance function of the future*, PricewaterhouseCoopers LLP, www.pwc.co.us/finance

16 = O'Connor, J. Schneider, L., and Willman, T. (2015), *The CFO agenda: key issues for finance in 2015*, Finance Executive Insight, The Hackett Group

17 = Fintouch (2015), *De effectiviteit van business control* [The effectiveness of business control], Fintouch B.V., Rotterdam

18 = Accenture (2018), *From bottom line to front line*, CFO Reimagined, www.accenture.com

19 = Eklund, S., Tam, M., and Woodcock, E. (2018), *New technology, new rules: reimagining the modern finance workforce*, McKinsey and Company

20 = Oxford Economics (2018), *How finance leadership pays off, six ways CFOs stay ahead of the pack*, www.oxfordeconomics.com

21 = APQC (2018), *Ten characteristics shared among best-in-class finance functions*, American Productivity and Quality Center

22 = Verbeeten, F., and Heinen, J. (2019), *Finance transformation in the digital era, acquiring new skills to drive the digital transformation*, Finance on a Mission (University of Amsterdam/Workday/PLUC!/Finance Transformation Forum)

23 = Essaides, N., Willman, T., and Dorr, E. (2019), *World-class finance: redefining performance in a digital era*, The Hackett Group, Atlanta

24 = Robert Half and the Financial Education and Research Foundation (2019), *Benchmarking accounting & finance functions 2019*, 10th Annual Report, Robert Half International Inc. and the Financial Education & Research Foundation

25 = Deloitte (2019), *Preparing for the future of finance – now*, CFO Insights, Deloitte Touche Tohmatsu Limited

26 = Gartner (2020), *Future of finance: 10 trends to watch now*, Gartner Inc.

27 = Agrawal, A., Eklund, S., Waite, J., and Woodcock, E. (2020), *Finance 2030: four imperatives for the next decade,* McKinsey and Company

28 = Essaides, N., Willman, T., and O'Connor, J. (2020), *2021 key issues*, The CFO Agenda, The Hackett Group, Atlanta

29 = Caswell-LaPierre, A., Kracklauer, S., Essaides, N., Dorr, E., Hall, B., and Willman, T. (2020), *Transforming finance to prevail in the next normal*, The Hackett Group, Atlanta

30 = Brennan, C., Ketchin, D., Caswell-LaPierre, A., Kracklauer, S., and Dorr, E. (2020), *Facts-tracking digital world class*, The Hackett Group, Atlanta

31 = Roos, A., Tucker, J., Rodt, M., Stange, S., Ego, P., Boudadi, A., and Sheth, H. (2020), *Lessons from best-in-class CFOs*, Boston Consulting Group

32 = McCaffry, R. (2020), *Finance transformation: the human perspective*, Association of International Certified Professional Accountants

33 = Farrar, M. (2020), *Re-inventing finance for a digital world*, Association of International Certified Professional Accountants

34 = Gartner (2021b), *Unlock your finance team's digital potential: 5 critical competencies*, Gartner for Finance, Gartner Inc.

35 = Tjandra, J., Swaminthan, A. and Jing Yi, P. (2021), *Finance of the Future: being a resilient CFO*, KPMG Services Pte Ltd.

36 = Grant Thornton (2021), *Values driving value, CFOs looking to lead on ESG*, Grant Thornton LLP

37 = Hippe, A., Roos, A., & Oberauer, A. (2021), *The Future of the Finance Function*, Boston Consulting Group

Appendix C: Scientifically Developing the HPFF Framework

In this appendix, the approach we used to develop and validate the HPFF framework in a scientific manner is described.[1]

DEVELOPING AND DISTRIBUTING THE RESEARCH QUESTIONNAIRE

When we performed the literature search to identify the movements in the finance function, we could not find a questionnaire that directly translates these movements into operational activities which could be tested. Therefore, in brainstorm sessions with experienced finance professionals, we developed a questionnaire ourselves. Several financial experts were asked to review and comment on the quality and comprehensibility of the questionnaire, after which it was finalized. Table 1 presents the resulting operationalization of the 11 movements in 34 operational activities, which are regarded as representing potential HPFF characteristics by covering all facets of each movement. In addition, the method of measuring the performance of the finance function was also operationalized.

Table 1. The HPFF movements and accompanying potential HPFF characteristics

HPFF Movement	Potential HPFF Characteristics
1. Increase efficiency and effectivity of the finance function	1. Implementing improvements is actively encouraged 2. Improvements are implemented in a structured way 3. People have enough time to make their work activities more efficient and effective 4. Improvement efforts are tracked and evaluated using performance indicators 5. Data is defined in a uniform manner so that there are no differences in interpretation
2. More focus on performing added value activities & business partnering	6. Less and less time is spent on routine activities 7. More and more added-value activities for operations are performed 8. Possibilities to create more added value activities for operations are, together with operations, regularly examined
3. More use of information technology to automate processes	9. Automation and digitalization have high priority 10. All routine processes have been fully automated 11. There is sufficient budget each year to accelerate automation and digitalization of the finance function
4. More cooperation with the business	12. The satisfaction of internal clients is structurally measured 13. In all the important processes conducted in the organization there is involvement of the finance function 14. Possibilities for cooperation and collaboration with operations is actively searched for by the finance function

continues on following page

Table 1. Continued

HPFF Movement	Potential HPFF Characteristics
5. More focus on looking ahead	15. What-if scenarios are regularly produced 16. Prognoses are proactively adapted on the basis of important developments 17. Priority during important management decision-making is given to the latest prognoses, as developed by the finance function,
6. More outsourcing and shared services	18. Processes are executed as much as possible in a uniform way and in one place, so that expertise about these processes is bundled and centralized 19. Whether insourcing or outsourcing is the best option for a certain process is constantly examined
7. More financial self-reliance of operational managers	20. Managers in the organization are sufficiently capable of interpreting and making decisions on the basis of the information offered by the finance function 21. Managers in the organization engage in financial self-service (* 'self-service' means that the managers have the opportunity to access and compose their management reports themselves, without the intervention of the finance function) 22. Managers in the organization mainly use the finance function for support with difficult and complex (financial) questions
8. Continuous attention for the development of financial professionals and for talent management	23. People receive sufficient technical training to be able to excel in their work activities 24. People receive sufficient personal development training to be able to excel in their work activities 25. All people in the finance function have a personal development plan
9. More involvement in strategic and decision processes	26. In each decision of strategic importance, the finance function has important input 27. Other departments regularly spontaneously ask the finance function for advice when taking important decisions 28. The finance function is seen as a serious partner during strategic discussions
10. Different behavioral profiles for financial professionals	29. There is a clear description of the technical requirements per financial role 30. There is a clear description of the behavioral requirements per financial role 31. There are specific development programs per financial role
11. More knowledge about information technology	32. The finance function has much IT application knowledge (IT application knowledge means having knowledge of specific IT software: what it can do and how it can help the organization) 33. The finance function is aware of the current and newest applications and possibilities of IT software 34. The finance function is capable of implementing the latest IT software
Performance of the finance function	35. The internal client is very satisfied with the finance function 36. Financials themselves are very satisfied with the finance function 37. The finance function always has an important role to play in decision-making in the organization 38. The finance function is very efficient ('efficiency' is the degree to which resources are used in the function in an expedient way) 39. The finance function is very effective ('effective' is the degree to which the finance function is successful in realizing its objectives)

The potential HPFF characteristics were collated in an internet-based questionnaire and its face validity was tested by asking several financial experts to complete it and provide comments regarding wording and understandability. After finalizing the questionnaire based on the feedback, financial professionals in our professional networks were approached to participate in the survey. In addition, when speaking at conferences, we asked delegates to complete the questionnaire. In total, 396 fully completed questionnaires were collected.

STATISTICAL RESEARCH RESULTS

To analyze the data we used an exploratory factor analysis (EFA). Components with eigenvalues higher than 1 were extracted through principal components analysis. Coefficients lower than 0.4 were removed (five in total) to increase the ease of interpreting the factors. The factor scores were used in subsequent structural equation modeling (SEM) analyses. The EFA returned six factors. Inspecting the results revealed that the sixth factor explained little variance and its item loadings were hard to interpret, so it was decided to run the EFA with five factors. This five-factor solution had a high Kaiser–Meyer–Olkin (KMO) measure (0.937), indicating excellent sampling adequacy. The solution explained 61.40% of variance. All factors had high internal consistency. Two cross-loadings were deemed problematic so these items were removed. Inspecting the factor loadings in the pattern matrix led to the following verbal interpretation of the factors: Factor 1 – Finance Function Improvement (Cronbach's alpha 0.820); Factor 2 – IT Focus (alpha 0.890); Factor 3 – Personal Development (alpha 0.838); Factor 4 – Role Clarity (alpha 0.842); and Factor 5 – Strategic Role (alpha 0.921). The underlying structure of the performance of the finance function items was analyzed in a similar manner. The EFA returned a one-factor solution and was named Finance Function Performance.

CONSTRUCTING THE HPFF FRAMEWORK

To investigate the influence of the HPO factors and HPFF factors on finance function performance, SEM was used. The model that was fitted connected each individual HPO and HPFF factor to finance function performance. Model fit was good and several connection weights were statistically significant. Figure 1 graphically depicts the results.

Figure 1 shows that the HPFF factor Strategic Role has the strongest correlation with finance function performance. It can be argued that the purpose of a staff function is to "serve" and support the business and its management as effectively as possible.[2] This is certainly the case for the finance function, as the HPFF factor Strategic Role, which aims to support operations has the most characteristics (nine) of all HPFF factors. Executing these characteristics properly will undoubtedly have a positive effect on finance function performance, especially for the elements "The internal client is very satisfied with the finance function" and "The finance function always has an important role to play in decision-making in the organization." The increasing role of IT in all organizational processes is reflected in the HPFF factor IT Focus showing a positive correlation with finance function performance: basically, the better the IT infrastructure and IT knowledge in the finance function, the better it can operate and cooperate. The HPFF factor Finance Function Improvement also shows a positive correlation with Finance function. This is unsurprising since all of these factor's characteristics have a direct impact on improving the function's day-to-day activities. The remaining two HPFF factors have a weaker or no direct influence on finance function performance. The HPFF factor People Development has a strong relation with the HPFF factors Finance Function Improvement and IT Focus, which shows that finance function members must be developed in the right manner, in both their technical and behavioral skills, to be able to execute their activities as effectively as possible. Interestingly, the HPFF factor Role Clarity not only has a logical relation with the HPFF factor Personal Development but also a direct, albeit weak, relation with finance function performance. A possible explanation is that the performance element "Financial professionals are very satisfied with the finance function" is positively influenced, as financial professionals know what is expected from them and can be sure that the organization will help them to meet those requirements.

Figure 1 also shows that three of the HPO factors have a direct positive influence on finance function performance. This was to be expected, as continuous improvement is an important activity of the finance function; long-term orientation is key to maintaining good relations with the organization's other functions and with external stakeholders (e.g., shareholders, the tax office), while good management is always required for a function to operate smoothly. It is only logical, then, for these HPO factors to show a correlation with most HPFF factors. The HPO factors Openness and Action Orientation and Employee Quality only have an indirect positive influence on performance through their correlations with several HPFF factors.

Figure 1. The HPFF framework

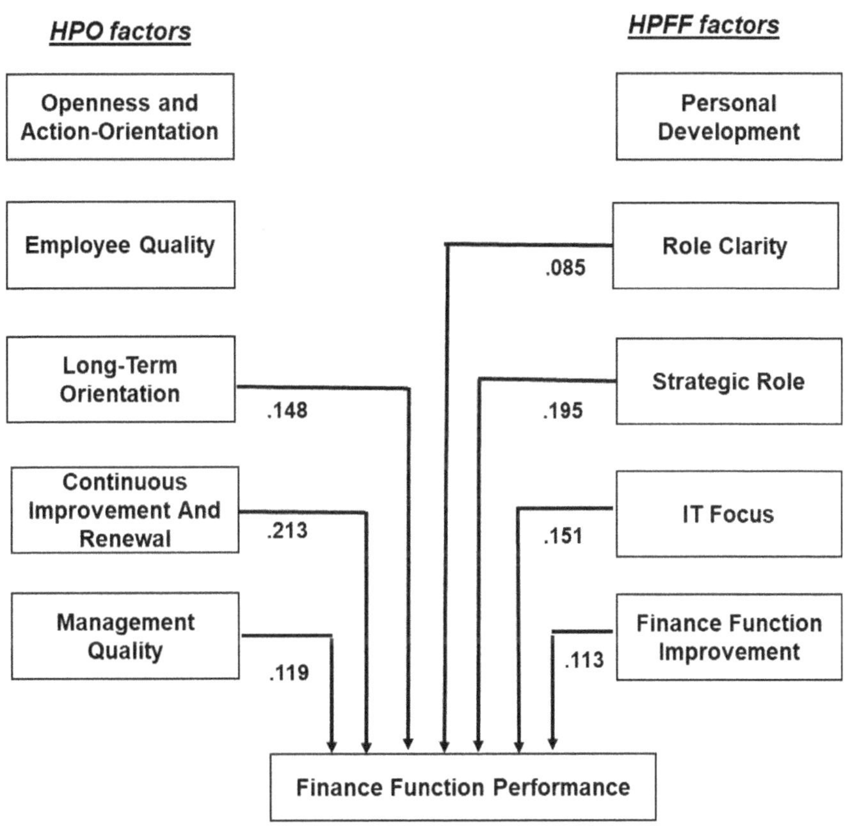

REFERENCES

de Waal, A., Bilstra, E., & de Roeck, P. (2019). *De high performance financiële functie in de praktijk* [The high performance finance function in practice]. Vakmedianet.

Kraan, D. (2017). Enhancing the finance function in line ministries. *OECD Journal on Budgeting*, *16*(2), 75–92.

Zoni, L., & Pippo, F. (2017). CFO and finance function: What matters in value creation. *Journal of Accounting & Organizational Change*, *13*(2), 216–238.

ENDNOTES

1 This appendix is derived from de Waal et al. (2019)
2 Kraan (2017), Zoni and Pippo (2017)

Appendix D: Overview of Roles in the HPFF Environments

In this appendix, the roles collected from the literature are summarized.

Type of studies	Year	Author	Number of roles	Type of roles
a. Studies on the roles in the finance function	2007	Wunsche	4	Steward, operator, strategist, catalyst
	2008	E&Y	4	Scorekeeper, commentator, custodian, business partner
	2018	Fourné et al.	3	Scorekeeper, watch dog, business partner
	2018	Eklund et al.	4	The core, the problem solvers, the specialists, the value leaders
	2019	Verbeeten and Heinen	3	Decision shapers, agile change makers, information architects
	2019	KPMG	5	Data modelers/scientists, Business solutions architects, Innovation and investment strategists, Business planning analysts, Business partners.
b. Studies on the roles of the CFO	2006	Hope	7	Freedom fighter, analyst and adviser, architect of adaptive management, warrior against waste, master of measurement, regulator of risk, and champion of change
	2014	KPMG	7	Guardian of performance and result growth, governance, efficiency/cost control and innovation. Big-picture visionary, owner of data agenda, developer of talent.
	2018	Accenture	3	The accountant, the business partner, the strategic enabler
	2018	Accenture	5	Strategy enabler, partner CEO, innovator, initiator of data agenda, developer of new talent
c. Studies on the skills and profiles of financials	2015	Ten Rouwelaar	2	Management service / business partner vs corporate policeman
	2019	NBA	5	The navigator, the sensor, the coach, the analyst, the gatekeeper
	2020	Caswell-LaPierre et al	5	Detailing digital transformation: digital engagement, digitally enable workforce and organization, digital service optimization, digital service optimization and analytics-driven business insight
	2020	AICPA	5	Technical skills, business skills, people skills, leadership skills. Digital skills
	2021	Gartner	5	Detailing digital competencies: technological literacy, digital translation, digital learning and development, digital bias management, and digital ambition

About the Authors

André de Waal (1960) is Academic Director of the HPO Center, an organization that conducts research into high performance organizations. He is also a partner at the Finance Function Research & Development Center, a company that aims to help finance functions to transform into high-performing units. André has been a consultant and partner with Arthur Andersen for 16 years. André also held a 13-year tenure as Associate Professor Organizational Effectiveness at the Maastricht School of Management. He has been guest lecturer at the Free University Amsterdam, University of Amsterdam, and Erasmus University Rotterdam, visiting fellow at Cranfield University UK, and senior lecturer at Wittenborg University of Applied Sciences. André holds a MSc in Chemistry from Leiden University (the Netherlands), an MBA from Northeastern University Boston (USA), and a Ph.D. in Economics from Vrije Universiteit Amsterdam (the Netherlands). His dissertation was about the behavioral aspects that are important for the successful implementation and use of performance management systems. André teaches and undertakes projects in the field of high-performance organizations and performance management in countries such as China, Vietnam, Bangladesh, Mongolia, Nepal, Mexico, Peru, Ecuador, Suriname, United States, UK, Italy, Belgium, Portugal, Poland, Saudi Arabia, Yemen, United Arab Emirates, Palestine, South Africa, Namibia, Tanzania, and Zambia. He was selected by managementboek.nl as one of the *Dutch Masters in Management*, 10 people who have influenced management thinking in The Netherlands the most in the past decade. André has published 440 articles (among which more than 140 academic publications) and 35 books. Among his English books are *Power of Performance Management, How Leading Companies Create Sustained Value* (John Wiley & Sons, 2001), *Quest for Balance, the human element in performance management systems* (John Wiley & Sons, 2002), *What Makes A High Performance Organization* (Global Professional Publishing, 2012), *Strategic Performance Management* (Palgrave MacMillan, 2nd edition, 2013), and *High-Performance Managerial Leadership* (Praeger, 2020). His articles can be read on www.hpocenter.com and www.andredewaal.eu.

Eelco Bilstra (1969) is a partner at the Finance Function R&D Center (FFR&D). Before co-founding this company, Eelco was a consultant with Finext for more than 17 years, a controller at Rabobank International for five years, and an accountant at Ernst & Young for two years. Eelco has a Masters in Business Economics (University of Groningen), field of study: Administrative Information Services. He has also completed a one-year post-doc course 'Steering changes in organizations' at SIOO (Interuniversity Center for Development in the area of Organization and Change, Utrecht). Eelco has more than 20 years of experience in the finance function in all kind of roles—as a business controller, project lead, initiative lead, product owner, advisor and coach—in all kind of companies in different sectors: telecom, banking, insurance, pharmacy, real estate, healthcare, and service organizations. His passion is improving the finance function, and through this helping the organization improve. In his view, finance should function as the spider in the organizational web, using its strategic position impactfully. His assignments are mostly positioned in the triangle of: organizational change, finance and data & IT. Eelco's areas of expertise are planning and budgeting, management information, cost management, performance management, and intercompany processes. His strengths are in the uncompromising analysis of an organizational dilemma and focusing on pragmatic execution in small steps together with the client, all in order to guarantee the sustainability of the solution and new ways of working in the organization. Eelco publishes on a regular basis about all kind of topics in the finance function, such as financial shared services, management information, and business control. In 2013, he conducted research with André de Waal on trends in the finance function; this formed the starting point of their journey into how to improve the finance function. In 2016, they wrote the first book about the concept of high performance in the finance function, with a strong link with André's HPO research. In 2019, they developed the HPFF framework, which essentially formed the start of the research and advisory company FFR&D (co-founded with Jacques Bootsman) with the aim of studying various kinds of areas in finance together with a network of finance experts, and to advise clients with an evidence-based and science-applied approach. You can reach Eelco via www.linkedin.com/in/eelcobilstra.

Jacques Bootsman (1967) is a partner at the Finance Function Research & Development Center, an organization that guides and supports finance functions to achieve and maintain excellence. Jacques has almost 30 years' experience in several finance functions in different industries. He started his career as a finance professional in a medical supplies and pharmaceutical company in an international environment where implementation of an international shared service center was on the agenda. Later, he was responsible for business control in a food factory and finance lead within a wholesale clothing company where improvement of working capital was necessary at that time. In the past 20 years, Jacques has been active as a consultant within the finance function in several roles such as (business) controller, program-lead, and advisor in the triangle of commerce, finance, and board of directors, helping organizations to increase the efficiency of their finance processes and to improve insights in the performance of the business. Because of his extensive experience with change management in finance, Jacques knows what is required to implement a new way of working within the finance function, taking into account the human factor in the change process. His drive is helping finance professionals to increase their impact within the organization. Jacques is also a member of the supervisory board of two scale-up companies in the healthcare sector. You can reach him via www.linkedin.com/in/jacquesbootsman.

FFR&D Center helps finance functions to become high-performing. The Finance Function Research & Development Center (FFR&D) was founded by enthusiastic professionals with decades of experience in implementing structural improvements in finance functions of organizations and who have a joint passion for continuously strengthening the financial function based on a foundation of evidence-based management research. To this end, FFR&D structurally invests in studies on the finance function that are conducted in collaboration with a community of finance experts. In addition, FFR&D regularly shares insights gained via workshops, seminars, books, articles, round tables, and blogs. This community of experts that shares knowledge and experience for the greater good of improving the finance function is thus an integral part of adding value through research to the finance function.

Index

A

accounting 6-7, 13-15, 31, 36, 48, 92-93, 98-101, 103-104, 113, 115-116, 118, 142, 155, 170, 215, 225, 235-236, 243
advanced data analytics 37
agile operating model 47, 105
Agile working 36
Analytics and business intelligence (ABI) 38
Artificial Intelligence (AI) 37, 48-50, 105, 204, 237, 264

B

Best Idea 208-209, 212-216, 218-220, 223-225, 227, 229-234, 236-238, 240-244, 246, 248-249, 251-252, 254-257, 260-262, 265
best practice 80
budgeting 8, 33, 35, 42, 47, 118, 170, 176, 205, 218, 224, 241, 245
Business Analysis 230
business forecasting 244-245, 264
Business Intelligence (BI) 37, 219-220, 224, 261

C

capital flows 8
career landscape 260-261
career paths 260-261
chain management 97, 218-219
change 14-15, 24-26, 31, 34-35, 43, 47, 49-50, 54, 58, 61, 80, 85-86, 92, 99, 102-104, 106-107, 118-119, 121-122, 125, 127, 134-136, 140, 143-145, 151, 155, 167, 179, 181-186, 197, 204, 216-217, 225, 227, 238, 243, 246, 248-249, 253, 260, 262, 267-268, 280, 282
Chief Financial Officer (CFO) 2, 6, 9-11, 13-15, 31, 41-42, 46, 51, 53-55, 72-73, 78-79, 81, 85-86, 88, 90-93, 99-100, 103-108, 122, 124-126, 140-145, 149-153, 156, 158-159, 168, 203-204, 219-220, 226-227, 231, 234-235, 241, 248, 257, 260, 263-264, 279, 281-283
cloud computing 38, 56
collaboration 10, 23, 25, 40, 47, 49, 59, 66, 72, 78, 101, 113, 120-121, 125, 128, 176, 192, 209, 214, 218, 240, 249, 254, 260-261
competitive advantage 24, 49, 142, 240
compliance 2, 6, 8-9, 51, 76, 93-94, 100, 104, 112, 114, 136, 155, 199, 201, 225-226, 230, 236
continuous improvement and renewal 20-21, 61, 66, 69, 72, 78, 194, 227
corporate governance 8, 104-105, 130
COVID-19 12, 14, 31-32, 36, 38, 40, 132, 142, 149, 163-164, 268, 270, 277-283
Cross-border migration 269

D

data governance 48, 85, 95, 108
data mining 95, 117
data warehousing 95
Delphi method 91, 196
Delphi study 171, 173, 196
digital finance function 108, 128-131, 133-134, 138-140, 279
digital transformation 14, 42, 48, 54-55, 108, 110, 116-117, 125-128, 130-144, 205, 234, 263, 281-283
digitalization 48, 116-117, 126-128, 132-133, 136-138, 141, 143
digitization 36, 49, 52, 64, 110, 112, 116-117, 126-127, 135, 204, 228, 234-235, 247, 263, 279
Director of Finance 6, 24-26, 40, 42, 191-192, 208-214, 227, 243, 245, 251-255, 257, 278-279, 281
disruptors 12-13, 40, 128, 135, 141, 266-267, 279, 281
dynamic reporting 36, 73, 75

E

Economic powershifts 268

E-invoicing 36
Employee Attitude 22
Employee Quality 21, 61, 67, 69
Enterprise Performance Management 95
environmental issues 268

F

Finance Academy 135, 168-169, 210-211, 254
Finance for non-financials 243
finance function 1-14, 24-40, 42-54, 56-100, 102, 104, 106, 108-113, 116-122, 124-142, 144-149, 151-164, 166-174, 176-206, 208-211, 213-217, 219-231, 233-244, 246, 248-249, 251, 253-263, 266, 273-279, 281-283
Finance Function Improvement 62-63, 68, 70, 73, 80, 125, 164, 206
Finance Function, Evergreens of 11, 22, 27-28, 31-32, 57, 78
Finance Operations and Reporting 6
financial managers 28-29, 142
financial processes 6-7, 10-11, 28, 31, 43, 45-47, 58-59, 64, 67, 73, 84, 88, 113, 170, 176-177, 203-204, 209, 213, 216, 227-228, 253
flexible employment 267-268
forecasting 8, 33, 35, 37, 40, 45-46, 49-50, 58, 61, 66, 76-78, 106, 118, 170, 224, 235, 237, 241, 243-246, 248, 264
funding 7, 201
Futurize! Process 141, 273-277, 281

G

globalization 31, 267
Governance, Risk and Compliance 6

H

high performance finance function (HPFF) 1-5, 11-13, 16, 26, 28, 35, 40-41, 55-58, 60-62, 64-90, 92-93, 97-99, 105, 111-114, 119-121, 123-125, 131, 144-170, 173-177, 179, 181-184, 186, 188-194, 196-206, 212, 227-228, 239, 249-251, 263, 266, 270-271
high performance organization (HPO) 2-3, 5, 11-12, 16-24, 26-27, 56, 61, 66-69, 78-79, 99, 124-125, 149-150, 156-157, 179, 181-182, 190, 205, 227
Horizontal and Vertical Finance 224
HPFF transformation 71-73, 76, 85, 145, 147, 149-150, 152-154, 157, 179-186, 188-191, 193-194, 196-197, 199, 206
HPO diagnosis 16, 22, 26, 150, 156-157, 227
HPO framework 5, 11-12, 16-17, 22, 27, 56, 205, 227

I

Implementation Capability 34
Improve Processes 220
Increasing inequality 268
Individualism 269
Information technology (IT) 1-12, 16, 19-20, 22-28, 31-38, 41-43, 45-48, 52, 57-59, 61-62, 64, 68-71, 73-89, 93-96, 98-99, 104, 107-108, 112-113, 116-122, 124-129, 132-140, 144-158, 160, 163-164, 167-171, 174, 176, 180-186, 188, 190-198, 200-205, 208-225, 227-240, 242-246, 248-249, 251-264, 266-267, 269, 273, 275-279
initial public offering (IPO) 8
Institute of Chartered Accountants in England and Wales (ICAEW) 6-7, 14, 54, 126-127, 142, 205
Integrated performance management 223, 265
intelligent finance function 45, 54
Internal Audit 9, 104
International Financial Reporting Standards (IFRS) 8, 31, 215
investor relations 7, 9, 50, 248

K

key performance indicator (KPI) 8, 36, 217, 220-223, 239, 279

L

Lean Finance 45
Lean Reporting 212
Lean Robot Process Automation 237
Long-Term Orientation 19-20, 61, 66-67, 227

M

making data reliable 33
management and control 6, 9, 216
management information 72, 77, 84-85, 89, 177, 198, 213, 216, 218-219, 225-227, 229, 238, 264
Management Quality 18, 61, 66, 69
master data 85, 95, 236
medium-sized organization 6
megatrends 12-13, 135, 141, 144, 248, 266-268, 270-271, 274-275, 277, 281-282

N

NBA/VRC 6, 144

O

Openness and Action Orientation 19, 61, 67-68
organizing 10-11, 136, 140, 191, 209, 213-214, 217, 220
outsourcing 7, 34, 58, 61, 225, 232

P

pandemics 38, 270
peak shaving 215-216
performance management 6, 25, 38, 50, 95, 117, 177, 223, 265
Planning, Budgeting, Forecasting, and Consolidation (PBFC) 224
primary financial basis 6
process mining 37, 102, 118, 232-233, 264

R

Regular Self-Assessment 227
regulators 10, 93
Resource scarcity 269
risk management 6-9, 31, 35, 37, 46, 56, 93, 104, 107, 118, 199, 213, 262, 277
robotic process automation (RPA) 36, 49, 102, 234, 236-238, 264
Robotics 30, 223, 231-232, 234, 236-238, 264
role portfolio 121, 252-253

S

self-service 47-48, 64, 75, 95-96, 101, 112, 202, 206, 216-218
Sensitivity Analysis 248
shared services 7, 45-46, 49, 58, 61, 208, 213-214, 221
shareholders 8, 10, 47, 93, 156
skill pool management 256-257
Skills mismatch 31, 267
Software as a Service (SaaS) 38
Speed of technological advancement 267
Stakeholder management 38
Standardize Reporting 208
Staying ahead program 155, 157
strategic management 6, 91, 243
Strategy and Risk 7
Supervisory Board 9-10, 93, 199, 277
sustainability 38, 46, 61, 69, 72, 79, 108, 267-268, 282
sustainable employment 267

T

talent development 59, 251
talent management 45-46, 99, 104, 257-259, 263
Taskforces 208
tax authorities 8, 10, 234
Taxes 6, 8, 10, 42, 46, 52, 72, 101, 115, 128, 136, 224-225, 234, 245
team composition 215, 251, 262
Team Cooperation 214
trainee program 255-256
trusted advisor 246

U

undercurrent 24-26
upstream 24-26
Urbanization 269

W

workflow automation 37
workforce composition 268-269

www.ingramcontent.com/pod-product-compliance
Lightning Source LLC
LaVergne TN
LVHW080644011026
849160LV00014B/1318